THE BANTU – JAREER SOMALIS
Unearthing Apartheid in the Horn of Africa

Published by
Adonis & Abbey Publishers Ltd
P.O. Box 43418
London
SE11 4XZ
http://www.adonis-abbey.com
Email: editor@adonis-abbey.com

First Edition, April 2008

Copyright 2008 © Mohamed A. Eno

British Library Cataloguing-in-Publication Data
A catalogue record for this book is available from the British Library

ISBN: 9781905068944 (HB), 9781905068951(PB)

Printed and bound in Great Britain

THE BANTU – JAREER SOMALIS
Unearthing Apartheid in the Horn of Africa

Mohamed A. Eno

ACKNOWLEDGMENTS

The enormous task that involved the undertaking of this work may not be complete without paying due respect to the individuals that contributed to its being and the others who truly inspired me in one way or the other. I am very grateful to Ali Jimale Ahmed and his family, Abdi M. Kusow and his family, David Le Cornu, Saad Hassan M. Abu Higail, Anthony Osambo, Naeem Al Momani, Mubarak Osman, Abdullahi M. Warsame (Adde Duqow) and Mohamed Hagi Ahmed (Hundhur) for their support and comment on this work; Agneta Svalberg, Abdi I. Samatar and Khadar Bashir Ali for their encouragement. I need to mention Rowdha Hussein, Fawzia Fereja and Lydiah Wanjiku as true friends who stood by me when I was initially putting this work together as my PhD dissertation. Many thanks go to all the traditionists and oral historians from the different Somali communities who allowed me to access the wealth of their knowledge about Somalia.

I am extremely indebted to my brother Omar A. Eno without whose advice and encouragement this work and my academic achievement would have never been of any significance, and also to his wife Ida Aju -- alias Dayu Eno. I am also very proud of my brothers Sayid-Ali, Jibril and Ahmed and my sisters Binti, Saida, Mariam, Boola, Batula, Nima and Shariffa for their support throughout the hard journey of my learning for a higher degree. I appreciate my wife Mariam-Betty and my kids Jamal, Ismail, Malik, Aziza, Jamil, Nassir and Khalifa for being supportive and very understanding about the limitation of my time when they really needed more of my attention. A strayed salvo on January 26, 1992 deprived Hagi Abdulkadir Eno, my beloved father, of witnessing this achievement which he had initiated the dream. My sister Amina and my brother Abdullahi too, did not live enough to see this occasion – May Allah rest all of them in eternal peace. My mother, Hagia Halima Hussein Hassan (alias Essow) has been inspiring all the way and her knowledge and memorically archived versions of oral poetry and history were immensely useful. I am very pleased to mention the special motivation from my nieces and nephews, Alma, Abdinur, Halima, Najma, Adna, Ahmed Jomow, Abdul and the entire group of Atlanta, very promising young learners.

Ahmed Keynan and Rasheed Farah, I dearly appreciate the knowledge you gave me about the Gaboye/Baidari Somalis. I thank Hussein Mohamud Mohamed, the counselor for Consular and Administrative

Affairs of the Somali Embassy in the United Arab Emirates, Mohamed Ba-Akaba of the Somali Consulate in Dubai, for helping me establish network with resourceful Somalis in the UAE, particularly in Abu Dhabi and Dubai. Many thanks are due to Ali Mohamoud Osman and his family, and also to Mohamed Ibrahim (Ibi), Jamal M. Hagi, Ibrahima Diallo, Markus Greutmann, Simon Malele and Jehan Zitawi – good friends and very helpful scholars. My utmost appreciation is also due to Eng. Jaha Juma Jaha, Saada Ibuni Swaleh, Farida Mtengeti Chabane, Radhia Mtengeti Chabane, Rahma Mtengeti Chabane, Abdul Ghasley, Hamza I. Midigo, Hamadi Kumula and Hagi Hibaal.

I need to mention the good working environment availed to me by the Board of Trustees of ADNOC Technical Institute as well as the ATI leadership including Omar Al-Hamed, Ismail Al-Sheikh, David Heuring, Ali Al-Maskari and of course Ahmed Kandil and Derek Korobkin. Your assistance was timely in that it came when I really needed a space of time to put sections of this book together.

All those who assisted me in one way or the other, but not mentioned here, please accept my heartfelt apology and gratitude for your contribution to this work. Last but not least, my thanks go to my publisher Adonis & Abbey Publishers, their editors, and three anonymous readers who fairly commented on this work and whose useful suggestions were taken on board. My sincere thanks to all of you.

DEDICATION

This book is dedicated to my late father, Hagi Abdulkadir Eno and my mother, Hagia Halima Hussein Hassan, whose strong commitment to the resistance of ethnic-marginalization inspired me not to give up in the quest for higher academic goals. The dedication also goes to the Bantu – Jareer people and the Gaboye/Baidari communities as well as to the rest of the racially and socio-culturally oppressed peoples who tolerate stiff social stigma in Somalia and elsewhere in the world.

Table of Contents

Acknowledgment   iv

Dedication   vi

Introduction   9

Chapter 1
The Debate over the Origin of the Somali People   15

Chapter 2
A Tale of two Bantu Communities: the Autochthons vs. the
Diaspora   65

Chapter 3
The Colonial Occupation of Somalia and the Stigmatization of the
Bantu People   105

Chapter 4
Post-Colonial Somalia and the Jareer Stigma: From Colonialism to
Neo-Colonialism   149

Chapter 5
Demographic Fabrication and Ethnic Marginalization: Looking into the
Background of the Enigma   193

Chapter 6
Endorsing Apartheid in a National Conference: The 4.5 Factor   215

Chapter 7
Amid Ethnic Marginalization and Identity Confusion: Who is a Somali
and What Determines Somaliness?   245

Chapter 8
Racial Discrimination in the Underbelly of Racial Homogenization:
Unearthing the Untold Apartheid   265

Chapter 9

Elaborating the Acts of Marginalization 275

Appendices 287

Conclusion 290

Bibliography 295

Index 313

Introduction

THE BANTU – JAREER SOMALIS
Unearthing Apartheid in the Horn of Africa

For a long period of time, a general belief has reigned in the academic and non-academic circles that Somalis are an extremely exceptional people, in that theirs is a homogeneous society composed of men
and women from one eponymous father from Arabia. They celebrate
same nomadic culture, and one Somali language! In the background of
all the said shared commonalities, this study argues that the Somali
people are made up of communities of different ethnic backgrounds,
each group practicing its own distinct mode of living and culture in the
midst of a conglomeration of a multi-ethnogenic society.

Therefore, parallel to the fluidity underlying the believed universality of Somali culture and origin, this volume aims at clarifying the
vagueness implanted in Somaliness or Somali citizenship itself. It reveals that certain sections of the distinct identities and cultures in this
Horn of Africa nation are ethnically stratified on the basis of geographical and genealogical nobility while others suffer ethnic marginalization within the fusion of Somali self-sameness. The core theme,
however, is to put in the limelight the social situation of the Ja-
reer/Bantu people amidst the racialist nature of a pastoral Somaloid
stock. Relatively, the study intends to investigate the complexity of the
subject by focusing on some basic questions such as:-

a) Does Somalia constitute a homogeneous society of Arab origin?

b) If Somalia is a truly homogenous stock, why do ethnic ramifications
and clan nobility and supremacy exist among this 'unique' people, who
are supposed to originate from the same eponymous immigrant Arab
forefather?

c) Why do some communities such as the Somali Bantu/Jareer people,
the outcast groups and others in certain geographical locations towards
the South suffer less-nobility and/or marginalization under the pretext
and banner of homogeneity?

d) In view of all these complexities, who is really a Somali and by what
criteria is the paradigm of Somaliness or Somalihood determined?

Prominent orientalists, nationalist politicians and a section of Somali scholars have often misleadingly featured the Somali people as a predominantly nomadic pastoral society whose relationships and political structures are based on segmentary kinship and clanism. However, recent 'revisionist' scholarship (Kusow 1995, 2004; Ahmed 1995, 1996; Luling 2002; O. Eno 2004; Eno & Eno 2007, 2008; Schlee 1994) suggests that Somalia's homogeneity and the Somali people's genealogical attachment to Quraishite Arabs, the tribe of the Prophet of Islam Mohamed ibn Abdullah ibn Abdul-Mutallib, cannot stand scrutiny. In any case, arguments of both faculties of thought will be mirrored in the next chapter.

This study defies the self-sameness theory by looking at Somalia from a different perspective and as ethno-cultural diversities in identity confusion. Amid these multiple patterns of identity confusion, it explores aspects of Apartheid, stigma and ethnic marginalization; this is to say that categories of Somaliness and their qualification become a subject matter for further analysis.

In a more radical nature, the author swerves from the paradigmatically customized clan-based classification of the Somali people to a more pragmatic categorization of 'Jareer" and "Jileec" as a reality on the ground. This phenomenon has become a basis for an untold type of apartheid exacted on the Jareer/Bantu in respect of their ethnic background as well as Negroid physical features. The study delves into a discovery of another version of Somalia as viewed through the socio-historical as well as socio-psychological tidings of this oppressed community suffering under the cover of an unsubstantiated mythical homogeneity.

In any case, after decades of colonial rule and upon unification of British and Italian Somaliland in July, 1960, Aden Abdulle Osman was nominated an interim provisional president till July of 1961, when he was fielded for presidential candidature against Sheikh Ali Jimale. Osman was re-elected to stay at the helm until 1967 when parliament ejected him out by voting in Abdirashid Ali Sharmarke as the second president of the Republic of Somalia. During the successive epochs of both Osman and Sharmarke, the political situation was marred by tribal rifts coupled with underdevelopment. The new nation-state became a victim of poor leadership, clan chauvinism and corruption in the corridors of the top administrative echelons.

Amid such pervasive rifts and internal political wrangles, President Sharmarke was assassinated in Laas Caanood by a bodyguard. The leadership vacuum created rift and disagreement among parliamentarians over the selection of the next president. The military coup by Siad Barre was hatched out of this political humdrum, nearly throwing the country into civil strife and political chaos. On 21 October 1969, Siad Barre and other high ranking army officers plotted a bloodless 'revolution' whose ideological propensity would cause socio-political transformation. However, on assuming power the military suspended the national constitution, dissolved the civilian government and the parliament, disbanded the existing political parties, detained or, as it is often euphemistically claimed, "held in protective custody" the political leaders of the former regime.

Unfortunately, most military leaders in Africa and elsewhere in the world have the tendency to claim the relinquishment of state power back into the hands of civilians after a short period, but it is a known fact that most of them cling to power longer than they had promised. The adamancy to power then plunges the nation into collapse, which in the Somalia case both collapse and anarchy became reality.

Dictatorial rule and clan-based politics have led to deterioration in people's living standard as new elite of army officers emerged to misuse their ranks as an avenue for achieving personal gains. Top civilian leaders also joined in the looting of public funds and expropriation of individually owned agricultural land of the inter-riverine Bantu/Jareer community. Competing classes rushing for the embezzlement of public resources rubbed shoulders in the financial institutions. The solicitation for unaccounted for loan facilities and individual development funds masquerading in the name of 'Iskaashato' cooperative society, and para-statal organization, became a common theme.

An enduring disaffection with Barre's dictatorial regime and ethnocentric aggrandizement has procured the uprising of a section of the society who took up arms against the regime of a brutal military dictator. However, the battle abruptly changed its face into a clan and subclan war whose mystery finds itself in the background of the ethnohistorical feuds in a society characterized as homogeneous.

Since Somalia's independence, the Daarood have utterly manipulated the political arena and the privileges associated with it. So the ousting of Barre, the notorious Darood dictator in early 1991, needed a robust group of armed Hawiye-militia to join forces to dislodge him from power. Under the factional symbol of the United Somali Congress

11

(USC), the Hawiye waged heavy street battles to which a die-hard Barre responded with massive artillery bombardment of Mogadishu, the capital city. Consequently, Barre was expelled from Villa Somalia, seat of the presidency. Whatever the effects, the war degenerated into anarchy and more atrocities that saw the dehumanization of the un-armed communities and abuses against the oppressed peoples, mainly the ethnic Jareer/Bantu population.

For over a decade and a half, endless conferences, alliances, self-imposed administrations, peace and reconciliation symposiums and billions of US Dollars in humanitarian assistance and development aid, could not lay the groundwork for the reformation and reconstitution of a functional Somali statutory structure. The 14th Somali National Reconciliation Conference, which was organized by the IGAD (Inter-Governmental Authority for Development) member states and well-wishers among the international community, was held in Kenya for a period of about two years. It was concluded with the formation of an interim federal parliament, an interim president and an interim cabinet, none of which is functionally effective as of now (February 2008).

This study bridges together areas of my interest in the Social Studies discipline. The prolonged 'civil war' (or more aptly Regional War) in Somalia, the social status of the Bantu/Jareer people and an insight into the conflicting identities of the Somali people influenced me to study the subject. The concentration, however, is not only in the social history of the people but also on the effects of the dynamics in the contemporary social life. Having a wide knowledge of the Somali peoples, their cultures and social systems, and involvement in various spheres in the academic and social development fields over the years, have become a basis for my desire to examine the realities about the different communities in Somalia and their interplay with, and effects on each other.

The reader may think of this study as a general discussion about the orientalists' Somalia, presenting the traditional culture of nomadic pastoralism in its entirety, but it is not. In fact it epitomizes to unlearn that culture (for a while) for the sake of introducing an entombed version of Somali cultural history. However, the bottom-line is to set the stage for an extensive understanding of the Bantu/Jareer people whose historiography and recognition of their ethno-cultural values have been denied the due locus they deserve in the history of the Horn, particularly in Somalia. In order to separate the Jareer and Jileec peoples of the society, Chapter One explores through the Jileec section of the Somali society while Chapter Two discusses the Bantu Jareer community. Chapter Three focuses on the colonial domination of Somalia and its effects on the Jareer. Chapter Four highlights post-independence Somalia and how the Jareer continued suffering under the administration of neo-colonial civilian regimes as well as how they were distanced from state administration. Chapter Five sets the trend by revealing the oppression against the Jareer people and the stigma they face in Somali social life as a community whose numerical enormity was tactfully but also treacherously obscured in pseudo-homogeneity. Chapter Six gives a reflection of an apartheid phenomenon dubbed 4.5 (four-point-five) social segregation system which divides the people into very-Somali and less-Somali categories of communities. What constitutes Somaliness itself and the nomad's self-invented criteria to determine Somaliness is explored in Chapter seven. In the last chapters, eight and nine, the study culminates in a quantitatively analyzed survey elaborating the status of the Jareer/Bantu and the stigma they tolerate under the guise of Somali 'homogeneity' and 'brotherhood'.

Chapter 1

THE DEBATE OVER THE ORIGIN OF THE SOMALI PEOPLE

Several approaches could be used to classify the Somali people, and which system to employ depends on who is using it, or for what purpose. According to Ioan M. Lewis,[1] a general perception exists in the fact that the clan stands as the center-pole of the nomadic political system. It holds the kinship together by suggesting the existence of about 4 to 6 clan entities. Others may extend the number to even more, by taking into valid consideration the separate units of Reer Xamar (Banaadiri), Barawaans (Reer Baraawa), Madhibaan (Gaboye outcasts), Jareer[2] etc., and the list could go on and on. In this way, Lewis thinks that the often memorized patrilineal genealogy is to the Somali the same as "what a person's address is in Europe."[3]

Another method of categorization would lump all the communities in the Somali peninsula into the two polar units of Jareer and Jileec (hard hair and soft hair) in other words Bantu and non-Bantu, without putting into context only the genealogical affinity of each group, but rather through a classification established on the basis of physical composition of the people themselves as Negroid and non-Negroid respectively. To the more conservative person, this approach may seem to intimate an indulgence in a system not utilized earlier, but we can try to make it the baseline of this study without violating the composition of the clan systems existing in their own traditional rights. Therefore, the adoption of this method represents yet [another] attempt of contributing to the ethnic classification or stratification methods, a useful categorization, which functions practically as the reality on the ground. So, in order to grasp the essence behind the Jareer and Jileec diversification, we start with the latter, the Jileec Somalis, in other words the Non-Bantu, Non-Negroid Somali people.

Versions of inconsistent traditions

The oral traditions go that, in the beginning, an Arab immigrant arrived somewhere along the shores of what is located in the northern coastline of Somalia. He was washed away on the shores after experiencing trouble with his dhow, which was wrecked. He was received by the local residents in the area, married from them and caused an unusual human germination of massive multiplication, demographically outnumbering the host community. One Sheikh Ismail Jaberti, as he was called, became a symbol of a rare case of an immigrant hero who later became the factor behind the biogenesis as well as genealogical 'transformation' of an entire race of black Africans into what Ali Jimale ironically describes as "Arabs with a tan."[4]

Douglas Collins writes about a tradition, which suggests that this 'noble' Arab was cast adrift many centuries ago as a boy and upon reaching manhood, fathered the Darod clan through his marriage to a local girl called Donbira. According to Collins, it was "Bereda, a small coastal fishing village," that his informant, Yusuf, told him as the place where "Darod, an Arabian noble, many centuries ago was cast adrift as a small boy and later in life married a Somali girl named Donbirro and so founded the great Darod section of the Somali people."[5]

A very peculiar situation arises in the implement of the traditions regarding the arrival of Darod as an individual, whether as a boy or a grown-up, or even if we consider, for the purpose of this discussion, that Jaberti Ismail begot him. Throughout the traditions, we are told about the coming of Arab Sheikhs: Ismail Jaberti (some put Jaberti first), Darod, Isaq, and so on, as individuals who married from the local communities. Later, we find in the lineage construction that all the Somaloid stock, including Digil, Isaq, Reewing (Mirifle), Darod, Hawiye and many others have descended from Samaale whose ascendancy is connected to Hiil, who counts back to Aqil and then further behind to Qureishite lineage of Mohammed, the Prophet of Islam.

In another tradition, *A Handbook of Abyssinia* presents that the eponymous ancestor, one Sheikh Jaberti "was wrecked on the NE. Coast where he settled and died, leaving a son Darod, the father of the Darod branch,"[6] who was later to foster the 'noble' people that make the great nation of the Darod clan. For this reason, the 19th century scholarship consisting of certain writers from the colonial regimes that occupied Somalia, have focused on the northern part of the country as being probably the cradle of the Somali nation since it was believed as the entry point through which the Arab progenitors had arrived. Commenting on one of such writers, specifically Lewis, Christine Choi Ahmed says that the "first and best-known scholar to examine Somali

16

society... almost all his field work was done in the northern Somaliland."[7] Yet Lewis himself acknowledged the paucity of factual substance in the content of the Somali traditions, often lacking in precision in dating and in names.[8]

The more peculiar scenario about Somali genealogy is in its lack of even two identical lineages in the more than five versions leading to the Arab ancestral father Aqil. Generations of people have kept the Arab-origin concept alive through the memorization of 'abtirsi' the ancestral name-count, not noticing the nature and origin of some of these names, which sound more Cushitic/African than Semitic/Arabian. Several names, supposedly of the same lineages, are also often counted inconsistent with one another; for example, whereas some count 23 forefathers to their ancestor, others do fewer generations (see also Luling, Somali Sultanate p. 101). The occurrences of such divergences and inconsistencies invite the notion that every Somali group has concocted at will a supposed chain of names to represent phony ancestors of unreal existence (see also Virginia Luling, Somali Sultanate, p84).

Some of these traditions narrate about the arrival of an Arab immigrant who dug a well in a strange newfound land. He helped a young herdswoman to water her flock from 'his' well. After sometime, her father who was so impressed by the healthy growth of his animals followed her. Upon arriving at the site of the well, the Arab immigrant refused to open 'his' well unless, and until the girl's father promised him a marriage to his daughter. After he was made the promise, the lonely immigrant removed the cover from the mouth of the well and watered the flock. Though doubtful the tradition is, it contradicts with the Somali saying of *"wax la yaqaan guurso, wax la yaqaan ha laguu dhalee"*, which encourages marriage to the one known so as to foster offspring whose origin is known and propitious.

This narrative though, seems to be a reconstruction of a modified replica of the Qur'anic story of Moses[9] who, after committing a crime, emigrated from his home to a strange land where he helped to water animals for two sisters. He was called for by their father and upon agreement of providing service for several years, Moses was promised marriage to one of them. After the completion of the stipulated duties, Moses married one of the girls and later acquired prophethood from God.

The dissimilarity of the two traditions lies in the fact that Moses was watering the two girls' small ruminants from an existing well whereas in the Somali traditions, Darod dug the well himself in a strange land. How only one man could dig a well in a territory where he was alien, and how he acquired the tools for digging are arguments that the oriental anthropologists and historians did not investigate substantively. The tradition also suggests that perhaps no other citizens either knew about this well or used it to water their flocks; or even possibly that Donbirro and her father were the only life existing in the area!

In the Darod clan family, a section of the traditions say that Darod himself, the noble Arab, was cast adrift as a young boy and that he got married to a local girl Donbirra upon his adulthood. Yet, it is bizarre that there is no mention of who Darod's foster parent/s were, since this version of the historiography suggests Darod as an underage child. More doubt also entails how and where he acquired the cynical non-Arab name of 'Darod'. Another question pursues about his 'nobility' because many immigrants fled from their home in Arabia due to persecution as slaves, and some or all those who might have allegedly escaped to the northern Horn region (if the Somali pedigree is one of them) could have as well been fugitive slaves who sought freedom away from their masters, the same story as we have seen in the case of the Wa-Gosha people of Somalia. But none of the various traditions and scholars thinks about other possible postulates, nor did the early orientalist scholars present a variant speculation of the topic except the suggestion of population pressure being the reason of the Arab immigrants seeking a safe haven in Somalia.

The historical construction as seen here needs more corroboration. Obviously, it is not by genuine coincidence that many foreign Arab immigrants arrived in the Somali peninsula at various dates while at the same time all trace their 'asal' origin, across variant routes, but to the same Qureishi tribe or 'Reer Banu-Hashem' the offspring of Banu-Hashem. Even if we accept the idea as that, how can we justify an Arab naming his children Sab and Samale, Cushitic names unknown to him?

For the section of the traditions which suggest Jaberti Ismail as the Arab newcomer marrying Dir's daughter Donbira, we encounter a controversy because we hear some traditions opinionating the descent of Dir and Hawiye from Irir, who also came from Samale, one who tracks Hiil as his agnatic forefather. This version seems to support the thought that Dir fathered both the Isaq and the Darod, as Ioan M.

Lewis illustrates.[10] More suspicion encompasses the origin of some of the names in the 'abtirsi' genealogy, such as *'Kombe'*, which can be classified as ethnic Bantu rather than a Semitic Arab name. Whatever the case, it is rather hard to regard credibility to any of these traditions because of their inconsistency and the controversies that make none of them plausible.

Most of the Somali progenitors have their traditions based on imitations of either ancient Arab stories or other Cushitic traditional heroes found on a tree or watering animals from a well. Abdalla Mansur's[11] details on the subject reveal not only the confusion surrounding the topic but they also devaluate the authenticity of Qureishite genealogy of those who deem a high regard for the affiliation of their identity to an Arab eponym.

This specification being a basis for Somalia's claim of Arab origin, which some scholars justify was exacted by population pressure from that region of Southern Asia in the proximity of Somalia, and a recent Somali migration from the north Horn to the south of the country, have misled many seasoned scholars by placing northern and northeastern Somaliland as the point of origin of the Somali race. As Professor Gunther Schlee enlightens, "Not only the more general historians (e.g. Low 1963: 321) but also the best specialists (e.g. Hunting Ford 1955:19; 1963:65-6; I. M. Lewis 1955: 45; 1980: 22-3) have succumbed to this error."[12] In a similar contention, Ali Abdirahman Hersi comments on the trend as "...puzzling," explaining the implausibility of the theory as he states, "Stranger yet is the fact that so many authorities have persisted in these far-fetched and untenable explanation."[13]

Another link to Arab genealogy is deemed to the Isaq clan. The supposed descendents of this forefather stand perceptually firm about their beginning from Sheikh Isaq. According to the traditions, Sheikh Isaq was an Asiatic-Arab from Kerbala in Iraq and stayed in Hadramut in Yemen for some years. He is claimed also to have been a close kin of the prophet of Islam, Mohammed, with some of the traditions placing that relationship as cousins.[14]

Sheikh Isaq, just like his other immigrant counterpart Sheikh Jaberti, lived among the local people. He married a local African woman of the Dir[15] community, and laid his name as the ancestor of 'mulatto' generations. Later, they would claim and uphold a noble pedigree that connects them biogenetically to Mohamed the Prophet as their consanguine relative. However, Sheikh Isaq's arrival in Somalia falls in a much later date than Sheikh Ismail Jaberti's, the eponymous ancestor of the Darod clan.

According to Georges Revoil, the arrival of the Darod clan's patriarch, whether Sheikh Abdirahman son of Ismail Jabarti or Darood or anyone else, is set at the 75th year after the Islamic Hijra from Mecca to Medina.[16] But in *The Modern History of Somaliland*, British anthropologist I.M. Lewis, renowned as 'authority' on Somalia, set the date at some time around the 11th century.[17] While former Ambassador Hussein Ali Dualeh avoids a possible controversy from the complications related to historical dating, Ali S. Muhamad was able to track Sheikh Isaq's arrival in northern Somalia to the year 548 A.H.[18] corresponding approximately to around 1153. Dr. Lewis opines his version as 12th or 13th century.[19] Whatever the arrival date, the unanimity as per the chronology of arrivals is unequivocal about Sheikh Ismail Jaberti or Sheikh Abdirahman or Darod preceding in the migration from Arabia than that of Sheikh Isaq, thus further defending the conception that the Darod (as far as the Somali context is concerned) have by far acquired their Arab pedigree earlier than the Isaq clan whose ancestor set foot in the Somali peninsula in a much later date.

Though both immigrants have the title of Sheikh [20] to their names, a title which is earned in more aspects than one, it is the latecomer, Sheikh Isaq that has done more teaching. But by analyzing the dates Hersi cited from Muhammad's article in the *Somaliland Journal*, if that is anything to go by, Sheikh Isaq came to Zaila in 548 AH, having left Baghdad in 498 AH.[21] By employing simple differential calculation, we see that Sheikh Isaq, though his age at the time of his departure from his point of origin or any other transit area was not satisfactorily established, landed on Somali soil at around half a century later than his year of departure from Baghdad. What age exactly he was at the time of the commencement of his incursion is not illuminated either beyond any reasonable doubt. If we assume that he was a mature and stout young man of 30 years when he departed from Iraq, upon his arrival on the north coast of Somalia he is already an old man of 80 years. Can we then assume that he was teaching Islam to his in-laws at that age for 16 years, tolerating painstakingly the effects of gerontology, as well as raising young children from his African wife/wives? The oral traditions then add that he later set on another journey to another territory, the Arussi area.

To increase the confusion, Lewis gives elsewhere in his volume

Saints and Somalis (p.14) that a certain Sheikh Ali Sh. Ibrahim who detailed the hagiography of Sh. Isaq, records 727AH as the year of Sh. Isaaq's death. Reconciling these dates becomes a constraint since logic denies rendering credence to one version against the other for their inconsistencies. The discrepancy is so wide that it ridicules Sheikh Isaq's life span to over two centuries, and that he was bearing children at that unthinkable age.

The extrapolation in this postulate somehow differs with the average rationale, regardless of how much benefit of doubt considered in its favor. For Sheikh Isaq to have begotten children at old age may not be the only point under contention, but more questions remain unanswered for the traditions regarding his eponymy to relate constructively. He was said to have journeyed with an entourage of about ninety people, but there is obscurity over what has become of the lives of the entourage. Who of them have reached Somalia with Sheikh Isaq? How many of them have also married from the local community and how many had come with their Arab wives? Have any of them returned to Arabia ever since, taking some of their offspring and/or wives with them? Which sub-clan/s represents the descendents of Sheikh Isaq's relatives among his entourage? All these and many more questions in fact lack the answers they beg for, hindering to facilitate the reconstruction cohesively for the clearer reckoning of the historiography of the Isaq nation of families.

Comparatively, the same investigation is applicable to Sheikh Jaberti as controversy also surrounds the identity of his wife Donbira, the so-called Somali girl married off to him. Some sources state that the early people to whom Donbira belonged were Galla/Oromo who lived in the region prior to the arrival of the Somalis. Other traditions have it as Hawiye or Dir whom Donbira belonged to. Whichever source we take into consideration, the conundrum toward the achievement of a satisfactory response to the hypothesis of immigrants of unsubstantial number exceeding their respective sedentary host communities does not only sound miraculous but also seems historiographically irresolvable. What has caused the disappearance from the scene of the local African people? Why are the Somalis more related to the Boran/Oromo, Baiso and Rendille culturally, physically and linguistically than to the Arabian people?

In another extreme but substantiated discordance with early colonial scholarship, current Somalists – Somalis and non-Somalis - provide

their argument based on well-elaborated hypothesis regarding the Somali phenomenon of Arab origin. "There is no way to reconcile this
erroneous view with the evidence of historical linguistics or cultural
history…"[22] Schlee disputes, with the postulation that Somalis need not
look far across the sea for their origin, but within the vicinity of the
East Africa region where other peoples of similar origin, cultures and
languages dominate. He observes significant cultural characteristics
and linguistic similarities among societies settled in various parts of the
Eastern Africa region before asserting confidently that "The general
attitude behind all these phenomena, namely the pleasure taken in
naming social events, in counting and calculating, seems to me to be so
deeply rooted in Lowland Eastern Cushites that personally I do not feel
the need to look to South-west Asian high cultures or elsewhere for its
origin."[23]

The cultural relationship of the Eastern African Cushitic settlers,
particularly Somalia and certain tribes such as the Rendille of Kenya
and the Galla – Orma, found both in Kenya and Ethiopia gives one the
assumption of a similitude whose attributes extend further back in history than something incidental. Nor could those customs and traditions
be regarded as an acquisition through minimal acculturation. But notwithstanding the close relationship covering multiple aspects of the
social life, the Somalis still have a deep predilection to come from an
Arab pedigree, an identity which in ancient times was used as a qualification for the gain of access to the top seat of rulership.

One of the most critical literatures on Somalia's Arab origin and
homogeneity as a nation came from contributors mostly consisting of
contemporary Somali professors and other distinguished scholars, in
The Invention of Somalia, the edited volume of Ali Jimale Ahmed. Somali
professor of history, Mohamed Mukhtar comments that the Somalis'
claim for Arab origin "remains enigmatic," arguing, "one would wonder, in the first instance, how the offspring of just two individual Arabs
could become not only the dominant people of the northern part of the
peninsula, but also the majority of the whole Somali nation today."[24]
However, Mukhtar blames the concerned scholarship and Somali authorities in his retribution that, "Efforts have been made to discourage
scholars from studying other Somali themes. Valuable sources for the
study of Somalia's past were ignored, among them, Arabic, Italian,
French and German sources."[25]

In his volume, Search for a New Somali Identity, Dualeh wrote in the opening pages that the Somali clans all come from different Arab immigrants who escaped from persecution in Arabia; their port of entry was Mait and that Isaq was the last to arrive – a reason why he (Isaq) established himself in Mait town on the coast of Somaliland. Dualeh writes:

> It is widely believed that the Dir was the first to arrive at the Somali coast, followed by the Hawiye and the Darod. The last to arrive was the Issaq clan, whose habitat today is the original point of entry for all the other Somali clans, the present Somaliland. The other Somali clans that preceded them have filled the hinterland, and therefore the Isaq was forced to live at the coastal areas.[26]

In his argument, the ex-army man turned diplomat points out that the Somali people belong to either one of the five groups of Dir, Isaq, Darod, Hawiye and Digil-Mirifle, all amalgamating into a one Somali tribe which otherwise consist of:

> "…A confederation of genealogically un-related clans. There are also a number of minority clans. There are no blood-links or other affinity between these five clans or for that matter between the smaller clans… The commonality is the language and the religion… The genealogical descent shows that the five main clans have no blood-links whatsoever."[27]

Dualeh contributes the philosophy that Sheikh Isaq, the assumed forefather of the Isaq clan of families as one who "…belonged to the Hashemite tribe…he got married to a Sudanese girl. She gave him four sons." He so certainly writes that when Sheikh Isaq arrived in Somalia, he came with his Sudanese wife and their four children. And after that, "In Mait he got married to a girl from the Dir clan…she gave him four sons."[28] These sons are then eight in total, but there is no mention of the whereabouts of the Sudanese wife's four children.

Dualeh's presentation of the narrative about Isaq relates all the praise of a legendary hero and his magical multiplication of a nation of nobles, but one acutely not short of controversy. Of more than four Isaq informants, including a woman, none was aware of their supposedly four siblings from the Sudanese mother. Nor did Dualeh explicate the names of Isaq's Sudanese/African firstborn children or whom their present-day descent lineages constitute, and whether they have returned to Sudan ever since Isaq's death. A clarification of the Sudanese woman's children would have enriched the discussion as an inceptive point for further study. Other oral traditions mention an Abyssinian first wife, but unfortunately Dualeh does not contribute any one of his sources.

In another observation, Dualeh presents Isaq and his presupposed compatriot Arab predecessors as arriving in numerous contingents of separate clans. He remarks above, "The other Somali clans...have [filled] the hinterland, and therefore the Issaq was forced to live at the coastal areas." Here Dualeh seems negligent of specificity in dealing with the subject. At one point he sounds to present individual immigrants before reproducing the same as nations of clans with each cluster clan moving into the Somali peninsula as a separate group of its own. Subsequently, his argument of the other clans filling the hinterland, thus earmarking high population density and/or population pressure inside Somalia, is better explained by Hersi who wrote about a quarter of a century ago Dualeh's book that, "Two hundred years ago the Somali population could not have been a quarter of its present magnitude."[29] Nevertheless, the indication we get from all these traditions exposes the extent to which the Somali genealogical myth had interplayed with the average social psychology. The intent was perhaps to pave way for the achievement of interest in the social pursuit for nobility and the attainment of power.

The debate on this subject heats up as two schools of thought encounter. The 'orientalist' school promoted the Arab genealogy of the Somali people, with the insinuation that all the Somali people, as an outcome of the 'abtirsi' which traces its roots back to the prophet of Islam, belong to a common ancestor. For that matter, they make a homogeneous nation who belongs to one genealogy. In this regard, and apart from I. M. Lewis, Dr. Thomas Eriksen also considers Somalia "...one of the few sub-Saharan states that are truly ethnically homogeneous..."[30] And Saadia Touval describes the Somalis as "...a rare case of a homogeneous ethnic group, inhabiting a large territory and united by culture, religion and tradition."[31] Yet in the widely read *Somali Nationalism*, Touval writes intensely about the composite groups of the Somali nation, without exempting the outcast communities and the artificially self-made cohort of noble clans.

On the other hand, the revisionist scholars do not only dispute the Arab genealogy but also stay firmly opposed to Somalia's ethnocultural homogeneity. Outstanding Somali sociologist, Abdi Kusow, presented some of the most recent radical theories regarding the subtlety of the Somali lineage system. Succinctly, he defines some of the reasons that led to the purportedly long-enduring homogeneity narrative as, "…an assimilative process [which] is in many ways made possible by the fact that the sponsors of the lineage-based narratives directly or indirectly controlled most of the post-colonial Somali political structures."[32] On that narrative, Kusow concludes: It assumes that the Somali society is homogeneous on an abstract idealized level, but in its everyday reality, consists of different groups with different social values and modes of production.[33]

In dehomogenizing the efficaciously traditionalized paradigm of Somali homogeneity, Kusow presents a self-axiomatic case of the outcast communities such as: Tumaal, Yibir, and the Madhiban, who represent a section of the oppressed populace under the homogeneity banner. He argues, "…despite the mythical equality, though, this narrative has been successful in effectively marginalizing and stigmatizing a significant portion of the Somali society as having an unholy origin."[34] In a similar sentiment, however, literary critic, and CUNY professor of comparative literature, Ali Jimale Ahmed, approaches the debate with a postulate of concern and notes, "These perceptions have contributed to the creation of a Somali that is *in* Africa, but not *of* Africa"[35] [Italics original]. From another perspective, Somali Bantu rights advocate and scholar, Omar Eno, clarifies the distinction authoritatively in a grand expression. He reiterates that "Somalia is a diverse nation holding together peoples from different cultures, traditions, languages, values and destinies. Somalia should celebrate the cultural differences that exist, which could ultimately be strength."[36]

In the paragraphs above, I have tried to present some of the pervading faculties of thought regarding Somali genealogy and homogeneity and the basis of their contentions. In this norm, the scope of classification within the Jileec group of Somalia varies. So far, our discussion was focused on the northern part of Somalia, as it is the place many scholars believed as the birthplace of the Somali nation. In the following section, the discourse will turn its course to the southern counterpart and the general predication of the comparative schools of thought, this time quoting written documents and oral traditions where necessary.

The Digil-Mirifle/Sab group and the link across the borders

In Somalia, the groups mainly constituting the Digil-Mirifle,[38] sub-branches of the Hawiye clan, and groups of the coastal area pursue different cultures and modes of living, but find themselves agglutinated erroneously into the nomadic culture of pastoralism. But the variant cultures, distinguished by settlement, ecology, and language are distinctly separate and stand as entities. This does not mean that they are out of the Jileec section of the society, but that there are distinct socio-cultural identities within the Jileec group itself.

Located in several regions along the riverine areas where the two rivers Juba and Shabelle stream their course, the Digil-Mirifle clan of families is symbolized by the distinctive texture of their Af-Maay[39] language. This medium, though different from the written Somali Maxaa-tiri chosen as the standard Somali script, enjoys a lingua franca status across various regions in southern Somalia - from Middle Shabelle to Lower Juba. Different communities do speak varieties of Af-Maay (Maay language). These varieties, though intelligible with one another, are quite distinct and unintelligible with the Maxaa-tiri Somali language.

Unlike their northern brothers, whose loyalty is vested vehemently in the dia-paying (blood-compensation) group or the kinship by lineage, the Reewing (Raxaween) culture puts '*Arlaada*' the country/the land, at the heart of its integrity. Selected elders lead the political hierarchy. They are respected for their wisdom and experience, inconsiderate of their wealth. This is unlike what characterizes the northern nomadic pastoral structure, where wealth influences the hierarchical framework of the society. In the execution of their social duties, the leaders are supported by "akyaar" - a council of elders. "The social organization of the Sab," compares Touval, "is much more hierarchical and formal than that of the Samaale."[40] Likewise, because they are settled, the Reewing, and for this purpose the entire cluster of the wider Digil-Mirifle confederacy are, yet in Touval's words, "less- warlike, less individualistic, more cooperative and more biddable than their Samaale brethren."[41] These cultural characteristics are clear distinctions between the inhabitants of the north and the south of the country, particularly the Sab and the Darood or the Sab and the Isaq.

The Reewing family of clans count their "abtirsi"[42] (patriarchal lineage) back to their ancestor Sab, the supposed brother of Samaale, ancestor of the stocks of clans comprised of what is mainly counted as the major clans: Hawiye, Darod, Dir and Isaaq.   As the late Helander informs us from the Hubeer, the Reewing sub-group he studied, the acquisition of membership is not necessarily only through ascription by birth but equally also by culture.[43] Helander bids reconfirmation to Mukhtar's definition about the gradual decline in the disappearance of 'abtirsi' or 'abtirsiinyo' as one goes further south of the country.[44] These cultural traits are some of the unmentioned differences within the Somali Jileec communities, but the major dimension of extreme genealogical polarity concerns the so-called eponymous ancestor, the father of Sab and Samaale as well as the disagreement regarding the original dispersal point of the Somali people.

The revisionist scholarship contends that contrary to the adherence to Arabness and blood relationship with the prophet Mohammed (PBUH), the Somali people have nevertheless originated not far from the region. Mukhtar provides several reasons why it would not be suitable for Arab migrants, who had escaped persecution in their countries, to have settled in a closely reachable territory where they could be pursued by their enemies. [45] His assumption is based on a premise that the area was unattractive to the Arabs due to four possible reasons, among them: -

i)"The region's proximity" to Arabia where these immigrants could be reached by their persecutors. Earlier incidents have been witnessed where missions were sent for the extradition of fugitives who had run away from persecution in Arabia.

ii) Lack of "urban centers" in the area: because the Islamic culture fostered in urban life, the predominant culture of nomadic pastoralism, symbolized by extensive wandering for the search of water and grazing land for livestock, could offer little attraction to a more civilized Arabian in pursuit of comfortable living.

iii) Absence of "natural harbors" and precarious maritime journeys on violent seas would make a migration to this part of Africa less attractive.

iv) "The lack of viable economic resources" was another disadvantage to choosing this area as a settlement.

These aside, cultural and traditional similarities among the

Galla/Boran, Rendille, Baiso and the Somali are so evident that one may draw a perception of contact which lasted over centuries. The similarities are astonishingly close and seem unobtainable in that complex nature through borrowing or brief relationship. Arguing against the Somali genesis from Arabian migration, Schlee discredits the theory as one not more than "a massive ideological construct."[46] This ideological construct is not only an image vastly accepted by the Somali people, but as we have seen earlier in this chapter, a belief to which the 'authority' on the subject have capitulated.

Disputing the north-south migration as the original movement of an Afro-Arabised Somali people, Kusow supports the opinion that the 16th or 17th century migration was preceded by a previous exodus which took the Somalis from the south to the north of the Horn. He thinks that the scholars who researched on Somalia had obviously based their hypothesis on the second migration which was actually reciprocity of the former south-north movement. Kusow clarifies:

Western anthropologists, particularly Cerulli and I. M. Lewis, postulated well-organized and rather elaborate north-south migration routes and trends based on an otherwise highly mythical but ideologically enduring northern Somali oral tradition.[47]

An examination of the chain of names leading to the ancestral father provides enormous discrepancy of numerous non-Arab names. How such names intruded into use by Arabs who were alien to the speech community, (if not by mythical Somali oral tradition) is also suspect and highly mysterious. Linguist Abdalla Mansur raises suspicion over how an Arab could use such name as "Kablalah"[48] and others that are so alien even in the southern part of the country.

As researchers shifted their speculation from Arabia and focus more on Southern and southeastern Ethiopia, the Cushitic factor of Somali origin developed more weight and credence. Murdock,[49] among other writers, holds the view that the Somalis could be related to other Cushitic groups like the Oromo, with the hypothesis that the original dispersal point was from southern Ethiopia up the northern Horn where Somalis settled for a time. Later on, Herbert Lewis[50] and Fleming[51] wrote in support of the same theme, which so far stands firm, albeit the difficulty in convincing a majority of Somalis about the new shift in their ancestral father from Arab to African. In fact the shift has increased the frustration since Africanity is an identity the Somalis look down upon. This disgust is revealed by their protest against the "status under the law of the Colony of Natives of Africa" which classified them as Africans, and against which they preferred that, "They should be recognized as Asiatics."[52]

Mukhtar's reasons (mentioned above) aside, historical linguistics elucidates that the southern-spoken Af-Maay of the Digil Mirifle ethnic community could have been the proto language spoken by a proto-Reewing proto-Somali people prior to the early south-north migration. In corroboration, Mohamed Nuuh Ali's lexicostatistical investigation illustrates the distribution of the language as it impacts on communities along the riverine south through central and upwards in the northern regions.[53] Ali's linguistic assessment produced heavier density of speech population of Af-Maay in the south, assuming gradual decrease across and over the regions towards the north. The result purveys an indication of the southern and southeastern Ethiopia territory in the vicinity of the Digil-Mirifle habitat as a possible original dispersal point. The probability is that those immigrants were the proto-Reewing -Somali ancestors, who, in Ehret's view, afterwards developed to a proto-Somali offspring.[54]

In my opinion, the fact that there are about three times more Af-Maay dialects in use today than the Somali Maxaa-tiri vehicle of communication further demerits the disputation of the latter as 'Somali proper' or original dialect. It also supports the Maay-Maay distribution hypothesis and its decline as we go along the north where not as many 'Af Maxaa' or 'Maxaa-tiri' Somali proper dialects are in practice among the nomadic communities in those areas. The decline in the dialect frequency, therefore, nurtures the presumption of the linguistic effect the geographical distance has impacted on the growth of multi-dialects as we move towards the north. After every caution is considered, I can safely argue about more Maay-Maay dialects than there exists of its "Maxaa-tiri" version of the Somali languages.

Another contention between north and south surrounds the interpretation of the name 'Somali' itself. Whereas the north bases the nomenclature on the imperative compound verb 'Soo-maal" interpreted as "go-milk", the Maay language presupposes the same but with an added connotation:

a) 'So-maal' = go milk (any animal) a term usable by both languages Maay and Maxaa, but which the northerners prefer for the camel.

b) 'Sa'-maal' = go milk (the animal referred being 'sa' a cow) specific interpretation to only Af-Maay.

The second sentence is suggestive of the agro-pastoral mode of the Reewing as well as some Hawiye sub-groups who herd cattle rather than camel. Touval gives a more variant interpretation and puts it as 'Zu-mal', which denotes a wealth-owner, and also as 'Soumahe', which is the Amharic equivalent to 'heathen'.[55] Being more analytical in his observation, Hersi acknowledges that, "out of five popular explanations, three are based on Arabic etymologies, the other two being naturally enough, from Amharic and Somali sources."[56]

Hersi's explanation enriches his consent with earlier explications given by Lewis,[57] Drake-Brockman[58] and Johnston.[59] But to overshadow history and limit the scope of knowledge, Somalia's curriculum and instructional texts, particularly in the Social Studies, were tailor-made to suit the ideology of Arabness and homogeneity. The impact of the mythical belief did not only compromise Somalia's identity but it also confused its Africanity. Of all the above-mentioned explanations, only 'soo-maal', 'go milk' was often highlighted in the school textbooks with the multi-ethnic communities in the country sausaged into one genealogical lineage of two ancestors that originated from Arabia.

The words 'zu mal' are Arabic and mean the 'owner of wealth'. If the nomenclature 'Somalia' is assumed to have been derived from 'zu mal', it does not inform us in the historiography about the wealth of this man and his offspring. The early scholars, historians as well as anthropological ethnographers, seem not to have analyzed beyond the concoctions and imaginations of their informants, possibly as a tribe. But when we leave Arabia and Arabic terminology, and come back to Africa, especially the greater Horn of Africa, I can safely assume a relationship between the tribe name Somalia and the sub-tribe name *Zamal*. My hypothesis leans on the fact that *Zamal* is one of four sub-tribes that belong to the Bilen or Bogos tribe. If we consider this notion, *Zamal* becomes a relative of sub-tribes such as "Sukuneiti, Ad Hadembes and Bet Gabru" who lived among the Tigre about a territory called Keren. There is also some relationship with the Agau tribe or group of tribes, neighbors of Abyssinia. The Agau were settled in the Lasta and Waag. Other groups are found in Agaumeder on the bank of Abai River, while the main language of Agaumeder is Awiya. (See *A Handbook of Abyssinia*, 1917)

The information provided here about *Zamal* makes us stumble, though accidentally, onto two linguistically important words. One is

'Waag' which is close to the Somali word 'Waaq' meaning 'sky'; also some people explain it as to mean a type of bird. The other one is 'Awiya', and is more important as it is very close to the name of the clan 'Hawiya', scattered in parts of southern Somalia. From here, one can 'albeit lightly' perceive a relationship between Awiya the language spoken in Agaumeder and the tribe or clan calling itself *Hawiya* which is established in parts of central and southern Somalia today. I need to note that in many historical events, when people migrate from their home territory to another settlement, they take with them a symbol of one or more of their cultural identities and keep for a long time to come as souvenir; hence retaining *Hawiya* as a tribal name reminiscent of the language the group used to speak. The second possibility could be that the foreign geographers, explorers or other visitors had taken the language name for the people too, since in many cases both conform to identity of a given people in a given place. (More in *A Handbook of Abyssinia*, 1917)

In any case, another mystery surrounds the inception of the name Somali. Its recent appearance in the history of the Horn could be an explanation of the beginning of a conglomeration of diverse peoples. Possibly they had had no blood affinity in the beginning, but joined later under that name. The reason for such unity could be to face together what might have been a universal threat they were unable to tackle as individual groups; the likelihood of this enemy being Abyssinia and the Christian culture.

My argument about the Somali-Qureishite pedigree is not intended to undermine the significance of the immigrant community: Arabs, Persians and other Asiatics who are mentioned in the Somali history. The effect of their varied roles in the cultural and commercial domain is remarkably vivid in multiple spheres affecting the wider Somali culture. But the re-evaluation of the traditions and the revisiting of the historiography of the country where necessary need to be regarded as tasks paramount for clearer understanding. In another sense, where a certain theory or a social belief has been investigated to produce a divergent result from what was the paradigm, then the amended version must be studied comparatively at par with the existing theory, if at all the old one is not discredited.

Horn culture in context

A further discussion takes us to a study of some of the cultures and traditions of the African peoples living in the closer periphery of Somalia notably those in the very neighborhood, their socio-cultural similarities and the possible relationship they might have harmonized with Somalia. Numerous customs and traditions believed in Somalia as part of the social culture, are also widely practiced by other communities in the neighboring countries, so we look at a very few of these practices.

'Tuf' (blessed spit)

We begin with the tradition of *'tuf'* or *'tufta'* which is often practiced in Somalia in thanksgiving and communal gatherings, during which a blessing is given by 'spitting' lightly onto someone sick or one to be blessed. Sometimes the spit is breathed into a bowl of water *'tahliil'* as a blessed/propitious drink for an ailing person suffering from a kind of disease or spirit possession. Alternatively, one may use the blessed medicine for shower in driving away sickness. This tradition might have been part of a culture derived from a proto-Somali people. Superstition apart, the proto-Rendille cultures of *"hanjuf"* the spit with the blessings, or the belief of the *'dahanti kulel'* the hot hand[60] that hurts, is primarily a presupposition of an earlier cultural contact between a proto-Rendille and a proto-Somali people. One may contend with the beliefs of paganism as entwined in this religious ritual, especially considering Islam as the faith of present day Somalia, but we are engaged in a discussion about socio-cultural beliefs that existed in pre-Islamic eras, specifically when paganism, sky-worshipping and idol-anointing were cherished prevalently as a mode of communication with the omnipotent, metaphysical being.

The second significance of this cultural practice is in its linguistic domain, which renders opulent etymological value to the relationship of the spoken word between Rendille and Af-Maay. The reason for this hypothesis is encouraged by the fact that the term *'hanjuf'* is semantically as well as phonetically congruent in both languages. The equivalent of *'hanjuf'* in the northern Somali Maxaa-tiri dialect is (*candhuuf*), while in a certain southern Somali dialect it is pronounced as (*cantuuf*).

'Megel' (real man/worthy- man)

Subsequently, the tradition of beneficence involving the gift to the needy, whether in camel or in any other commodity, is invariably also part and parcel of the cultural life of the Somalis' closest cousins, the Rendille. The act gives the benefactor an attribute as *'deeqsi'* (generous), and hence 'a man'. In Rendille culture such a person is called *'mejel'* (man enough) for being a daring benefactor who parts with a camel as a gift.[61] Again, despite a slight variance in the phoneme situated in the middle consonant 'j', the terminology is very intelligible with the Af-Maay word *'megel'* (man); it would very likely qualify for a version of the multiple dialects which the Maay-Maay language is a medium in many regions of the country.

'Arbaca mugdi u dambeeyso'

Another paganic-like tradition, one which has endured over the centuries, is the avoidance of the last Wednesday of the month, popularly known in Somalia as 'Arbaca-mugdi-u-dambeyso' meaning the last Wednesday falling in the dark period of the waning moon.

This day is often avoided in the initiation and undertaking of social activities such as ceremonies, engagements, business ventures and marriages. The 'dark' Wednesday is associated with misfortunes and disadvantages; therefore it is depicted as a matter of great fear for its presumably negative future consequences. It is not by coincidence, however, that the same socio-cultural beliefs are shaped in the social customs of the Boran, the Oromo and the Rendille living in the East Africa region, particularly in parts of Kenya and Ethiopia.

'Dab-shid-ka'

Cerulli expressed in another tradition that the Somali New Year[62] is celebrated with a festival of *'dab-shid'* the lighting of fire. Unaware of Cerulli's research at that time, but conducting an independent study for Heegan newspaper, local English weekly, I commented severally about *'dab-shidka'* cultural event. One of them is reproduced here:

In the evening before the Aw-Dangole performances are over, everybody on either side of the bank [of the river] lights a small heap of fire in front of the house, and everybody steps over it saying,

"BAASOOW BANAAN BAX – BARAKOOY IMAAW," which means "BEGONE, EVILS, BEGONE – COME BELSSINGS, COME," in order to usher in the new year and its blessings. This is what is known as DAB-SHIDKA (The fire-lighting), and it is observed in many parts of the country too.[63] (clarification in parentheses recent.)

However, '*Dab-Shidka*', the fire-lighting, is one of several ways to mark the celebration and festivities observed in welcoming the New Year. Other equally enduring traditional activities like '*Istunka*' stick-fighting are held in some parts of the country, Afgoie being the most famous town for the stick-fighting. As Schlee manifested in writing, the chants performed during this fire-lighting ritual, the Rendille, Boran/Oromo and Sekuye tribes remind one of the "...remnants of their earlier Somaloid (proto-Rendille-Somali) language which have been preserved in this conservative ritual context."[64]

Dr. Hersi tends to deem '*Istunka*' stick-fight as a custom adopted from the people of ancient Egypt, who also have a similar event known as 'tahtib'.[65] But considering the numerous cultural concordances Somalia shares with the Cushitic neighbors, I would personally make the basis of my argument that, though an in-depth study on comparative cultural studies is beyond the scope of this work, the custom has emerged not far from precincts within East Africa rather than the postulate of its importation from a country as far as Egypt on the North of the continent. The support is that the Oromo do have and perform the same as part of their celebration for the new year.[66]

In southern Somalia, Shanti-Aleemood, a sub-branch of the Digil-Mirifle, settled in Wanla-Weyn (Daafeed) between Afgoie and Bur-Hakaba, are also practicing observers very fond of the stick-fight. In Bay, it is observed regularly. To mark the occasion, even unorganized or little organized youths perform it in their own way by conducting a simple replica of the fight in some districts. By doing so, Ismail Ibdi Issa narrates that "the youth enjoy the welcoming of the New Year so that they too get its propitious blessing."[67]

In Afgoie, the southern Somalia town whose name is often coined with '*Istunka*', the inception of the stick-fight is attributed neither to Egypt nor to the Cushitic race in Eastern Africa. The inhabitants rather believe that the five male children of an earlier ruler called 'Au-Adeer', who at the time held the hegemonic leadership in Afgoie, have started this traditional performance. Again, considering the fact that Au-Adeer was a Gobron who migrated from Upper Jubba, the area closest to the

Oromo settlements in Ethiopia, with Maay being the sociolinguistic medium of the Gobron, one might be tempted to postulate an Ethiopian connection here with *Istunka*. I am not ultimately making a conclusion on the originator of the custom, but this is part of the tradition as related to me by elders of almost a hundred years old at the time of my interview with them in the late '70s and early '80s as part of my personal interest in the culture of '*Istunka*':

> Whenever Istunka is mentioned, its roots go back to the five brothers born to one of Afgoie's most famous of ancient Sultans, Au-Adeer, called Shanta Au-Adeer (the five of Au-Adeer), who first were the brains behind what stands at the present day as one of the most celebrated festivals held in the southern regions of the Somali Democratic Republic.[68]

In Afgoie, the elders are great repository of the history and traditions as these are passed from one generation to the other. As far as '*Istunka*' is concerned, most of them have been participating (in the words of one of my interviewees) - "...ever since we opened our eyes."[69]

Although Afgoie and other areas in Somalia may undertake the New Year festivals of *Istunka* and *Dabshidka* as their neighboring Oromo and other peoples elsewhere, it carries much more cultural significance for the Afgoians. The occasion avails every able '*laashin*' bard with an opportunity to produce his poetic talent in the creation of spontaneous '*mar*'[70] verse, to which the background chorus group can dance and chant. The '*Shirib*' or '*Shurub*'[71] as it is called, a chanting procession, is an opportunity for the rival groups on either bank of the river to visit their counterparts, to criticize and taunt their rivals poetically of the lewd or indecent acts committed by any of their kin over the years and particularly since the last '*Istunka*'. As such, it is a very significant celebration embedded with socio-cultural values. It marks an unadulterated connection between the society and their culture, an aspect which gives considerable importance to the reason why the '*Shurub*', '*Dab-shidka*', '*Istunka*' and other related celebrations are culturally interwoven values of the social identity.

Though I deal with Afgoie/Istunka theme elsewhere as an independent study, I may throw here just an illustrative example of the social connection to the celebrations and subsequently why we consider the oral traditions and oral literature so indispensable, by studying the next verse:-

A *'laashin'* bard from the west bank and his team crossed to the east and produced this *'mar'* verse:-

Ninki Sheey dad qaato Shuqulaa u yaal
Shukri ii Shariifoow Sheelaraa la geeyi.[72]

Translation:
> Whoever squanders public property, takes oneself to task,
> For, lying in custody at Sheelaro remain Shukri and Shariffoow.[73]

This verse bears multiple significances. First, it corresponds to an article by Virginia Luling, an anthropologist who studied Afgoie from the perspective of the Gobron Sultanate. While conducting her research in Afgoie, she wrote about the municipal administration where she says: "...During my stay in Afgoie, however, this office was there in abeyance since its last two incumbents had been imprisoned for embezzling funds..."[74] At the time of her visit, Luling was probably unaware of this verse, which now re-strengthens her story of the incumbents under custody for embezzlement of public funds, and how the local traditional intellectual measured the event in his bardic verse.

A brief deductive analysis of the verse takes us beyond the incident as an isolated event, and shows us:

a)   The connection between the verse and the two incumbent office-bearers Luling mentioned in her article though she did not give names, that actually these two were Shukri Sheikh Giireey and Shariff Hassan, alias Shariffoow, two prominent social figures in the district of Afgoie whose imprisonment was a town-talk at the time. Also many more verses exist but will be cited elsewhere.

b)   How in the oral literature, the traditional intellectual/poet produces his creativity related to social events as realities of the day, and the disgust the community expresses on misappropriation of public funds and abuse of office and authority.

c)   The significance of the verse (and other social festivities of Istunka/Dab-shidka) to the social history as a retrievable material archived in the human/social memory of the local people who are conscious of their cultural way of life.

d)   That historical narratives archived safely in the human/social memory can be accessed in times of necessity for the recounting and narration passed from one generation to the other via memorization, very useful approach to reconstructing social history of the people. When I (author) first heard the verse, I was a young boy in my early teens, but in my late forties now when I quote that same verse effectively as part of a historical reconstruction linking the verse to relevant evidence which a foreign scholar (Luling) had published in an academic journal.

The extrapolation given here is not to explore in detail about the prominence of the *Istunka* and its *Dab-Shidka* festival, but to show a reflection of the people's adherence to the customs as events worthy of commemoration, hence their collection and memorization of the verses reminiscent of *Istunka* as an occasion of particular social significance.

As I noted earlier in this study, the Arabo-Persian immigrants in particular and Asia in general, has achieved a memorable historical place in the Somali society in multiple continuum. Long time maritime links were established as Hourani explicates that, "Persian relations with the African coastal regions were largely via this maritime trade networks."[75] As far as China, the land of the Berbers (Somalia) was known to seafarers and geographers in pre-Islamic periods, with a noticeable un-Islamic culture[76] which Duyvendak elucidates, among other writers, where references of toponyms such as 'Bobabi' (Somali) were given.[77] Although in the 12th century Al-Idris[78] writes about the Somali coast of Zeila as yet a city under Christian influence, a few centuries later, Asian travelers witnessed how Islam was flourishing along the Somali littoral, including Brava (Baraawe), Mogadishu (Muqdisho) and Zeila (Seylac). Ibn Batuta[79] comments on these towns as important sources of commercial commodities like rhinoceros horns, ivory, hides, tortoise shells and aromatic merchandise rarely available in other parts of the world. These commodities, according to the historians, were supplied to Asian countries and Egypt. To say the least, the Islamization of Somalia is as a result of the arrival of Asian immigrants, whatever their other motives might have been.

Notwithstanding the commercial connections, the most visible legacy from Asia is the generations of people who originated from there, but took residence on the coastal towns of Somalia. With them, they brought in a culture and civilization that marinated a harmonious interplay with the cultures, traditions and general mode of living of the host communities. But when all the credit due is adequately acknowledged, we are left with no satisfactory evidence of traces of agnatic link with Qureish as it is claimed in northern Somalia. All the justification we have for this relationship doesn't go beyond the fabrication of chains of patrilineal names leading to a humdrum of Cushitic and Arabite mixture.[80] Because former scholars and others who listened to the traditions have taken them at face value, without questioning the intricacies within, a homogeneity myth of Arab origin has dominated the Somali historiography.

Moreover, early explorers provide a clear account that they had not encountered any meaningful evidence attributable to Arabness in culture, character or otherwise in the areas mentioned as the first arrival points of Somalia's Arab forefathers. Instead, it is cities like in the Banaadir coast, where a genealogical relationship to Arabia could be claimed. Here exists proven cultural, technological as well as architectural evidence, but the case is quite vice versa in the northern part of the country. This particular territory, where the cradle claim is most purported, Hersi acknowledges, has provided little attraction to Arab immigrants and thus much less mention in the records, a theory which enhances more approval to Mukhtar's four reasons referred above in this chapter.

Further shedding more light on this particular coastal area allegedly affected by population pressure from Arabia, and which is situated between the north of Mogadishu and east of Zeila, Hersi registers:

> Medieval geographical and historical sources are all but silent about this Coastal stretch. An immediate and also the most reasonable interpretation of this silence would regard it as meaning that there were no significant Arab settlements or activities along that coast. [81]

The identity dilemma

Certainly, the conundrum allied with the Somali identity is a multilayered puzzle of kaleidoscopic internal and external dimensions. The entanglement finds Somalia in a very tight situation, an unavoidable dilemma of choosing between an African identity which it has denigrated (see above note No. 52) and an Arab origin which has failed proof in all the tested genealogical conceptions.

Critical of the ideology of Arabness and the ensuing homogeneity which offered little or nothing to respect equality among all the communities, Omar Eno deplores the former constitution of Somalia as a document that had "...no clear criteria for citizenship qualifications ..." He further emphasizes, "The constitution [to be enacted after the civil war] must therefore clearly define who is a Somali."[82] (Elaboration in parentheses mine)

In the shadow of Omar Eno's strong criticism lies Somalia's appointment to top positions of Somali--Kenyan and Somali--Ethiopian citizens as Mariam Arif reconfirmed later:

> ...a Somali born in Djibouti, Kenya or Ethiopia had the right even to become a president of the republic of Somalia... One of the former Ministers of Defense was originally born in the Northern Frontier Districts of Kenya and had served as a Kenyan Military Officer for many years... There were members of the Supreme Revolutionary Council, army and police generals and officers, Ministers, ambassadors and other high-ranking government officials who were treated like any other Somali citizen.[83]

In the pretext of predilection for Arabness, Somalia has deliberately compromised the identities and cultures of diverse communities in the country. They suffer due to their ethnic African origin and/or with regard to invented forms of tribal hierarchy. This reality, as Kusow[84] would agree with me, agitates the debate that Somaliness itself is determined primarily according to pre-set limitations governed by geographical location, and effectively ironed out through clan categorization. The psychosocial dictum concealed in the distribution of the degree of Somaliness is well preserved as a medium for creating self-ennoblement and superior clan and cultural identity. In a more elaborate fashion, it means that those closer to the cradle where the mythical Arabness had had its initial contact with Somalia (by clan and location) are contextually genealogically more Somali than others whose geographical settlements and patrilineal adjacency are metaphorically distantly located. This system of dichotomy and stratification has been cautiously 'midwifed' that it engineered an artificial deficiency for every component of culture and clan in Somalia, while 'pure nobility' is regarded only to the immediate descendants of Darod and Isaq, the offspring of the two immigrants allegedly hailing from Southern Arabia.

As a discussion on the topic may lead us way beyond the limits of this study, an understanding of the phenomenon remains worthwhile. As I already argued about the *Jareer* and *Jileec* division of the Somali people, we are still in our exploration for the understanding of the clan divisions paramount within the Non-Bantu *Jileec* communities of Somalia. We have focused thus far on the Digil/Mirifle and the so-called descendants of Sheikh Isaq and Sheikh Jabarti. These have successfully 'ennobled' themselves as the supreme descendants and Somali proper. The ennoblement has become a divisive tool to demean the rest of their brethren into a lower status than theirs, but somehow higher than the others outside that genealogical bracket. We now turn to the Hawiye clan of families and the phenomenon of linguistic supremacy in a society claimed to share the same language.

The Hawiye

Categorically, the Hawiye make a part of the *Jileec* Somalis. The widely believed traditions describe them as descendants of Hirab who is a brother of Darod. In unraveling through the multiple lineage and genealogical patterns, it is really hard to select one authentic version, an episode that narrows the reliability of any of them.

The four sub-clans of Abgaal, Murusade, Hawadle and Habar-Gidir mainly numerically dominate the Hawiya clan. In settlement, the Habar-Gidir share boundaries with elements of the Darod in the central region while their Hawiye brothers are towards the south. The Abgaal allegedly constitute the largest number and are found in several areas from somewhere in the proximity of the central towards regions in the south, comprising pastoral and agro-pastoral cultures of living (see Ali J. Ahmed 2008). The Hawadle are adjacent to the Habar-Gidir in the central part and share sections of the Shabelle River with the Reer Shabelle, Makanne and Reer Isse *Jareer* communities. The Murusade sub-clan's settlement is subtle. Some of them live in parts in the central, others in the neighborhood of Ethiopia, while more segments live in various regions in the south. The Murusade are said to be related to the Karanle Hawiye who settle in the proximity of Ethiopia, living with units of the Sheekhaal, also of the Hawiye.

Except the Habar-Gidir who depend on nomadic pastoralism, the other three sub-clans practice a mélange of pastoralism and farming, although certain units among them may engage in these modes separately according to their environment. Sometimes the mode of living depends squarely on the community that accepted them earlier as 'Sheegad' clients, like the Murusade in parts of the south as well as the

Abgaal and Habar-Gidir who settled in locations away from their de-marcated ethnic territories. The next chapter will give a brief discussion about 'Sheegad/Sheegato' client phenomenon.

Linguistically, the Hawiye communicate in a unique dialect of the Maxaa-tiri Somali language. They also communicate in other southern dialects as conditioned by their geographic location as well as the sociolinguistic community among whom they live. For instance, linguistically, it is indistinguishable between a Jareer speaker and an Abgaal counterpart who grew up both in Jowhar. Likewise, some Murusade, Garre, or Gaaljecel in Afgoie and its environs all speak Afgoie dialect of the Somali Maxaa-tiri version although they may also speak fluently one or more Maay dialects as spoken by the sedentary residents. Additionally, every community's tongue is in its own distinct dia-lect of the Somali language, an accent that typifies the particular clan of the speaker, especially if one is brought up among one's own sociolin-guistic community. May be a few sentences can help to compare the familiar Abgaal dialect to that of the north, and contrasting them simul-taneously with Af-Maay:

Af-Maay/Maay language	Ab-gaal/Hawiye (southern dialect)	Woqooyi (northern dialect)	English
Maay fathaase?	Xaad rabtaa?	Maxaad dooneysaa?	What do you want?
Surungkuungaa ka neebsat-hooyne	Mahaanaan isaga ba-jeeynaa.	Halkan baan isaga na-saneynaa.	We're just resting here.
Meelaa iska roog. (Meelaa surunaaw)	Rabtaan iska joog. (Mahaaga iska rorog)	Halkan iska joog. (Halkaaga taagnoow)	Just stay here. (Be where you are)
Igaarti kooyteey?	Igaarti ma timid?	Wiilashi ma yimaadeen?	Have the boys come?
Ikorooy	Iikaadi	Isug	Wait for me.

Source: by the author

Apart from the genealogical unification, it is relevant to note that linguistic stereotyping constructively exists in Somalia. I may agree though, with Allport,[85] about stereotypes not being always negative, but only when, in the opinion of Taylor and Simard, as explained by Hewstone and Giles, "...that out-group stereotypes may lead to the positive outcome of mutual social differentiation."[86]   But, like in the genealogical domain, the sociolinguistic registers, styles and variations in accent are categorized as less pure as we move from the north to the south. The variances of these modes of communication are therefore thought of as adulterated versions of the 'pure' or 'standard' Somali language as spoken by the self-ennobled clans. The basis for this stratum does not take into account the paradigmatic reality of social status and geographical area reflected in the speech-community's language. Often it is extended well beyond the communicative tool it is and to mean the formation of superior ethnic identity. Linguistic stratification and negative stereotyping, in the Somali social etiquette, run parallel with clan stratification, opposing the linguist's method of measuring or assuming one's language according to one's class.

Sociolinguistics, in the Somali context, is an area not yet sufficiently researched on, but nevertheless a useful tool utilized as a basis for ethnic stratification where the further one is from the south, one's language is deemed more 'noble', better and purer in form and lore. Situations are usually witnessed where a speaker from the southern regions is prejudiced: *"Af-Soomaali ma yaqaan"* doesn't know Somali language, although that speaker is a citizen of the country by birth and breed (see also Luling, *Somali Sultanate*). This episode happens simply because one doesn't belong to the sociolinguistic group of the northerner person criticizing. For this reason, linguistically the Somali language itself plays a more divisive role than its external display as a unifying factor.

Contrary to the northerners' belief of their dialect as the uncorrupted original accent of the language, the southern speakers think the northerners speak 'sullied' Somali, hence their reference to their northern brothers as 'Soomaali khaldaan' which is 'mistaken or error-bound Somali' - a phrase denoting that the northerners are incomprehensive in the dialect of their spoken Somali.

According to this observation, ethnic nobility does not give justification only in the genealogical composition of the northerners but also a superior rank for their dialect of the Somali language. That divide has been effectively legitimated through language policy and language planning (LPLP) during the standardization of the Somali orthography and upon its inception in 1972. The dictatorial leader of the nation who was from a sub-clan of the Darood clan, has used his powers to that end and therefore above the common man's disputation.

Some southern intellectuals like Jamal Mohamed Hagi[87] admit that the Somali social system operates from a self-ennobled nomadism. That indoctrination simply but emphatically determines that whatever is related culturally to nomadism is by any standard superior to all the rest. Because there is little understanding of the language science, we may find very few who would accept that all dialects of the same language have equal importance to the speech communities concerned rather than inferiorate them due to the psycholinguistic substance conditioned by their society and environment.

The most peculiar stratification is that Hawiye, who are also considered as the descendents of the Arab-Qureishite forefather, are adjusted in a social place better than others but lower in degree than the higher premise occupied by their northern Darood and Isaq brethren. Because genealogically, geographically as well as linguistically they are situated away from the cradle point where Somali nobility was born, it has become adequate reason to deny them full noble status and equal ethno-social place.

The outcast groups and the un-islamic phenomenon in Somalia

These are groups who are despised. Their social place is not considered even at the bottom of "homogeneous" Somalia, but in fact outside of it. As the *'raagaay'* (old tradsitionists) said, the outcasts are akin to the aforementioned Somali nobles. Their trouble began when their ancestor *allegedly* ate to satisfaction meat from an animal not slaughtered in the *'halal'* accepted Islamic way. Though the traditions suggest his hunger during the commission of the act, ever since that unknown day, all the descendants of that forefather have been ostracized as unclean human beings. Due to that impurity the generations from the lineage became subject for social exclusion. The 'nobility' decided these are unapproachable for social relationships like marriage, but fit for undertaking occupational tasks such as iron-smithing, circumcising children and other menial activities which the 'pure' clans scorn doing.[88]

We need to envisage here that according to the traditions, the forefather of the outcast communities committed the act *together with* his brother, the pedigree of the noble branch. They allegedly *both* fed on the meat of the 'decayed' animal, but strangely enough, the act didn't affect the purity or status of the group that claim nobility. The reason given for the retention of their purity is because he had not eaten to satisfaction as his sibling had done.

These communities are called diverse names some of which are related to occupational tasks rather than tribe or clan. Examples of them are: - Tumaal, Yibir, Yaxar, Midgaan, Madhibaan. These communities all come under the confederation of Gaboye, which is a nomenclature derived from the quiver which these groups keep their arrows as hunters and as warriors. (Read more about the Gaboye in Eno and Eno, forthcoming)

The outcasts are subject to a continuum of attachment to and detachment from a clan as per the dictation of the 'noble' group they are associated with. These so-called outcasts are normal human beings like others: polite, respectful, born-Muslims, respectable, pretty, intelligent and inseparable by look and complexion from the claimants of nobility, but they suffer under perpetual social castigation administered against them by none other than their own Somali brethren. As a result, they can't enjoy equal status in the society.[89]

Ioan M. Lewis, for whatever motive, has embraced Somali pastoralists to a title of a volume *"A Pastoral Democracy"*, when in reality these outcast groups have encountered unfair mistreatment under undemocratic pastoral society. As has been enlightened by Lewis himself, they (outcasts) are not allowed to sit and contribute their point as equals in the nomadic council of meeting. The pastoral 'nobles' consisting of the lineage members in the '*shir*' meeting, as the tradition recognizes, reach the decisions. In such segregation, one may query with concern why a scholar of the caliber of Dr. Lewis failed to demarcate between discrimination and democracy! Or possibly he needed not know see the reality except from the eyes of his 'noble' informants.

The claim of 'pastoral democracy' contradicts the values of democracy on the platform of an artificially molded social stratum in contravention of the principles of Islam and of homogeneity. Exclusion garnished with debasement of any magnitude do not foster accommodation to democracy when important elements of the social grain are marginalized due to idealized divisions set on the basis of ethnic self-ennoblement. Analyzing the situation, Marian A. Enow opines that the dominant nomads, to the social disadvantage of the dominated, determine social places.[90] Under these circumstances, the reality behind the concept of "all men are councilors and all men are politicians,"[91] serves as a continuum of oppression.

Generally, egalitarianism cannot exist in synchrony with pervasive discrimination in the decision-making ranks but should encourage the provision of unbiased access for equal distribution of wealth and other opportunities for social mobility - vertically much so as horizontally. But the antithesis, to democracy, is that the status of the outcast groups uncovers a hidden system of prolonged unjust which smears indignity to the philosophy of democracy and practice of egalitarianism. If anything, Lewis had better reserved his comments on the pastoral injustices that regulate and inform the culture of the Somali nomadic life than celebrate it as democracy.

Equal status, opportunity and distribution of power and resources are concepts entwined with the ethics and cultural values of any given society, but in the Somali pastoral structure, elements of moral decay such as discrimination and degradation are pursued pragmatically, and by the day. Such realities have laid a demarcation line that places the privileged in the egalitarian status and the underprivileged or unprivileged off it in the periphery. In my view, the thesis, in form and character, absolutely disqualifies the ideals of either democracy or egalitarianism.

The inference from the revelation renders that the decisions reached by members of the so-called nomads in the '*shir*' council meeting, are not in any way based on just regarding the proliferation of interested-party interference. For, in the sad eyes of the discriminated outcasts, the practice is tantamount to localized imperialism void of any moderate consolation. The social institution itself constitutes nothing short of a promoter of ethno-political preponderance, which decides the limitations of the rights of the 'other' group within the community! The cultural behavior has developed disintegration among a society so characterized by an outward homogeneity, thus prompting another contending statement by Eno who writes:

> Normally within a homogeneous ethnic group, an intense feeling of group solidarity develops and an attitude of egalitarianism becomes evident. However, there is no solidarity whatsoever to be seen in Somalia. The ethnic dichotomy is in fact much deeper than in any other heterogeneous society on earth.[92]

In her article, "Caste Discrimination", Smita Narula describes the cast system as "...a hidden apartheid of segregation, modern-day slavery, and other extreme forms of discrimination, exploitation and violence."[93] By contrast, the Somali outcasts undergo similar oppression and abuses as mentioned by Narula. They have been systematically kept off-board the societal framework. The ethnocentric system of the Somali society has denied these groups even the ownership of a tribal land (See Mohamed-Abdi Mohamed 1997.) In essence, they cannot settle as an independent social body of their own, unless they are attached to other clans as dependents and subordinates.

Like the Osu of Nigeria, the Baraku of Japan and the Dalits of India and Sri Lanka, the Somali outcasts suffer under extensive social oppression and are subject to permanent social prejudice. They are demeaned as pollutants within the social fabric. Moreover, Somalia's widely exaggerated uniqueness as a homogeneous nation of one society sharing the same origin, one language, same religion and so on, declined to accommodate and address the outcasts with an equal status. They live as a very low social class and as subordinate humans. "Midgaan-Madhiban have never had any secure rights or protection in Somali society. Even in overseas Somali society, they still face hatred, harassment and abuse," reveals Asha Samad,[94] who articulated her concern in a paper about the undesirable social situation of the Somali outcast communities.

I partly agree with Dipankar Gupta on the notion that "caste-based stratification displays very different characteristics"[95] in that it constitutes, in the Somali perspective, multifaceted phenomena under the manipulation of the perpetrating 'noble' groups. One of these characteristics is that, although in the U.S.A. or in other racial societies, blacks and whites etc. may contract into marriage, it is highly impossible in Somalia for such a social institution to bring together an outcast and a 'self-ennobled' into a unit of one family, irrespective of sameness in color, clan or creed. Still, within the context of the characteristics of cast-based stratification, I disagree with Gupta on the misplaced opinion in his study of 2000 which reads in part, "No caste would agree that members of other castes are made up of substances better than theirs,"[96] which he emphasizes again in his later work '*Caste, race, politics*' when he says, "No caste would like its people to marry outside the community. No caste would like to merge its identity with any other caste."

First of all, and for all practical purposes, the cast system is employed in multiple ways than one. Each method of practice in the institution has its orientation as a result of the cultural effects on the belief and social behavior of the community concerned. But one aspect of castism dominates everywhere, taken as a form of racism or otherwise: that it is an inhuman social phenomenon based on the oppression of an advantaged group against a disadvantaged breed whose social identity is often under suppression and stigma. Under this reality, the matter of concern should not be displayed in the simplistic symbiosis adopted on personal opinion, as Gupta wants us to condone, but conversely holistically in the context of the wider destructive impact it holds on the wider societal dimension. We should not overlook the burden that the cast institution is heavily worshipped by the oppressors, culturally and socio-psychologically, as a sacred component of the social values.

Secondly, because the awareness inherent in the ill practice of castism lives with us through the tutelage of our social culture, no individual would indulge in his/her desire for exogamy, marriage beyond the societal confine, which the cast system has mapped the borders. The oft-coveted principle of the 'upper' society designed the psychological framework under which it implemented the delimitations and cynic social demarcations as a burden the 'others' cannot cross beyond.

Thirdly, because castism encompasses identity, superiority, alienation, degradation and other symbolically abstract beliefs, it would inflict more loss of identity to the superficially constructed high cast 'nobility' than the socially excluded because, as Marian Enow believes, "'Equality for all' poses threat to the beliefs of supremacy and nobility of the oppressors."[97]

Finally, social mobility in the spheres of politics, economy or in any other individual   achievement (by a lucky few) in the metaphors of the physical world cannot be adjudicated as a variable of meaningful inferential compensation for counter-balancing the afflictions of moral devastation accrued against the outcast communities. The consequence extends well beyond any degree of privileges or achievement - call it Sanskritization or whatever. These privileges amount to nothing more than individual opportunities acquired by a few. When we consider the generations of helpless 'others' born into an inherited, socially ascribed stigmatization and oppression into a down-trodden class as   social scum, I don't imagine whether the entire world can remedy the nature of that psychological wound. But in retrospect, if social interaction is harmonized with respect for human value, dignity and equal opportunity, even the learned Gupta would not need to postulate about the newly developed class of "upwardly mobile sanskritizing caste," because the mobility should have rather been based on meritocracy than on castocracy or ethnocracy.

The concern, in holistic term, engulfs into the confines of the metaphysical domains affecting the social conscience, consciousness, values, and morale. The intuitive properties of the person, both in mind and attitude, should dignify every human nature with a desire to be appreciated. Put in another way, if a certain opportunistic group has bankrupted the aspirations and social esteem of a sector of the community, in order to validate the maintenance of identity supremacy, the outcome transforms the societal network into a hub of a clinically supervised disintegration, which Somalia is contemporary evidence.

In the Hindu system, Das and Choudhury believe that "caste perpetuates social distance with the help of religious sanctions." Similarly, Somalia's Islamic priests, doctrine, and concept of homogeneity and self-sameness remain all silent about equality of all Muslims especially when it concerns the purpose of caste equality.[98] And as such, Somalis are strong believers and adherents to a rigid caste system and social stratification.

However, when all is said, there is no concrete evidence whatsoever to substantiate the exact source of the alleged impurity of the outcasts as per the allegations devised by the 'noble' clans. The pastoral traditions that related the allegations of impurity of the Gaboye community as well as the orientalist scholars who purportedly reported and celebrated the caste impurity in their academic writings remain silent about core evidential issues as the place of the 'fallacy' and the approximate date thereof are not mentioned. Relatively, the invention of the 'Nasab-dhiman' (dented-nobility) outcast system by the 'nasab' noble predecessors must be deeply rooted in the nomadic avarice for surfeit in a culture characterized by lust for power and quest for superior identity, a complexity which Islam denounces its indulgence.

When examined comparatively to its Indian counterpart, the Somali outcast system appears eccentric in nature. In India, it is alleged to have begun as an issue of two races: the light-skinned Aryans invading the dark-skinned Dravidians with the imposition of an unfamiliar stratification which misconceived the dark-skinned as unequal, inferior and uncivilized people. In the Somali situation, one observes that the color, clan and creed of both the discriminating majority and the socially distanced outcast minority are utterly inseparable and basically one and the same people, Somali and Jileec by composition. They are in fact indistinguishable in every sense by their features and racial background. This culture, which in the Somali social organization depletes the human value of such a social sub-group, leads one to disagree with Ghurye and Risley[99] who view cast as an institution that celebrates its birth as a result of racial divisiveness; because in the Somali situation, there is no evidence of racial difference although the system has taken an equal dimension in a different form and construct.

Actually, varieties of the traditions and the scholars suggest blood affinity between the so-called 'nasab' nobles and the 'nasab-dhiman' outcasts, and how the status of this group was dropped (Burton 1987; Cerulli 1919, 1927; Drake-Brockman 1912; Kirk 1904). How that consanguinary relationship was terminated to debase one and not the other, when both brothers had eaten together the meat from the dead animal, is not a point the nobles would be pleased to take for further discussion or under scrutiny. Nor does anyone among the scholars or the traditions that initially purported or framed the caste institution ask the type of the animal concerned: was it camel, cow, goat, or sheep? Or was it a wild animal whose consumption for human nutrition Islam had forbidden? The approximation in time of the event is not so clear either. The traditions are contained in absolute silence about the answers to such questions.

This uncorroborated episode of unproven evidence, which has probably occurred in Somalia's pre-Islamic days, cannot in any circumstance be a contemporary justification to undermine the rights of any citizen, regardless of his ethno-cultural or religious background. In general, unproven allegation is not reason enough to ennoble one offender at the expense of the de-ennoblement of the other. "It is an artificially created system of deliberate inferioration of the non-nomadic societies and cultures, aiming at the gain of legitimacy for self-promotion," argues Abukar Mungai,[100] a Jareer surveyor in Mombasa.

The Asharaaf

Another perplexing case in the Somali lineage metaphor is the group calling themselves Asharaf. Members of this group claim they are more respectable, more praiseworthy and more honored than the rest. The significance in that belief is borne in the title 'Shariff' pre-fixed to their real names. According to their traditions, they have descended right from the prophet's household, hence their double purpose of the term Shariff which serves as a personal title distinctive only for this stock, and its common noun version Asharaf (Ashraf) which suits as the clan name, legitimating the title 'Shariff' for every male and 'Shariffa' for the female from the community. The Somali 'claim' Hashemite descent just like the Asharaf but none sticks to the use of 'Shariff' as a title before their names. But the Asharaf, who favor themselves as more Hashemite than the non-Asharaf Somalis, feel offended if the title is misplaced elsewhere other than their extraction.

In linguistic terms, the Arabic word 'Shariff' comes into use as a name of an individual's choice. Secondly, it may be used as an adjective qualifying or describing a noun in the case of one, anyone, irrespective of clan or origin, who is regarded for one's respect and honor to others and by others. As the Arabic saying (transliterated in English) goes, *"Man Sharafa nafsahu, fahwa Shariff* – whoever honors himself (abstains from doing evil to others) is certainly honorable (by others).

The Arabite origin of this sub-group of the Somali social thread is also suspect because they narrate diversified traditions. When I posed a few questions to some elderly Ashraf informants in the course of my discussion with them, they were unable to respond satisfactorily. The three of them could not agree on the lineage of one progenitor. They could not provide comparative definitions concerning the Asharaf among the Banadiri, the Asharaf of the Reewing and the numerous Asharafs scattered among the Somali subgroups. Surprisingly, the *'Abtirsi'* genealogy sometimes gives queer elements of non-Arab names, which no informant could explain. Shariff Hussein Shariff Mohamed (about 87 years old) was eventually inclined to agree that the nature of the Asharaf relationship to the Arab is not any different from that of the Somali tribe with the Qureish, "because they all belong to a Qureishite pedigree." [101] This suggestion encourages us to believe the existence of a finely woven genealogical myth also in the traditions of the Asharaaf.

When I asked them why they give their tribe name first-hand as Asharaf, and not Qureish or Banu-Hashem because the Qureishite do not use "Asharaaf," as a tribal identity, they were quick to react that the Somalis know them by that tribe name, while one of them, Shariff Osman Shariff Samad Shariff Ali, answered that it was actually the Somalis who first gave that tribe name to the Asharaaf. Then I asked how Somalis, as outsiders, could confer a name on a whole tribe without first knowing its ethnonym from the ethnic community. In response, they said that they were not there when it happened but that I (author) should not doubt their Qureishite/Hashemite origin.

In another question, I asked them to discuss about the distribution and distinction between the Asharaaf in the Somali sub-clans living in the north and south of the country, in parts of Ethiopia and their agnates found also in parts of Kenya. Was it only one Shariff who came and fathered all the Asharaaf in the diverse regions or were there many Shariffs who arrived in Somalia at various dates and places as to assume the Asharaaf affinity to the Somali tribes/clans of the distinct modes of living? The responses were incongruent: Shariff Osman held the opinion that all these groups of Asharaaf came from one immigrant Shariff and acquired his offspring by polygamy with women from diverse Somali clans. In a variant view, Shariff Abdinassir Elmi Shariff Mohamed (alias Quleel) thought many Asharaaf immigrants came and settled among the Somali clans at various dates and points. He also speculated that the Asharaaf among the Banadiri and Barawans came later than those living among the Somali proper. Then I reminded the early arrival date of some of the Barawaans and the later arrival date of some of the Banadiri Asharaaf in reference to Banadiri traditions, and what they could make of those histories; the Asharaf informants were not anywhere near a suitable response.

When I mentioned the difference in the lineages of all these Shariffs who suggest a connection to the prophet of Islam but who do not know or are not recognized by their kinsmen in other regions in Arabia, one informant responded that [possibly] the Asharaaf in Arabia must have forgotten their migrated kinsmen. Shariff 'Quleel' however raised the possibility of the Arab Qureishites ignoring or debasing the Somali Asharaaf as a result of the latter's marriage relationship with the African women. I also sought their recognition of what Ioan M. Lewis wrote about the Asharaf that, "...a group of sheiks assumed prominence and formed the Asheraf tribe," (Lewis, *Peoples of the Horn of Africa, p.36*). They opinionated that even some of the tribes to whom they joined have also in time come to be known as Asharaaf. Since they have lived together for a long time, they said division and separation of the community wasn't necessary. Despite all the desire for closer consanguinary relationship with Prophet Muhammad (PBUH), "...the claim is disallowed by the Sherif of Arabia, who look on the Somalis as an inferior race" (*A Handbook of Abyssinia*).

After two days of discussions about the subject, my Asharaaf informants seemed short of reconciling the distinction between their own genealogies and that of their ethno-history regarding their migration. Some of the stories sounded as a copy of the Somali myths in search of a more 'reputable' identity than the African one that haunts the average Somali nomad in the northern regions. The ethno historical data I collected from the three historians are not corroborative any more than the multiple Somali versions of their origin. Similar to the Somali traditions, the Asharaaf myths cannot be considered as valid stories of truth-value, since Somalis are not only capable of forming and attaching themselves to identities, but also with ease. Professor Abdalla Mansur reveals a situation in which a Somaliland community "created in Kenya the 'Isaaq Sharif Community,' claiming that their ancestor was the cousin of the prophet Mohammad, in order to obtain the best treatment in that multiracial society…In 1948 this new genealogy was published in a book printed in Cairo…" (Abdalla O. Mansur 1997:124-5).

The coastal dwellers

Next in the discussion come the coastal dwellers, the Banadiri (Reer Xamar), the Bajuuni and the Barawaans. These are speculated as the descendants of immigrants from Arabia and Persia although the Amarani of Baraawa, according to I.M. Lewis,[102] and other sources, are alleged of being the descendants of Israelite escapees who might have fled from their ancient settlement in the era of Islamic expansion.

The Barawaan

The Barawaans are sailors, traders, fishermen, and are famous artisans in hand- made/embroidered hats and in shoemaking, popular in Somalia as '*koofi Barawaan*' and '*kabo-Barawaan*' (Barawaan hats and Barawaan shoes) respectively. They are active merchants and speak Chimbalazi, a language which the Somalis simply call *Af-Baraawa* (the language of Baraawa), but which scholars classify as a Swahili dialect. They have arrived several centuries ago and became part of the social fabric. They are scattered along the coastal areas in Somalia, Kenya and even Tanzania.

Unlike the outcast groups who are not accepted by the Somalis into marriage, there has been a relatively low intermarriage with the Somalis who do not despise the Baraawans like they do to the other '*kabo-tol*' shoemakers of the outcast Somalis. Though sometimes seen as Diaspora, the Barawaans have (as *Jileec*) achieved a certain degree of upward mobility regarding their officers in the army and navy of Mohamed Siad Barre's military regime, as well as other civilian posts in the administrative and diplomatic functions. In any case, the Baraawaans are numerically a minority and subject to harassment due to their non-Somali origin. Regardless of their origin, within the *Jareer* and *Jileec* classification, the Barawans are *Jileec* and are thus technically but temporarily (for the purpose of this study) deliberately lumped with the rest of the Jileec population.

Upon first hearing, the ordinary person assumes Baraawa as a clan or tribe but it is a toponym of the territory rather than a fiber of consanguinary lineage composition of its multiethnic/multiracial population. It is a settlement for people of diverse background consisting of the indigenous local community and their counterpart from Persian and Arabian Diaspora. Although certain elements within the community claim descendency from Ashraf, it cannot be conclusively confirmed, particularly with regard to the fact that sections of those who claim Barawanese citizenship had been associated with Israel rather than with Qureish.

As a coastal city-state, Barawa shares a long history with the other Swahili city-states that emerged along the East African coast. This history, in my opinion, is not exempt from paradoxes when we examine this ancient city-state from two dichotomous standpoints paramount to its social activities. For one, Baraawa stands as a cosmopolitan ancient city-state that has produced great Ulama (religious scholars) like Sheikh Uwees (Uways), Sheikh Nurein Sabir Al-Hatimy, and Moallim Nuri and so on. These scholars, according to Mohamed Kassim, [103] were leaders who were 'mufti' well-educated and erudite in a variety of disciplines in the field of Islam. Indeed, they contributed invaluably to the spread of Islam in the country and overseas.

The second axis, by which Baraawa became famous, emerges in the realm of slavery and as a slave trade hub. From this conception, we see a city-state keeping in parallel rivalry two repellant social paradigms: Islamic education and slavery institution. But for whatever reason, the

Somalist scholars are numb on the latter subject. Exposing some slave-related evidence, Robecchi Brichetti[104] has analyzed Baraawa around late 1800 or early 1900 as having not less than 800 slaves among a community Guillain[105] estimated at about 5,000 people in 1847. The figures imply an average of one slave to every six people, in other words, one slave to every family of six members.

Though the contribution to the proselytization process has been praised with due appreciation, Somali scholars, particularly the learned elite from the south, shy away at the threshold of discussions surfacing the theme. But Sakawa Abu, a member of the Tunni community of Baraawa believes, "Except very few genuine scholars, most of the so-called Ulama were protecting their own interests, individually and socially."[106] The statement of this Tunni elite and the revelation of slave ownership by Brichetti surmise a postulation at discrepancy with what is traditionally preferred about those religious scholars.

In general view, these clerics are portrayed as sagacious and erudite and capable of establishing reputation across the border as prominent crusaders of Islam, great proselytizers in the wider East Africa region. What often is deliberately downplayed though is their failure to achieve the same for the abolition of slavery. In their own abode and among their own community, we have in record neither success nor even a tangible attempt by these priests to come forward crusading for the abatement (if not altogether the abolition) of the dehumanization of disadvantaged people, including women and children under slave subjugation in Baraawa and its environs. And as we shall see later in one of the next chapters, they might have even been compromised by the colonialists, from whom they received gifts and other materials, hence betraying both the cause of Islam and the obligation to the community.

The thriving civilization of Baraawa, therefore, to say the least, did not emerge only as a result of the immigrant community who arrived with their different cultures and skills but also by the vast economy and accumulation garnered at the cost of wagelessly exploited human resources; men, women and children who were made '*hanti*' human property, either through the *Ulama*'s misinterpretation of the Qur'an to suit special social interests or through their negligence in denouncing the unholy practice. The resources and profits realized under heinous circumstances founded on human exploitation nevertheless played a remarkable role in thrusting Baraawa into fame as a coastal city-state, while one cannot exonerate the town-elite, past or present, as direct or indirect beneficiaries of that slave economy. As Sakawa Abu (alias Abti) emphasizes, "From the so-called Asharaaf to the Amaraani, they were all slave-herders."

I may, at this point, opinionate that as long as the Ulama ignored criticism of the booming slavery business and its religious implications, the common slave masters remained as devoted followers. The Ulama, as witnessed from the social life of their day, probably concentrated on selected areas of Islam, which avoided elite collision with regard to slave trade and slave exploitation. On the vice versa, then, if extremity in Sufism has reputed the Ulama, its opposite in slavery certainly remains a living disrepute to them.

The Banaadiri

The Banaadiri people are also called Reer-Xamar and are featured as being of Arabian descent. They live mainly in the Lower Shabelle coastal town of Marka and the capital Mogadishu. They are business people and sartorial skills men, but some of them practice fishing too. Certain versions of the oral traditions say that, after arriving in Mogadishu centuries ago, they opted to change their original tribe names and affiliated themselves to the Negroid Zenji as "Sheegad"[107] clients. Certain sources of the traditions suggest that the main Banaadiri subgroups are Dhabarweyne, Bandhowow, Moorshe, and Iskaashato. These subgroups consist of a mixture of indigenous and immigrant communities. The names are not based on strict clan lineage but rather consist of a combination of communities who formed an alliance under the toponym Banadir for mutual social purpose and coexistence.[108] Some of the Diaspora communities, according to a section of the traditions, are said to be of Russian origin, others of Persian while another portion is associated with the Zenj stock representing the indigenous Negroid Jareer people. Some of the traditions relate that certain groups of the immigrant Banadiris have originated from Iraq.[109]

However, there is no reliable evidence to confirm the link or otherwise between these immigrants and their suggested places of origin. Nor can anyone confirm with certainty their status prior to their arrival in the Coastal towns of Somalia and their exact motive for abandoning their home areas. But unlike the Barawaans who acquired a surplus identity as members of the larger Digil-Mirifle confederation, thus counted among the Digil sub-groups, the Banaadiri/Reer Hamar stand on their own in the socio-political domain and pledge loyalty to their own ethnic party. Although they suffer minority status, also related to their ethnic background as immigrants, they do not suffer from low status qualities like the Bantu/Jareer or the outcasts. They are eligible for intermarriage with the Somalis although this does not happen very often as they keep that social institution endogamous.

According to the traditions, upon the arrival of the Reer Xamar the local Zenj Negroid, in other words the Jareer autochthons had Mogadishu under their hegemony. They have settled the *'gibil-cad'* light-skinned Banaadiri of mixed origin across different periods. The Somalist scholarship is controversial about the leadership of a Jareer (Swahili-speaking) ruler in Mogadishu. In a way, Chittick's speculation of a Swahili-speaking ruler in Mogadishu or Shungwaya and the traditions by the Banaadiri historians support each other. However, more about this subject is the concern of the next chapter.

The Banadiri and Barawaans are less aggressive people and peaceful by culture. The sedentary social groups with whom they interplayed shaped many aspects of their local social life. Though they are accorded a status not much desirable as that of the Somali proper, they occupy a social stratum above the outcasts and the Bantu/Jareer communities.

The Bajuuni

The Bajuni, like the Barawaans, stretch their social relations from the southern coast to the East African coastal towns of Lamu, Malindi and Mombasa in Kenya and Zanzibar and Tanga in modern Tanzania. They speak a Kiswahili dialect and fishing shapes their living economy. They are a minority and are therefore at the lower end of the hierarchy of Somaliness. They are not considered as an outcast populace but the non-Somali ethnicity frequently stigmatizes. Maintaining marital affinity with their Bantu neighbors and intermingling with other Swahili people makes them undesirable for closer ties with the nomads of the northern culture.

It is noteworthy mentioning that the Bajuni are considered by some sources as a sub-branch of the East African Bantu population while other sources suggest an Indonesian origin or culture (I.M. Lewis, *Peoples of the Horn of Africa*). Whatever their lineage, their cultural context, language and the sound interaction with the Bantu around their environs have acquired them an enviable multicultural-ism in unity. Mzee Juma Bakari notes, "Many say we are Arabs, others Iranians; intermarriage with them (Arabs and Persians) cannot change our culture as Bantu."[110] In his view, another elder from the same community, Mzee Hamisi Othumai Mwakwafasa, expresses his indig-nation because "These (scholars/researchers) who write about social history write from *'dadka xukunka haayo'* – the ruling elite – not from us."[111]

The latter oral historian's remorse represents the non-nomadic So-malis' disapproval of the contamination of their true identity and cul-ture under a pseudo homogeneity which categorically identifies them with the nomads, denying the fact that theirs is a culture quite inconsis-tent with nomadism or even pastoralism in all practice of their social life.

Conclusion

This chapter reflected on the debate about the origin of the Somali people and the subsequent migration from north to south, which revi-sionist scholarship has overturned with new evidence based on culture, language and geographic location. This thesis falls in accordance with an earlier south-north migration, suggesting a dispersal point in the eastern/southeastern lowland of Ethiopia and a most likely origination from or genealogical affiliation with Cushites of a probable proto-Reewing people.

We have seen how the Arabs and Persians had interplayed with Somalis through commerce, culture and intermarriage, but without a tenable evidence of Somali genealogical link with either the prophet, the Qureishite people or with any other traceable Arab tribe to that connection. The different clans and cultures were also briefly dis-cussed, and their respective relationship and status in the Somali social thread with some light on linguistic stereotyping. The discussion now guides us to turn to the Jareer people who are the subject matter of the next chapters.

Notes and references

1. Lewis, Ioan M., Peoples of the Horn of Africa – Somali, Afar, Saho. London; International African Institute (1955: 96-97). Usually Somalis like to divide the clans into what they term as 4 major clans and a minority group. See also 'A Pastoral Democracy by the same author.
2. Jareer refers to 'thick hair', 'kinky hair' etc., also sometimes called 'timo adag' in Somalia; the reference is attributed to the Bantu, Negroid community who are counted outside the Somali clan lineage and eponym. 'Jileec' means soft, and is an attribute given to the non-Bantu Somali, and signifies softness of hair and "nobility". According to this significance, other clans who are not even Somali proper like segments of the Reewing, the Banadiri (Reer Xamar), the Barawaans, the Midgan, and Madhiban and so on, come as one unit since they all use the word 'Jareer' as a derogatory term preferred to call the Negroid stock.
3. Lewis, I. M., A Pastoral Democracy: A study of pastoralism and politics among the Northern Somali of the Horn of Africa. African Publishing Company (New York. 2nd edition. (1982: 2), (First Published in 1961.)
4. Ahmed, Ali Jimale., "Day Break Is Near, Won't You Become Sour?" in Ahmed, Ali J., (ed.), The Invention of Somalia. Red Sea Press Inc. (1995: 140.)
5. Collins, Douglas, A Tear for Somalia. Jarrolds Publishers London Ltd.(1960:110)
6. The British Naval Staff, A Handbook of Abyssinia, vol.1, June 1917, Intelligence Division. (Kenya National Archives – Nairobi) p.148
7. Ahmed, Christine C., "Finely Etched Chattel: The Invention of a Somali Woman", in Ahmed, Ali Jimale, (ed.), op. cit., p.162.
8. Lewis, I.M., Historical Aspect of Genealogies in Northern Somali Social Structure. Journal of African History, III, (1962: 35-48).
9. The Holy Qur'an: English translation of the meanings and commentary. Revised & Edited by the Presidency of Islamic Researches, IFTA, Call and Guidance. King Fahd Complex for the Printing of the Holy Qur'an (Sura 28: 23 – 29).
10. Lewis, Ioan M., Peoples of the Horn of Africa. op. cit., p.15.
11. Mansur, Abdalla O., 'The Nature of the Somali Clan System', in Ahmed, Ali Jimale (ed.), op. cit., pp.117 – 134.
12. Schlee, Gunther., Identities on the Move: Clanship and Pastoralism in Northern Kenya. Gideon S. Were Press, (1994: 43-44).
13. Hersi, Ali Abdirahman., "The Arab Factor in Somali History: The Origins and the Development of Arab Enterprise and Cultural Influences in the Somali Peninsula." Ph.D. Dissertation 1977. University of California, Los

Angeles.

14. A Handbook of Abyssinia, op. cit., pp.147-148
15. Dualeh, Hussein Ali., Search for a New Somali Identity. Printed in the Re-public of Kenya. (2002: 9).
16. Revoil, Georges., La Valle Du Darror, Paris: Challamel Aine, Libraire – Editeur, 1882.
17. Lewis, I.M., The Modern History of Somaliland: From Nation to State. New York: Fredrick Praeger – Publisher (1965: 22)
18. Muhammad, Ali S., "The Origin of the Ishaq People", Somaliland Journal, (Hargeisa, Dec. 1954). Cited in Hersi, The Arab Factor in Somali History.
19. Lewis, I.M., The Modern History of Somaliland, op.cit.
20. In Arabic Language, Sheikh may mean 'an old man,' 'a religious scholar'
21. Hersi, op. cit.
22. Schlee, op. cit., pp.44.
23. Ibid., p.90.
24. Mukhtar, Mohamed H., 'Islam in Somali History: Facts and Fiction', in Ahmed, Ali Jimale (ed.), op. cit., pp.9 & 15.
25. Ibid., p.21.
26. Dualeh, Hussein Ali., op.cit., pp.9 – 10.
27. Ibid.
28. Ibid.
29. Hersi, A.A., op.cit., p.25.
30. Eriksen, Thomas H., 'Ethnic identity, national identity and intergroup Conflict: The significance of personal experience' in Ashmore, Jussim and Wilder (eds.), Social Identity, Inter-Group Conflict, and Conflict Reduction. Oxford University Press. 2001, pp.42-70.
31. Touval, Saadia., Somali Nationalism – International Politics and the Drive for Unity in the Horn of Africa. Harvard University Press, Cambridge, Massachusetts 1963:29.
32. Kusow, Abdi M., 'Contested Narratives and the Crisis of the Nation – State in Somalia: A Prolegomenon', in Kusow, Abdi M., (ed.), Putting the Cart Before the Horse. Red Sea Press (2004:8).
33. Ibid., p.11.
34. Ibid., p.3.
35. Ahmed, Ali Jimale, 'Daybreak is Near - Won't You Become Sour?' op.cit., p.141
36. Eno, Omar A., 'Sifting Through a Sieve: Solutions for Somalia', in Janzen, Jorg (ed.), What Are Somalia's Development Perspectives? Proceedings of the 6th Somali Studies International Association (SSIA) Congress. Berlin, Dec. 1996. Das Arabische Buch – Berlin (2000:64)
37. Dia-paying: "Dia" is a kind of blood compensation paid by the kinship of a killer to the kinsmen of the victim.
38. Digil-Mirifle is composed of a confederation of clans whose kinship is

based on mutual co-existence among all the settlers, rather than clan affiliation or genealogical relationship. However, they have their ancestor Sab who is the brother of Samaale who fathered the other Somali clans.

39. Af-Maay, also known as Maay-Maay, is a language spoken mainly in Southern Somalia, particularly along the majority of the riverine belt of Juba and Shabelle. It is not intelligible with the Maxaa-tiri version of the Somali language.

40. Touval, Saadia., op. cit., p.16.

41. Ibid.

42. Abtirsi (ancestral counting): is the genealogical count from the father back to the eponymous ancestor. In the Somali tradition, it is patrilineal although the matrilineal opposite exists in the Gosha area.

43. Helander, Bernhard., 'The Hubeer in the Land of Plenty: Land, labor and vulnerability among a Southern Somali clan'; in Besteman, Catherine and Cassanelli, Lee V. (eds.), The Struggle for Land in Southern Somalia: The War Behind the War. Haan Associates – London(2000:50).

44. Mukhtar, Mohamed H., 'Islam in Somali History', in Ahmed, Ali Jimale, (ed.) op. cit., p.17.

45. Ibid., pp. 8-9.

46. Schlee, Gunther., op. cit., p.26.

47. Kusow, Abdi M., 'The Somali Origin: Myth or Reality' in Ahmed, Ali J., op. cit., p.84.

48. Mansur, Abdalla Omar., op. cit.

49. Murdock, George P., Africa: Its people and their culture history. New York: McGraw Hill, 1959.

50. Lewis, H.S., 'The Origin of the Galla and Somali', Journal of African History, VII, I (1966) pp.27-46.

51. Fleming, H.C., Baiso and Rendille: Somali outliers: Rassegna di studi Etiopici, XXC (1964), pp.35-96.

52. The East African Standard, 18th August, 1930. Various issues at the Kenya National Archives and other documents.

53. Ali, Mohamed Nuuh., 'Somali History: Linguistic Approaches to the Past,' in Kusow, Abdi M., (ed.), Putting the Cart Before the Horse. op.cit. Also see an article by the same author in Ali Jimale Ahmed (ed.) the Invention of Somalia. Red Sea Press.

54. Ehret, Christopher., "Cushitic Prehistory" in Bendar, Lionel (ed.) The Non-Semitic Languages of Ethiopia., pp.85 - 96.

55. Touval, Saadia, op.cit., p.10.

56. Hersi, Ali Abdirahman, op. cit.

57. Lewis, Ioan M., Peoples of the Horn of Africa. op. cit., p.14.

58. Drake-Brokckman, R. E., British Somaliland. London: Hurst & Blacket Ltd (1912: 15; 71).

59. Johnston, C., Travels in Southern Abyssinia. London: J. Madden & Co.,

(1844: 13).

60. Schlee, Gunther., p.56.
61. Ibid., p.57.
62. Cerulli, Enrico., Somalia: Scritti vari editi ed inediti. Vols. I, II, III. Roma.
63. Eno, Mohamed A., 'The Istunka Festival – A traditional Mock-fight at Afgoie. HEEGAN NEWSPAPER, Friday, July 20, 1984; p.3 (see also Virginia Luling "Somali Sultanate".
64. Schlee, Gunther., op. cit., pp.67 – 71.
65. Hersi, Ali Abdirahman., op. cit.
66. Interview with Oromo elders in Pangani Estate, Nairobi, 2004.
67. Ismail Ibdi Issa; Discussion in Nairobi. 2004.
68. Eno, Mohamed A., "ALL ROADS LED TO ISTUNKA (A Grand Mock-Fight at Afgoi)" in HEEGAN NEWSPAPER, Friday, Aug. 1, 1986; and Part II, Friday, Aug. 8, 1986.
69. Au-Isman Sadiq – Interview in Afgoi, July, 1980. Such idiomatic expression is used to refer to what one remembers since childhood.
70. 'Mar' sometimes 'Magac' is a poetic verse, which has an equated level of rhyme and alliteration according to a key phonemic sound.
71. Shrub/Shirib: The two can sometimes be exchanged. A kind of traditional, processional singing, dancing and chanting in which singers in two parallel lines recite the verse by sharing it as the front group and the rear group, taking turns in their singing. Each group repeats its part after the other until the 'Laashin' traditional bard whistles to compose a new verse.
72. In this verse, two municipal officers, Shukri and Shariffo, had been arrested and summoned in court in Mogadishu for misappropriation of public funds, so it was a good opportunity for the rival group to taunt these culprits and their kinsmen of the disgraceful acts they committed. They were later charged and dismissed with disgrace.
73. Sheelaro is a mispronounced Italian word 'Accelaro' used for the quick response unit of the police; it was also the name of a police station in Mogadishu.
74. Luling, Virginia, "Colonial and Postcolonial Influences on a South Somali Community"; Journal of African History, Vol. 8, No. I Spring, 1976.
75. Hourani, G., Arab Seafaring in the Indian Ocean in Ancient and Medieval Times. Princeton, 1951.
76. Duyvendak, J.J., 'China's Discovery of Africa'. (London School of Oriental and African Studies, Occasional Paper, 1949).
77. Ibid.
78. Al-Idris, Abdi – Abdalla Muhammad. Kitab Nuzhat al-Mushtaq, Bodelein, Oxford.
79. Ibn-Batuta, Abu Abdalla Mohamed., Rihlat ibn Batutta (Travels of Ibn Battuta), edited by Abd al-Hadi al-Tazi, 1997.
80. Mansur Abdulla O., op. cit.

81. Hersi; Ali A., op. cit.
82. Eno, Omar A., 'Sifting Through a Sieve'; op. cit., p.68.
83. Gassim, Mariam Arif., Somalia: Clan vs. Nation. Printed in U.A.E. (2002: 77).
84. Kusow, Abdi M., 'Contested Narratives and the Crisis of the Nation-State in Somalia'; op.cit.
85. Allport, G., The Nature of Prejudice. Reading, MA: Addison – Wesley; cf. Hewston, M. and Giles, H. – 'Social Groups and Social Stereotypes', in Coupland, Nikolas., and Jaworski, Adam (eds.), Sociolinguistics: A Reader and Coursebook. Palgrave. (1997: 271).
86. Hewstone, M. and Giles, H., op. cit., in 85 above.
87. Jamal Mohamed Hagi., (alias Salad) personal communication in Portland, Oregon, USA, November 2004.
88. Kusow, Abdi M., 'Contested Narratives...' op. cit.
89. Ibid.
90. Marian A. Enow., personal communication, 2004.
91. Lewis, I. M., A Pastoral Democracy, op. cit.
92. Eno, Omar A., 'Sifting Through a Sieve: Solutions for Somalia' op. cit., p.69.
93. Narula, S., 'Caste Discrimination.'
http://www.india-   seminar.com/2001/508.
94. Samad, Asha S., 'Brief Review of the Somali Caste Groups' – statement to the Committee on the Elimination of Racial Discrimination, Aug. 2002 - The International Dalit Solidarity Network. http;//uk.geocoties.com/internationaldalitssolidarity/cerd/Somalia2002.html.
95. Gupta, Dipankar., Interrogating Caste: Understanding Hierarchy and Difference in Indian Society. Penguine Books, New Delhi. 2000.
For more on the subject, read also Appadurai Arjun, 'Right and Left Hand Castes in South India', Indian Social and Economic History Review, vol. II, 1974. p. 216 – 260.
96. Gupta, Dipankar., 'Caste, race, politics'.
http://www.india-seminar.com/2001/508.
97. Marian A. Enow., Personal communication, 2004.
98. Das, Hari Hara., and Choudhury, B.C., Introduction to Political Sociology. Vikas Publishing House PVT Ltd. Second Reprint (2002: 262).
99. Sir Herbert Risley and Dr. Ghurye, quoted in Das and Choudhury, op. cit., p.263.
100. Abukar Abdullahi Mungai., Interview in Mombasa, 2004.
101. Shariff Hussein Shariff Mohamed., Interview in Parklands Estate, Nairobi. 24 - 25 Dec. 2004. He was among a team of three Ashraf elders to discuss about the Ashraf community of Somalia.
102. Lewis, I.M., Peoples of the Horn of Africa.

103. Kassim, Mohamed M., 'Aspects of the Banadir Cultural History', in Ahmed, Ali J., (ed.), op. cit., pp.29-42.
104. Brichetti, Robecchi., Dal Benadir, Lettere illustrate alla societa Antischiavista d'Italia. Milano, 1904., p.203.
105. Guillain, Captain C., Documents sur L'histoire, le geographie et la comerce de L'afrique orientale, 3 vols., Paris: Arthur Bertrand, (1856: II - 520).
106. Sakaawa Abu., (alias Abti), Discussion in Nairobi, 2003.
107. Videotape shot during a workshop in Mogadishu, 2003.
108. Ibid.
109. Ibid.
110. Mzee Juma Bakari, formal discussion in Mombasa with 6 Bajuni elders from Somalia and Kenya, 2003.
111. Mzee Mohamed Hamisi, Mombasa, 2003.

Chapter 2

A TALE OF TWO BANTU COMMUNITIES: THE AUTOCHTHONS VS THE DIASPORA

The Bantu - Jareer Autochthons of Somalia

The Bantu/Jareer people of Somalia have their settlement in the in-ter-riverine area, along and in the hinterland of the country's two riv-ers, Jubba and Shabelle. They heavily occupy nine out of the country's eighteen regions, though other sources mention ten regions. Apart from Mogadishu, which is a more concentrated cosmopolitan city, there is likelihood that they constitute the majority of the sedentary community in all these regions.

The Bantu people practice mainly, but not exclusively, an agrarian mode of living, making use of the rivers that pass in their regions. While agriculture is the main lifeline of the rural Bantu, in urban areas the Jareer consist of the largest number of skilled technicians: masons, electricians, mechanics, carpenters, and plumbers etc., know-how ac-quired usually by years of apprenticeship. The tendency towards these skills and occupations has been intensified among the Bantu, partly due to the Somali's despise. Accordingly, these and a variety of other occupations are not regarded much by the nomadic culture, which ap-proves that only non-nomadic, low people should live by such 'dirty' jobs.

Jareer, as a word, means 'hard hair', 'kinky hair', 'thick hair', or 'coiled hair'. It is an epithet (though more acceptable than other terms) fully loaded with a connotation whose descriptive implication reflects African genealogy rather than an Arab origin as claimed in nomadic Somalia. Other pejorative terms such as 'Habash',[1] 'Adoon',[2] 'Bidde',[3] are also often used for the Somali Bantu as a manifestation of their dis-tinct ethnic origin.

The Jareer, distinguished by their physical features typical of the black African muscular frame, are a community of heterogeneous eth-nic composition. They celebrate accommodative cultures diverse in kind but otherwise existing in complex harmony. They are different because according to settlement, some live along the river Shabelle while others are settled along the river Jubba, each of which belong to a unique culture of its own. All the Somali Bantu/Jareer share unrestricted social interaction among themselves – including intermarriage – regardless of creed, allowing their cultures to communicate as a fountain of fusion. To many, the cultural communication and cross-cultural cooperation has led to inseparability of the two Jareer peoples. It may surprise many, scholars and ordinary lay people, that the Somali Bantu belong to two distinguishable histories that are neither often discussed by scholarship nor acknowledged by the Somali people. The Bantu along the bank of Shabelle river and in the interior are suggested by recent scholarship to constitute "...Negroid groups present before the Somali migration."[4] The statement is supported by a report saying that "some are descendants of pre-Somali Bantu population; others are descendants of slaves from East Africa."[5] Except very few researchers, almost the entire Somalist scholarship has followed one of three groups:

a) Scholars who, due to avoidance of controversy, express difficulty in separating the autochthons from the Diaspora.

b) Researchers like Turton who opted for an accumulative sum up of all the Jareer as slaves or their descendants, despite abundant evidence and means for classification in written records and traditions;[6] and

c) Authors who take a precautious, non-committal position when writing about the issue of the Negroid/Jareer people of Somalia.

In the Shabelle River area, the historical tiding differs from that of the 18th or 19th century importation of slaves from parts of Tanzania, Malawi and Mozambique. Aside from the disregard of the separation of these two histories by scholarship, the local oral traditions, archival records and an attachment to the exploitation of the land offer tangible evidence. A panel of expert anthropologists who investigated the subject made a conclusion, saying, "...we may reckon those [Bantu/Jareer] tribes in all probability represent remnants of a pre-Somali population..."[7]

Derek Nurse observed the undermining by Somalist scholarship as they portrayed all the Bantu people in the country as either slaves or the descendants of slaves. This inadequately investigated subject, which saw all the community qualified in the same characterization as slaves, was probably a plot aimed at serving favorably the economic interests of both the Italian colonial system and Somali slave owners. Therefore, Nurse gives his opinion on the Somalists' indecisiveness on earlier Bantu presence in the present day territory of Somalia. He claims, "The possibility of earlier settlements is admitted but not emphasized."[8] The opinion is well placed, considering the negligence with which the specialists have approached the area, falling short of exhausting the topic to considerable satisfaction rather than justifying the neglect as a 'difficulty' in distinguishing, though none has mentioned impossibility.

Over the years, very rich debates have been going on about the separation of the historiography of the Bantu people. The ensuing engagements contributed more knowledge, not only to this particular episode, but also some which necessitated scholars to conduct studies on other relevant peoples in neighboring Kenya's coastal and Tana areas. Communities comprising the Segeju, Mijikenda, Pokomo, Duruma etc. were studied to determine the relativity of their oral traditions regarding a dispersal region or regions in Somalia. As it turned out, without disregarding slight differences, most of the tribal traditions maintained consistency in the unanimity of their answers. They repeatedly narrated about a migration from Shungwaya centuries ago, after having been living there for a long span of time prior to their exodus.

Shungwaya is not free from controversy, according to views and findings of researchers. It is of relevant interest to review the Shungwaya phenomenon and the possible connection with the inter-riverine Bantu of Somalia. The review, however, is brief as it is intended just to shed some light on the debate scholars had on the subject.

Abdi Kusow quotes Turton, who believes in the lack of significant evidence suggesting that these pre-Cushitic inhabitants were Bantu speakers. He further argues that both archaeologists and linguists have failed to furnish reliable information in support of such conclusions.[9] Referring to Turton in the same manner, Mohamed Nuh Ali somehow daringly acknowledges, by adding "… even though there are Swahili speaking communities in Barawa and the Bajuuni islands along the coast."[10]

Both Somali scholars, Kusow and Ali, for whatever reason, seem to adhere to Turton who, likewise, had derivatively borrowed the theory from Morton's suggestion directed towards the Shungwaya. The Somali scholars, in their part, do not impart sufficient corroboration adding to the Turton hypothesis and opinion. Nor do they produce any attempt for investigation through the available literature for grasp of the other equally mention-worthy version of the historiography before the rapid conclusion denying pre-Somali Bantu presence in the territory.

In different chapters of the same volume, they both mention (through Turton's work) the lack of archaeological and linguistic evidence, contrary to the documented fact that these, to some considerable extent, if not satisfactorily, are available in the literature of outstanding research scholars' publications who dealt with the topic from the aspects of variant traditions as well as proven substantive linguistic perspectives. Turton, however, portrays the suggestion that the Bantu–Mijikenda Shungwaya issue in the *Kitab-al-Zenj* (the book of the Zenj), which contained the Mijikenda-Shungwaya migration and ethno-historiography was suspect because the tradition does not arise in other documents.

First of all, there is little dispute about the existence of Shungwaya. A substantiation of that evidence is clearly provided by Morton who, despite his argument, acknowledges some evidence, which stands as a support to the traditions, and the Kitab-al-Zanuj:

> There seems to be real evidence that a city called Shungwaya once stood on the southern Somali coast. It is so placed on (one) British and (several) Dutch maps, the earliest being the Linschoten chart, 1596. Versions of the Kilwa and Pate chronicles mention Shungwaya, the former as an important city in the Shirazi colonization of the coast, the latter as a city brought to heel along with Kismayu, Baraawa and Mogadishu by Sultan Omar of Pate in the fourteenth century. The Portuguese mentioned Shungwaya (Jungaya, etc.) but apparently they had never stopped there.[11]

Morton, however, happens to slap invalidation on the Kitab al-Zanuj with the claim that the Mijikenda and the coastal Arabs had an interest in continuing the custom of retaining early traditions and customs about marriage such as pawning of women and postponing bride wealth, which the British colonial rule was enforcing its abolition. If, agreeing with Morton, the Mijikenda and the other coastal tribes had a custom-based interest, we can ask about others who collected equally important information. For instance:- What interests did the British and

Dutch have particularly in mapping and locating Shungwaya in their cartography as a place opposite Pate Island or at/around Bur Gabo in Southern Somalia? What special interests underlie the Kilwa and Pate chronicles for having mentioned Shungwaya? What about the ancient authors who recorded an event of Shungwaya sending an Ambassador to China? Finally, where do all these evidences fit in satisfying the interest of the Mijikenda custom about marriage? The answers to these questions militate against Morton's hypothesis and reveal its unsubstantiveness.

Chittick is among the scholars who criticized Morton for misquoting Cerulli. Morton wrote that the *Book of the Zenj,* according to Cerulli, was a document used in court by the *qadi* (Muslim judge) in the course of fulfilling his legal matters. In responding to Morton, Chittick writes, "In fact Cerulli says nothing of the sort; on the contrary, he compares the document to other historical chronicles of eastern Africa," (H. Neville Chittick; the Book of the Zenj and the Miji Kenda; IJAHS, Vol.9. pp. 68-9). Regarding its authenticity, Chittick argues, "*The Book of the Zenj*, like many such historical chronicles, is a compilation from more than one source...The core of the earlier part of the *Book of the Zenj* is, as its title indicates, principally concerned with the Zenj of the southern Somalia region, who are called Kashur in the account, and their migrations." Chittick states, "Morton postulates its being produced in court but provides no evidence to support this, and the document does not appear to have been mentioned by the officials concerned."

Turning to Mohamed Nuh Ali, and particularly on the issue of linguistic evidence, which he recognizes as a "diachronic record"[12] regarding its historical function in reconstruction, I am tempted to think that we need to consider a semantic evaluation of the root forms of the etymological properties of the language (dialect) spoken by the farming communities of the Jareer people, or to present results of any studies the scholar conducted on the historical ethnography of the claimants of Shungwaya – be them the riverine Somali Bantu or their kinsmen who migrated to Kenya as a result of intolerable male castration and attacks by the Galla/Cushites[13] and the "Wa-Katwa" Somalis. And regarding the "diachronic evidence" which Ali postulates, I indulge to take the liberty of arguing that every language enjoyed a synchronic period before taking its diachronic phase and that neither Ali nor any other scholar has taken the initiative to produce the synchronic nature and living characteristics of the language he refers only to its "diachronic" status, derived from an evaluation of what it is now rather than what it was then. If one cannot effectively reproduce the synchronic properties of the language at the time of its referred existence, all what is said amounts to a hypothetical guess work lacking in conclusive evidence.

Doke introduces a linguistic argument about phonetic misspelling, possibly committed by whoever translated the original Arabic version. The right transcription should have been 'Bilad-ul-Bont', but in English orthography without any justifiable reason adopts it as 'The Land of the Punt', undermining the linguistic reality that pragmatically an equivalent of 'p' is absent in both Arabic and Somali scripts. Therefore the 'p' stays as a misrepresented sound since its presence in phonetic terms is linguistically unjustified. The speculation thence leads us to consider 'Bunt', 'Bont' or 'Bantu' which may sound possibly the same for the non-native speaker.[14] From another angle, Derek Nurse reasons:-

> Somali society was predominantly pastoral, the Bantu-speakers predominantly, though not exclusively, agricultural. If such a contact situation lasts for more than a short time, some form of mixing or symbiosis is likely to occur, and the most obvious linguistic signs would be loanwords. Specifically, we might expect some southern Somali dialects to have absorbed words relating to agriculture taken from one or more Bantu languages.[15]

Therefore to satisfy his intuitive academic curiosity, Nurse took an excursion of what he calls "…among a community of agricultural Somali between Mogadishu and Merca… and produced the following:-

Yambo	'hoe' (cf. Swahili jembe, northern Swahili yembe).
Bangat	'machete' (cf, Swahili panga)
Kombe	'coconut' (sic) (cf Swahili ki-kombe
Jiko	'cooking stove' (cf Swahili jiko)." [16]

Linguistically, Nurse classifies Miini (ci-miini) spoken in Baraawa, as a "(northern) Swahili dialect."[17] Later postulating the possible relationship between Miini and the Sabaki-speakers (Pokomo and Mijikenda), he reconstructs his analysis and the presumable inducement as below:-

> Much more likely is contact in Somalia. Both the Mijikenda and the Pokomo claim to have "come from" "shungwaya," which in the words of the Book of the Zinj had at least the twin components of town-dwellers and people along the Juba who cultivated and kept stock.

> If we assume the town-dwellers spoke Miini and the people on the Juba spoke Pokomo/Mijikenda, then we would have an explanation for the foregoing contact-induced borrowings. Miini was the language of the town or towns, but was also used as a trading lingua franca by the people on the Juba. Since it was not the first language of the latter they misused it, modified its verbal morphology and the modifications were ultimately adopted by the first speakers of Miini.[18]

In addition to the hypothesis and loanwords suggested by Nurse, more corpus could be injected in to the list which, in my opinion, may sound loanwords to the non-Bantu Somali-speaker but a normal tongue for the Jareer person. These are:-

Somali/Bantu etymology	Kiswahili	English
Lin, lim	ku-lima	to dig (farm)
Kumi	kumi	ten (cents)
Taano	taano	five (cents)
Uumid (uun)	ku umba	to create
Cambe/Cambo	mwembe	mango/es
Boombo	boma	abode, farm
Baamiye	bamia	Lady's finger
Qalinfur	karafu	Cloves
Dan	damu	Blood
Nyaanyo	Nyanya	Tomatoes
Moxog	mohoga	Cassava
Ruux	roho	Spirit/heart
Mardaaf	madafu	Coconut
Mashaqo	Mashaka	difficulty, problem,
Maaji	maji	Water
Hoodi!	Hodi!	anybody at home?

Source: by the author

The above are some examples of a vast linguistic corpus, which augment Sutton's idea that "Swahili culture has its origin in the first substantial contacts between the coastal Bantus and the Islamic world." He also gives Kilwa, Mombasa, Malindi and Mogadishu as examples.[19]

Morton, Turton and other authors might have some reasons, albeit their weakness, but Shungwaya is neither the historians' myth nor the traditionists' creation. It is preserved in voluminous records, including human memory of successive generations and proven by expert historians and linguists who examined, re-examined, evaluated and re-evaluated their findings. Thomas Spear, who has devoted a considerable period of his academic life to the Mijikenda and Shungwaya narrative, has this to contribute:

> We have seen how the Singwaya legend can be viewed equally on different levels as a charter of social institution and as a coherent historical narrative of a 16th century migration. As narrative, the intricate interweaving of several traditions, the identification of spurious elements and the addition of documentary, linguistic and cultural evidence all established its accuracy.[20]

Spear retorts firmly in noting,

> "The fact that Swahili originated along the Somali coast around Brava makes it imperative that Sabaki speakers were present in the immediate hinterland of Shirazi settlements there to have given rise to the pidginized language."[21]

Yet in another linguistic evidence, the renowned Spear quotes,

> "Hinnebusch is quick to admit that there is nothing in the linguistic evidence to dispute possible Singwaya[22] origins for his Sabaki group..."[23]

Spear was commenting on linguistic findings presented by Hinnebusch who had a disagreement with an earlier study done by a different method. Sounding satisfied with Hinnebusch's "genetic classification of Swahili within the Sabaki group,"[24] he writes convincingly,

> "Swahili shares a common proto-language or origin, with the other members of the Sabaki group – Mijikenda and Pokomo... there must have been historical interaction between Sabaki and Arabic-speakers somewhere along the northern east African coast... the earliest permanent Arab residents on East African coast settled around Brava and Mogadishu. These settlers probably arrived in the 9th century. The African components of this syncretic culture were more than likely contributed by Sabaki - speakers dominating the hinterland of Brava, and the most important one was undoubtedly Swahili language."[25]

Spear's postulation definitely leads us to the hypothesis that, upon arrival, the Arab or other migrants in Brava and Mogadishu were not significant in number. Secondly, they were not Swahili-speakers either upon their arrival. Thirdly, with their small numbers, they wouldn't have settled in a strange land without obtaining first-hand information regarding security and socio-cultural regulations of the landlords/hosts by which they were to abide if they were to be accommodated in that country. Jacob Kimaryo notes the belief that cultural and linguistic transformation of certain Swahili African communities "originated in Shungwaya alias Shirazi." [26] But strange colonial documents always fond of obscuring the contribution of the African culture, credit immigrants onto the East African coast as first settlers, early settlers etc., while the indigenous African people and their culture are reduced to a 'receiver-status' with no meaningful recognition of their contribution to the socio-cultural interplay.

In spite of the existence of this version by reliable expert scholars, Ali seems to have posited different views over the Shungwaya issue as a contentious subject poor in archaeological evidence, without putting in place a substantive argument of his own but simply reflecting on a single version of what otherwise has been academically challenged. This uncorroborated invalidation of a pre-Somali Bantu settlement in the country is partly, notwithstanding the scholarly discussion, an agitation whose contemplation is based probably on the grooming of an ancestral as well as linguistic origin, whereby a history none other than Rahaween precedence prevails in Somalia. With that underpinning, a pre-Somali Bantu presence may disrupt or, in other words, interfere with the entire hypothetical set-up of the proto-Reewing-Somali origin theory. Needless to say, the infirm quotations of Morton and Turton are not rather plausible, noting that their works on the Shungwaya topic were not only academically disputed but weakened by experts.

In any case, "Ruins of a fortified settlement together with Kwale-ware pottery dating from the 11th to the 15th century at Munghia near Brava suggest Bantu occupation, as does the continued presence today of some autochthonous Bantu-speakers in the Juba valley..."[27] This being aside, scholars have provided copious research and results to correct and criticize Morton in his theory of the Shungwaya legend. Neville Chittick posed his argument, as Allen tells us, "...largely on internal evidence, that the Book of the Zenj could not be fraudulent in Morton's sense."[28] Chittick also published his proposition on the availability of documentary evidence written before 1895, which agree on Shungwaya and the Mijikenda origin, "...implicitly if not explicitly."[29]

In a succinct elaboration of the traditions and the Book of the Zenj, especially name places and/or name transference, Chittick notes, "a town of the same name [*as Shungwaya*] at the modern Bur Gabo," as he cites Grottanelli.[30] (Emphasis added)

Needless to list all those toponyms transferred to later settlements in commemoration of the earlier home settlements, a few such as outlined below, may serve the purpose of evidence too:

1) In the late 17th century, a settlement further south in the Pate region carried this name.[31]

2) By about 1914, Sungwaya was a kaya on the northern side of the Sabaki River west of Malindi.[32]

3) The name Kirao appears also to have been transferred. Morton locates the place west/ northwest of Malindi.[33]

4) Mangea lies west of Malindi, significantly, the Book of the Zenj tells us that the Kashur moved the Juba to the place named Giriama beyond (or after) Munghia. More interesting is the location of a Munghia on the Somali coast between Merca and Barawa; this is a Bantu name, and we have here another example of the transference of names.[34]

5) At Munghia are the ruins of a fortified settlement, and the pottery picked up at the site is of the period from the eleventh/twelfth to fifteenth century date.[35]

In his Doctoral Dissertation entitled, "The Arab Factor in Somali History," Dr. Hersi neglected to emphasize Bantu presence in pre-Somali epochs while the evidence was idiosyncratic in several of the documents he cited:

1. In *Awdah Al-Masalik,* Ibn Sibahi provided an illuminating distinction between the people he describes as he wrote "the Berbers (Somalis) were a nation…between the Abyssinians and the Zenj."[36] In this statement, Ibn Sibahi mentions (a) Berbers (or Somalis or whoever that might have been), (b) the Abyssinians and (c) the Zenj. This mention is a clear evidence of Zenj or Bantu or Negroid presence, despite the interchangeability of the group names, including Jareer.

2. Al-Idris's 12th century visit recorded in his *Nuzhat Al-Mushtaq* illustrates the south as "The country of the pagans…They take erect stones as their gods…eating fish, shellfish, frogs, snakes, rats…and many other animals which are not eaten." We cannot relate the characteristics of this episode to the Somali whose mode has always been

linked to nomadic pastoralism. Also the pre-Islam Somalis wor-shipped 'waq' or 'waaq-waaq' which is often narrated to refer to the sky or sky-God, and at times a kind of bird. In terms of alimentation, we expect a pastoralist's meal to contain '*cad iyo caano*'[37] a piece of meat and milk, paradigmatic of the Somali nomadic culture. Traditionally, the nomads have expressed disgust for the smell of fish and its nutri-tional value as a diet. Burton tells us that noble Somali despise fish-eaters.[38] In his volume entitled *The Road to Zero*, former diplomat Mo-hamed Osman Omar mentions how after the Revolution in 1969 of dic-tator Mohamed Siyad Barre a national campaign was introduced in a measure to encourage the consumption of fish, because it had earlier been disdained. This brings us to the speculation that the fish-eaters were possibly the Zenj or Bantu people of the pre-Somali occupation, most probably the indigenous Jareer that presently strengthen the so-cial thread of what is indiscriminately enmeshed together as Banadiri. As mentioned earlier, these are the autochthons, who occupied the re-gion before the appearance of any of the others, be them Hawiye, the light-skinned Reer-Xamar migrants from the Diaspora or any other Somali or Galla arrival.

3. Hersi noted northern Somali loanwords such as:- "doobi, Miis," and so on, in display of early Indian presence in the northern Somalia, ignoring the alternative reference of the linguistic legacy in the agronomic culture as we have seen above.

4. We see often that ancient Somalia was rich in the export of commercial commodities such as ivory, ostrich feathers, leopard skins and rhino horns; but Hersi does not enlighten the veracity that hunting has never been a pastoral occupation and that, if anything, it is a living mode detested by the Somali pastoral culture. There is a section of the traditions suggesting that certain northern tribes or sub-clans are loathed and despised by the dominant Isaq clan for that practice. As Ioan M. Lewis proposes affirmatively, "Noble Somali do not them-selves hunt."[39]

Therefore, if we cautiously examine the different socio-cultural modes of the Somali social segments as we see them today, and consid-erately think of the quantity of merchandise involved, I conclude that such activity would require exceptional expertise and skills in over-coming the hazards involved in hunting and approaching such ani-mals.

Here again, this item leaves us with a hypothesis that these people should have been professionals in hunting, thereby positing the Eyle and other people of the Jareer ethnic community as the possibility. This hypothesis is strengthened by the oral traditions of the Eyle themselves and facts in the academic books that the group resorts also to agriculture as a substitute subsistence occupation only in times of rains.[40]

5.   Elsewhere, scholars mention ruins of medieval settlements on the Shabelle valley[41] and discoveries by colonial officials of old agricultural settlements in some parts of the north before their decline.[42] When taken into account the Somali nomads' disdain, disgust and disrespect for the pursuance of agriculture as a means of living, a thought begs for postulation as to who those people could be who were mentioned as the sedentary community who practiced agriculture in those localities Hersi mentioned in his study!.

6.   A substantial proof, which Hersi fell short of emphasizing, but which the traditions, Neville Chittick[43] and Shariff Aidurus[44] are all in accordance with is that, not only about early Bantu residence but much so in leadership. Chittick suggests that a Bantu ruler who spoke Swahili ruled in Mogadishu, and the traditions are in consent with that. Relatively Shariff Aidurus's book recognizes pre-Somali Bantu settlers in Somalia with the picture of a Bantu youth displayed in one of the pages, most probably as an illustration distinguishing the Bantu from the Somali; but Hersi dared not hint at that – for whatever purposes!

7.   Trade and commerce are activities, which are the engagement of a sedentary culture. Pastoralism, specifically nomadic pastoralism as we know it in the Somali culture and tradition, is a form of living characterized by extensive wandering, constant mobility, migration, instability, and rampant with factionary feudal warfare. At this juncture, the question begging for an answer remains: who could be the sedentary, stable people pursuing the oft-mentioned trade with foreigners? Most of the merchandise mentioned by the early writers are available in the hinterland and therefore would need people living in the hinterland to hunt them, prepare them and bring them for sale. Which Somali culture endures this type of odd work? Which community among the Somali society is characterized as hunter-gatherers? Certainly we know of the Eile, who are Negroid/Jareer in all aspects of their life, as one possibility; but what about communities of the Somali-Arab lineage: who among them pursues a hunting mode of living? Hardly any 'noble' Somali accepts this as part of his culture, according

to the information they provided to Lewis.

The above evidence encompassing traditions, documents, archaeology and genealogy pertinent to Shungwaya and the migration of its ancient settlers before they lost their dwellings to Somalis and Galla, we may now focus on the traditions and available records of the Somali Bantu with specificity to the autochthons of the riverine south.

First of all, Chhabra reminds us that "History is a witness that all over the world ancient civilizations developed on the banks of rivers like Indus valley civilization, Nile valley civilization etc. In the ancient past, all important cities were founded near river banks."[45] For centuries, the Shabelle river valley has been a center of agricultural settlements of thriving polities within their own territories. The dwellers of this valley constitute a consortium of peoples who remained behind during what oral historians describe as *"dudka"* the exodus, or the great Bantu migration in the 16th and 17th centuries in the wake of Somali and Galla insurgencies in the area.

Virginia Luling, who accomplished an extensive research period on segments of these people admits, "Before the Somali penetrated the area in sixteenth and seventeenth centuries, a population of Bantu-speaking cultivators inhabited the river lands."[46] The inhabitants of the area believe, in their own traditions, that they are the autochthons of the riverine, the earliest settlers. Their adaptation to and control of the environment informs us a lot. The division and delegation of social activities are elements of proof that only a keen observer can learn. As one oral historian, Ismaaciil Aliyoow Baxaar[47] put it, "How can this land be claimed by anyone other than a Bantu? Who can control the crocodiles, hippopotamus and the other species in the river bed, other than a Jareer?" He convinces to answer proudly that unlike what Luling wrote about the mythical narrative of the Gaalabax 'kooyto' comers in Afgoie, "All the Baxaar[48] everywhere along the rivers are Jareer, and none is Jileec."[49]

We can also consider Faay Muudeey Shongow's statement of the Baxaar duties belonging to her Jareer people as was also quoted by Luling,[50] who maintains in another substantiation that one of her informants " ... claims that the area once belonged to short people with flat noses, strong muscles and big jaws, mostly living by the rivers, whose descendants are still here".[51] Perhaps we can also multiply our evidence demonstration by invoking another one from Faay Muudeey Shoongow, a local female elder, telling Luling, "Our ancestors were born here; they did not come here."[52]

The Jareer and the Jileec live together in many towns and villages on the banks of the rivers, but it has since time immemorial been an indispensable social duty of the Bantu/Jareer as the owners of the land, to bear responsibility of control over the species in the river. The Jileec would have developed means of control over these creatures had they been the earlier inhabitants to live in the area. They would have developed a means of taming these species by utilizing the river.

No matter how much learned or respected one may be, once the Bantu/Jareer *Baxaa*r sanctions the suspension of the use of the river, no other settler can lift the ban, be he a Sultan or Sheikh or any other member of the community. The ownership and operation of the boats as means of transport is another duty, falling also under the ancestrally designated responsibility of the Jareer. The managers and caretakers of these social tasks are the Bantu. It is their sense of belonging to the environment and closer attachment to it that separate them from the *"kooyto"* comers who settled with them first as *'sheegat'*[53] but later overturned the mutual co-existence into serfdom, only after gaining support from kinsmen from far. But whatever the trends and tidings of time, the Jareer stay attached to their land which is a significant indication of their *"maguuraan"* (sedentarism, immobility) despite perpetual attempts to uproot them either by war or by coercive attachment to a Somali clan.

The traditions recount endless events of how the non-Bantu Jileec communities were initially accepted as new settlers and associates into *'gunta'*, the community. Mentions have been neatly narrated in well-preserved Jareer poetry, three of such being the following:

(a) Shiikh ii Sharaf-kiina Sheegataa-tihiin,
Minaa i-Shumeeynin waa nii Shawihaa.[54]

Translation
> From Sheikh to Sharif (of the Jileec) clients (of ours) you all are
> If you disdain kissing (my hand in respect), I will chase you (out of my land).

In another verse the Jareer poet reminds the Jileec about time past when they were destitutte, living in the bush:

(b) Duurka ii Dugaagtaa Diriskaada ahaay
Anaa ku Dadeeyi Deeganka ku siiyi

Translation
> A neighbor of the wild species in the jungle you were
> (It is me that) I made you live like human by giving you the settlement

The Bantu bard laments the Jileec settlers of hypocrisy and recalls:

(c) Mugii Aradneedoo Afkaada Uraayi
Aboow Ileheed Adoon ma Eheen!

Translation
> Shabby when you were (unworthy) and of malodorous mouth,
> You wouldn't dare call me 'Adoon' (slave), but instead called me 'Abow'
> (respected older brother)

The above verses envisage the different positions of the Jareer/Bantu as the autochthons and the Jileec as *'kooyto'* comers/immigrants. Said in another fashion, the Jareer feel pride in their precedence in the land, and such verses are recited to communicate displeasure with incidents of Jileec arrogance, ennoblement or foolish pride.

Traditionally, before one is qualified and accepted as a member of the *'gunta'*, he would approach *'Akhyaarta'* or *'Ul-gaduudda'* the council of elders, present his proposal and procure a formal acceptance or decline. Upon the procurement, the person acquires membership but under a *'sheegato'* client status. He becomes part of the community culture and the institution of the social customary charter then protects the new member, as he is also obliged to abide by it. "But these *'sheegato'* clients from the Jileec have caused us betrayals and irreparable damages,"[55] Aaw Bukoow recalls. "At the beginning, they plead for mercy and help, later when they are satisfied with their number, they breach all the *'gaanuun'*, the customary social canon regulation, and pose a threat,"[56] explains Aaw Diinle Aliyow. Ioan Lewis,[57] the anthropologist, would agree with these elderly historians, in his evidence that Somalis become strong by forming alliances to face a common enemy.

In ancient times when the Bantu were the only settlers in the interriverine, the period leading to sometime after *'dudka'* the mass exodus of the Jareer migration took place; the Somali were joined to the community as clients. Cerulli, the Italian ethnographer who wrote extensively about Somalia, mentions members of Hawiye sub-clans including the Hilibi, the Moobleen, the Daa'uud, the Baadi-Cadde and the Moolkal who initially settled along the Shabelle River as clients under the patronage of the sedentary Jareer farmers. These members were not merely absorbed on client basis but were even assimilated and have left their pastoral culture to adopt farming instead. Other remarkable instances are the Waceysle who have been long inhabitants of Shanlo village[58] while others are scattered in adjacent villages like Dhagaxow.[59] In yet another more interesting evidence, Francesca Declich writes about the possibility that such social interactions may also lead to linguistic impact.[60]

In a similar occurrence, the *'gunta'* community of *'Aruundaale'*, present day Afgoie (Afgooye), welcomed the Gobron and the entire Geledi confederacy, upon their arrival from the vicinity of the Ethiopian lowlands in Upper Jubba area. The Eelqode communities, possibly the Aytire leadership at the time, welcomed them as religious people, and were later assigned as bird-controllers who would read Qur'an and give propitious blessing to the production and multiplication of crops. Writing about this group, Lewis explains, "Their blessing protected the crops from birds – the same power attributed to saints elsewhere in the farming districts of Somalia."[61]

The Gobron were religious people; not only that, they are very well known for their sorcery and superior spiritual powers. They were experts in unleashing strong magical powers (*caziima*) to enemies and other undesirables. Normally, in those days, their task would categorically involve on the prediction and occult manipulation of the results of the wars. Their knowledge of that supernatural magical maneuver of *'saac'* - the favorable timing of operations, and the employment of other spiritual powers to disadvantage the foe, were among the advantages that have facilitated - if not accelerated – the synchronous decline and rise of the Aaytire and the Gobron respectively.

The Geledi, who some scholars describe as warriors, have experienced an intolerable duration of Silcis occupation and slavery to the extent of paying tribute even for the use of the water from the river and from the harvest of their crops. In addition, there were other unbreachable customs and traditions, such as that of (*Todoweeysi*) – honeymooning of a Silcis man with every Geledi bride before contact with her husband.

However, this subjugation was terminated after the arrival of the Wacdaan who overran the Silcis in a devastating battle. The oral tradition, one of the *'Istunka'* stick-fighting festival, produced in response to the Galadi's taunting of Shukri and Shariifow (mentioned in Chapter One), confirms that custom in this couplet:

> *Tuug waa Tiriseen waa Tilmaansateen*
> *Wax luu Todoweesti Tolkeeya ka keen.*[62]

Translation:

> You have counted and (virtually) marked culprits/stealers (from my kinship), But you can not mention from among my community (a female) who has honeymooned the 7-days with a male (other than with her husband!)

The 'Laashin' poet from the community of Shukri and Shariffoow, on the east bank of the river, was exasperated by the taunt of the rival group and 'bixii' produced/cited the above 'mar' verse, which in retaliation caused vexation among the entire Geledi population on the west bank of the river. It was morally more painful in taunt because it revealed a historical shame of the sultanate, which many Geledi people (especially those who exalted themselves to self-ennoblement) avoid reminiscing.

Still in the topic of *'sheegat'*, client, it would be fair to take the Ceelqode issue as instance. The name *Ceelgode* (Eelqode), which is said to have been given to the Tolweyne, is in fact the eponymous ancestor of the real Ceelqode clan who are the sedentary population of "Oraxsin" west Afgoie, the indigenous Jareer settlers. Luling (2002) did approach the tradition about Ceelqode only from the perspective of her hosts, the 'nobles'. The other version, which she admits the 'slaves' denied her accessibility, is the subject under elaboration. The previous version of Luling seems irreconcilable with some of the known traditions in several ways. Linguistically, the etymology "Ceelqode" is the equivalent of the English 'well-digger' or 'borehole-digger' and pronounced in the official local Maay language as "Eelqode". My argument now follows: -

If the Tolweyne are the 'nobles' as they claim, and 'Eelqode' is the digger of the well or borehole: who digs the borehole according to *"Jiinka"* riverbank tradition, the noble or the ignoble? There is no tradition or history whatsoever which suggests that 'nobles' in Afgooye ever engaged themselves to the hard task of digging wells. It is a heavy duty and therefore belongs to the undesirables at the lower stratum of the social hierarchy. Let me also add for the sake of ethnological bene-fit, that people who don't dig the grave [of] their own deceased kin are least expected of digging a well [for] everyone else, including the igno-ble or 'slaves'. In this case, since the name is attributed to someone who qualified to dig wells, and it is the Jareer that undertake this kind of activity, it is plausible only to consider the tickling fact that the so-called 'nobles' of the Tolweyne have adopted by subscription the name of the Jareer borehole-digger, Eelqode. For this matter, we may politely accommodate the presumption or even perception that the one whose name has been adopted so widely as the ancestral eponym of the whole clan/lineage is most certainly the original settlers.

The indigenes offered leave for settlement to the immigrants who later '*sheegteen*' adhered to their ancestral name. To put it otherwise would sound irrational, more peculiar, and of course demeaning for a "noble" clan to have accepted in any other circumstances, to take the name of a low man, and in this case Eelqode – well digger. Here again, my predisposition sustains that the multipurpose Somali phenomenon of '*Sheegat*' as narrated by many Somali and non-Somali scholars might have been promptly abused, this time by the Geledi and the entire so-called 'noble' people attached to the Eelqode of Afgoie. The Aytire who are the descendants of Aw-Elqode were reduced to slave status with-out having been enslaved by anyone.

The pastoral societies of Somalia are often dependent on the '*sheegat*' system for grazing opportunities and other social relations. For the urban dwellers from the nomadic culture, one often associates with another community through marriage or even at times by other dubious ways of identity manipulation and misinformation as Gunther Schlee witnessed in Kenya:-

> I once asked a Marsabit businesswoman from the 'Idagalle of Isaaq, who claimed that "idagalle was just another name for the Rendille clan Elegella, how she came to believe this. She pointed to the similarity of the two names, an argument that did not convince me. She then gave her argument a pragmatic turn: 'It is much better to have people than to be alone.' That is why she and her family '*shegdeen*' Elgella since their arrival in Kenya, had become known as 'the Somali of Elgella' to the Rendille. Many Somali traders relied heavily on the help of such Rendille 'brothers' in the beginning and only later, when they had ac-

cumulated wealth, developed cultural arrogance towards these 'pa-gans'.[63]

Schlee expresses astonishment over this experience and notes, "I have not met a Somali who regarded this ubiquitous type of relation-ship as shameful."[64] The above paragraph defines one of several as-pects; some mentioned here, which the Somalis exploit to attach them-selves to a *'buur'* a mountain – in other words, a strong tribe or clan, for reasons clearly marked on interest. The nomadic culture teaches about the habitualization of this suspicious tradition, as it advises: "*Buur noqo ama ka mid noqo*", others putting it as "*Buur ahow ama mid ku tiirsanow*" which respectively mean 'either be a mountain (strong tribe) or ad-here/adjoin yourself to one' and "Be a mountain or be leaning on one."

Another illuminating factor in Professor Schlee's statement is how the Somali revert to arrogance and superiority immediately upon achieving their goal. This negative description fulfills the argument of the traditions of the two Jareer historians Aaw Bukoow and Aaw Di-inle, referred above in 45 and 46 respectively, which the Jareer poets have also commented on the dimensions of its treachery in disgust.

An aspect of the *'Sheegato'* client phenomenon of clan affiliation ex-tensively stays vivid among the Digil-Mirifle confederacy of tribes. The traditions and even written documents mention sub-clans like the Hadama who absorbed numbers of people from the Dir and the Daarood.[65] Many people previously believed as part of the Digil-Mirifle social organization, who shared lineages cognate to the Reewing, have in a dramatic somersault re-allied with their reactivated original Daarood sub-clans like Ogaadeen, Dhulbahante and Majeerteen. The self-detachment from the host clan and resuscitation of one's 'original' clan, took their toll in the wake of the civil war when shifting alliances and clan confederacies became the resort for protection, a paradigm so characteristic of the nomadic way of life. Against the Digil-Mirifle, those previously most attached to the clan, i.e. born and bred in *Baydhaba Jannaay* and its affiliate Reewing territory inflicted the most devastating havoc during the Somali civil war.

The negative legacies which the indigenous Bantu people inherited from the settling of the Jileec Somalis into their social system are char-acteristically variable, but the most damaging are the loss of their an-cestral identity, language and culture which all disappeared as a con-sequence of assimilation under the guise of Somali 'brotherhood'. In time, the brotherliness was betrayed, culminating in a serfdom status of the Jareer community who otherwise deserved respect as beloved hosts and human philanthropists.

The previously accepted collateral communal relation, as cited by Schlee, changed into arrogance and intolerable lust for hegemony. The traditions reveal endless wars that were fought between the Somali pastoralists and the Bantu remnants that waged persistent protest against Somali wish for subjugation.[66] Most of these battles were fought due to the aboriginal Bantu people's hatred of dominance whereas for the Somali, with their fondness and belief of slave ownership as their Qur'anic right,[67] it was regarded shameful for them to have been re-sisted by the Bantu, especially after overwhelming the Galla into sub-jugation and reducing them to *'Qowsaar'* pastoral slaves.[68] "As the *'Raagaay'* (ancient forefathers) passed to us, in one day over 40 Somali Jileec fell *'goobyaal'* (battlefield casualty). The Jareer lost a few as they were in *'gaadiilo'* tactical ambush. After that battle in Balcad, Jareer went out in peace."[69]

These traditions, acquired from different sources, and supported by written documents, could not convince Somalis and colonists Italy as well as Asian immigrants from categorizing all the Bantu people as slaves. The most plausible rationale behind this categorization would put the Somalis in a class of their own and above the Jareer so that their claim for Arabness would be superiorically but superficially main-tained. In his opinion, historian Omar A. Eno refutes this unscholarly misinformation and argues,

"A myth perpetuated by Somali officials and by some scholars sug-gested that the entire Jareer population in Somalia consists of a small number of imported slaves from East Africa, an argument which is not supported by any historical or anthropological evidence."[70]

In my contentious view, for all the Jareer/Bantu to have been im-ported as slaves for cultivation, the masters should have been seden-tary settlers along the rivers prior to their acquisition of the slaves; but it is the other way round because the Jareer remain until today the only race with dominance on the river banks, even after the departure of their kin. Alternatively, the so-called 'imported slaves', notwithstand-ing their previous occupation, would have been made *'Qowsaar'* pas-toral slaves herding camels or attending to other pastoral livestock, the nomad's area of economic domination.

To strengthen his point, Eno cites none other than Turton[71] who conceives that in their process of expansion, the Galla and the Somali encountered Bantu-speaking people as their main rivals for control over grazing land in order to achieve a complete control over large areas in the riverine region.[72] Apparently, if this particular group under discussion, the Bantu-speakers, were imported slaves, they wouldn't have had a right to land ownership as they themselves were 'owned' by the Somalis. Had this been the situation, the pragmatic slave-master relationship would disagree with the notions of an "encounter" because slaves would not be expected to dare disobey their masters. Put differently, in the Somali Jileec thinking, a property cannot own another property. With that in mind, therefore, the "encounter" to uproot them envisages concrete evidence that they were the indigenous settlers whose land was, for all perceptible purposes, the bone of contention for the Galla, the Somalis as well as the Italians.

From the picture of this argument, we can screen that the Bantu population have found themselves between the hammer and the anvil: at one end were biased scholars who relied on the nomadic version of the traditions, at the other end were the Somali pastoral nomads seeking clan supremacy through mythical Arab identity. These two antisocial forces have, at different times and degrees, sufficiently orchestrated the contamination, if not contemporary demise, of the historiography as well as distinct ethno-cultural identity of the entire Bantu community. A brief discussion of the motives is sprinkled throughout the study.

Ancient maps and archival documents all support invariably the presence of non-Somali, non-Arab and non-Cushitic peoples in what they called 'Bilad - 'l Punt' which highly suggests 'Land of the Bantu'. Some of these documents carry descriptions of Negroid or Zenj physical characteristics; features which are loathsome to the noble-claiming Somali people and which to them are biological properties and complexions of 'low-born' inferior Africans.

What happened in what is today known as Somalia conceptually resembles the emigrational phenomena that took place in other parts of the world where a continuum of human transplantation and cultural importation have caused the concealment of the aesthetics of the indigenous people through domination. The migration I am referring to, in our limits within the Somali case, was the creation of what Omar

Eno termed "Landless Landlords and Landed Tenants."[73]

In my perception, so as to account for the complex factors of identity, mobility, cultural supremacy and ethnic-ennoblement, self-Arabized Somali nomads had to work out an ethnic stratification policy, which places them above the sedentary Jareer people. The wider effects, though, led to the creation of slavery and Slave Empire, ethnic marginalization, political domination and cultural genocide. According to Adam Kheerow, "There was already black colonialism in our midst in Somalia against the 'mano fero' (iron hand or Jareer people) before the arrival of the white colonist."[74] Shiikhe Ismaan Sadiiq adds, "The arrival of European colonialism has played [only] a complementary role to the localized Somali colonialism of the Jareer because both colonists, Italians and Somalis, were in mutual concordance in the colonization of the Bantu/Jareer people and the expropriation of their land."[75] Both systems have, from the Jareer view point, led to the marginalization of the Jareer as an inferior people with little human 'value' and 'cognizance'. Their social place and human potential was not considered beyond the boundaries of the lowly and burdensome duties derided by the artificially 'Arabized' Somali nomads.

Historians have undertaken fabulous studies concerning the East African coast, but the investigations carried out on the interior, particularly in the hinterland of the Somali coast of Banadir; seem to be scant and therefore inadequate. Until recently, there was lack of interest to study this area, the interior. Consequently, it created intricacies for scholars to distinguish between the Bantu Negroid population in the country, namely the indigenes and the Diaspora whose migration was recent. For instance, just to mention a few among these communities, we have such as:-

a)   Bantu/Jareer who consist of a considerable number of what is cumulatively lumped as Digil-Mirifle, whose association is not genealogical but a heterogeneous confederation of population of diverse ethnic backgrounds. Whatever the social status might be, formerly or currently, the keynote is the affiliation and social interaction that interlock the Jareer peoples to the rest of their Jileec counterparts. The *Hubeer*, the *Gabaawiin* and the *Harin* represent examples of such mixtures, even making it safe to say that in a properly conducted census, the Jareer would probably count numerically higher than their Jileec 'brothers' in the same sub-clan. The *Elai* and *Eyle* need no further mention in their quantitative supremacy as they are often categorized as distinct Negroid groups bearing identical physical recognition in contrast to the Jileec of the Reewing.

If, due to their culture and mode of living, the Sub (Digil-Mirifle or Rahanweyn) are despised by their Somali brethren of the nomadic pastoral culture, they thought being Jileec acquired them a qualification to look down upon the Jareer/Bantu Negroid people living among them. The nature of their contemplation is epitomized in veritable terms, appellations and epithets like 'boon', 'madde' and other words equivalent to the Af-Maxaa version of 'Adoon', 'Bidde', 'Habash' etc., which are all low strata-related derogatory registers used by the average Jileec in degradation of the Jareer.

b) The two main Aaytire tribes, the autochthons of the Geledi territory in Afgoie, make another stock of Bantu people, so numerical but co-existing with Jileec peoples of Digil-Mirifle origin. In fact they were the early settlers who accommodated the Gobron as Ulama (religious men), and other clans of the present Geledi confederacy of tribes in Afgoie district who themselves admit to have come as 'kooyto' immigrants. Dissatisfied with the formation of artificial genealogical supremacy, the Aaytire have reneged against the social hegemony of the Gobron sultanate and re-crowned their Sultan separately. Currently, at the helm is Suldaan Abdullahi Baansa, whose coronation was held in a fabulous ceremony in Afgoie, an even which the Gobron and their Jileec Geledi affiliates saw as a great dishonor to their social leadership.

c) The Tuni are composed of a broad segment of Jareer population who, in spite of the linguistic difference, many outsiders may confuse them with their counterparts in Baraawa. They are absorbed in the Digil-Mirifle confederation which represents them under that alliance. Among the people they live, they keep tolerating the effects of an adversely stratified social class.

Within the inter-river area, among the Reewing and as a branch of the Digil segment, these people's ethnography as well as ethno-history have erroneously been associated with lineages they have no ethnic relationship with. To the effect of that controlled interplay, it incites dissatisfaction in some quarters at the mention of the separate identity of this people.[76]

The superficially 'shared' and externally celebrated identity apart, "The Jareer are very rarely accepted by the Jileec into exogamous social institution with the 'brothers' and 'sisters' outside the Jareer genealogical bracket," insists Hassan Faqay,[77] a member of the Jareer community in Lower Shabelle region. But as a certain category of these Jareer people may be classified as descendants of ex-slaves, the fact is that they are residues of the indigenous Sabaki/Bantu speakers who could not make it during the Mijikenda-Pokomo-Wa-Nyika migration up along the Tana area and other parts of the Kenya coast.

We can analyze the Bantu/Jareer precedence by building on another analysis based on Professor Kusow's[78] thesis about the link in authority between the first-born and the water and/or land usage system, which determines the ownership right to the property. The tradition as explained by the methodologist and sociologist may probably be right with relation to particular groups within the Reewing community. However, examining the same postulation from another perspective, this time from that of the sedentary Jareer agriculturalist, there exists a more complex social institution in which land and water usage is vested, and which constitutes a hierarchical organization with each level fulfilling a given obligation at that stage or level, according to the dispositions of the *"gaanuun"* canon customary regulations of the Jareer people.

Therefore, since the latter system (of the Jareer) offers a wider divergence in the regulation of these essential social activities, there is more reason to think that the system might have universally been practiced by the Jareer/Bantu agricultural communities, before its adoption at a later date by the Reewing pastoralists, including the Maay-speaking portions in Afgoi. Logically, if the Somali brethren of the Reewing were migrating across the long distance from the Ethiopian eastern lowlands up the northern Horn in search of territories where they were to be 'first-born', they would have probably left certain assimilations traceable to them, except the few Jileec whom they might have left as *"Sheegat"* among the Jareer.

However, if a mechanical contention is imposed to validate this theory, then it will agree with the other parallel but more tenable concept of an early settlement on the Somalis' migration routes by Bantu farmers who were then the 'first-born' compared to the others who had to settle away from the riverbanks and as far as the less fertile land in the northern regions. Therefore, considering the hypothesis of the 'first-born' oft-referred in Somali nomadic culture, it will determine the Bantu, and not a proto-Reewing proto-Somali people, as the earliest settlers in Somalia beyond any reasonable doubt. Explaining it otherwise would mean that the Somalis, who had earlier on dispersed from the Ethiopian Lowlands in their first migration South-North, would have settled all the Bantu populated areas as first-borns, a golden opportunity which would help the 'nobility' to claim ownership and deny the Jareer a claim to the productive land. But the fact that they pushed the Sabaki-speakers (Mijikenda/Pokomo) in their second (return) migration from the North to the South in search of a better environment, and the current distribution of the Jareer people in the south, especially the largest productive areas, I don't think we can suggest other than these 'Negroes' (whether 'Habash', 'Adoon', 'Boong', 'Maddo', 'Jareer', 'Bidde', 'Beyle-Sanbuur' or 'Sankadhudhi') being the first-borns to their respective areas of settlement. One wouldn't think of better evidence than their dual access to the most important environment for survival namely: - the water from rivers Jubba and Shabelle and the arable land adjacent to them. Until now, these remain as part of the socio-historical identity of their cultural attachment to the area. In comparison, the Jileec are on the hunt for the acquisition of the same territory by blunder, extortion, expropriation and by bloodshed.

In another observation of the Somali's well or borehole (*war*) and first-born authority regulation, it gives us a want to consider the arrival of the proto-Somali ancestors in water abundant areas along the rivers Jubba and Shabelle, not as first-born, but as migrants themselves in search of habitation. The distance away from the water points and further migration to a domicile suggests the clan's search of a country to exercise as a first-born stock akin to that settlement.

In any case, the Bantu/Jareer people's proximity in wider part to the easily accessible water points, i.e. living in the majority of the villages and towns in the vicinity of the rivers and the interiors extending there from, remains a clear indication of who were the first-born. In the given theory where the first settler becomes the first-born of an area, it would give us how many first-borns! The concept of first-born, according to the general norms, functions in true biogenetic paradigm where by birth the child, (male child in patrileneal cultures) is the first one born to a lineage, and the thesis may bear negative consequences for its application to dry land farming.

For all practical purposes, the dry land farming hypothesis may stand a bit shaky since the Jareer farming communities normally cultivate on adequate land whose distribution and availability do not depend on who is first-born or non-first-born. Newcomers, in this case, are either given a parcel after acceptance for settlement, or denied altogether. If the practice exists among the agro-pastoral Reewing people, I believe that it cannot cover all farming communities because the Jareer is born to a settled people who are already in possession of land and water and who are first-born in the village or villages where they live. Therefore, they have been saved from migration elsewhere, wandering in search of open land to claim first-born status. In fact, it is this kind of migration of the proto-Reewing/Galla-Somaloid peoples that supports the indigenousness of the Jareer in Somalia because all the known Somali traditions mention their origin from an eponymous immigrant father. None, in fact, has related any tradition of earlier attachment to the land or precedence to the Bantu/Jareer people, but ubiquitously origination from places distinct from what we know as Somalia today.

The loss of identity following the migration of the bulk of the Wa-Nyika tribes has expunged the remnant groups into affiliation as 'subordinate' humans to the bellicose Somali as the dominant lot. Due to the subjugation by various Somali sub-groups perfected against them, it ultimately resulted in the disappearance of their ascendant lineages and consanguinary tribal identities that became remote up the generations.

However, there was coercive adherence of the Bantu to a Somali tribe or sub-clan which had specific as well as common goals of the tribes concerned.. The Somalis needed to exploit the Jareer male as manpower in the events of warfare in which the Somalis encountered each other frequently. Traditionally, when the Jareer person's 'Abtirsi' ('ab' means ancestor; and 'tirsi' = is from the term 'tiro' meaning count, number) patrilineal count to the forefathers has been absorbed into the Somali tribe or sub-tribe, though artificially, the Jareer had no safer alternative but to abide by the cultural norms and values of 'his' Somali kinship.

Further deteriorating the situation were the colonial scholars. They wrote about the Bantu/Jareer people while conducting most of their fieldwork, if not all of it, without properly accessing the traditions from the relevant community. When crucial ethnographical and socio-historical study was undertaken about the Bantu many of these scholars were based among remote communities away from the primary subjects of the study. They relied on biased sources, interested parties who themselves lacked proper knowledge about the Jareer background. Those scholars and authors have certainly become part of the hindrances that misinformed about the reality of the Bantu history, by publishing inferential data of mendacity. The few who claim to have carried out their fieldwork in the south have not taken much opportunity to talk to the Jareer people as their initial contacts. From the tendency of their interest, focus and language, one can reveal symptoms of the social philosophy of the Jileec as 'nobles' of a hybrid genealogy against a socially worthless Negroid people, all of slave descendency. This is to argue that certain researchers have been "investigating" the Jareer community while the bulk of their information was sourced from the dominant Jileec who form the so-called 'leaders', 'elders', 'nobles' and 'sultans'; those situated at the top of the social structure. Accordingly, data collected through such measures and tools were used to study the social and historical aspects of the Jareer, and produced results incongruent with the true history of the Jareer we know.

Even in the case of contacting an autochthonous Jareer informant, possibility is that he may not express the status of his identity independently. In the presence of the Jileec people as interpreters or self-made nobles, the Jareer interviewee finds himself under pressure because of the Jileec who want to make sure that the Bantu informant doesn't contradict their misinformed version. Dr. Catherine Besteman encountered the undesirable effects against the Bantu social situation during her long study on a section of this community in the Jubba Valley regions. Her comment was, "A stigmatized identity does not create ethnicity."[79] Appalling situations of this nature have also played a part in obscuring the daily reality about the situation of the Jareer, historically as well as socially.

Quite a number of Bantu people interviewed in the presence of the Jileec, either as interpreters or otherwise, must have given a series of answers to please the third person than to present the actual truth. On the other hand, a section of these investigators might have arrived at the field with the misconception of researching on 'Jareer slaves', ignorant of the ethno-historical variation between the imported Diaspora Bantu and the indigenous, thereby floundering into dissatisfaction and information inaccessibility. Virginia Luling has encountered a similar situation in Afgoie. In her own words she admits that she got her information "...partly, from accounts given to me by Nobles, since those former slaves that I met were uncommunicative."[80] My guess to such embarrassing experiences suggests that the inaccessibility occurred due to a possibility that the informant was not a 'habash' or a member of "former slaves" but instead a "Jareer aborigine" or a 'Bantu indigene."

This kind of situation may be experienced when the unaware investigator compromises certain processes such as overlooking prior arrangement with the 'habash' informants for familiarization and building rapport. For instance, Besteman informs us how she took care of the issue concerning confidence--building during her fieldwork in the Juba Valley. Therefore in the former's case, as a reaction to what they saw as identity misinformation and socio-psychological torture in the presence of one claiming to be 'noble', the 'habash' opted to air a message of protest by boycotting to respond, hence justifying Luling's concentration to collect data from the opposite group, the 'self'-ennobled Jileec.

To sum-up this discussion, let us now turn to the other history of the second Bantu/Jareer community consisting of the Diaspora, immigrants who were brought to Somalia as victims of Arab slave trade.

The Diaspora Somali Bantu

The second history of the Somali-Bantu population belongs to a section of the Jareer people who are mainly the citizens of the Juba valley. They consist of heterogeneous peoples composed of an autochthonous nucleus and an immigrant counterpart who settled along the valley about two or three hundred years ago. Ethno-historically therefore, the valley is a composition of fugitive run-away slaves and indigenous groups who lived there before them, but united as a community. Numerous names are used for these peoples, such as 'Gosha' (people of the un-inhabited forest), 'Mushunguli' (could refer Mshungwaya?), 'Dhal-Goleed' (the offspring of the un-inhabited bush) and so on. They are described as "distinct groups like the Zigua, Zaramo, Magindo, Makua, Manyasa, Mushunguli and Yao".[81]

The traditions and archival documents tell us that there was famine in the original settlements of these people in Tanzania when Arab merchants lured them with promises of a more productive land and better living. Later it happened to be a deceitful promise, which Grottanelli[82] explains exhaustively. Subsequently, they were transported in dhows and sold into slavery to the coastal Somalis. Understanding the deception and the exchange of hands between the Arabs and the Somalis, the ill-fated victims of slavery had to make a decision for emancipating themselves, an opportunity which did not come rather easy. Defining that episode, Mzee Mkomo says, "The mistreatment and malnourishment were intolerable to the Mushunguli for they had neither expected nor experienced slavery."[83] Omar Eno[84] cites Lt. Christopher's report on the latter's visit to the Benadir in 1842, concerning the Somali mistreatment of slaves, a thesis that supports Mzee Mkomo's story. Robert Hess, in evidence, describes the inhuman condition of the slaves as "…often kept in manacles and fetters, overworked and underfed."[85]

As a consequence, the malnourishment and mistreatment by the Somali spiraled to devastating proportions, mentally much so as physically. Several plans were made after secret contacts among the people have been established. Women and children would be the heaviest burden in the wake of an engagement in battle en route to emancipation, but nevertheless, everybody had to face the burden together. Commenting about the intricacy of the trend, Mzee Mberwa termed it as *"kufa na kupona"* [86] (very strong Kiswahili expression meaning "to die and be relieved"), in other words 'do or die'. In connection to slavery, therefore, the Bantu victims from the Diaspora had to cope with the complexities arising from the dreadful implications of a bestial institution away from home, which in the late Walter Rodney's comments "…meant migration of labor in a manner one hundred times more brutal and disruptive."[87] The only difference of the Mushunguli case from Rodney's Western slavery is the color of the master which, in their situation, was a mythically Arabized black African Somali.

The Gosha people's determination to free themselves from subjugation at any cost would not please the Somali slave owners, particularly the Reer Hamar, the Amarani, the Biimaal and other Hawiye groups who pursued realizing high economic ambitions by means of exploitation. Robert Hess notes that without slave labor, "The Biimal who had the nomadic Somali's traditional disdain for agriculture would be reduced to subsistence economy."[88] Being the might and machinery for the income generation, there was no possibility the Jareer could abandon their work stations en masse without sacrifices and presumption of the obvious fatalities. They had to prepare for possible engagements, especially knowing that the base of social prosperity and other Somali trade economy was built on the grain produced by the slaves.[89]

With the passage of time, some of the slaves managed to escape and disappear, while others did so by sacrificing their lives for the freedom of generations to come – although the stigmatization of an unending slave status would live permanently with them. The leadership of the escape plot rested over the shoulders of a female, Wana-kooka (others call her Wanakoocha). She was a seer who gave instructions that there would be no looking back once the journey to freedom had started; also, anyone who abandoned his people would be dealt with by the ancestors' wrath and curse. She boosted her army's war psychology by reminding them the harsh inhuman penalty and punishment awaiting a failed escape attempt, so it would be a manly act for one to die rather than live a submissive life under Somali oppression. Elaborating on the consequences of escape failure, Lt. Christopher of the British Naval Army concedes witnessing an instance of escapee punishment in which a shackled slave was fetching water from a well to supply laborers about four miles away![90] (More about Wanakoocha and waGosha Diaspora read Eno & Eno 2007).

As Mzee Juma Chivalo narrates, "When the Mushunguli reached the Juba valley; they were received and absorbed into other existing Bantu aborigine/Negroid communities who were scattered in small and large villages on both banks of the river."[91] The traditions sound more emphatic on the later arrival of non-Mushunguli runaways as well as individual escapees who had lost the way and reached up to Afgoi and Mogadishu before tracing their kinsmen back in the Juba valley. Upon settling in the valley, each village had a leader and every few small villages had a structure under one leader. Here they established themselves as polities with strong social interaction, united under the banner of wa-Gosha people, harmonizing the differences of their multi-ethnic background. The oral historians I met in Tanga, Dar-es-Salaam, Kakuma, Marafa, Swaleh Nguru and Jomvu, were unanimous about Wa-Gosha engagements in several wars. The instigations behind these battles had mainly had their causes from Somali desire for re-enslavement of the fugitive Gosha ex-slaves, with the inclusion of the indigenous freeborn Jareer. I video-taped Jareer elders in Mogadishu who mentioned about vicious attacks by Somali pastoralists attempting to dispel even the Jareer autochthons from their areas; most imminent of these wars were two fought separately with the Biimaal and the Ogaden. Between the two, more reminiscent is the battle in which the Ogaden were severely subdued.

Under the leadership of Nassib Bundo,[92] around 1890, the wa-Gosha people had established autonomous villages and cultivated abundantly. They had been producing surplus to trade with other communities and practiced fishing to exploit the river. The Somali were envious of the improvement of the living situation of the Bantu and the order and stability prevailing in their settlements. In reference to the situation, Somali historian and slavery expert Omar Eno confirms that "The state of Gosha was surrounded by enemies, the Somali nomads."[93]

As a result, suspicions of war with the Ogaden have been precipitating for some time because quite often the belligerent Ogaden pastoralists were intruding the Bantu by derogatory abuse, trespassing and grazing their livestock on mature crops and sometimes beating children. All these aggressions represented acts of provocation but the Bantu persevered, concentrating on their economic improvement and the maintenance of good neighborliness. In time, the Ogaden had received support men from their clansmen, which explains deliberate intentions of an attack for a long time.

When Nassib Bundo was informed about the provocation of an Ogaden build up for war, he summoned several elders in a secret meeting at night. They discussed thoroughly about the possibility for war. Within a few days, the elders reported to Nassib on their support in another meeting, which lasted till dawn. However, the Ogaden, as it appeared, were not aware of wa-Gosha preparation in a unified defense; and on that fateful day when the battle erupted, they were overrun overwhelmingly beyond their expectation. The Bantu ran amok. The Ogaden pleaded for mercy but Bantu vexation piling up over the years has exploded beyond normal bounds of tolerance. The traumas from earlier grudges of Somali mistreatment and inhumanity under slavery have now found a healing mechanism for vengeance in this war, and the Ogaden had to bear the painful burden. The damage was immeasurable. The magnitude of the Ogaden devastation, in man and morale, would remain unrecoverable for decades to come; and the peace that prevailed in the region thereafter brought more restoration of pride and dignity for the 'Dhal-Ooji' children of the Oji/Jareer in the Juba valley.

The most significant phenomenon of this war, which is reminiscent of the present situation, is the Ogaden plea for mercy in the battlefield, constantly repeating the three-word sentence 'Ooji-yoow abuur reeb'[94] which means: - Ooh Ooji (Gosha people), leave some offspring behind; don't exterminate all of us, please! [95]

Reviewing the sources of the multiple traditions gives the inference that several core factors have contributed to the defeat of the Ogaden:-

1.   The leadership at that time, Nassib Bundo and his council of elders at the realm of the villages were wise. Nassib had sought the opinion of the elders who then won the trust of the masses before their stipulation for war. The quality of leadership reminds us of Palmer and Perkins who argue that in the absence of strong and sound leadership, "morale is totally useless, if indeed it can exist at all."[96]

2.   By seeking the elders' opinion, Mzee Bundo was evaluating the community's morale because he wouldn't dare a defeat in the duel once he had committed the community into it. He and his council were probably adept about social morale as during crisis, according to Morgenthau, "it permeates all activities of a nation, its agricultural and industrial production as well as its military establishment…its presence and absence and its qualities reveal themselves particularly in times of crisis."[97] And this was a time when the freedom of the entire Gosha was at stake.

3.   The people had experienced a very successful harvest in the previous season and as such had adequate grains to survive in the event of a prolonged battle.[98]

4.   The Wa-Gosha were inflated with exasperation because the Ogaden had sent several threats to the Bantu, suggesting either a) to submit to clientele and serfdom status, b) to quit the valley or c) to prepare for war.[99]

5.   Determination was a key influencing factor, according to the traditions. According to Omar Muya, the Wa-Gosha had to choose between repulsing the Ogaden once and for all, or suffering perpetual slavery; because even in the event that they relocate elsewhere after a defeat, more Somali temptation for their conquest was imminent. Finally it would mean changing only masters but not status. They opted for war as an ultimate solution.

The Ogaden – Bantu war has an undertone of remote as well as immediate causes. Among the dynamic agents was the Ogadens' desire to convert the entirety of Jareer of Gosha into slaves looking after their livestock and undertaking other menial jobs, and/or working for them on agricultural bush land, cleared by the Gosha farmers and cultivated in favor of the Ogaden who would then reap the profit. However, the immediate cause that accelerated the war, according to a section of the traditions, was the murder in Mofi Village of Mamgala Maligo Mazale, the sister of Mkoma Maligo Mazale, the Sultan of Mofi at the time.[100]

In this particular incident, the Ogaden, led by Sheikh Ambulo,[101] waged a surprise attack without any provocation whatsoever. The people escaped to take cover in Mukuy Gamila village across the river where the wa-Boni people live. Mamgala was pregnant and reluctant to flee, because she wanted the people to defend themselves. When the Ogaden found her, she was tortured against her refusal to make a confession of the whereabouts of her people. She resisted after which they cut her womb open, killing her and her unborn baby boy. When the men returned, they were disgusted with the callous act of the Ogaden.

Messages were communicated to the other Bantu Sultans who joined for the burial of Mamgala and her premature child. Prominent leaders like Shongor Mafula, Mzee Chaima of Hindi (Bula Mareer), Mzee Kalindima of Kwak-Kwam (Bandar-Jadiid), and Nassib Bundo of Kamsuma, had a big task in their hands. The anticipated fatal incident was more likely and even much closer.

After strategizing their people within a short period of time, they sent a mission one night and the Ogaden leader Sheikh Ambuulo, was abducted from his residence.[102] He was brutally murdered in vengeance for Mamgala's death. The Ogaden were deeply astonished and embarrassed upon the knowledge of their leader's mysterious disappearance and subsequent death. They got boosted with a massive reinforcement from their different clans and tribes for a final strike to engage the Jareer and subdue them into another Somali conquest.

An amalgamated Ogaden force under the leadership of Mohamed Heren Daboolo, Omar Godane and Leflef took up arms and attacked from different fronts, including Migua, Bulizaga, Miono, Kamsuma, Makalango, Mofi and Mugambo, in different battles. However, the miscalculation of the Ogaden was that they had not anticipated a pan-Jareer conglomeration of forces to go into battle side-by-side. As a consequence, one Ogadeni leader, Heren Daboolo, was killed in Mukuy Gamila. Omar Godane was shot with a poisonous arrow while drinking water from the river at Chirua (Lama-daad) and instantly fell dead there. The third Ogadeni war leader, Leflef, was '*goobyaal*' (death casualty in the battlefield) in Migua. In the course of these annihilations, the Ogaden realized that the Bantu were irresistible. They were dispersed, sought after, overpowered and humiliated. They had neither recourse nor intercession as they pleaded "*Oojiyoow abuur reeb! Ooji-*

yoow abuur reeb! Oojiyoow abuur reeb!" It was too late, as the Bantu puss of anger could no longer be kept in the bulging wound of perseverance.

Sheikh Murjan, a respected Bantu clergyman, convened a high-level inter-clan reconciliatory meeting in Mwana Mofi between the Bantu and the Ogaden, as the latter felt survival heat at the imposition of tribute for watering their livestock in the river. At times, their tribute was rejected with orders forbidding them from approaching the vicinity of the wa-Gosha/Jareer settlements. With the reconciliation meditated by Sheikh Murjan, however, the relationship was normalized and peace and tranquility were restored.

Whatever the cost of the war, the Bantu Diaspora's intolerance to slavery, their victory over the Somalis coupled with self-pride, and an astounding leadership recognized by their Somali rivals, provided them some consolation and self-esteem. Nassib was probably the only leader in pre-independence Somalia and even after independence, to rally a willing and formidable army estimated from twenty to forty thousand men.[103] Kenneth Menkhaus (PhD Dissertation) and Catherine Besteman (PhD Dissertation), who both conducted superbly refined studies in the Juba valley and on the Gosha Bantu/Jareer communities, have visited this version of the oral traditions about the Ogaden-WaGosha war in their respective research.

Diplomatically, Sultan Bundo was in a class of his own. He developed relationship with all peoples of good intentions for mutual co-operation. Many countries recognized his authority as a Sultan of the Gosha. He had respect for his colleagues and the community as a whole. He was against injustice and was kind to the people in times of need. He was not dictatorial and was less bellicose, though he was a shrewd military leader and good strategist in time of war.[104] Due to his resistance to colonial injustice, the Italian colonial administration incarcerated him in Mogadishu until his death.

Conclusion

Separation of the two historical backgrounds of the Somali Bantu/Jareer people was long over due. Until recently, it has been very difficult for the pre-Somali indigenous inhabitants to have their history distinguished from that of the Somali Bantu Diaspora. The former remain in their current settlements as residues of the Sabaki speaking groups related to the Shungwaya/Mijikenda. Connection to the environment, the traditions, and written archival materials present clear evidence of the distinction between the two Bantu communities. But for the sake of ethnic supremacy and a long enduring search for nobility, the Somali Jileec clans have opted to present all the Bantu population in Somalia as nothing but imported slaves. Surprisingly, the Somali people have also a habit of shying away from acknowledging the Bantu people's resistance to slavery but often dramatize the issue as if they were satisfied with the status quo. The wa-Gosha people's determination out of bondage and struggle to oppose slavery for ever was also highlighted with some reflection on the war against the Ogaden Somalis. Bantu leadership in war and in peace, polities and prosperity should also be given the honorable place they deserve in Somali history; not the erroneous way they are often presented as imported slaves, but the other true version that they are also the autochthons of the territory.

Notes and references

1. Habash - is a derogatory word applied to the Bantu Somalis. It means Abyssinian pagan.
2. Adoon - means slave. It is pejorative and is used to abuse all the Jareer/Bantu Somalis regardless of status.
3. Bidde and 'Beyle-Sanbuur' are the equivalent of Habash, Adoon etc. The northerners to derogate the Jareer often use them.
4. Montclose, Marc – Antoine Perouse de. The French scientific Research Institute – www.ceped.ined.fr/cepedweb (Also read Report on Minority Groups in Somalia: Joint British, Danish, and Dutch Fact Finding Mission to Nairobi, 17-24 September 2000.
5. UNDP Human Development Report – Somalia 1998: 23-24.
6. Turton, E.R., - "Bantu, Galla and Somali Migrations in the Horn of Africa – A Reassessment of the Juba/Tana area." Journal of African History 16 (1975):519-537.
7. Bulletin of the International Committee of Urgent Anthropological and Ethnical Research; pp.28-29. No.3, 1960; with the help of UNESCO.
8. Nurse, Derek. - "Shungwaya and the Bantu of Somalia: Some Linguistic Evidence. Kenyatta University College.
9. Turton (Ibid.)
10. Ali, Mohamed Nuuh, "Somali History: Linguistic Approach to the Past", in Kusow, Abdi M., (ed.), op. cit. p.24.
11. Morton, R.F., "The Myth of Shungwaya Origins of the Mijikenda: A Problem of Late Nineteenth Century Kenya Coastal History" , The Interna-

tional Journal of African Historical Studies 5 (1972):397-424. Also at the Kenya National Archives – Central Government Library: (83-528) – 149. 3MOR.

12. Ali, Mohamed Nuuh, op.cit., p.18.

13. Ibn Sibahi, - "Awdah al-Masalik, op. cit. See also Lewis, I.M., Peoples of the Horn of Africa, p.45.

14. Doke, C.M., - "The Earliest Records of Bantu" reprinted from Bantu Studies – vol. XII, No. 2; June 1938.

15. Nurse, Derek, "Shungwaya and The Bantu of Somalia – Some Linguistic Evidence, Kenyatta University College.

16. Ibid.

17. Ibid.

18. Ibid.

19. Sutton, J. E. G., "Early Trade in East Africa"; Historical Association of Tanzania. First Published 1973. East African Publishing House.

20. Spear, Thomas T., "The Kaya Complex – A History of the Mijikenda Peoples of the Kenya Coast to 1900, Kenya Literature Bureau, Nairobi (1978).

21. Ibid.

22. Thomas Spear uses Singwaya instead of Shungwaya.

23. Spear, Thomas T., "Traditional Myths and Linguistic Analysis – Singwaya Revisited." La Trobe University. (1977).

24. Ibid.

25. Ibid.

26. Kimaryo, Jacob L., "East African Coastal Historical Towns: Asiatic or African? A paper presented to the Conference: U-landsforskning 2000. January 13-15, 2000, University of Gutenberg, Goteborg, Sweden.

27. Spear, Thomas T., "Traditional Myths..." op. cit.

28. Allen, James de Vere, "Shungwaya, The Mijikenda, And The Traditions." International Journal of African Historical Studies; vol. 16(3) 1983 pp. 455-85.

29. Ibid.

30. Grottanelli, V.L., "A Lost African Metropolis," Afrikanistische Studien Berlin, 1955, 231-242.

31. Krapf., Travels., c.f. Chittick, op. cit.

32. Champion, A.M., The Agiryama of Kenya; Royal Anthropological Institute Occasional Paper No. 5 London, 1967: 6-7.

33. Morton, R.F., "Shungwaya" 401. cf. Chittick, op. cit.

34. Cerulli, :Libro degli Zenj," 253, n.3; cf. Chittick, op. cit.

35. Chittick, H.N., "An Archaeological Reconnaissance of the Southern Somali Coast," Azania, IV(1969), 118-120.

36. Hersi, A.A. op. cit.

37. "Cad iyo caano" – respectively mean 'piece of meat and milk', the supposed diet of Somali pastoralists.

38. Burton, R., First Footsteps in East Africa. London (1894:109).
39. Lewis, I.M., Peoples of the Horn of Africa, op.cit., p.75
40. Notes from videotaped Somali Bantu oral historians, 2003. Mogadishu – Somalia.
41. Hersi: A.A. op. cit., p. 172.
42. Ibid. 173
43. Chittick, Neville cf. Hersi op. cit. (fn 81 pp 103-104).
44. Aidarus, Sharif Aidarus Ibn Shariff Ali; - Bughyat al-Amal – fi-Tarikh – As Sumal; Mogadishu, Stamperia A.F.I.F. 1955. I have also had several personal discussions with Shariff Aidarus in his residence near the border zone between Hawl-wadag and Wardhigleey (near Radio Marina) in the 1980's and he personally gave me a copy of the book. The Shariff was a friend of my father and a close friend of one Hagi Sufi of Bondheere, who was also my father's friend.
45. Chhabra, S.S., Fundamentals of Demography (2001) Surjeet Publications.
46. Luling, Virginia, "Colonial and Post-colonial Influence on a South Somali Community". Journal of African Studies, Spring, 1976 volume 3, number 1.
47. Ismail Aliyow Baxaar – personal discussion in Saudi Arabia and recorded audiotapes 2002.
48. Baxaar – is the caretaker of the species in the river such as crocodiles and hippopotamus and so on.
49. Ismail Aliyow Baxaar, see No. 47 above.
50. Luling, Virginia, Somali Sultanate op.cit. p.118, fn.9.
51. Ibid. p.117. fn.7.
52. Ibid. p.116
53. Videotaped workshop for Bantu elders, op.cit.
54. (a) Sacdi Mumin Hassan, (b) Maxmadeey Ismaan, (c) Muridi Maaxi Mumin
55. Aaw Bukow Ahmed – personal interview, 2003, Afgoie.
56. Aaw Diinle Aliyow – personal interview, 2003. Dhajalaq village, District of Afgoie.
57. Lewis, Ioan M., Peoples of the Horn of Africa. op.cit. p.14.
58. Cerulli, Enrico, - Somalia, Scritti editi ed inediti, vol.III (1964) Roma: Istituto Poligrafico dello Stato.
59. Shanloow and Dhagaxoow are two villages of the Shidle Jareer community in Middle Shabelle region. They are at times read together as 'Shanloow – Dhagaxoow' without the conjunction.
60. Declich, Francesca, "Fostering Ethnic Reinvention: Gender Impact of Forced Migration on Bantu Somali Refugees in Kenya. Cahiers d'Etudes Africaines, 157, XL-1, 2000 pp. 25-53.
61. Lewis, I. M., Saints and Somalis: Popular Islam in a Clan-based Society. London. Haan Associates, (1998:86).

62. Laashin Sacdi Mumin Hassan.
63. Schlee, Gunther, op. cit.
64. Ibid.
65. Lewis, I. M., Peoples of the Horn of Africa. op.cit. p.40.
66. Videotaped workshop. As above.
67. Speke, cited in Besteman, Catherine L., "The Invention of Gosha", in Ahmed, Ali J.(ed.) op.cit., p. 49.
68. Ibid.
69. Sheikh Abukar Gaafaay, in videotaped workshop in Mogadishu. op.cit.
70. Eno, Omar A., "Landless landlords and Landed Tenants" in Kusow, Abdi M., (ed.) op. cit.
71. Turton was an opponent against the Bantu settlement in the riverine area and the associated Shungwaya issue. In an abrupt turn-over, he suggests an encounter and rivalry between the Somali/Galla and riverine Bantu.
72. Eno, Omar, A., "Landless Landlords". op.cit.
73. Ibid.
74. Eng. Hagi Adam Kheerow – personal discussion, 2003 Afgoie, Somalia.
75. Shiikhe Ismaan Sadiiq – personal discussion, 2003 Afgoie, Somalia.
76. Eno, Mohamed A., "Jawaab", Wargeyska Runta – 16-30 Maajo, 1996; Cadadka 10aad, Bogga Saad.
77. Hassan Faqay. Interview in Nairobi, 2003.
78. Kusow, Abdi M., "The Somali Origin: Myth or Reality", in Ahmed, Ali Jimale (ed.), op.cit. pp.81-106.
79. Besteman, Catherine, "The Invention of Gosha", in Ahmed, Ali Jimale, op.cit.
80. Luling, Virginia, Somali Sultanate, op.cit., pp.126-127.
81. U.S Department of State; Human Rights and Labor – March 2000.
82. Grottanelli, Vinigi., "I Bantu del Giuba nelle tradizioni dei Wazegua." Geografia Helvetica, VIII, 3, p. 254.
83. Mzee Muya Mkomo, personal interview in Kwedhi - Kwazu, Tanga- Tanzania, 2004.
84. Eno, Omar A., "Landless Landlords". op.cit.
85. Hess, Robert L., Italian Colonialism in Somalia; The University of Chicago Press, 1966:87-99
86. Mberwa Muya Mberwa, personal conversation in Magalia, Dar-es-Salaam, Tanzania. 2003.
87. Rodney, Walter, How Europe Underdeveloped Africa. East African Publishers. 2001
88. Hess, op.cit.
89. ASMAI – Archive Stoic del Minister degli Affair Ester, (Roma, Italia) 1905.
90. Christopher, William. "Extract from a Journal by Lt. William Christopher, commanding the H.C. Brig. Of War Tigris on the East Coast of Africa. May 8th,1843." Journal of the Royal Geographical Society 14 (1844: 76-103).

91. Mzee Juma Chivalo, personal interview in Kwedhi Kazoo, Tanzania. 2004.
92. The traditions say his real name was Makanjira but was popularly known as Nasib which was a name given to him by the man who found him as a young boy and fostered him. Nasib means 'luck'.
93. Eno, Omar A., ' "Gosha/Heer-Goleet" (people of the forest): Runaway slaves in the Juba valley of Southern Somalia'. Unfree Labor and Revolt in Asia, University of Avignon.
94. Ooji, or Oji is a derogatory term often used to refer to the Juba valley people. Despite its referral use, the exact meaning of the word is obscure. Some sources suggest that it is derived from the Italian word 'Oggi' the equivalent of 'today' in English, because of Gosha people thinking that it is limited only to what is today and not beyond or in the future. But obviously the word must have been used earlier than the arrival of the Italian colonialists. In the Shabelle valley, the reference is attributed to someone who has been enslaved and it is used (not in their face) for people who are known to have been enslaved; the Jareer also use that to a known descendent of slave.

    The expression 'abuur' means seed/s, and 'reeb' stands for 'to spare, to leave behind'; therefore 'abuur reeb' symbolizes not only the admission of defeat and submission for mercy, but also an imminent annihilation and wanton extinction of a generation or generations, hence the pleading to spare some 'abuur' offspring as a future evidence of the existence our present generation under extinction.

95. Arbo, Mohamed Ramadaan, Personal discussion (several occasions in the late '90s) on the historical background of the wa-Zigua people.
96. Palmer, Norman D., and Perkins, Howard C., International Relations; Third revised edition; A.I.T.B.S. Publishers and Distributors, 2002.
97. Morgenthau, Hans J. Politics Among Nations: The Struggle For Power and Peace. Sixth edition. (2001) Kalyan Publishers.
98. Extracted from the manuscripts of Omar Muya Mberwa, Kakuma Refugee Camp – Kenya, 2004.
99. Ibid.
100. Mberwa Muya Mberwa, Chairman of Somali Bantu Refugee Community in Kenya, discussion in Kakuma Refugee Camp, Kenya, 2004.
101. Sheikh Ambulo: the Wa-Gosha call him Sheikh Mambulo.
102. Majority of the sources say that extensively administered magical power was used for Sheik Mambulo's abduction to Mkoma Maligo's house in Mofi.
103. Mukhtar, Mohamed H., in Kusow (ed.) op. cit.
104. Hadija Msharemo Mwali, discussion in Chogo Refugee Camp, Tanzania, 2004.

Chapter 3

THE COLONIAL OCCUPATION OF SOMALIA AND THE STIGMATIZATION OF THE BANTU PEOPLE

The Berlin Conference of 1884 - 1885 is a vicious historical event of a rare kind. Several European countries, particularly Britain, Germany, France and Portugal embarked on a transcontinental mission across Africa for the exploitation of African resources in man and material. Indeed, it was the implementation of the philosophies exchanged during the various sessions of this convention that later caused to Africa multi-dimensional problems some of which triggered several transnational wars, ultimately transforming forever the living conditions of many Africans.

Europe's penetration into Africa characterizes a unique formulation by the individual powers concerned, not exempting the option of force and coercion in order to realize each country's set goals for its colonial expedition, with no consideration to the will of the local people. In the epistemological work of Olatunde Odetola and Ade Ademola, "It was a case of imposition of foreign rule upon an indigenous people irrespective of the wishes of the people concerned."[1] In a more generalized sociological undertone, Kayongo-Male and Onyango state:

"European and Arab contact with Africa initiated highly disruptive changes which affected African life. New economic systems changed family production systems; political actions led to forced labor, racial segregation and alienation of land - all of which had implications for family life; and religious proselytization altered the symbolic meaning of family life."[2]

The colonial powers, specifically Britain and Italy, had similar objectives of exploitation but engraved in different attributes. After stationing a garrison in Aden, Yemen, in 1839, Britain developed the concept of working out some measures of importing livestock from Somalia. Thereafter, the British started settling in the northern coast of the country right in the vicinity of Yemen. To that effect, erudite economic geographer, Professor Abdi Ismail Samatar writes that the livestock sub-regime at the time was "the most important commodity in the Somali trade with the outside world."[3]

In the southern part the interest was in the agricultural sub-sector, which the Italian colonial administration desired to develop and exploit for its own benefit. Before the partition, the Sultan of Zanzibar had the Benadir Coast under his rule. This consisted of Barawa, Mogadishu, Merca and Warsheikh. However, Egypt showed her interest in the country around 1875, but due to other commitments in the Sudan, her presence was brief and rather insignificant. Nevertheless, it was after Egypt's arrival in Somalia that the European concept of colonization gained momentum.

The Italian government assigned explorer Antonio Cecchi to conduct an expedition, an idea which was suggested by then Foreign Minister Pasqual Mancini. Among Cecchi's assignments were to see about the situation of southern Somalia and attract Said Bargash, Sultan of Zanzibar, into commercial relationship. The Italians were present in Zanzibar because Filonardi, prior to expanding his business activities into Somalia, had established commercial operations in the archipelago, dealing in cloves, in which Zanzibar still deals actively even today. It was after negotiations and recommendations that Filonardi got a grant for business expansion from the Bank of Rome[4] in simultaneity with an approval as Italy's representative in Somalia.

Archival documents show Italy's interest in the acquisition of Kismayo by purchase from Bargash[5] but it did not materialize. In another development, the European states of Germany, France and Britain were determined to edge the Arab Sultan out of the East Africa Coast or at least make away with a chunk of the territory under his control. Sultan Said Bargash found himself and his rule in extreme threats from stronger European states willing to create havoc. France, Britain and Germany dared Bargash to the extent of sanctioning delimitations on his areas of control in the Banadir coastal towns, not exceeding about 10 kilometers into the hinterland.[6] The area constituted Kismayo, Merca, Brava, Warsheikh and Mogadishu.

On the Italian side, after the death of Bargash, Filonardi was still pressing hard his successor, Sultan Said Khalifa, for the acquisition of Kismayo. In a quick diplomatic turnaround, Said Khalifa approved the transfer of the Kenya Coast to Britain in 1888, operating on the institutional name of the Imperial British East Africa Company (IBEA). But Italy finally succeeded to seal the Benadir coast deal in August 1892. A British official named Portal represented Sultan Said Ali of Zanzibar and Cottoni signed on behalf of Italy. The amount involved was

160,000 rupees, which as a result legalized the Benadir concession.[7]

Before the arrival of the Italians, the pastoral Somalis used to manage booming businesses in the sale and purchase of slaves, often transported from the Tanzanian coast in Arab dhows, and in the exploitation of the slaves for their human resources in the agricultural sector. The previous chapter mentioned how slave muscle was responsible for the attainment of material benefit for many Somali tribes. But the new Italian administration announced the expropriation of all land as the property of the Italian government. The second matter was that, according to the Italian policy, slave trade was no longer tolerable and had to be abolished.[8]

Filonardi tried to establish his business empire in Somalia but that did not come rather easy. The amounts he received from the Italian authorities in subsidies were less than adequate to cover his operating costs. Despite the efforts he exerted, the results were much less than the aspirations. Occurring in time with that was the Italian defeat by Ethiopia in 1896, which brought about the downfall of the Crispi administration. Italy was ashamed and internal criticism mounted due to this incident; a European colonial power devastated and humiliated by an African country. Therefore, as far as the new Italian administration was concerned, Filonardi had to be replaced by what was known as Societa del Benadir or the Benadir Company. Through this period of changes and debacles, Britain took over the northern part of Somalia, France chunked off Djibouti, the territory of the Afar and Issa, Italy colonized Southern Somalia while Britain later annexed Ogaden to Ethiopia and the Northern Frontier District to Kenya. Both of these last territories were under British hand upon their attachment to the respective countries.

Although the concessions for the Benadir and the approval to occupy Kismayo were signed in November 1889, decision had not been made on the boundaries of the territorial administration separating both colonial powers, Italy and Britain.[9] Italy was considering these trends in its favor because it was mainly Britain that played quite significant role in Italy's success in obtaining these concessions.[10]

During that time, the settlers of the Juba valley, Kismayo and the vast area of its surroundings were living in autonomy. They faced threats and harassment from the neighboring bellicose pastoral Somalis, but they maintained a high degree of concentration on tilling and the enhancement of their production and livelihood. Menkhaus reports that the Juba valley community "produced regular yields of surplus grain which they sold to trading posts of the sultanate of Zanzibar."[11] They also enjoyed trade relationship with the interior where business people purchased from them either by barter or by money. But Italy had the intention of utilizing colonial mechanisms to produce abundantly and realize vast accumulation by export supply. In the Shabelle area, several communities were self-dependent on their low, subsistence scale of production while surplus was marketed often to urban marketplaces for family income.

Apart from grains which contained the staple food maize, and other crops like sesame, beans and a variety of other vegetables and fruits, many rural farmers had constructed 'dool-shini' beehives and produced honey for the household as well as for the market. Many Jareer communities had members who possessed herds of cattle, producing milk and butter, though scholars don't often mention the practice of the latter mode of production as they prefer to describe the Bantu as a purely agrarian economy, overlooking this other sub-sector.

However, slave trade and slave exploitation have gained economic advantages to many communities in the Shabelle river area. The Bimaal, Mobleen, Reer Hamar, Amarani, Geledi, Wa'daan and other tribes were the prime beneficiaries of slave economy as they utilized the slaves for different purposes; as concubines, domestic servants and as the basic workforce in the agricultural production. Due to these vital economic advantages, Italy's announcement of intolerance to slavery and slave trade had a long way to go with Somali convincement. The pastoral Somalis were not willing to relinquish their "right" to slave ownership, claiming that their Islamic faith was the basis for their entitlement to own people as 'hanti' property.

Upon the replacement of Filonardi Company, Antonio Cecchi came to Somalia presumably for several purposes but, among others, the two evident objectives were: (a) to support the influence of the newly appointed Societa del Benadir, and (b) to stop Ethiopian expansion in Luuq, Baidoa and other riverine areas in Abyssinia's proximity. An anticipation of a possible danger from the Ethiopians has led to Cecchi's seeking of alliance with the Sultan of Geledi. The operation of the Societa del Benadir, which Cecchi had recommended to take over from Filonardi Company, was marred by delays. The prolongation of the inefficiency of the new company was also partly due to the Italian government's lack of clear-cut policy in meeting the financial prerequisite towards the company's coffers.

In late 1890, Cecchi organized an army of men including hired Somalis and Italian sailors to move to Baidoa and Luq area to contain the Ethiopian expansion. His encampment at Lafole came suddenly under attack. The askaris abandoned the caravan and fled for their lives. The devastation was so enormous that the commander of the caravan, Cecchi, was killed there. All, except a very small number of less than ten men, survived the incident.[12] After the humiliating defeat by the Ethiopians in Adowa, Lafole was another Italian shame under African fighters, a blow which the colonial administration had to deal with seriously. In fact, as a schoolboy, once when we passed Lafole area on the way to our farm in Dhajalaq, Afgoie district, my father told me about how "a dying Italian soldier swallowed his gold ring, before a Somali cut his belly open and removed the ring".

After a few months, Commander Giorgio Sorrentino was sent to find out the causal attributes of the Lafole massacre. Through his investigation, the Commander concluded that the incident had no relationship with nationalist sentiments. Rather, it was an incitement triggered by two Arabs in Mogadishu. It was discovered later that the two were actually one named Islam bin Mohamed and the other Abu-Bakr bin Awad, an interpreter who enjoyed a good status and reputation at his employment in Filonardi company.[13] They were threatened by the new appointment of Societa del Benadir and thus sought to cause disruption. They instigated the local Wa'daan and Geledi tribes to wage a surprise attack on the Italians. They were apprehended and later sentenced outside Somalia, probably in Zanzibar.

What was not secret though, was that Filonardi and Cecchi were both aware of the existence of slavery in the Benadir coast, but they were lenient. Cecchi was also reluctant about abolition of slave trade, with some of the sources noting that he had a female teenage servant of the Galla tribe. Sorrentino realized the slave situation and servitude problems in the Somali coast of Benadir but he too, could not jeopardize the delicate relationship between his country and the local people.

In the north of Mogadishu, on the coastal strip of the Majertinia, the land of the Darood, the Italians were availed with an opportunity to colonize by the local pastoral inhabitants, through their Sultans. The colonial archives reveal that as early as 1888, Sultan Yusuf Ali sent a delegation to Zanzibar. His message to the Italians was that he was seeking protection from that country.[14] Robin Hallet supports these colonial documents about the Majerteen call for Italian protection, and writes, "Early in 1889, the rulers of two northern Somali sultanates with capitals in Obbia and Alula decided for reasons of calculated self-interest, to place their territories under Italian protection."[15]

Barely two months after the visit, Yusuf Ali formally leased his sultanate for about 1,200 Maria Theresa thalers, the currency at that time, and officially signed agreements chartering Italy as the protector of his sultanate. Subsequently, his son-in-law, Sultan Osman Mohamud who ruled Alula entered into negotiations with Italy and struck a similar deal for protection in April of the same year.[16] Some sources suggest that Osman Mohamud had made an earlier offer to Germany to put his sultanate under them on September 6, 1885, but that it had not been ratified in Germany.[17] In a similar trend, certain colonial documents evidence the signing of an agreement between Yusuf Ali and Germany in November 1885, with Claus von Anderson signing as a representative from the German East Africa Company.[18]

In the Benadir area, several local traditional chiefs in el-Athala have signed treaties of cession with Italy after an earlier resistance and infliction of casualty on the Italians.[19] The exchange of hands and the Italian purchase of favor from the notables of the tribes and the elites continued even through Sorrentino's tenure, as Hess informs us that "At Brava, Merca and Mogadishu, Serrentino presented the walis, notables and cadis (religious judges) with gifts of turbans, Arab garments, syrups, incenses and Maria Theresa thalers. It was an inexpensive total investment of 296 thalers in gathering friends for Italy."[20]

In the northern Somali coast, the first treaty with the British dated to the year 1827 when an English crew suffered shipwreck off the Somali coast. This was approximately twelve years before the British conquest of Aden in 1839. It was however the Aden occupation that carries a greater significance in the establishment of business treaties between the Somalis and Britain. At any rate, the British expansionist policy was facilitated, like it happened in the south, by tribal treaties that brought under Britain all the territories of what came to be known as a British Protectorate. Jardine, a former secretary to the administration of Somaliland (British Somaliland), described the economic capability of the territory as "the only country in our East African Empire that was then self-supporting."[21]

The statement from the former official of the protectorate convinces us that Somaliland at the time was being heavily exploited by Britain more than could be in favor of the local people. And considering the fact that export commodity from this region heavily consisted of the small ruminants of goats and sheep, the effect must have substantively frustrated the productive policy of pre-colonial pastoralism; an economic tragedy scholarly presented by professors Samatar and Samatar as they elucidate, "The rise of commercial pastoralism principally affected small ruminants and therefore, the economic domain of women and children."[22]

This negative effect was the birth child of the British colonial strategy which had to fulfill the dual purpose of meat supply to Aden and an access in reigning part of the Indian Ocean where they could monitor maritime movements to and from India. Another purpose could as well be to ward off total domination of the area by rival European colonialists. So, with these strategic architectures and tribal treaties facilitated through payments and promises for protection, vulnerable Somali territories, north, south and any other zone, fell prey to colonial expansionists. In any aspect, a very analytical observation of the economic impact on the rural Somali, whether pastoral or agrarian, concurs well with O'connor's concept of the functions of imperialism, defining it as a "formal or informal control over local economic resources in a manner advantageous to the metropolitan power, and at the expense of the local economy."[23] It was a tragedy Somalia would never recover for the rest of her life.

Although horrendous drawbacks were suffered in relation to the subversive tentacles of colonial contact, the contrast between Italian and British Somaliland in the pre-colonial era and during colonial domination is that the latter was characterized by the intervention, and may be invention of a class of profiteers who garnered accumulation for personal capitalistic gains without meaningful change in the welfare of the rural producer - specifically the family (see Abdi I. Samatar 1989), while the south had a reputation for basing the family production on the abuse of human ethics and values, and the exploitation of a labor force from slaves, economically boosting the social status and income of the slave owners.

The picture we get from this analysis shows the existence of two distinct social cultures, embracing also distinguishable means and processes of production. In elaboration, whereas the northern pastoralist could sell his livestock at wish, albeit the strangled commodity prices, he was exercising his liberal individual right in accepting or declining primarily the investment of labor in the mode of production and subsequently the offer made to him for the product. In the south of the country, a potential human 'superpower' owning a socio-ethnically disadvantaged human being as property '*hanti*', was the controller of the price stipulation while the labor input was materially exhausted from the muscle of a shackled slave or from the forced labor of a freeborn indigene.

Slavery scandal and resistance of certain Somali clergymen to abolition

With time, the escalation of anti-slavery campaigns in Italy and humiliating exposures in the Italian papers has given reason for an investigation. The drastic situation, which the colonial government found itself in, was aggravated by lack of total commitment over a prolonged period of time which the regime left the colony in the hands of representative companies. As Eno suggests, "Italy's initial concern was to promote efficient colonial administration in Somalia than to abolish slavery. As a result, some of the Italian officials turned a blind eye to the ongoing slave trade."[24]

The debate on the rampant situation of slavery in Somalia was put into the limelight by disclosures contained in the report of Chiesi and Travelli.[25] The two-man commission, of whom the latter was a renowned lawyer, illuminated the extent as well as intensity of slave trade and slavery in Somalia. They detailed the indifference with which officials of the chartered Italian companies responded regarding the containment of the widely diffused problem.

In a measure to deactivate the heightening global criticism over its colony, Italy couldn't pursue a better framework than direct government administration in southern Somalia. The colonial regime's action dissatisfied the slave-holding Somali tribes as they sensed the inevitability of their disenfranchisement from the lucrative slave business. Protests and uprisings were marked in a bid to display to the Italian administration the magnitude of dissatisfaction and contumaciousness in the slaveholding quarters. Some of these protests, in writing and in rebellion, were made by highly regarded 'Islamic primates' of respect for their knowledge of the doctrine and their reputable position in the society.

The sultan of the Geledi and his slave-owning people were among the strong voices advocating for the retention of the status quo, continuation of milking slave muscle. Chiesi and Travelli cite their complaint:

> We have protected the trade routes and remained faithful for fourteen rainy seasons. Now our slaves no longer get returned to us. Ill will grows among our people, especially among the poor who, having only a few slaves, when these flee, lose all means of earning a living and don't know whether to leave or stay.[26]

Despite the grievances by the slaveholders, the Italian occupationists had to find a solution to ease the pressure off the government at home. The ordinance of abolition had to be upheld, whether for better or for worse. It took a reasonably long time, about 12 years or so, from the time Filonardi first moved into Somalia and when the government directly took charge. The period also marked dismissals of officials linked to the chartered companies, culminating in the revocation from Filonardi and Societa del Benadir their rights as representatives of the Italian administration. In early 1905, the government took over the administration.

Feuding hostilities led to several confrontations between Italy and the Somali tribes. Eno reveals, "Merca, Jilib, Jesira and Dhanane are some of the notable battlefields where the Bimaal (Hawiye) pastoral tribe engaged colonial soldiers constituting Somalis."[27] Nevertheless, revelations such as by Italian naval officer Gaetano Bossi had already done the damage. He recommended the need for a more organized government role. Commander Onorato di Monale who undertook an investigation upon the early announcements of the Benadir Coast slavery scandal wrote another equally discrediting report. Some excerpts of the report, including information given by the local chiefs and other outstanding figures of the community, read:

> ...not only did slaves enter Benadir ports, but that the last slaves to enter the town date back only to last December. Slaves are bought and sold in the Benadir towns, not only under the eyes of Italian authorities...but according to registry of the cadis of Mogadishu...with the sanction of those authorities. In the Benadir, a slave can be bought, sold, imprisoned, inherited, given as a gift, exploited, and rarely liberated. Far from taking steps towards the gradual disappearance of domestic servitude, the company is perpetrating it and

aggravating the condition.[28]

In a gesture to consolidate its colonial activities firmly, Italy succeeded in the purchase of the Benadir ports for an estimated amount of 3,600,000 Italian Lira, the equivalent of 144,000 British pounds. It was an achievement seen as a step forward in Italy's quest for gaining larger Somali territory. But within the colony, as Italy was aware, resistance was unavoidable since some tribes were discontent by the abolition policy.

The Somali slave owners, as is paradigmatic of the nomadic psychology, tinted the abolition policy as a religious issue in a bid to gain legitimacy for their cause of war and sympathy from other clans, under the philosophy of Jihad (holy war). Mohamed Abdulle Hassan, the Mad Mullah and leader of the Dervish, assisted the Bimaal cause to that end. The colonial administration recruited soldiers to face the arrogant and belligerent Bimaal. When the battle erupted, several Bimaal villages were torched off. The Bimaal, in retaliation, made several attempts to overrun the Italian askaris in Dhanane, situated between Merca and Mogadishu. They were all in futility until the Bimaal were relentless subdued.

In a diplomatic move to step up the scale of 'pacification', the colonial officials approached chiefs and notables of the various tribes to win their support and maintain good relationship between the colonists and the colony. The Somali pastoral tribes seized the opportunity. The two ensuing reasons were for access to the colonial officials (as a medium between the Italians and the community), and secondly for the payroll which displayed a recognition of their social status as the leadership. The Sultan of the Geledi was one of such leaders who subscribed wholeheartedly to this kind of colonial appeasement.[29]

Skirmishes between the Bimaal and the Italians continued for quite some time, though intermittently.[30] The colonial troops got a breakthrough and eventually penetrated the towns of Bariire, Malable, Audegle (Aaw-Dheegle) in the Dhoobooy area of Merca, and Afgoi a few kilometers from Mogadishu. The event has finally tamed Bimaal resistance, widening the aspiration for peace and liberty.

Sheikh Hassan Barsane's resistance to the abolition of slavery

One Sheikh, who was exaggeratedly honored as a hero in Somali history, was Sheikh Hassan Barsane. He resisted to the abolition of slavery to the extent of misinterpreting the Holy Scripture – the Qur'an, by writing to the Italians:

> "All our slaves escaped and went to you and you have set them free. We are not happy with the [Antislavery] order. We abandoned our law, for according to our law we can put slaves in prison or force them to work."

And what law was the 'respected' Sheikh referring to?

> "The government has its law and we have ours. We accept no law other than our law. Our law is that of God and of the prophet.... "God has said: The few can defeat the many. The world is near its end; only 58 years remain...It is better to die following Muslim law. All Muslims are one.[31]

In the preceding statement, Barsane has committed not less than three discrepancies contrary to the Islamic faith. But a Jareer poet, who was against enslavement of Muslims, and its un-Islamic practice, sets the main response in this verse:

Ninki Ashahaato Adoon ma Ahaado
Amar Eebe diidi yaa kaa Aqbalaayo[32]

Translation:
Whoever announces the oneness of Allah in submission, no longer remains a slave;
So, nobody abides by your orders regarding what Allah has illegitimated.

Sheikh Hassan Barsane is one of a few heroes honored in the history of Somalia. He is, as far as we have seen in the history curricula of schools in the country, dignified as a sharp protestant against the Italian colonialists, and one who died for the cause of nationalism. But on the contrary, he died due to his rejection to free Muslim lives in the campaign for the abolition of slavery and of slave trade. As far as Islam is concerned, a good model is Abubakar, the Apostle of Mohammed the prophet (PBUH). He paid money to purchase Bilal's freedom after the latter converted to Islam. In this case, the two acts of Abubakar and Sheikh Hassan Barsane are contrary to each other, but the former's gesture accommodates well with the harmonious tenets of Islam and the preservation of human dignity. Barsane's, in retrospect, amounts to a villain's misuse and abuse of the Holy Scripture to gain his own personal interests.

Previously, many scholars have written concern over the obstruction of the truth about Somali historiography, social anthropology, culturology and other areas, with the focus and scope of criticism succinctly directed onto the nomadic pastoralist in the north. In fact, it is now in the south that we learn about religious scholars engaging in both misuse and abuse of the Islamic faith for personal gains. And rather than condemning their ill effects on society, the Jileec pastoral authorities have eulogized their villainy by building monuments and naming academic institutions after the great sinners.

Drawing from archival evidence, Sheikh Hassan Barsane and a large number of the Somali people of his day (and even today) have been correctly described by colonial officers as corrupt people. They have been accused of contaminating the Islamic faith by twisting it for personal goals. An extract of the nature reads:

> *Sir,* With reference to attached - in my opinion the Somali...accepts the Sheria just as far as it suits him. He claims to be a Mohammeddan but during my service...both Sir Reginald Wingate – Serdar and Major General Von Slatin Pasha, told me that they did not consider the Somali as a true Mohammeddan...[33]

That this is a persistent paradigm of Somali attitude can also be seen in recent events in the civil anarchy period when the so-called Islamic courts discriminatively arraigned the unarmed and ethnically oppressed communities like the Jareer.[34] Suffice it to say that many religious scholars have used their Islamic knowledge as an income generation project rather than to preach the doctrine of peace and equality for all Muslims (*See Chapter One, The Barawaan*).

After the war of words, a number of confrontations took place between the Galjel (Gaal-jecel) of Hassan Barsane and colonial forces, which pressed the former into submission. Eventually, the so-called religious leader was captured, as his kinsmen could not save him in their plea at submission. They were disarmed while Barsane was taken to the dungeons in Mogadishu and sentenced to death. Later the death sentence was revoked to life imprisonment where he remained incarcerated till his death.

Italy and the expropriation of Bantu-land

An exhaustive feasibility study by Romolo Onor, an Italian agricultural economist, suggested to his government the establishment of "large-scale agricultural development in the area."[35] Towards the implementation of the objectives of this colonial plan, an arable land of about 46,000 hectares on the fertile areas along Juba and Shabelle rivers was illegally written off in concession by the colonial governor. This huge land was conceded to only 15 concessionaires who could not induce the required labor force because the Bantu cultivators were unwilling to work on land other than their own and for the benefit of their own families.[36]

The colonists were caged in a fix. With the pastoral Somali's scorn for cultivation, one described as "...lazy... preferring to live by war and rapine,"[37] the Jareer muscle was the most viable option for Italian exploitation. The multilayered tragedy exposed to the Jareer farmer was not just the expropriation of his land on the one part and the exploitation of his human resource on the other. It further developed so much psychological agony in passing from one type of slavery to another, i.e. from Somali 'African' repression to white Italian oppression. Vigorously criticizing the situation, Omar Eno emphasizes, "The Bantu/Jareer people were caught in the middle of a dilemma between two devils."[38]

Colonial Italy had to engineer a way out of its mess. As a result, it introduced the 'kolonyo' (corvee) forced labor system that was among the prime factors of socio-economic disintegration and labor disorientation of the Jareer community. It became also a cause for rural migration, as the male youth could not live freely in their rural villages and among their families. The agenda of the Italian colonial economy denied them sanctity among their people; hence their involuntary divorce from their abode.

Simultaneously, on the part of the Somali ex-slave-owners, the grudge over the abolition policy has been redirected on to the Jareer population. They unscrupulously entered into a new type of solidarity with their colonial masters, coordinating the conscription of the Bantu youths to the Italian plantations. Although from one perspective they revenged against the effects of the emancipation through abolition, the other one served their socio-psychological satisfaction, which placed them in a stratum above the Bantu. The impact was that they realized their exemption from the 'kolonya' as former masters, 'nobles'.

For the Bantu, the situation was from slavery to slavery, literally meaning from a local colonialist to a foreign colonialist in collusion with the former local colonialist. To a considerable degree, the colonially supported stratification has indiscriminately devastated the social morale and human dignity of the Jareer people, since it was [only] the Jareer, whether emancipated or conscripted native, who supplied the (corvee) work force. Rodd Ronnell had to describe the fascist regime's agricultural enterprise in the interriverine as "...a labor policy of considerable severity in theory and actual brutality in practice...indistinguishable from slavery."[39] Obviously it was slavery, a modernized form of colonialistically modified slavery; one in which the Somali people severely antagonized the Jareer Muslim in favor of a European colonialist.

In her view, Sylvia Pankhurst portrays the episode as a scheme projected to bankrupt the indigenes of their land, marching them to the Italian plantations by coercion and oppression.[40] A bulk of oral historians unequivocally support Sylvia's argument. For instance, Mohamed Hussein Hassan, alias Jawaani (Giovanni), narrated occasions in which newly married bridegrooms were deliberately targeted for conscription without the knowledge of the brides or their families.[41] They were deprived of their rights as their civil liberty was infringed. Also, the Jileec elders forcibly celebrated marriages to conscripts against the will of the brides and their families.

One Aaytire man known as *Deedeeysamoow*, had just returned from work one day when he was told that his daughter had been wed off by the Jileec sultan to a conscript scheduled to depart the following day. He followed the man to his house. He saw him from inside through a crack in the door and stayed in the room silently. Deedeeysamoow waited for some time without success. He was vexed beyond control, ran amok and stabbed almost every Jileec male he met in the street, killing several people.[42]

Another tragedy, also by the Aaytire of Afgoie, took place after three relatives were conscripted. They were taken to Mogadishu wherefrom they were put on transport headed to the Dhoobooy area (around Merca). Upon reaching Wiliyoow Cadde (near the modern

People's Assembly) they drew out their *'galmaax'* daggers and stabbed the Sagaalle/Jileec (Somali pastoral) elders escorting them. There was a huge pandemonium from the frantic scene, and the men escaped in the commotion. Later the elders of the escapees gave a reasonable account of the agitation. The injuries inflicted were settled on customary tribal basis and the men were freed.[43] Certain sections of the traditions suggest that after that fatal incident, conscription in Afgoie was brought to abatement.

SOMALI NATIONALISM: CLOUDY CLANISM

A Jareer Poem for Prologue

> *Xaq minaad warrantood xaqiraada dhaafto*
> *Xurnimo Xabashaa ku Dhammaadi, Xabbadda Xooggeeda*
> *Xil iskama saarin Leegada Xarbigi dhoobooye*
> *Laakin Xeeraraad dejiseen ood Xukun ku qabateene;*
> *Xaabsee Xandha-lahaaw leed dhammaan isku Xineeysiine*
> *Xoolo Xad ee ku Xarakoo Xilkas-la'aan waaye*
> *Xamar soo deg lee miyaa Xurnimo-doonkiina.*[44]

Translation:

> In talking reality, without a sense of prejudice
> It is the Jareer that succumbed in the struggle for independence and to the merciless bullets
> The SYL (as leadership) maintained indifference towards the Dhoobooy confrontation (Keli Asaayle)
> But (SYL) enacted a constitution and gained self-determination
> Otherwise, your (leadership's) concentration is gauged only to compete for accumulation;
> But misappropriation and arrogance are not symbols of wisdom
> Is the essence of your nationalism based only on a migration to Mogadishu?

According to the Bantu-Jareer social thought, the emergence of Somali "nationalism" and the "struggle for freedom" (*halgankii gobanimodoonka*), [seem] to have been exaggerated and propagated in post-colonial period when, borrowing Ali Jimale's words, "The political sifting process did not develop an apparatus which could separate the chaff from the seed".[45] Apart from the political end, Somali nationalists

119

have a long way to go to achieve an admirable credibility for worship as national heroes and models, at least in the eyes of the Bantu citizen.

The political end, of course, was to elevate to national status characters that otherwise had been notorious for their ruthlessness, antagonism, tyranny and opportunism. The blueprint for their acclamation to heroism and national stardom were born with the new class of Barre's military leadership. Barre's military junta succeeded in shelving away the various controversial descriptions and negative biographies of the so-called 'nationalists' of their own clans. They employed their political hegemony, the available national resources and media propaganda to refigure certain characters for recognition to heroism.

The premeditation responded to a triple objective: (1) to envisage the military Junta's nationalistic spirit; (2) to create positive image and recognition for certain groups thus erecting some of their own kinship on national monuments to obscure their evil deeds in the historical records; and (3) to pave the way for the modern recreation of a new national historiography of nomadic protagonism, employing simultaneous inventions and insertions all the way.

The most celebrated national heroes, in the northern nomadic version, come in the persons of Mohamed Abdulle Hassan, Ahmed Ibrahim Al-Ghazi – (known to the Somalis as Axmed 'Gurey' (the left-handed) and Ahmed 'Gran' to the Abyssinians) and Hawo Osman Tacco, popularly known as Xaawo Taako. For reasons known to Siad Barre and his kinship, these were made the celebrated heroes and heroine. Their recognition was depicted with national monuments, exclusively towering through the skies of Mogadishu.

Ahmed Ibrahim Al-Ghazi (Gurey): identity amendment or historical error?

Somali history portrays Ahmed Gurey as a hero who in 1533, while leading a multinational army, conquered and heavily defeated Ethiopia. The invasion has gained Ahmed Gran an enormous territory, "…putting him in complete control of south and central Abyssinia."[46] Though Ahmed Gurey has been celebrated as a national hero Somalia's history curriculum does not elaborate his true identity. His Arabness has been erroneously subsumed into Somalia's search for heroes of national class, hence the Somali school-children's mistaken belief and portrayal of Gurey as a great Somali hero. The Somali historiographers and curriculum designers also shied away from mentioning the multi-nationality of Gran's army, thus exposing all his army as brave Somali warriors.

Such works of historical misinterpretation and hero impersonation have been part of the pastoral authorities' agenda to conceal the true historical picture of the country. The negative consequence affects even today the product of that curriculum, the likes of Cabdi Maxamuud Maxamed (Goobe) and Cabdullahi Cusmaan Cumar (Shakespeare). They have unsuspectingly co-authored the same misleading material in a history syllabus for the consumption of Somali primary students. An example is the Social Studies syllabus for Grade 6 (Cilmiga Bulshada 6) where the two co-authors wrote confidently, saying "*Axmad Gureey wuxuu ahaa Geesi Soomaaliyeed,*" which translated means, "Ahmed Gurey (the left-handed) was a Somali hero." The sad part was that UNESCO had heavily invested in the project, without engaging proper material in expertise. After the publication of the book raised complaints and protests, the financiers of the project, UNESCO and UNICEF, opted for the discontinuation of the volume from classroom teaching.

Mohamed Abdulle Hassan: mad Mullah or macabre madness?

Somalis gave Mohamed Abdulle Hassan the honorary title "*Sayid*", lord. But to European scholarship he is known as the 'Mad Mullah'. He is another figure of frequent appearance in Somali history: (a) as a leader of exceptional nationalist spirit in fighting the British colonialists in northern Somalia, and (b) as a poet with a great talent in oral literature, particularly in oral poetry.

Sayid Mohamed Abdulle Hassan's legendary history has been looked from the often-promoted version preferred by the Somali ruling elite, the pastoral nomads that stage-managed the political domination of the country. In that narrative, he had the ardor and charm as well as leadership potential to put together a large army of nomadic fighters – Dervishes. He engaged the British colonialists in several fierce battles and inflicted upon them a lot of casualty. He was the only or first African anti-colonialist hero whose troops suffered aerial attacks. Among others, he is reputed for defeating the British-led colonial forces in several confrontations, including one in which a British commander was killed.

Sayid Mohamed's oral poetry regarding the ill-fate of this officer, Mr. Richard Corfield, has in Barre's days been among the compulsory literature in the school syllabus emphatically recommended for memorization. A few of the verses go as follows:-

Adaa Koofiloow jiitayoon dunida joogeyne
Adaa jidkii lagugu waday jimic la'aaneede
Jahanama lageeyoow haddaad aakhiro u jahatay.

Translation:
   Oh Corfield, gone you are from this world
   Driven through the merciless path thou art
   Towards the hereafter you are; destined into hellfire.

After almost twenty years of disruption and devastation, Sayid Mohamed and his Dervishes were defeated. They ran away in disarray and he died in 1920, after disease and starvation plagued his camp. He was buried unceremoniously, perhaps due to the ugly situation prevailing in his encampment at the time. .

The other version about Sayid-Ka

The hidden version that also shapes the acts and personality of this leader entices our attention in order to treat history with a due balance of truth, regardless of consequential dissatisfaction in certain quarters. Unlike the known religious leaders, Mohamed Abdulle Hassan's followers mainly consisted of his own Ogaden sub-clan of the pseudo-nobility of the Darood clan. The method he used to employ to obtain support and followers remained incompatible with Islam because of the tools he applied; in that, Hallett asserts, "He resorted to the most ruthless methods,"[47] because "members of the local Muslim establishment were outraged by his attacks..."[48] as "...doubtful followers ran the risk of summary execution."[49] In another page about Mohamed Abdulle Hassan's tyranny, Michael Tidy and Donald Leeming remark, "Muhammad again resorted to military activities against various Somali communities."[50]

Among the discredit in the mainstay of Sayid Mohamed's theological profession (if it can be called so) is his announcement of being the Mahdi, a statement which no Islamic scholar in his right senses would ever dare say. He kept wandering and attacking communities in order to coerce them into his accompaniment. "The men were flogged until, sworn on the triple divorce oath [*"xila-fur"* in Somali], they agreed to obey him"[51] [emphasis mine]. Dissonant with the behavior requisite of an Islamic scholar, the Mad Mullah must have been a chronic impostor and a slanderer of the highest proportion by claiming the possession of powers to turn the white infidels' bullets to water.[52]

By reading Jardine, one may assume of exaggerations contradictory of this popular Somali character, but a variety of his poetry confirm the kind of heinous policy he engaged and the quality of tyranny he employed. The concealment of this reality about the man's true life in the social history is an attestation of the military regime's hypocritical attitude in dealing with the historiography of the country and its people. To contribute to the thesis of the hidden picture of the Sayid, Professor Abdalla Omar Mansur cites a verse from a great Somali poet, Ali Dhuux, who looted camels and in defense referred that even a man regarded so 'religious' as Sayid Mohamed Abdulle Hassan permitted and actually took leisure in looting other people's camels.[53]

The likes of the above attitude and other indecent activities of the Sayid in oral literature or in the traditions, and the military government's super-humanization of the so-called hero have fallen apart with a Jareer poet. He was alternatively concerned about the top military officials' expropriation of Bantu farms in the riverine areas of Juba and Shabelle. He recited:

Tuugadii Tolkiina Taalaa u dhisteene,
Tacabkeeyi haleeyseen maxaa ka Tireen?[54]

Translation:
You erected monuments for (even) the looters among your kinship,
But what is the fate of my expropriated lifeline?

Another poet and a Jareer compatriot responded to him with a clear definition of the situation and the disparity between the Jareer and the Jileec:

Tuugga reer Tolkiisaa Toowraadaan ka buuxo
Yaa ku Taagsaheey oo Tiir kuu naqahaayo?[55]

Translation:
> The thug's kinship dominate the ruling Supreme Revolutionary Council,
> You (Jareer) don't have a center-pole to lean on!

The revisionist scholarship acknowledges the insincerity of the ruling elite. One of such scholars is Mukhtar who wrote: "Historical sites were set up where there were no signs of history. Religious heroes were made up where the practice of Islam has been insignificant".[56] Citing Jama Mohamed, Professor Cassanelli enlightens, "The dervish wars and the dislocation of nomadic groups caused by them left a legacy of mistrust and bitterness which was typically preserved by clan poets in series or "cycles" of poems that kept these rivalries alive."[57] The Somalist scholar, in more elucidation of the theme, writes, "For example, the mutual suspicion that has characterized relations between Isaq and Darood Somalis for most of this century almost certainly originated in the events of the dervish period."[58] Ascertaining the tyrannical leadership of Sayid Mohamed Abdulle Hassan, Dualeh highlights, "His religious movement became despotic. He would kill and loot the tribes that would not lend him support. The tribes in British Somaliland, with the support of the British authorities, took up arms against him. He was finally defeated".[59]

In southern Somalia, many communities and pious religious personalities and sects (tariqas), particularly the Qadiriyya, know Mohamed Abdulle Hassan and his Dervish henchmen as unreligious villains operating under the cover of Islam. In one of his acts of outright thuggery, Mohamed Abdulle Hassan assigned a team of his Dervish to assassinate Sheikh Uwees, one of the most celebrated religious leaders of the Jareer in Somalia, in the famous rural town of Biyooleey. After the sad and cold blooded gangland style massacre, the Qadiriyya religious poets composed the following (dhikr) religious song in a couplet:

Afaraay Ahaayeen Uweesaay dileen
Owliya Allaayaay ka Inkaar-sadeen.[60]

Translation:
> Four they were who murdered (Sheikh) Uwees
> And (as a result) accumulated curses from all corners of the pious ones of God.

And the righteous of the Reewing, in whose territory the renowned Sheikh Uwees was assassinated, went in pursuit of the culprits as they sang:

> *Ankaaraneegii Abdoow (Abdulle) Hassan Aragteey?*
> *Usii Amuuthee Ileey madii Aragdo.*[61]

Translation:

> Who can tell me the whereabouts of the cursed Abdulle Hassan?
> Death will be his fate upon my sight of him.

All these evidences from Somalis and non-Somalis, scholars and non-scholars, expose the quality and character of the man for whose aggrandizement so immaculate a monument was towered into the skies of Mogadishu. The dubious military administration under the ideological tutelage of nomadic political doctrine deliberately forged a Sayid Mohamed Abdulle Hassan history, an agenda to exonerate him and his Dervish militia. They successfully, during their time, exonerated him from the genocide he and his henchmen committed against innocent peoples of diverse Somali communities in the north as well as in the south.

Unlike other leaders, the policy that Mohamed Abdulle Hassan exploited was partly reinforced by his people's unlimited desire for wealth in camel and for women. He more often than not preached, contrary to the sound teachings of Islam, the lawfulness in misappropriating the wives of those non-compliant with his way of life. Jardine confirms, "The wife of one of our Somali native officers was divorced from her husband by the Mullah and appropriated to his own harem."[62] His despotism negated all Islamic and human boundaries that "Until they promised to obey him, the tribesmen found their property plundered, their women ravished."[63]

And Aw Yuusuf Yaabisow recites from an anonymous poet who was displeased with the ravishing of women by Abdulle Hassan and his Dervish. Despite the powerful message it carries, the poem was downplayed in the Dervish camp and circles. The verses, however, blaming Abdulle Hassan and his Dervishes of::

> *Beryo badan waxaad laheyd Booqasho aan aadno*
> *Ma Bilcaan un Bay noqotay Barakeceenii*
> *Boobka habluhu miyaanan anagu marna ka Bogsoonin*

Bidceynugalnaye Bulshooy Baaba' hurimeyno

Translation

The visit for several days you advised we were to make
Seems to have become only a search for women (to ravish)
Are we not ever to refrain from ravishing the females?
By this we surely are a society astray and destined to devastation

Hawo Osman Tako

The other martyr is a heroine, Hawo Osman Tako. Without a credible reference though, the traditions say, especially in the words of Nuruddin Farah, "She was in the Jihad against the Italian infidels and a Somali whose son is now a governor of a region, hit her. The arrow was poisoned, and she died of it."[64] Controversial narratives make a definitive understanding of Hawo Tako's killer somewhat indefinite and inapprehensive. One version notes that protesters were demonstrating against the Italians. Commotion was rife. In the course of the melee and confrontations, one Somali group was on the Italian side which some sources suggest consisted of the security apparatus stationed there to restore law and order. Others think that among that group contained pro-Italian Somalis who were ready to take on their own countrymen in a tough engagement.[65]

I am not quite certain about Nuruddin Farah's source(s) – whether he was actually an eyewitness to the event or received the account of a reliable eyewitness; or whether he was actually sending a tribalistic rhetoric in a novelist's delivery fashion. The inclination of the notion, with all due subtleties, convinces the reader of Nuruddin's '*A Naked Needle*', that the 'culprit' might have been known by many, long before Farah's condemnation of the man. If it was so, then we expect the shooter would have been identified with equal ease and apprehension from both sides -- by all or even a few more of the victims as well as some more of the culprits. Following that opinion, the credibility of Nuruddin's crucifixion of "the man whose son is now a governor of a region" could be accepted with more viable trustworthiness, and beyond the sentiments of tribal rhetoric.

Considering the large number of people involved in the fracas in Mogadishu that day, it might not have been simple to identify an archer shooting from the midst of wildly agitated crowds. Secondly,

was it only one man that had a bow and arrow or was it a weapon con-
ventionally used that day – by one group or both confronting parties?
Thirdly, if that were true, and the culprit was not enjoying any kind of
immunity, he would have either been taken to custody by the authority
or revenged against by Tako's tribesmen or by the zealous on her side
under the nationalism euphoria. Of all the casualties on that fateful
day, Mohamed Siad Barre and Nuruddin Farah appear to have similar
sentiments over the Tako issue. Why neither Barre nor Farah gave
equal importance to the other Somalis who suffered casualty in one
way or the other on that day, is a clear subject in line with clan bias.
Two Jareer men, namely Mohamed Isse (*Shiidle* tribe) and Haji Osman
Sabdoow (*Kaboole* tribe) were among the dead casualty while scores of
others including women were seriously injured. But they bear importance for neither Barre nor Farah. "Because these are Jareer victims,
they are never mentioned in any of the Somali records of the events on
that day," stresses Ismaaciil Caliyoow Baxaar.

But reviewing Ali Jimale Ahmed's literature reveals Nuruddin's intention. Through Koschin, the protagonist in Farah's prose (namesake
of the author's son), Nuruddin transposes the impact of tribalism on
nationalism and vice versa, hence Ahmed's assumption that, "Opposing political views within Somali society are evaluated in terms of the
consciousness of Koschin."[66] Relatively, Ahmed's disclosure of Farah's
tribal image, imparting elements of political consciousness impreg-
nated with clan sentiment, are characteristics dominant in the ethnocentric Somali society. So, when Ahmed interprets the essence of the
monument, Koschin's feeling to the lady of the monument with the
arrow pierced through her chest, the donkey-waterman (in Somali
"*woo-biyoow*" or "*biyoole*") and then the killer of Hawo Tako, they definitely signify a clear demonstration of Nuruddin's ethnocentrism (at
least at that time?). He attempted to encapsulate his feeling in the person of Koschin, a name he deliberately borrowed from his son, closest
of kin.

I have surfaced this part of the debate in order to show that records
of Somali history are not set straight, not even by erudite scholars of
world fame like Nuruddin Farah (at least 30 years ago), specifically
when it comes to clan chauvinism. As Ahmed analyzes, Nuruddin's
version of the historiography is more of discourse intended to twist
and manipulate the real history.[67] Nuruddin Farah's ethnic consciousness (or ethnocentrism?) is borne in the essentiality of his prose fiction

and the strong message it conveys in the interplay between Somali history and Somali politics on the one part, and Somali intellectuals and ethnocentrism on the other.

In concluding this piece about monuments and Somali intellectuals' temptation in the manipulation of the national history, I cite a discussion in poetry between two Jareer bards. They were also disturbed by the controversy surrounding the killing of the heroine Hawo Tako. The venue was Haji Aden's house in the District of Hodan in Mogadishu where the two poets met incidentally. After talking about various topics, the theme of Hawo Tako's killer came up. One of the poets enquired:

Taarikhda Tubteeda yaa ku Toosihaayo,
Taakow ninki Toogti meel iigu Tilmaamo?[68]

Translation:
Who can set the historical record straight,
(and) Reveal to me the shooter/killer of Hawo Tako?

The other bard recited poetically a laconic elaboration of the incidents on that day. He described the mood of the people, the political goal, the objective and significance of the protest, the roles and political ideologies as well as individual interests of the various clans before culminating his response in two instant but separate couplets. In the first verse he elucidates:

Taariikhda Tubteeda Turxan kaama Taalo
Taakoowne Tolkeedaa Tawaanta u deesti [69]

Translation:
No clouds or mists can overshadow the path of history
Her own kinship exacted the infliction on Tako (the 'heroine').

The second couplet is a reaffirmation of the first one. Here the bard becomes more emphatic by expressing himself more authoritatively in the first person singular, as one who has no much doubt about the episode, at least in the view of the section of the society who have an opinion contrary to that of either Barre or Farah. He volunteers to illuminate:

128

Taariikhda Tubteedaan kuugu Toosihaa
Taakoow ninki Toogti Tolkeed Tiradeed! [70]

Translation:
I set the historical record straight (for your benefit) that
Tako's killer is her kinship, lineage.

Of course the opinion given here is not in any way a conclusion on who killed Hawo Tako. Nor does it suggest support for or bias against any party. Mine is to demonstrate, as much as possible, that contrary to the cultural and intellectual prejudice smeared on the Jareer people, they possess a primordially effective awareness of the historical and political events evolving in the distance of the societal span. But the wealth of a social culture cannot enjoy its aesthetic value against Ahmed's shocking revelation of the 'intellectuals' of the Somali Academy of Arts and Sciences when he states that "Some of these 'intellectuals' were of the opinion that certain parts of the country did not have literature."[71]   Nomadic pseudo-ennoblement and ethnic prejudice apart, these so-called 'intellectuals' of the Academy lacked the understanding that no society could exist without literature as it is part of the cultural fountain nurturing the social life of all the human race.

Alongside such 'intellectuals'' prejudice lay a precarious cultural antagonism which negates, in social terms, the celebration possible in the harmonization of unity in multiculturality. The effects of the looming disaster of a prejudicial, stereotypical nomadic intellectuality engaged on the destruction and denial of a people's culture is an outright degradation of what p'Bitek summarizes as "[t]he philosophy of life of a people,"[72] and in this context, of the Jareer people. In other words, as Kanwar Mathur says in his work in *Intercultural Communication*, "Ignorance of values causes inter-cultural misunderstanding," in the sense that whereas the nomad despises and degrades the agrarian culture, the latter feels that a pastoral nomad who is often associated with livestock may not develop sound thinking skills. The above extrapolation was meant to cement the framework for the next corpus of discussion about the core element containing Somali nationalism.

The subtlety of Somali nationalism

Somali nationalism, in similitude to other African countries, has been born out of the furor of colonialism. It was a tool, a weapon devised by the elite in their attempt to dismantle, with the full moral force of a united society, the exploitative grip which colonialism had been exercising over the local people. But what are the various definitions of nation or nationalism? Some of these can be classified as:

> a) A group of communities settled in a certain geographical location in the principle of which they can be distinguished from other nations or communities of nations; hence nation as a form of identity.
> b) Nationalism necessitated by common or shared historical circumstances, which a society has experienced together in a holistic manner, and which is built on an ideological framework, a belief of some sort.
> c) Nationalism begotten out of social/public consciousness; a kind of social awareness that puts forward the implementation of a social and political agenda that looks into the common good of society at large.

Several other categories can be added to the above. But in Somalia, constituents of polyethnically heterogeneous communities, the term nationalism enhances ambiguity, etymologically as much as perceptually. Prior to the amalgamation of the tribes or clans into a cohesive national body, each clan or sub-clan was conducting its own cultural liberty/democracy as a nation. Terms like *'Waddanki/dalki baan ka imid'* (I am from the country/nation.) used to refer to one's area of origin have universality in Somali social life. Therefore, to every group or sub-group exists a nation much closer to his heart than the newly constituted peripheral nation binding together the diversity of nations for the common purpose of decolonization. The latter type of nationalism, unlike tribal nationalism, was exploited by the pastoral political elite to unify a society whose "basis for political allegiance is blood kinship or genealogy"[73] rather than the common good of society. This kinship factor, which displays the veracity of the Somali pastoral culture, is what I.M. Lewis, the social anthropologist, gives a perfect description as he writes, "A Somali does not ask another where he is from, but whom he is from."[74]

In comparison to that, Frederick Hertz thinks of nationality as a group of people "...formed by the will to be a nation."[75] Ernest Barker presents his definition that what actually is represented as a nation is, "a body of men inhabiting a definite territory, who normally are drawn from different races, but possess a common stock of thought and feel-ings acquired and transmitted during the course of a common history."[76] Approaching it from an intuitive spectrum, we can refer to Arnold Tonybee's statement that it is "a subjective psychological feeling in a living people."[77]

When we measure against these definitions, we may perceive that the theory of Somali nationalism emerged primordially as a splash of anti-colonialism, a thesis of a good substance of credit to Professor Hassan Omar Mahadallah.[78] But the causation that agitated and instigated what he precisely termed as "idée-force", in my contention, comes partially from the Somalis' displeasure with the status quo vis-à-vis the abolition of their internal colonialism practiced in the slave institution and over the Jareer people, as far as the southern part of Somalia is concerned.

We have to consider this; upon its inception, the Somali elites' notion of nationalism was amiss of concrete fundamentals functionable from genuine philosophy of nationalistic ideology. At that far time, we know that nationalism built its foundation on a shaky and fragile 'collectivity jargons' which in effect were seen as a framework for depriving the people of their more attached tribal identity. Particular victims of that identity were the settlers in the fertile riverine regions and more specifically the Jareer and the Digil-Mirifle confederacies.

Investigating the question about Somali nationalism, Mahadallah discusses and differentiates between the various aspects of nationalism; cultural, linguistic, territorial, religious and historical, before adducing to the conclusion that Somali nationalism was devoid of all these binding factors that are necessary for creating a morally cohesive nation; one united by a psychological will that would put the nation over and above individual and ethnic interest. His proposal of "traditionalism" and "anti-colonialism"[79] as the two forces behind Somali nationalism would stand firm against any pertinent scrutiny, in my view. But for the sake of corroboration, I would allow myself to extend the debate a bit further.

Reflections of Somali clan segmentation are very visible against the milieu of the society's ethno-history. But traditionally, whether ancient or recent, Somali people have formed a larger tribal nation to face together a common threat or enemy. Some instances can be drawn from events very ancient and others of recent occurrences:

a) The unification of the clans in time of war under Islamic or nationalistic ideology has been celebrated under Ahmed Gran, (Axmed Gureey) the left-handed leader whose real identity has never been clear in Somalia. Anyway, in Gran's duel against Abyssinia, Somalis (*in conjunction with other nationals who are not often acknowledged in Somalia*) united into the coalition that raided and overwhelmed Abyssinia;

b) The Galla war is very reminiscent of its legacy of pastoral slavery that Somalist scholarship has not yet sufficiently unraveled;

c) The battle on the pre-Somalia Bantu settlers that significantly uprooted a majority of the Sabaki/Bantu population from their land and coerced the remainder into brutal life of submissiveness represents remarkable Somali clan-alliance;

d) The Wa-Gosha encounter has joined together a giant Absame/Ogadeni composition of Darood tribes to form an alliance to edge out the Jareer from the Jubba Valley;

e) The Somalia-Ethiopia wars of 1963/4 and 1977 are still fresh in the Somali mind; and

f) The 'liberation' struggle to gain the Northern Frontier District (NFD) of what is now the Northeastern Province of Kenya; have all been unifying factors, because what is characteristically uniform about all these wars is the merger of the otherwise disgruntled clans into unity as 'Somali' and in 'defense of the motherland'. As the emotion against the 'collective threat' wanes, so disappears the spirit that amalgamated the clans; instantly melting away the coalition of these otherwise separate nations of clans. Comparatively, the struggle against 'colonialism' is not from a sentiment very different from any of those unifying factors. In all of them the interest was forestalling a threat from what was seen as a common enemy.

But other factors too, have contributed to decolonization, not only in Somalia but Africa as a whole. In Professor Ochieng's assumption, "America, which emerged from the Second World War as the richest nation on earth, and with a glut of capital, was looking for investment possibility all over the world and this was being frustrated by European colonies."[80] Ochieng', and later Maloba, both agree that external global dynamics also played a significant political and economic role in the decolonization process of Africa.

Colonialism was being squeezed into a tight corner as the Italian Anti-Schiavista groups pulled the lid off realities of the decay in its colony, Southern Somalia. Similarly for the north, internal pressure was mounting on the British government, mainly from the public, spearheaded by political institutions. The USSR, in its part, for whatever reasons, was criticizing colonialism as a plunder and economic sabotage of the young colonies. Raising communist concern, R.H.A Merlen proposed the necessity:

> "...to reach the Somali peasants first... and have a series of heart-to-heart talks with them ... that the Somali Intelligentsia merely want to use them as tools for their own gains.... Otherwise we shall experience in Somaliland the sort of thing, which is now happening in Java and Malaya... Ethiopia and Somalia are danger areas for Africa as a whole from the point of view of communism... The tragedy is that a few semi-educated Somalis have been encouraged by the press of the Left and by their appearances before the United Nations."[81]

In the environment of these realities the attainment of independence in Somalia, like elsewhere in Africa, was accelerated by the West's policy of discouraging the colonies' fondness for communist ideologies and the reception of financial assistance from the Soviet bloc. Undoubtedly, some countries did, on the basis of political interest, causing a painful blow to Western political domination in some Third World countries. Equally important was the economic concerns of the metropolitan countries which in fact suffered drastically as a result of the war, a reality which prompted the USA to design the Marshall Plan to save its allies in Europe from further economic devastation. These dynamics, which are least discussed in the Somali nationalism discourse, and the ill will the colonial regime inherited as the legacy of abolition of slavery, have coincidentally but efficaciously contributed to change the political atmosphere leading to the rejection of colonialism in southern Somalia.

As experienced in other colonies, the circumstances leading to Somalia's independence have at some point come as a result of the fact that at least "there had to be local demands for independence,"[82] insofar that this could be seen as a justification for decolonization.[83] But at a glance in the Somali situation, the issue of abolition of slavery as a persistent factor at the social interest level of the pastoral Jileec, cannot be overlooked at all.

Basically, the Somalis' preach of nationalism was a mere verbal precipitation of what otherwise constituted clan-based protest movements, each one of which pursued a covert tribal agenda. Only that this agenda was enshrouded in the vague verbosity of nationalism. This is the reason why, in veritable mode of nationalism, Somalia or the SYL has not produced a founding father recognized locally or internationally, equal or comparable to what colonial Africa has experienced and produced in the wake of the struggle towards decolonization and formation of independent nation-state.

For the sake of the debate encompassing Somali nationalism, I may contribute in reminiscing the point that initially it was the Somali clans or tribes that have tempted or rather offered a leeway to the colonialists [voluntarily], and the right to be colonized in the guise of seeking protection. They stipulated treaties with the colonialists in exchange for annual payments, monthly stipends and other benefits which the local Sultans, elders, chiefs and notables of the clans received as acquiescence for solidarity justifying their solemn willingness to welcome the interested colonial powers.

The Somali Youth League: where the ills all started

Political elites like Hagi Mohamed Barrow, Omar Abdulle, Aw Bukoow, Aw Shantey Omar, and Aw Shidow Hirale show that the SYL's collaboration with the Italian colonial administration had multidiagonal aspects. But, as they reiterate, the main ones include: (a) Political independence as seen separate from economic independence, which had its own dimensions. The idea was not to bring to the surface the economic complexities and frustrations entailing the issue of the white-settlers' land expropriated from the Jareer communities in the riverine area; (b) the safeguarding of the Italian interests in the post-colonial independent state. Of course land was anticipated to be a contentious issue and the Italians would not have considered a hand-over of power to SYL without first putting in place the interests and welfare of their settled citizens in the colony. According to these elders, that the Italian concessionaires continued production and accumulation unabated on the expropriated Bantu land, even upon attainment of independence, gives room for the speculation of government approval on the Somali side.

Notwithstanding the achievement of independence, the colonial policy was visibly intact in the administrative and economic systems of the new government. The pre-colonial promises and the strong nationalistic jargons were transformed into a bed of neocolonialist attitudes designed to serve the political and economic interests of the colonialists. At the cost of all this mayhem, as the Jareer elders believe, the Bantu farmers had to bear the burden as the SYL government deliberately ignored engaging the Italian authorities for compensation over their atrocities and expropriation against the autochthonous agrarians.(Also see Ahmed Qassim Ali 2004).

The new Jileec elite in power found themselves in hot competition for resources, nepotism and clanism and imitation of the lavish living of the replaced colonizers. They procured to themselves a status and class at par with their former masters and embarked on a long journey of corruption and wealth accumulation. They took over from the colonialists, from privileges to the purse. The new nomadic elite reduced the essence of nationalism and value of independence to the Somalization of the eating of the Republic. The newly acquired power, according to the urbanized nomads, equaled a powerfully accelerated vehicle to access riches and capital wealth, opportunities lacked in their impoverished life before independence.

Indeed in Somalia, the SYL is synonymous with nationalism, decolonization and independence. But surprisingly enough, its formation was initially from Sakhawaddin, Jareer elite, extensively supported by Britain; and the idea of a 'greater Somalia' as a nation under one flag belonged to British Foreign Secretary, Ernest Bevin. By Dualeh's confirmation, "It was a British invention."[84] Upon its induction in May 1943, apparently with the approval of the British Military Administration,[85] the institution was known as the Somali Youth Club. It was actually in 1947 that the name took a political shape and official responsibility under the Somali Youth League (SYL), popular in Somalia for "Leego/Leegada" simply meaning 'the League'.

As a political party, the SYL is comparable to the two sides of a coin. On one side, it was the uniting force of a sector of the masses, spearheading an ideology of a Greater Somalia (though at a later date); on the other, it had its base on the two most tragic elements to nationalism, namely: - self-interest and ethnocentrism. In a real sense of logic, the SYL's clanism and silent clan competition for future posts upon independence have entirely jeopardized the true spirit of nationalism. That selfish attitude was responsible for the disorientation of the psychological variables of integration. It compromised cheaply the unison of the nation and the motto of nationalism, prioritizing responsiveness to clan interests rather than safeguarding the sacred national interests.

When a learned political scientist like Professor Mahadallah labels Somalia's struggle for independence as *"A Pithless Nationalism,"* in the title of his essay, we can conclude from his comments that Somali nationalism was not a genuine endeavor driven by the ingredients of intrinsic societal love for a wider Somali nation. Looking at the SYL from the hidden side of the coin leads to the track record of the ills and evils the party leadership had committed. The afflictions caused by internal party rivalry between Hawiye and Darood have derailed the ideological force of focus and national ambitions and goals of the other communities.

Touval observes the political situation before writing:

> "Political parties are based upon tribes or tribal lines... Recruitment to the police force and the army is also conditioned by the need to preserve a tribal balance... Yet the most westernized Somalis, the most modern ardent nationalists who violently oppose tribalism, are not oblivious of their tribal connections."[86]

By analyzing Touval's discourse, one may respect with all academic epistemology, the precision in Mahadallah's analytical postulate of 'Pithless Nationalism', a rare kind of essay contemporarily debating Somali Nationalism. In conclusion, the Somali intellectual summarizes, "With the exit of the colonial powers, Somali nationalism lost its twin pillars of anti-colonialism and traditionalism."[87] The gist of this rhetoric guides us to the belief that, by losing the pillars of the objectives, the proponents of Somali nationalism then and now, have reeled the goals off rail; and by far remain to be a group hovering, "Off the beaten sterile trail,"[88] borrowing Ahmed's words.

The SYL's treachery becomes evident in its treatment of the non-Hawiye non-Darood members, in a well orchestrated act of tribalism. However, the implicit political as well as ideological gimmick was that "the political parties and the various tribal groups were mainly occupied with capturing the positions which the Italian trusteeship administration was gradually transferring to the Somalis."[89]

On this precarious political scene, where every individual went in the hunt for post via clan importance or strength, one should not be taken by surprise why true founding father like Abdulkadir Sheikh Sakhawaddin suffered mysterious death; others like Haji Mohamed Hussein were dismissed on evenly calculated ethnic grounds; while the assassination of Ustad Osman was a Somali plan which the SYL government later ignored to investigate while the culprits were still alive. The probe into Ustad Osman's assassination would have been made easier by first summoning the man (friend) who had lured him out of his house on that fateful day. According to Ismaaciil Baxaar, Hassan Mohamed (Maanlaawe), Hagi Iidleh and Omar Abdulle, prior Osman had just concluded his preparation to travel abroad in a few days' time in order to pursue the recognition of the political identity of the Jareer and their accommodation in the forthcoming Somali administration. That "friend" was a known member of the Jiddo community in Lower Shabelle, and might have spilled the beans had he been interrogated over the assassination plot, in which he had played a major role.

Deeply dissatisfied with the internal wrangles of the SYL, its unethical power sharing and the alienation of the Jareer and Abdulkadir Sheikh Sakhawaddin, a young poet expressed the Bantu-Jareer community's sentiments concerning the mischievous grievances:

> *Suleeqa iyo Saxarla nimbo Sadaa gaari/Sakhaawe*
> *"Somaali ma ahaa" tireen, "Sanbuur weeye" / Silacne*
> *Sakhaawaa badnaay Saxarla Soofkeedi/*
> *Sixinki minaa maashi Salaanti waa diidi/*
> *(Wallee!) Sir nin qabo Saadaadkaba Samaan kuma Sifeeyne.*[90]

Translation:
> Everybody (clan) got a share of Suleeqa and Saxarla
> (She camels symbolizing independence) / But you
> alienated Sakhawe (diin) (the Jareer) for his ethnicity,
> saying "he is of the (flat nose)" / Though in the search for
> Saxarla (independence) it was Sakhawa that bore
> The brunt of burden / Once you began enjoying
> The butter you became arrogant and above everyone/Begone!
> For Almighty God has not praised the treacherous lot.

It has never been postulated until recently the other relevant version about Somali nationalism. The post-independence ruling elite, and almost the entire Somalist scholarship either distorted or ignored the significance of the relationship between the effects of the abolition of slavery, the Somali tribal leaders' solicitation for foreign occupation in the guise of protection, and the uprising of slaveholding Somali clans. The following may clarify the argument:-

1.   When the Italian companies first came and ignored the existence of slave business, there have been neither sentiments of nationalism nor anti-colonial uprising, nor skirmishes, nor confrontations. If anything, the Jileec Somalis have not only accelerated colonial occupation but facilitated it by rendering services for the settlement of the colonizers through their tribal chiefs, elders, kadis (religious judges) and other elite of good social standing, who accepted to be employed in preparation for the overwhelming domination.

2.   Confrontations started only after the abolition issue became serious and upon the withdrawal of the companies that were leniently tolerant to slavery.

3.   The reasons for the 'anti-colonialism' zeal in the years following abolition, are manifested in letters and verbal protests the Somali tribes made regarding the retention of their slaves; some of them justifying the practice as their legitimate Islamic right.

4.   After abolition and full occupation for conquest, the Somali clans collaborated with the same 'colonialists' in conscripting the Jareer community – autochthons and ex-slaves alike - to forced labor for Italian concessionaires exploiting the land expropriated from the very Jareer community.

5.   The attacks the slave-holding Somali tribes engaged on the settlements of the freed ex-slaves to repossess them, provides sufficient reason to support the motive for uprising as being economic interest and not with regard to love and affection for the nation.

What one should be conscious of is that, in the first place, nationalism did not take its birth in Somalia as an original stimulus created out of conscious love for the nation. It came as a spurious duplication of what was happening in Europe as a result of the World Wars and the emergence of the formation of young nations on that continent and elsewhere in Africa and also in Asia. As we have learned from the written literature as well as the traditions widely paradigmatic of Somalia, the nomadic Somali who had always been portrayed as an egalitarian enjoying a pastoral democracy, having his loyalty to his lineage, always had his national integrity attached to his abode.

Outside this settlement, which he shared with his closest of kin, he did not have a scope or focus to call a Nation, as it did not exist genuinely in the patterns of his social consciousness at any time in the history of the Somali nomadic life. Clear evidence can be taken as the creation of the so-called SYL, the party praised to be the forerunner for Somali independence. According to history, the SYL was not the brainchild of socio-political consciousness but as an impetus of the British colonial regime that disconcerted the Somali people due to the former's political rivalry with Italy over the control of the Somali peninsula in its entirety.

Different from sedentary societies which have social cohesiveness as a result of their communal nature of living, the pastoral nomad did not have a sanctified moral orientation towards membership of a wider nation. A wider national conception would come as a possible motivation only when inspired by spoils or opportunities towards political hegemony as seen achievable through tribalism. Mine is to suggest that even within the SYL and the independent administrations in the country, there has not been an emphasis or orientation that drew a common destiny agenda or a nation as it did inversely for individual sub-clans and clans of those who were the purveyors of the nationalism school of thought.

Nor could it be contended by all elaborative means, that economic nationalism could be a figure of attribution to nationalism since the country lacked the basic infrastructure necessary in the mobilization of the exploitable productive sectors. Significantly, communication network across the regions, particularly north and south of the country was not properly streamlined. In a personal discussion in Nairobi Dam in 1994, ex-army man Ali Atosh related how linguistic intelligibility was another cause of deterioration to the whole nationalism and unity set up, particularly after witnessing that certain public officials and functionaries from the northern regions were unable to work among sections of the southern communities without an interpreter.

The north-south polarization, further complicated by distinctiveness in prevalent socio-cultural diversities, was a depriving issue that could not enhance an economic nationalism, due to uncoordinated intelligentsia and disparities in elite thinking. This is perceivable in the context that whereas the nomadic culture maintained an enduring belligerency in stock-rustling for resource augmentation and wealth accumulation, the southern economy had been fostering with slavery as its industrial machinery.

Based on the two benchmarks of exploitation and disdain for hard work, it differs from one's understanding of the notion that economic nationalism could be a dynamic force behind Somali nationalism. The elite enterprise at the time had not developed an integrative mode capable of accommodating all the masses within the structure of an economy-based community toward national conscience. Therefore, the abstractness of the elites' nationalism ideology, avarice for resource control (legitimated through political incumbency), and other prevalent degeneracy have been inimical to the processes of nationalism for it to have been born out of historical, social, cultural, political or psychological commonality.

While considering the other universal factors that had their contributions in their own manner, my argument is that the dissatisfaction with the abolition of slavery was the remote cause in continuum, with feuds and grudges which took a rebirth in a modified sense and under newly created terms like 'independence', 'anti-colonialism', and 'nationalism'. I contend that Somalis have lived independently, nationalistically (at clan level), and colonialistically (subjugating the Jareer) prior to their solicitation for the arrival of the Europeans and the enactment of abolition. The so-called 'nationalist' sentiments are not the genuine reflections of an intuitive love for nation because no lover of his nation would implore for money in exchange for its exploitation by another, unless otherwise the Somali's concept of love for the nation is different.

It also sounds rather ironical that the same people who had received monetary gifts and made treaties with the colonialists would react against their 'protectors' once they had given them leave to settle and protect them. After these related evidences are examined, abolition of slavery was the major factor that at threshold drove a wedge between the protectors (rephrased 'new colonialists') and the protected (rephrased 'former colonialists'), in the Bantu-Jareer viewpoint, and hence the conditioning of the instigation and sentiments to broader degrees, causing the battle engagements that followed suit.

Differing with the pastoralists' idea of nationalism, one Bantu/Jareer poet chastised the Jileec Somalis for their double standard:

*Tuugsi ii Tereesaa Talyaani ku keenti
Tujaarnimo gaaraa Tolkiin u gadeen![91]*

Translation:
    You gave leave to the Italians (to settle) by begging for their money (Maria Theresa thalers)
    You sold your country/people (purposely) due to your rapacity for wealth.

The other quality accorded to Somali nationalism, as criticized above in Mahadallah's and other scholars' theories could not stand verification. Similarly the notion of the SYL as a nationalist political body ignites a lot of doubt especially when the frame of their slogan "nationalism" was not the product of national love but one of clanism. In the first instance, the SYL was dominated by the offspring of the same people who '*sold*' their territory to the European colonialists and were as such educated possibly from those resources. Their agenda was the repossession from the colonial power of a larger territory, now that the opportunity to use slogans like "nationalism" and "Greater Somalia" as tools for ethno-political motives were commensurate with the fervent atmosphere instigated vehemently, among other things, by the long standing grudge of economic imbalance between former local black colonialists i.e. Somali slave owners and newly settled European colonialists i.e. Italian fascist regime.

So, in the grim thick of nationalism and anti-colonialism persisted a consciously hidden conflict of interest over the Jareer manpower and land, between the former Jileec slave owners and the Italian colonial administration. The Somalis felt unpalatable the disenfranchisement of their economic source (slavery), which the new colonialists were now exploiting in the mode of forced labor. In the circumstance, the Bantu land and free labor force were the bone of contention but of different wording for the respective colonialists, Italians and Somali pastoralists.

Another perspective shows that 'nationalism' had variable meanings, relative scopes and interests for the diverse communities. While the SYL had its territorial scope mainly within the borders of Italian Somaliland and later British Somaliland, its ambition for a Greater Somalia was very superficial and minimal until later when the greed for grab multiplied. There were no records at that period to support Somali definition of the area constituting its territorial limits and confines other than the claim that certain Somali speaking people lived in certain places (Mahadallah 2004), a desire that disregarded the mixture of the non-Somali speaking population making part of the cultural thread of those settlements.

The establishment of SYL offices in neighboring countries was done for political sabotage and manipulation between European colonial powers – Britain and Italy. SYL presence therefore should not be approached on the basis of either stimuli for a Greater Somalia tutelage or support from the entire Somali people living in those countries. Colonial archival materials reveal that it was a matter of "for and against" as the leaderships of certain clans were actually opposed to the presence of the SYL in their areas:

> The leaders and elders of the Ajuran tribe in Kenya saw what was happening. They realized that the undermining of the British Administration means also the undermining of the tribal law and consequently the elders' authority since the British ruled through the indigenous institutions. Luckily, they realized this whilst they had control of their people and accordingly when they prohibited Ajuran tribes from belonging to the Somali Youth League the minority opposition with which they met was eventually quashed.
> Executive committee (of the SYL) started hearing and deciding cases concerning Mohammedan Law and custom...Pressure, in many forms, was brought to bear on any person failing to comply with an order given by the committee.[92]

Regarding the understanding of nationalism in perspective of the distinguished clans, we should not afford taking the risk of overlooking the social psychology of the communities, the basis of their social belief and behavior as each had its interpretation of what it knew as nationalism:-

1. To the Darood, the interpretation of nationalism could have been gauged to a variety of sultanates (communities) to be put under the rulership of one sultan and his council from the hierarchical lineage, and all to be ruled by one Darood sultan;

2. The Hawiye thought the right to the numerical majority should be theirs, after all the capital Mogadishu, "belonged" to them. Other Hawiye groups, specifically the Abgaal, foresaw the political process as tainted and implausible, thus nurturing the idea of nationalism through the perspective of their own kind of liberalism, hence the crea-

142

tion of 'Partito Liberale Somalo';

3.   The Digil-Mirifle idea of nationalism had shunned any interest in the nomad's 'barren' territory in the north but limited within the concerns and interests of their people spreading only through the confines of their specified territorial boundaries, hence federalism, regionalism (Rewin-ism; Digil-Mirifle-ism) rather than nationalism;

4.   The Jareer anticipation was so optimistic as they thought of nationalism as the return and repossession of their expropriated land and the recognition of their rights as equals according to the tenets of Islam and values of their cultural beliefs; and that they should be compensated for the damages caused by both Somali and Italian colonialists;[93]

5.   The yardstick of Isaq nationalism was erroneously calculated from the belief of submerging and overshadowing the existence of the non-Isaq population in the north in order to access a larger portion of the national pie, in other words the nomad's *'Maandeeq'* the she-camel that is often a symbol of nationalism and independence;

6.   The non-Isaq population in the north might have thought of nationalism as the dilution of an Isaq-dominated political hegemony and economic disequilibrium and hence the support for unification beyond sectoral or regional nationalism; a unified Somali nation that would recognize them a place (as an independent entity) in the sharing of *"Maandeeq"*, i.e. the benefits of independence.

The fluidity of the alignment and coalition of tribes uniting under the roof of one party and the deceptively persuasive campaign slogan of "Greater Somalia" soon surfaced the reality. Loyalty was withdrawn from the party and integrity was rapidly shifted along tribal lines and not along national cause. A party that was internally suffering from the pandemics of clanism has been entrusted with the enormous responsibility of governing a nation, after negotiations and assurances of safeguarding colonial interests.

During the ten-year period of UN trusteeship in southern Somalia, negotiations were going on for some time for the unification of British Somaliland in the North and Italian Somaliland in the south. On June 26, 1960, the northern regions achieved independence and unified subsequently with their southern brothers on July 1 of the same year, upon the declaration of self-rule for the south. Although sovereignty and self-determination were achieved, what apparently was lacking at the time was, to borrow from Ngugi wa Thiong'o, "Decolonizing the Mind"[94] from colonial tutelage, ruling the country with a balance mind and under the doctrine of equal opportunity. But this did not happen as we shall see in the next chapter.

Conclusion

The colonial occupation has impacted on the Bantu Jareer people more negatively than other communities in the country. It has devastated the entire economic as well as all other social development factors of the community. However, the Bantu Jareer dilemma can be looked at from the colonial appropriation of Bnatu land, the forceful exploitation of the Jareer manpower as well as the Somali people's siding with the colonialists. Being on colonial payroll as middlemen, the Somali people colluded with colonial Italy in the conscription of the Jareer to work on Italian concessionaires. The belief is that neither the SYL nor the legendary religious elites have raised the issue of Bantu rights. In essence, Somali history has tried to deliberately obscure the reality about the Somali interplay with the colonial administration as far as the Bantu issue is concerned. But on the contrary, the same regimes acknowledged as heroes certain politically formed heroes and heroine with no much history to admire. To make things worse, the post independence regimes have not taken the initiative to remedy the Bantu Jareer grievances but instead embarked on further demolishing the subsistence economy of the Jareer by expropriating more Jareer land.

Notes and references

1. Odetola, Olatunde T., and Ademola, Ade., Sociology: An Introduction of African Text. Macmillan. (1985: 34).
2. Kayongo - Male, D., and Onyango, P., The Sociology of the African Family. Longman, Third Impression. (1991: 1-2).
3. Samatar, Abdi I., The State and Rural Transformation in Northern Somalia 1884 - 1986. Madison: University of Wisconsin Press. (1989: 32)
4. ASMAI., galleys 331 - 2.
5. Filonardi report, (Zanzibar) ASMAI, position 55/1, f.4, October 1886.
6. Hertslet, E., The Map of Africa by Treaty (Third Edition) London. His Majesty's Stationery Office, 1990, I, 304 - 8.
7. Cottoni communication to Brin, July 1892, Zanzibar. ASMAI, pos. 55/5, f. 37
8. Provisional Ordinance for the government and Administration of Territory

Under the Protection of Italy. Filonardi Report No. 171; Sep. 16, 1894. ASMAI, pos. 75/1, f.3

9. Hertslet, E., The Map of Africa by Treaty, III, 948, 1091 – 93; London Post, November 21, 1889.

10. Mackinon's communication to Crispi, August, 1888, London. ASMAI, pos. 55/1, f. 8.

11. Menkhaus, Kenneth John, "Rural Transformation and the Roots of Under-development in Somalia's Lower Jubba Valley", PhD. Dissertation., op.cit.

12. Hallett, Robin. Africa Since 1875. Surjeet Publications. Second Indian Reprint. (1999: 131).

13. Giorgio Sorrentino, Ricordi del Benadir. Naples: Trani – (1912: 27 – 28)

14. 'Libro Verde', doc. 2, p.27, containing communication between Filonardi in Zanzibar and Crispi, the Italian Prime Minister.

15. Hallett, Robin, op.cit. p.130.

16. 'Libro Verde', doc. 11, annex 1, p.40. Treaty of Protection.

17. Launay (Berlin) communication to Crispi, in March 1889. ASMAI, pos. 59/1, f.8.

18. Yusuf Ali's declaration in Alula, April 7, 1889, ASMAI, pos. 59/1, f.5.

19. 'Libro Verde', doc. 29, annex II, p.69

20. Report of Commander Sorrentino, cited in Robert Hess, op.cit., p.33.

21. Jardine, Douglas., The Mad Mullah of Somaliland., op.cit., p.34

22. Samatar, Abdi I., and Samatar, Ahmed I., "The Material Roots of the Suspended African State: Arguments from Somalia." The Journal of Modern African Studies, 25, 4(1987), pp. 669-690.

23. O'Connor, James., "The Meaning of Economic Imperialism," in Rhodes, R.I., (ed.), Imperialism and Underdevelopment. New York: Monthly Review. 1970a: 118.

24. Eno, Omar A., "Landless landlords" op.cit., p.143.

25. Chiesi, Gustavo, and Travelli, Ernesto., Le Questioni del Benadir. Milano: Bellini. 1904.

26. Cited in Cassanelli, Lee V., "The Ending of Slavery in Italian Somalia: Liberty and the Control of Labor 1890 – 1935", in Miers, S., and Roberts, R., (eds.) The End Of Slavery in Africa. The University of Wisconsin Press (1988:318). See also Robert Hess, Italian Colonialism in Somalia pp.80-83, and Omar A. Eno, "Landless Landlords and Landed Tenants" in Kusow, Abdi M., ed., Putting the Cart Before the Horse, pp.135-154.

27. Eno, Omar A., "Landless Landlords..." op.cit., p.144

28. Onorato Di Monale report, ASMAI, pos. 75/6, f.56. Feb. 1903.

29. Hess, Robert., op.cit., p. 90.

30. Cassanelli, Lee V., The Shaping of Somali Society. Philadelphia: University of Pennsylvania Press. (1982: 201ff), Also Hess, Robert, Italian Colonialism in Somalia; Eno, Omar A., "Landless Landlords and Landed Tenants" in Kusow, Abdi M., ed., Putting the cart Before the Horse, Red Sea,

2004; Mukhtar, Mohamed H., "Somali Response to Colonial Occupation," in Kusow, ed., op.cit.

31. De Vecchi di Val Cismon., Orizzonti d'impero: Cinque anni in Somalia. Milan: Mondadori. (1935:10)

32. Sacdi Mumin Hassan, a very popular poet in Afgoi with a lot of contribution to Poetry at the social scene in Afgoie.

33. A communication: letter from the District Commissioner's Office, Kismayu, December 2nd, 1916, signed by the Assistant to the Provincial Commissioner. (Kenya National Archives - Nairobi).

34. Eno, M.A., Wargeyska Runta Bogga 4 aad; Warar Qubane ah; Waxa isku soo dubarriday Eno. 5th - 20th Juun 1996. Cadadka 11aad.

35. Eno, Omar A., "Landless Landlords" op.cit.

36. Guadagno, Marco., Xeerka Beeraha/Diritto Fondierio Somalo. 1981:179.

37. Incoronato report No. 90, Zanzibar, Dec. 1893: ASMAI, pos. 75/1, f.3.

38. Eno, Omar A., "The Reasons Behind the Somali Tragedy and the Vulnerable Minority Groups, Particularly the Bantu/Jareer." A paper presented at the African Studies Association, November 3 - 6, 1995, Orlando, Florida, USA.

39. Ronnell, Rodd., British Military Administration of Occupied Territories in Africa. Londra. 1948: 162.

40. Pankhurst, Sylvia., Ex-Italian Somaliland, p. 90.

41. Mohamed Hussein Hassan (Jawaani). The late Jawaani was my uncle. He often talked about *Kolonyo* and *teen* (term?) many times when he visited us in Mogadishu and also when we spent some of our school holidays and Istunka festivals at his place in Afgoi.

42. Videotaped workshop in Somalia in which Jareer elders discussed ancient as well as the contemporary history of their community, 2003.

43. Ibid.

44. Aw Yusuf Yaawisoow recited this poem lamenting the selfish activities of the SYL. He was a very strong anti-colonialist. He was also among 15 or 17 young men who had sought arms from Sayid Mohamed Abdulle Hassan to fight colonial establishment in the South.

45. Ahmed, Ali Jimale., Daybreak is Near...: Literature, Clans and the Nation-State in Somalia. Red Sea Press. (1996:95).

46. Dualeh, op.cit., p. 4.1

47. Hallet, op.cit., p. 132.

48. Ibid.

49. Ibid.

50. Tidy, Michael, and Leeming, Donald., A History of Africa 1840 - 1914. Volume Two. Arnold Publishers., p. 108.

51. Jardine, Douglas, The Mad Mullah of Somaliland, p. 43.

52. Ibid. p. 44.

53. Ali Dhuux, cited in Abdalla Mansur., "Contrary to a Nation: The Cancer

of the Somali State", in Ahmed, Ali Jimale, ed., The Invention of Somalia; op.cit., pp.109 -110.

54. Ismail Aliyow Baxaar, a Jareer poet and oral historian currently resident of Jeddah, Saudi Arabia.

55. Abdullahi Abdulkadir (Aw Jaalle), a poet with a composition of so many poems of contemporary Somalia.

56. Mukhtar, "Islam in Somali History," op.cit., p.21.

57. Cassanelli, Lee V., "A Historian's View of the Prospects for Somali Reconstruction", in Janzen, Jorg., (ed.), What are Somalia's Development Perspective?, p.37.

58. Ibid.

59. Dualeh, op.cit., p.88.

60. Traditionally Qaadiriyya dhikr (religious song) is sang for praising Allah, the prophet and pious religious scholars. But in this incident, it was constituted to inflict an accumulation of curse onto Mohamed Abdulle Hassan and his Dervish.

61. Reewing folklore song of a classic Af-Maay poem composed in reaction to Sheikh Uwees's assassination by Mohamed Abdulle Hassan's Dervish..

62. Jardine, Douglas., op.cit., p.51.

63. Ibid. p.50.

64. Farah, Nuruddin., A Naked Needle. London. Heinman. (1976:104).

65. Hagi Adimow, in Bantu elders' discussion in Jeddah, Saudi Arabia, 2002.

66. Ahmed, Ali Jimale., Daybreak Is Near..." p. 96

67. Ibid., p. 93.

68. Mohamed Ali Isman (Weershe) Mogadishu 1970s.

69. Abdullahi Soomoow (Ul-Qalin) Mogadishu, 1970s.

70. Ibid.

71. Ahmed, Ali Jimale, "Daybreak is Near, Won't You Become Sour?" in Ahmed, Ali J., ed., op.cit., p.140.

72. P'Bitek, Okot., Artist the Ruler: Essays on Art, Culture and Values. East African Educational Publishers. Reprinted 1994, p.22.

73. Lewis, I. M., "The Land of the Living Dead". Sunday Times, August 30, 1992.

74. Ibid.

75. Frederick Hertz, quoted in Nationality in History and Politics. London. (1915:13) cited in Palmer and Perkins., op.cit.

76. Ernest Barker, quoted in Palmer and Perkins, op.cit., p.19.

77. Tonybee, Arnold, J., quoted in Nationality and War., cf Palmer & Perkins. op.cit.

78. Mahadallah, Hassan., "Pithless Nationalism: The Somali Case", in Kusow, Abdi M., ed., op.cit., pp.59-74.

79. Ibid.

80. Ochieng, William R., 'The Mau Mau, the petit bourgeoisie and decoloniza-

tion in Kenya', unpublished paper, Kenyatta University, 1984, 8. quoted in Wunyabari Maloba, "Nationalism and Decolonization, 1947 – 1963", in Ochieng, W. R., ed., A Modern History of Kenya 1895 – 1980. Evans Brothers Ltd. 1989.

81. R.H.A. Merlen, East Africa & Rhodesia, Jan 13, 1949. Kenya National Archives, Nairobi.
82. Maloba, Wunyabari., "Nationalism and Decolonization, 1947 – 1963" in Ochieng', W. R., ed., op.cit.
83. Ibid.
84. Dualeh, op.cit., p.39.
85. A communication dispatch from District Commissioner's Office, Wajir, Northern Province, 19th April, 1948. KNA, Nairobi.
86. Touval, Saadia, op.cit., pp.85-86.
87. Mahadallah, Hassan O., op.cit.
88. Ahmed, Ali Jimale, "Off the Beaten Sterile Trail"; A paper presented at the 47th African Studies Association, New Orleans. November 2004.
89. Touval, Saadia., op.cit., p.87.
90. Mohamed A. Eno, Extracted from the poem "Saxarla, Suleeqa iyo Sanbuur".
91. Maxmedeey Ismaan, A couplet selected from miscellaneous verses Maxmedeey had recited on various events.
92. A communication letter from the District Commissioner's Office, Wajir, Northern Province, 19th April, 1948. (Kenya National Archives – Nairobi).
93. Hagi Mohamed A. Roble (alias Maadeey Barakaale), a Jareer elite and participant in the Jareer meetings in Saudi Arabia, 2003.
94. Wa Thiong'o, Ngugi., Decolonizing the Mind is the title of Ngugi's book discussing the politics of language in African Literature. It is the book Ngugi promised to be the end of his writing in English. He says, "This book, Decolonizing the Mind, is my farewell to English as a vehicle for any of my writings. From now on, it is Gikuyu and iswahili all the way." p.xiv. East African Educational Publishers.

Chapter 4

POST-COLONIAL SOMALIA AND THE JAREER STIGMA: FROM COLONIALISM TO NEO-COLONIALISM

Upon the rubrics of fictitious nationalism, a government of unity was formed and a ten-year period of UN trusteeship known as *Amministrazione Fiduciaria Italiana della Somalia* (AFIS) under Italy was brought to an end. Prior to independence, there existed a legislative assembly, which was chaired by Aden Abdulle Osman. Under the Assembly, an internal Somali administration was established in preparation for the 1960 take-over. The administration was composed of a Prime Minister, Abdullahi Isse, and five cabinet ministers including Sheikh Ali Jimale, Mohamed A. Nur, Muse Boqor, Haji Farah A. Omar and Salad A. Mohamud. The formation was imbalanced and Hawiye domination was visible from the cabinet picture. Consequently, the Darood dubbed the internal administration "Governo Sacad" rather than Governo Somalo, the legitimate standard term. The reflection of this attitude relates back to tribal differences and inimical feuds long existing between sub-clans of the Prime Minister Abdullahi Isse of the Sacad (Hawiye) and rival Darood sub-clans in their territorial settlements. The implication of the transformation of Governo Somalo to Governo Sacad, the Prime Minister's sub-clan of his Hawiye clan, meant Darood disapproval even if the dissatisfaction was not made official by open disagreement or protest. It was the first blow of mistrust in the approach towards independence. As Gassim elucidates, the SYL at the time, "...was not a feasible tool towards statehood..."[1] highlighting political immaturity with a scope not beyond the clan domain.

Soon a fracture developed from the disparity in the power sharing system. The Darood withdrew their support and loyalty to the internal government while the Hawiye were more than justified to put their weight behind it. The analysis of political activists like Haji Mohamed Barrow[2] posit the situation as an acid test for the SYL leaders' platform for gaining political momentum at both clan and national levels. The Darood's minimal representation in the internal government, by and large, had a dual effect: (1) That clanism is always superior to nationalism in Somali socio-political life, and (2) That the Darood had to retreat, strategize and then come up with a more effective political roadmap to support their clan supremacy, the psychological food for pastoral pseudo-nobility. From the humdrums of this thought, we can see that the spirit of nationalism has waned off into the doldrums. Clan sentiments and identity not only effectively prevailed but were reinvigorated as the most powerful vehicle to the top. With this provocation, untended wounds of centuries suppurated in this political divide of no ends.

In the north, the situation seemed more favorable. The parties of the day shared the parliamentary seats. These included United Somali Party, Somali National League and the National United Front. When the first administrative body of British Somaliland was established in 1959, the seats were allocated in accordance with tribal system. But even so, it is not to rule out that the process was free from anomalies and manipulations.

After unification, the Somaliland members of parliament and politicians felt caught up in an overwhelming Hawiye-Darood dominated political hurricane. Although they were given some cabinet positions in the new government of national unity, they were not the least impressed. Their anticipation was a power sharing structure of north-south, which was not responsive to the tenets of the greed that was haunting the southern leaders at the time. It was an all-Jileec affair, since the Jareer aspirations to parliament were effectively thwarted by the SYL bigwigs.

When Aden Abdulle Osman was elected the first president of the Republic of Somalia, a Hawiye southerner married to a Darood woman, the northern politicians expected the Prime Minister would be nominated from them, which did not happen. Instead, Abdirashid Ali Sharmarke, a Darood from the SYL, was nominated to the helm of the cabinet, probably as acquiescence to the Darood on the one hand, and to SYL supremacy with strong control in the government on the other. A fifteen-member cabinet was entrusted with the administration of the Republic. The clan representation was uneven as Hawiye and Darood scooped the largest numbers, with the Issaq at par with the Digil-Mirifle and the Gudabursi at much smaller representation.

The Isaq found themselves deeply ditched into a double tragedy. For one, the sharing mechanism did not favor them in terms of north against south as per their presumption. For the other, since the north is characterized also by ethnic diversity, they had to concede some of the seats to representatives from the other northern communities. Dented by the new political trends, the Isaq aspiration stood daunted and as such vulnerable to northern elite criticism.

In retaliation, some northern officers embarked on a reckless mission to heal their grievance. They attempted a secessionist plot, which was soon averted and landed them in jail. The new government had difficulty determining the fate of the officers involved. The problem was bifocal; part political and part social. To contain the heightening political as well as social temperaments, the government took the raw option that was the release of the officers, but only after a symbolic court hearing.

In this nature of affairs, nepotism, clanism and individualism became the forces of substitute to the outwardly promoted nationalism. To the state coffers, every individual at its vicinity had to help himself and his kinship to the best of his ability, if not to the best of his satisfaction. The syndrome of "the culture of eating"[3] eroded the national development aspiration. Giving a critical analysis of the situation, Abdi Ismail Samatar argues:

> The competitive and Xeer-less nature of the post-colonial social system made state revenues, including foreign assistance, the bone of contention in a stagnant economy. In other words, those first on the scene could reward themselves and their clients.[4]

The pastoral crave for avarice respected no borders. The government policy was mistranslated into a go-for-the-grabs system, breaking all ethical bonds and moral obligations as leaders. For Sabine and Thorson believe, "Unless the state is a community for ethical purposes and unless it is held together by moral ties, it is nothing, as Augustine said later, except 'highway robbery on a large scale.' "[5]

The preceding theories of state class, presented as "Xeer-less" in Abdi Samatar and "highway robbery on a large scale" by Augustine, refer to two societies of the same immoral image. But in the Somali context, it is not presented in better hypothesis than Abdi Samatar's observation:

> The main way to get access to state funds was to become an elected political representative or, even better, a Minister, and this goes a long way to explain the increase in both the number of parties and candi-

dates in the 1964 and 1969 elections. Mainly because of the understanding that the upcoming contests were all about the 'privatization' of state largesse – indeed, many senior civil servants resigned in order to participate in the electoral gamble.[6]

From a stagnant economy, Somalia couldn't cater for its needs internally and externally. Persistent constraints created enormous disequilibria in its balance of payment. As a result, it became among the largest recipients of foreign aid in the world. A UN report confirms thus:

> Somalia, throughout its first three decades of independence received one of the largest per capita levels of foreign aid in the world. Unfortunately, most of it was squandered on inappropriate projects or lost to massive corruption thus earning Somalia a reputation as a "graveyard of foreign aid."[7]

But as the political squabble continued, the focus was diverted from national development. More concentration was given to clan politics. Nationhood literally lost its due value, since it was a tool for trade only through the decolonization process. For same as seen in many African ethno-cultural contexts, "It was practically developed during independence,"[8] and in effect had no deep roots for it to contrast to the deeper clan affinity and kinship.

The Somali President ignored to contain the brewing clan struggle amid his government. The elite competition for misappropriation of public resources, the expropriation of agricultural land and worsening inter-clan rivalry which characterized the subsequent regimes, have had their foundation laid in Aden Abdulle Osman's period. By allowing the appointment of the cabinet on clan formula, Osman legitimated the emergence of what Lipset calls "a society divided between a large impoverished mass and a small favored elite."[9]

As a result of this competition, rural migration was intensified in search of opportunities for the acquisition and accumulation of '*hanti qaran*' – public resources. Within a short period of time, competing immigrants flooded the urban areas, particularly the capital Mogadishu. Members of the cabinet and other top civil servants recruited their newly arrived kinsfolk. Many of these immigrants, like one of our former tenants, were not only on stipend from public coffers without rendering any service to the public, but were 'ghost workers' employed in more than one ministry!

The person I am referring to belonged to a nomadic community in the eastern regions of the country. He lived with his family in a separate apartment of our house till the military take-over. It was after his illegal salaries were terminated that he confessed to my father about the loss of all the three separate wages he had been earning for the past eight years. He was no longer able to pay for the apartment. He was given two or three months rent-free during which he looked for a room somewhere in the outskirts of Mogadishu. Later, he had to go to Saudi Arabia where he got employed as a casual worker.

Many top officials resorted to emulating the white colonialists. They stepped up their hunt for wealth and luxury and acquired plantations in the fertile land of the Bantu, along the Juba valley and in the Shabelle regions, many of them by expropriation. Kenneth Menkhaus agrees that in the 1960s, "Most of the Somali plantation owners were deputies in the national parliament or had other high positions of authority."[10] Needless to say, these were all Jileec Somalis in pursuit of public looting.

The chronology of past events reveals that Somalia has been associated with clan feuds, looting and livestock rustling. As Bloom and Ottong emphasized, "The stability of a community depends upon the quality of the groups that compose it."[11] And the quality has been, in the above paragraphs, described as "Xeer-less", meaning defiant of the traditional morals and the customary law. When, from a sociological perspective Bloom and Ottong hypothesize, "…corruption is associated with societies…in which there are no widely - accepted norms of sharing power,"[12] they would agree with me to have classified Somalia into that category of societies. The attitude and the moral decay of the ruling elite were prelude to a situation which would make Ahmed comment about three decades and half later that, "… it is impossible in this age to run a "tribal" government or regime. All trials in this direction have come to nothing."[13]

Hagi Barrow expresses how the cabinet and the whole administration was infinitely suffering from lack of inter-group and intra-group adaptation, mutual adaptation to one another, while the first president's intervention was ineffective. According to this elder, the majority who constituted the government were barren of either of the desirable human qualities in life, namely, virtue and knowledge. Arrogance utterly inherited the place of wisdom. And the cause of the conflict, in addition to other factors, was what Mary Getui would admit as, "The superiority complex of one group over another."[14]

Corruption and squandering of public coffers became the regular business of office duty. The elite built modern villas and purchased property in posh areas, for speculation and profiteering, from the tax-payers' money. Ahmed Qassim Ali reiterated that the expropriation and land looting with its effects of retrogression and economic vulner-ability to small-scale farmers, "was aggravated by successive post-colonial Somali administrations... by coercion and violence."[15] He la-ments that the lack of redress for the colonial mischief and grave viola-tions of human and property rights against the farmers, "...justifies only the failure of the successive Somali administrations to affect a land reform system."[16] Ali, despite its internal wrangle, censures Aden Ab-dulle Osman's regime for inefficiency and unpatriotic sentiments by accommodating the wish and interests of the colonial administration. He acknowledges, "The FR (First Republic) was by no means the right government to solve the problems of agriculture in southern Somalia. It maintained the status quo and contributed to the decline of produc-tion and consequent deterioration in the farmers' means of livelihood. It also postponed land reform indefinitely."[17]

When the first post-colonial regime could not address the com-plaints of the Jareer/Bantu regarding the land reform issue, economic participation, political recognition and social development in general, the elite of the day were convinced that the regime was neocolonialist in ideology and anti-Jareer by policy. Several Jareer '*Laashimiin*' poets interpreted the social feeling of their community, criticizing the presi-dent as unpatriotic who shared something in common with the coloni-alists:

Aadan ii Alberto Uurkooda halwaaye
Arladeey Isticmaarkaa loogu Aabayeeli.[18]

Translation:
Adan and Alberto (the Italian colonialist) are of the same (colonial) ideol-ogy
(No wonder) that my land was made an appeasement to the colonialists

154

Minaa Onoraato Amarkiisa yeeshi
Ismaan Istiqlaalki waa Aamin darreysi[19]
Translation:
>   If you accepted to abide by Onorato's orders (neocolonialistically)
>   You (Osman) rendered freedom worthless (of the struggle).

Arrinti Asaayle Aadan waa Ogaaye
Intareesadissaaw An Ii Arkiwaayi.[20]

Translation:
>   Adan was knowledgeable of the Asayle massacre,
>   But due to his self-interest, ignored to remedy our (Jareer) grievances

Onor ii Onoraataa Ushaada Udhiibti
Aadanoow Adduun yaa kuugu Aaminaayo![21]

Translation:
>   Once you have pledged allegiance to Onor & Onorato (colonialists)
>   (Aden) You are no longer trustworthy on this earth!

Abdi I. Samatar and Ahmed I. Samatar, who conducted studies on the functional nature of the post-independence Somali civil administrations, give a scholarly corroboration, one in agreement with the Jareer poets' verses. They delve into the subject by stating:

> The birth of the Somali post-colonial state was the outcome not of a long and broad-based social struggle, but rather of an accommodative arrangement whereby the cost to the colonial regimes was to relinquish visible power but not to lose decisive influence.[22]

To put it bluntly, in Aden Abdulle Osman's era, the genre of the political sociology, in other words the relationship between the nomadic social background and the existing/functional political institutions, shared the same imagery. Therefore, the political behavior of the parties was the emerging product of the social behavior eminent in ethnocentric nomadic culture.

In a broader sense, these persistent characteristics can be measured as interrelated variables in a continuum in the social psychology of this group, interacting symbolically in different stages and environments. In that framework, and according to the nomadic philosophy, the po-

155

litical party was used as an advanced device for attaining clan representation at the national level. The clan system, which functions as the law-making institution according to the ideals of I. M. Lewis' 'pastoral democracy', now transposed into a political establishment with an urbanite outlook, put in place to shape the national legislation that would satisfy violent pastoral avarice.

Certain scholars, Somalists in particular, tend to approach with promotional philosophy the formational and functional nature of the post-colonial regimes before Barre, particularly the first regime, as 'democratic'. When Somalis describe Osman's regime, the major basis of the explication of democracy is often delimited only to the process of formation of the structural body of the government as an institution, hence a "democratically elected government" and a "democratically removed institution". One of the problems of this thesis of delimitation of democracy to the electoral process only was perhaps encouraged by loud propaganda outside academic relevance or merit.

Alternatively, we can give democracy due consideration in terms of its social effects and relations - in the aspect of the ethics of political sociology - but not only the compatibility of the electoral system with democracy. By and large, the underlying concept of democracy should embrace the foundational principles of equal opportunity, fair social mobility, meritocracy and reciprocal loyalty between the elites in office and the society that entrusted them with both the power and authority they exercise.

The absence of an atmosphere conducive to the encouragement of the above factors is itself a shortcoming to democracy. In this stance, I contend that, apart from the racially/ethno-politically manipulated electoral processes; none of the post-colonial civil administrations was democratic in practice. According to Held,[23] democracy should be viewed as a political system capable of encouraging the purpose and practice of political equality, the protection of liberty and freedom, the defense of common social interests, the response to the requirements of the citizens, the promotion of moral self-development and the ennoblement of unbiased decision-making that takes every citizen's interest and well-being as a priority. But, when the 'democratically elected' members abuse their offices, it is nothing short of violation of the fundamentals of the very democracy that empowered their election into office. In retrospect, the violation of democracy illegitimates, technically and procedurally, the institutions and structures occupying the abused offices. As a consequence of this philosophy, I strongly argue that the first regime was not operating from the ideals recommended for 'democratic government' since it contravened the basic principles of democracy.

Despite the sentiments in her ethnic bias in approving Aden Abdulle Osman, Mariam Arif Gassim[24] is one of very few Somali authors who acknowledge the political alienation of the Jareer. Although she praises Aden Abdulle (alias Aden Adde) lavishly, perhaps it did not dawn on her why such a "praiseworthy" president could not see about the Jareer what she could see about their alienation. Secondly, Gassim does not seem to regard as a problem or an issue the enormous areas of farmland expropriated from the Jareer and their conscription to forced labor. But had the same fate of the Jareer affected the Hawiye, the President would have reacted with a different attitude to address the situation on his clan's behalf, thereby facilitating in his capacity as the president the reclaim and restoration of their property, with possible demand for reparation as well as an apology. Thirdly, had the oppression the Jareer experienced been exacted on Gassim's sub-clan and the president remained indifferent, Gassim's comment would have acknowledged the tribal bias to her sub-clan more than the mere mention of the Jareer and Jileec racial divide she hinted at, but without detail.

For the average Jareer/Bantu people, the reaction to Somali democracy has been manifested in the poetry above. The neocolonialist policy of the post-independence civil administrations, Aden Abdulle Osman being the foremost leader, had their roots firmly laid prior to the SYL climb to the top. Mariam Arif hints, but neither emphasizes nor elaborates, as she writes, "The Italian administration began to negotiate and be on good terms with the nationalist party...,"[25] but in his essay *"Land Rush in Somalia"* Ahmed Qassim is clear about the government's conscience. David Laitin confirms also in his volume *Politics, Language and Thought (p. 100)* that "the Italian Administrator appointed Cabdullahi Ciise as the first prime minister of an all-Somali government... for Cabdullaahi and the then SYL president, Aaden Cabdulle Cismaan, were both on good terms with the Italian administration."

As I noted earlier, the most critical issue was the illegal concessions and acquisition of Jareer land by the Italian colonialists and their settlers, which was further aggravated by Osman and his colleagues in office as the leaders of the first 'democratic' government. By depth, the Jareer poet did not say *"..Intareesadiisaaw An ii Arkiwaayi,"* out of sheer vanity or fantasy. He was a voice advocating for the most oppressed people in the peninsula. In such a situation, pain is best felt by the sufferer as the Jareer remind Osman:

Mugi Colka yiili Ciidanaan eheene
(Caddoow) Cashadoo hunkeed maa iiga soo Caraawdi![26]

Translation:

During the struggle, we were participants in the war,
(Oh Adde!) Have you now abandoned us (Jareer) because of a dinner (a personal interest) offered to you by the white colonialists!

Regarding Gassim's reiterated statements of "no consideration to Jareer" on pages 41, 43, 46, and "the Jareer Weyne of today did not have a special status", also on page 46, the Jareer bard had clarified the point in a flurry of oral literature much earlier than the author's published work:

Tiro ii Tagoog ii Tacab leeyma gaaro
Tiinteeya hunkeedaa leegu Tiiksahaa![27]

Translation:

We are unmatchable in Number, and strength in production
But we (Jareer) are alienated (persecuted) due to the
(distinctiveness) of our hair (ethnicity as Jareer).

Aadeey ilmihiisoo Itaaliya joogo
Onor ii Onoraato Eed loo helimaayo. [28]

Translation:

As long as Aadeey's (Aden's) children are studying on scholarship in Italy
Onor and Onorato (Italian colonialists) remain blameless (fulfilling their part of the bilateral interests).

In another stanza, the same poet throws a consolation verse to the Jareer community after displeasure with the first president's disregard to address the agony of the Bantu community.

158

Ismaan Ilmihiisaa Istuudiyo Aasti
Isticmaarka Ilaahaa kaaga Aargudaayo

Translation
> Osman solicited Scholarships for his offspring (so expect no remedy from him) And Allah will reward you against the colonial mistreatments

Apparently, as we can grasp from the sentiments of the victims of the first civilian government's neocolonialist policy, what Gassim describes as "decent parliamentary president... His valid role of adviser to the government and the National Assembly was very much appreciated," is contrarily described by a section of the community as "indecent, cold, inactive, ineffective and politically shortsighted."[29] And by observing Mariam Arif Gassim's discourse in another statement remarking, "and president Aden was looking the political equilibrium of the country only from the Darood /Hawiye angle,"[30] is in itself a satisfactory evidence of the first President's ineptitude and political shortsightedness.

As the leader of the nation, and as a "decent parliamentary President," the head of state should have been beyond the "Darood/Hawiye" rhetoric, and should have in essence developed political maturity with a national focus instead. His imprudence and sheer myopic political vision are also discussed in Dualeh:

> The 1960 Somali State, through the fault of President Aden Abdulle Osman, and his southern supporters, was clearly built on unjust edifice...When Somali history is finally written, President Aden Abdulle Osman and not President Mohamed Siad Barre, as some people erroneously believe, would shoulder responsibility for the agony, death and destruction that emanated from his deliberate historical error. Unfortunately for Siad Barre, he inherited President Aden Abdulle Osman's unjust legacy... Unfortunately for the Somali people, President Aden Abdulle Osman was neither a visionary nor a great nationalist.[31]

Through his unwise action as the first President of the newly independent Somali Republic, Aden Abdulle Osman, has sown the seeds of disenchantment and disintegration of the embryonic Somali State. His action was a setback to the vigorous Somali nationalism and its aspirations to unite all Somali territories. It sent the wrong signals to the other territories that were not part of the union. The signal was, "Don't join us."[32]

With the emergence of new claims and criticism, this study opens a long overdue version about the hidden subtlety of the first president. The new version of diatribe and discourse should therefore be deemed fair audience by any scholar exploring the nature of democracy the first administration practiced, particularly the covert attitude of the first president against the rights of the Jareer ethnic community, and his leniency towards the colonial regime. But when all is said and done, it is academically, historically as well as socially shameful and hypo-critical to attempt an exoneration of the moral guilt of the incumbent while crucifying the lower ranks in his court as is often done in the is-sue of the Somali civilian regimes. It has become almost a tradition for certain scholars to condemn and criticize corruption and embezzlement by the officials of the state administrations while embarking on exalta-tion and glorification of the incumbent at the helm of the same graft-ridden institution.

As SYL executive member and as President of the Republic, the politician turned agrarian committed blunders, particularly in plotting against the Jareer people, by imposing and nominating non-Jareer can-didates in Jareer-dominated constituencies, on SYL ticket, and subse-quently rigging the votes against the will of the Jareer majority.[33] This attitude of 'highway robbery on a large scale' does not make the in-cumbent or anyone in his bandwagon pioneers of a people-driven de-mocracy in the country. Often the first government's system is erroneously purported by a section of the Somali society and even possibly scholarship as a democratic institution led by a democratic leader. But the various communities of a society look at their leader from different angles, and if some portray the first president as democratic, then oth-ers see him from the opposite perspective. Jileec nationalist philosophy aside, the Jareer do not see their first leader and his administration as bringing any change from the colonial rule, but instead reshaped it to look neocolonialist. His system of governance was covertly operating under the aegis of clanism and ethnocentrism, thus "ethnocracy" should be a more convenient term.

For instance, the constituents in this poetic verse gave an aspirant of a parliamentary seat on SYL ticket a strong message of disapproval because they wanted to elect one of their own into parliament:

Dambartii la nuugi aa la Doorahaa
Waa Diidi Dayuuro mi'iigu Dageeyso.[34]

Translation:
> We are in favor of electing one of our own
> We reject to be landing zone for an airplane (foreigner).

The aspirant was exasperated by the message and publicly talked of the importance of his vote in the presidential election, and therefore his assurance of unlimited support [by] the President and the party (SYL) "ad ogni costo", at any cost; come what may. Finally, when the votes were cast and the SYL candidate was nowhere near victory, the returning officers from the people's opposition party, the (SNC) Somali National Congress, were thrown out of the counting room,[35] thousands of voting cards in favor of the opposition were sneaked out and burnt,[36] while the results were announced prematurely in favor of the SYL, before even opening most of the ballot boxes returned from voting stations heavily populated by the opposition.[37] However, this is just one example of numerous cases of rigging and electoral injustice which the President's party and men immorally sought office, but the enumeration of them all is a matter that will be discussed elsewhere.

Another sober contention in Gassim's excessive commendation of Osman suggests that a diplomatic debacle, as delved in the author's own words, "Prime Minister Abdirashid signed the military assistance agreement without neither (sic) informing nor (sic) consulting the President"[38] could have been avoided and handled with the maturity it deserved had the President shown loyalty, absolute integrity and a sound atmosphere of working relationship between him and his administration. The kind of discrepancy Gassim envisaged uncovers "the precarious political divide at the top and the irresponsibility with which crucial national issues were prone to barren nomado-politica (Hassan Maanlaawe), under the "weak leadership traits in the person of the first president," Sheikh Hassan Suleen.

After independence, in 1961, the U.S International Cooperation Administration conducted a study in the Inter-riverine, coded (Inter-River Economic Exploration). According to the report, the aim was "to evaluate the potential productive capacity of the Inter-River Area of the Somali Republic."[39] The experts assessed the area as capable of improving the livelihood of the people in the area:

"The resources per capita are relatively high. The ratio between the population and the potential resources is such that the per capita income could rise to a level at which people can live fairly well and even begin the processes of saving... Any investment in physical plant must be accompanied by an active, vigorous educational program. A combination of developing the latent skills and the natural resources in the Inter-River Area could provide a backbone of economic stability for the Republic. It is stressed throughout this report that both skills and facilities must be upgraded concurrently...[40]
The report assesses the economic potential of charcoal and says:
"If charcoal production is conservatively and systematically carried on under appropriate management, it will bring an income which can partially pay for the development of the project."[41]

The dating of this study falls in the presidential tenure of Aden Abdulle Osman. The report reminded one of a discussion in mid '70s between Hagi Bashir (a former minister?) of the Majeerteen sub-clan, his right-hand man nicknamed 'Lugo-god' and Hagi Abdulkadir Eno. Hagi Bashir contracted Hagi Eno for the rehabilitation and renovation works of some of his property in the capital. The venue was Hagi Bashir's residence in Mogadishu, on the Shabelle-Km 4 road, between Cinema El-Nassar and ex-Fiera Ground. As the political history revealed, Hagi Bashir disclosed the unexpected, "If not for Aden Adde, the agrarian people and the entire country would have been prosperous." Hagi Eno asked for explication. Hagi Bashir replied, "Several investments were ready but the president would not approve." Hagi Eno again asked, "Why?." Hagi Bashir responded, "They were Americans and the President was pro-Italian." Hagi Eno contributed ironically, "Or development was being denied for the Jareer." Hagi Bashir admitted, "That was obviously there."

According to Osman Kamula Mofi, after meetings with some top Kenyan officials in July - August, 1962 in Mogadishu,[42] Aden Abdulle and the entire Somali government officials' hatred of the Jareer people increased. Mofi recounts, "Sackings of the very few Jareer officers in the army and in the police forces were unprecedented while the massive transfers of the junior staff were absolutely uncalled for."[43] The old Mofi recalls the untimely summons of the two or three remaining Bantu officers: "The late Omar Abdulle used to be under continuous harassment though he resisted till his unjustified sacking by Siad Barre."[44]

Aden Abdulle's anti-Jareer sentiments and neo-colonialist attitude, as evidenced above, are supported by Hagi Bashir's statement in the precedence. Significantly, apart from Mofi and the Jareer poets, the other sources are non-Jareer Somalis of diverse ethnic background; Darood, Isaq and Hawiye. Former ambassador Mohamed Osman Omar's volume *Road to Zero* reveals more on Somalia's first civilian administration.

Giving me some insights into the colonial and post-colonial politics before his resettlement in the U.S.A, ex- Police Colonel Omar Abdulle was of the opinion that "it was due to Aden Abdulle's political failure, indecision and excessive pro-Italianism that mainly contributed to the disintegration and mistrust among the members of the SYL party, the government and the Somali people as a whole." The aptly 'democrati-cized' Aden Abdulle was practicing in the dark, according to the elite, a policy and personal ideology only Abraham Lincoln could practice in public, though similarities remain vivid, while differences need not be ignored.

Former U.S. President Abraham Lincoln supported the freedom of the Negroes, as multiple Grammy Award winner Stevie Wonder re-lates in a song, "...And the leader with a pen, who signed his name to free all men, was a white man."[45] But according to independent thinker, Professor Ali Mazrui, the same Lincoln was of the notion "...that blacks and whites did not really 'belong' to the same Republic."[46] In the So-mali case, although Aden Abdulle did not support Bantu/Jareer free-dom (dissimilarity), but on the contrary upheld colonial laws and en-actments regarding acquisition and expropriation of their land. The first President's silence over the Jareer grievance amounted to his de-nial as their representative; within the concerns of his interest-based moral obligations, they did not indeed 'belong' to the same republic as the other citizens in the country. If anything, he sustained their effec-tive alienation and neglected to seek remedy to the Italian atrocities against the Jareer community

However, to the majority of the people, nationally and internation-ally, Siad Barre's misdeeds and dictatorial hegemony by far overshad-owed the trace of the mistakes made in the civilian regimes. But as the fact remains, all administrations, civilian or military, have to take re-sponsibility of their actions. Of course there are differences in the degrees of moral and material devastation which the Jileec administrations have caused to the Bantu community, but the bottom-line of the argument is that pragmatically all the post-colonial leaderships have, in multiple ways than mentioned, repressed the indigenous Jareer people into the submission of *"sheria ya mwenye nguvu mpishe!"*[47] (roughly meaning "the law that 'might is right!' ")

In this framework, and according to the nomadic philosophy, a political party was established as a modern instrument replicating clan representation at the national level. The clan system, which functions as the law-making institution at the rural society by *'xeer'* and *'dhaqan'*, (customary law and tradition) was transposed into political party with a look of urban modernity. But by so doing they could not eclipse the fact that "[I]n moving from one group to another an individual generally brings with him certain inclinations, sentiments, attitudes and values, that he has acquired in the group from which he comes,"[48] giving attribute to the nomadization of the political culture and the economic behavior of the country. The conceptualization pertinent to the first regime was its misapprehension or rather misinterpretation of what Gaetano Mosca theorizes as a relationship developed between the ruler and the ruled, as opposed to dominance by the ruling elite over the masses.

After defeating Aden Abdulle Osman in a presidential election in 1967, new President (former Prime Minister) Abdirashid Ali Sharmarke did not prove any better than his predecessor. In fact the situation deteriorated. Heavy rural migration resulted in urban population pressure and the culture of nomadic parasitism; wanting to live better without contribution of labor to the economy. The administrative officials were in office to misappropriate public funds in preparation for the upcoming parliamentary election in what Abdi Samatar accurately termed "a political gamble", that was also understandable from an artist's song aired from Radio Mogadishu:

> Dibutaati inaan noqdaa baan Doonayaa
> Dawladda anka qeybgalaa baan Doonayaa
> Ama waa ley Dooran
> Ama Daadku iqaadye.[49]

Translation:

> I am set to be a Deputy
> I desire to participate in the (forthcoming) government;
> So, either elected shall I be

Or swept away in the torrential rains (of political gambling) shall I be.

The connotation suggests participation in the government as a crucial goal because that would put oneself in a position where one could siphon public funds for one's individual and ethnic gains. Come the next parliamentary elections, certain ethnic groups had a sizeable number of political parties. The biggest ridicule followed soon when almost all the opposition parliamentarians crossed the carpet over to the ruling party, undermining multi-party-ism in favor of a one dominant party in Somali parliament. The reason behind the shift of loyalty from one's party to the ruling body is calculated on pure personal interest. More explicitly put, it was an approach by which an individual parliamentarian 'sold' himself off to the most powerful man in the country in exchange for an appointment to a cabinet position where one could undetectably drain public coffers dry. This fashion of governance which was duplicated from milking one's own she-camel at will, began during the first civilian regime and continued throughout all Somalia's post-colonial administrations.

Before the new members could adjust to achieve their goals, the most unexpected (to some) happened as President Abdirashid Ali Sharmarke was shot dead by one of his kinsmen while on a tour in Las Anod, probably paying the price for the electoral irregularities. Inter-parliamentary rifts and wrangles ensued regarding a successor, although the constitution was clear about succession and its legal modalities. The death of the President did not only increase the insatiable lust and avarice of the pastoral parliamentarians, but it also emerged that claims of dynasty were deteriorating the situation as certain pastoralists thought it was their prerogative right to lead the country.

From dubious democracy to dictatorship

During the crisis over the president's death, another class of the same pastoral culture but of different political dogma was closely monitoring the situation of the parliamentarians. General Mohamed Siad Barre and a group of his army colleagues took over power in a bloodless military coup d'etat. Here opens another chapter of Somali life and brings in a historical change that did not only subscribe all the citizens to an abrupt nomadic configuration but also to ruralization of urban life. Mariam Arif Gassim presents the episode amazingly but analytically:

"The "ruralization" process was accelerated by the recruitment of pastorals into the Somali National Army and Police Force. In a relatively short time after the takeover, the majority of government high-ranking officials were of pastoral origin."[50]

Interpreting the situation from its nomadic mentality, Abdalla Mansur also demonstrates the mayhem conspicuously in his assumption that "The state property which consisted in great part of foreign aid became the best "Mandeeq" to raid."[51]

The coup leaders, *'Golaha Sare ee Kacaanka'* the Supreme Revolutionary Council, through excessive media coverage and nationalistic rhetoric, won the heart of the masses. They announced zero tolerance for graft as they put the cabinet of the civilian government in prison. The civilian constitution was shelved and a new charter was drafted and approved by the SRC.

Several episodes preceded the military coup. President Sharmarke and his Prime Minister, Mohamed Hagi Ibrahim Egal, were not comfortable with Siad Barre, who had been nominated as the Commander-in-Chief of the Somali Armed Forces by former Prime Minister Abdirizak Hagi Hussein, during the tenure of the first president Aden Abdulle Osman. He was seen as a little educated old officer, compared to a better trained younger generation in the army, mainly graduates from Italian military academies; some of them specializing in military administration.

Barre was also sympathetic to former President Aden Abdulle Osman in his presidential race against Abdirashid Ali Sharmarke, and when the former was defeated, Barre's survival as the top-most army man in the land was hanging on the balance. He had a good degree of trust and understanding with Yassin Nur Hassan, a strong Majerten politician in the cabinet, but Barre was sensing his imminent troubles from the distance. "He realized later the mistake he had made by siding with first President Aden Abdulle Osman who was neither a strategist nor an effective role-player in the political game."[52]

Signs of a coup in the making were flickering far in the political backyard, but the civil government was extremely absorbed in the milking of "Mandeeq" (the she-camel that symbolizes Somali independence). The death of Sharmarke has also given ample time to Barre and his colleagues for final touches to their milestone operation. Many of the pastoral ministers and parliamentarians, for their separate individual interests, were attempting to manipulate the constitution by harassing Sheikh Mukhtar, the President of the National Assembly from the Reewing/Digil-Mirifle community. According to some analysts, rumors of a coup were downplayed; underestimating the underlying potential in Siad Barre's little education.

But even so, the coup situation was an all-Jileec affair, considering the composition of the players in both camps: members of the civilian administration and officers leading the army coup. Neither the 25-member SRC nor their nominated cabinet members had a member of the autochthonous Jareer community. Not only that, the Jareer suffered the first casualty of the Supreme Revolutionary Council by having several of their top officers relieved of their duties in the forces.[53]

But the worst had to come for other communities when within one year of the Revolution members of the senior coup leaders were arraigned in military tribunal, court-martialed and condemned to death by firing squad. It was clear symptoms of Barre's tyrannical behavior and political doom in Somali social life, but most of all an effective means of airing a message of ruthlessness to his colleagues in particular and to Somalis in general. Many zealous 'revolutionary' workers demonstrated in the streets of the capital in support of the death sentence by the military court against the three accused, chanting: "Qoorsheel Qoorta-gooya; Gabeeyre Geedka Geeya" – Korshel, cut his throat; Gaveire, execute him by firing squad.

With General Salad Gaveire Kedie and General Mohamed Ainanshe Guled, Abdulkadir Dhel Abdi, was also to die by firing-squad. Mystery surrounds the alleged coup attempt; whether it was fabricated to avenge personal vendetta or otherwise, is not yet a matter open to public knowledge. It left a very painful multidimensional social enigma. Very few, if any, are in possession of the plain truth regarding the nature of the treason case instituted against the three. It is not even clear whether the source of the information was Barre's national security apparatus or whether the KGB, numerous and close to Barre at the time, had an involvement in phone bugging or in any other high-tech surveillance. But the news bulletin from Radio Mogadishu, partly read:

Maxamed Ceynaanshe Guuleed, Salaad Gabeeyre Kediye, Cabdulqaadir Dheyl Cabdi, saddexdaba, maxkamad militari ah waxay ku xukuntay in la daldalo, hantidoodana dawladda la wareegto,

Translation:

> A military court has found Mohamed Ainanshe Guled, Salad Gaveire Kediye and Abdulkadir Dhel Abdi, guilty of an attempted coup. The court has sentenced them to death and the dispossession of their property by the government.

The execution of prominent members of the SRC (Supreme Revolutionary Council) by firing squad was a pre-notification of successive events of devastating nature that were to come in the future. In later years many citizens had to meet their fate by firing squad, including 10 clergymen, executed in one morning.

In spite of the colossal damage and the message of tyranny, the national political ideology was driven into a new subscription rhymed to the heavy drumbeats of Scientific Socialism, locally called *'Hantiwadaagga Cilmiga ku-Dhisan'*, although Barre himself was not known for knowledge of any science, including quality military science.

The political atmosphere had an impact on the lore and literature of the socio-political arena because *'geela'* (the camel) and *'heesaha kacaanka'* (revolutionary songs) took the trend of the ordinary discourse in the offices and in normal social life. Everybody had to be a member of *'bulsho kacaan'* revolutionary society, and one way of admitting self-subscription to such a society was by showing one's loyalty either by praising that discourse or by listening to it very often. Accordingly, one would not claim membership to *'bulsho kacaan'* wholeheartedly if one was not affluent in *'heesaha kacaanka'* and *'suugaanta geela'* camel literature, or more precisely, all that appertains to the nomadic culture.

Knowledge of the camel complex was quite necessary because it was the culture of *'Aabe'* Siyaad, the father, and his entire Darod Jileec kinship. It would perfectly decide one's acceptance and place as a 'child' of the nation and a 'pupil' of (*macallinka kacaanka*) the teacher of the revolution. After accepting this rhetoric intuitively, the loyalty had to be pronounced also outwardly, thus traditionalizing the singing of praise songs of the 'father' every morning by adults and youngsters alike, at the start of work and class respectively. A number of delays to the routine would put the "wrong-doer" into the undesirable category of *'dib-u-socod'* or reactionary to the cause of the revolution and hence attract a negative consequence such as sacking from one's job or suspension from school.

With the Scientific Socialism came the establishment of various para-statal institutions. Notorious among these were the Agricultural Development Corporation (ADC), the Somali National Cooperative Union, Ente Nazionale di Commerce – E.N.C. (National Agency for Commerce) and others responding to political and tribal purposes.

The Ente Nazionale di Commercia (ENC) was 'reputable' for hoarding goods and manipulating market prices by creating artificial shortages in the importation and supply of essential commodities – sugar, cooking oil, wheat flour, and other consumables. The society had to respond with integrity as *'bulsho kacaan'* with silence and by queuing for the commodities in the wee hours of the night in front of their respective supply/retail stations before these open in the morning. A Jareer poetess could not hold her anger and disgust over the inconvenience the society was undergoing as a result of these long queues to which the 'father' of the nation had no immediate solution. She communicated her disenchantment in this canto, with the first line explaining the nature of the quandary and the second asking 'the teacher of the revolution' why it was that essential commodities were getting scarce:

Sokor ii Sariiraan Saf oogu jirnaaye
Seergooye Siyaadoow Saan maxaaw ahaay?[54]

Translation:
We are queuing for (basic commodities) - sugar and cooking-oil Siad, the one wise in policy-making, what is it that we are experiencing?

The Somali script

The introduction of the Somali script, just like the clan-based monuments, was celebrated as a major revolutionary, nationalistic achievement through *'hantiwadaagga cilmiga ku qotoma'* meaning scientifically driven socialism. It was in fact an achievement, cumulatively to the subscribers of the culture of the camel complex. It was a bright opportunity for the imposition of their language and virtuously their dialect on the masses at large. It was the decision of the Supreme revolutionary Council, and in accordance with *'mabaadii'da kacaanka'* meaning the principles of the Revolution, to have an official national language whose derivative influence from the camel culture and the central/northern dialect have been unanimous on the determination of its purity.

It was a bright opportunity because the urbanized camel culture had at their disposal all the necessary devices and avenues prerequisite to it, from policy and planning, to implementation and adaptation. However, the core incentive lay in status planning, making the language official. More explicitly, even if this particular language and/or dialect did not have functional base as *lingua franca* among the poly-ethnic nations of clans, it could be raised to a higher status at the na-tion-state level. By being at the hegemonic rank of the state, the policy-making pastorals did not only design the thematic substance in plan-ning, but by doing so brought for legalization the corpus from their own dialect, so that the agrarian and agro-pastoral southerners would be obliged to transform *hastily* their cultural corpus to the *"superordi-nated"* aesthetics of the northern nomadic pastoral commandments.

The main hidden agenda, as would be evident later, was not the nationalist step advertised through the mass media but to nomado-culturalize the whole system of governance as well as society at large. Subsequently, they had to conceive a plan of massive urban-implantation of their rural people, with unlimited participation in all the social activities, particularly desirable posts for accessing easy pub-lic money. The agenda of the Somalization was set according to the understanding of the pastoral elite that "formal language policy mak-ing...plays a crucial role in the distribution of power and resources in all societies ..."[55] Obviously, the role would fall in a theoretical dis-agreement with Renan's idea of language as an effective instrument in civic nationalization because this, contrarily, was national-ethnicization!

Whether the ruling group was aware or not, it was borrowing heavily from Italian communist Antonio Gramsci,[56] whose work sug-gested hegemony as a system in which the ruling elite would influence the rest of the society or classes to adopt or assimilate their own cul-tural and moral values. Perhaps it eluded the great communist thinker that communities of diverse cultures and background cannot be of the same moral and cultural values because, as Kanwar Mathur defines, "[t]o be truly part of a culture, one must grow up in it."[57]

A powerful ideological force was put to work. Just as occupation-ists and colonialists have imposed their language and culture on the indigenous population for colonial gains, Barre and his ruling kinship were designing in advance a formula with the same aim and objective, but in a different context. Put in simple form, it was a means of maintaining parity between the prospective rural migrants and the rest of the non-nomadic urban culture. The scheme was aimed at reinforcing the philosophy of cultural domination by the former against the rest of the masses.

The context of this argument is not only to be seen in the linguistic form of the Somali language as spoken in the wider sense, but also the effect of standardization of one language or dialect of a language as spoken by a group who were in control of the process of its standardization. In addition, the status in cultural and linguistic mobility given to the speakers of that language or dialect as "official", in contrast to speakers of other languages or dialects of that same language, bears an authentic clan definition. The economic aims and achievements underlying the impact of acquisition and standardization, moral vulgarity and decline in social values, need to be examined wisely before drawing a definitive conclusion to decide the rate of success of that language.

From another view, the effect of the Somali orthography on the alienation and degradation of other living languages and cultures in the country need also to be studied carefully in order to make a constructive assessment of the persistent disadvantage variables. My linguistic reference here is quite separate from mere accent, which is seen as "only a difference in pronunciation."[58] For a better comparative understanding of their intricacies, David Abercrombie classifies:

> Accent and dialect are words which are often used vaguely but which can be given more precision by taking the first to refer to the characteristics of the medium only, while the second refers to characteristics of language as well.[59]

Janet Holmes makes it even more elucidating; though her referral language is English, our assumption is in Somali:

> The dialect we grace with the name Standard English is spoken in many different accents. But, as illustrated in the discussion of regional dialects, there are also many standard Englishes.[60]

Although Holmes seems to have fallen into the trap of Somali myth of monolingual society, an embarrassing trap many unsuspecting scholars trampled into,[61] I agree with her in the fact that in language standardization or planning, "Numerical dominance is not always what counts, however, political power is the crucial factor,"[62] and that is the factor which, in the Somali social domain, determined the linguistic bias of standardizing a nomad's language and dialect for adoption by all other social cultures regardless of their own mother tongues.

Commenting on the work of Hodge and Kress, Coupland and Jaworski write, "For them, language styles have symbolic meanings that represent different positions in social conflicts, such as class interests and associated power struggles."[63] By that note, the standardization of one dialect against the other, or in global terms, the nationalization of one language at the disadvantage of others, is in conformity with the avoidance of the cultural diversity prevailing in Somali social life; in other words an act of linguistic imperialism or the domination of the tribal language of one group in power against others who lack it. Self-endorsement of a culture and language in which one was not born means the acceptance of the devaluation of one's cultural values and identity to a subordinate class, and this was the hidden vision of '*Aabaha Ummadda Soomaaliyeed*' - the father of the Somali nation/people, and his henchmen towards other cultures. The subject is beyond the coverage of this chapter and will be dealt with elsewhere in the course of the study of my EdD in Applied Linguistics and TESOL.

The Cold War

Somalia had a constantly brewing problem with Ethiopia for centuries, over territorial rule and accusations and counter-accusations of expansionism. Barre, viewing the Soviet Union's growing interest in gaining bilateral relations with Ethiopia, felt discontent. With signs of discomfort within the army and earlier promises and aspiration of the myth of 'Greater Somalia', he had to find a way out of his simmering political hotbed.

The Ogaden movement, Western Somali Liberation Front, intensified its subversive guerilla warfare before the situation degenerated into a horrific conventional war of massive man and material damage on both countries, which make up the poorest of the world. As the Jareer population can remember, the 1977 Somalia - Ethiopia war was one of the worst periods ever for the community. The youth were dis-

172

criminatively conscripted and sent to the warfront for a country where they never enjoyed equality, human dignity, liberty, or good social life and status.

The war bore humiliating impact on Somalia, politically, economically and militarily. It had further complicated to worse the entire social infrastructure which Barre's Scientific Socialism had aggravated. After the formidable Somali troops had overrun the Ethiopian forces in an overwhelming military convention, disgruntling them into disarray and pushing them to less than a hundred miles to the capital Addis, Russian, East German and Cuban troops had to save the day for Ethiopia and rescue the new Soviet ally. The stronger communist forces, with their more sophisticated military arsenal sent the advancing Somali forces into a quick retreat. Literally, Somalia defeated Ethiopia on one on one basis, but the Soviet and Cuban troops ultimately won the war for Ethiopia.

Not surprising enough, the Somali officers met some of their Russian trainers and advisers upon their retreat after ceasefire. According to Colonel Mahdi Mohamed Issa (then a Captain), one Russian expert told him, "You made us proud militarily, but ashamed us politically."[64] The senior Russian officer's statement had strong connotations with mixed reaction; one was the 'victory' of the Russian trained Somalis equipped with their Soviet-made military arsenal devastating American investment in Ethiopian army over the years; the second was that diplomatically, the Somalis shunned the Soviet proposal of a federal system, bringing together several of its allies within the neighborhood of the Horn.

As Lewis said, "Siad's mother was Ogaden and her clan looked to him for support."[65] Accordingly, in Somalia, the war was justified at twofold, nationally as well as ethnically. Even if the ultimate goal recapturing the Ogaden was not achieved, at least Siad's affinity to the Ogaden was paramount as the wider Darood clan and the entire Somali clans witnessed Barre's sacrifice to his mother's people.

The return from the war, or the psychology of a forced defeat, has tremendously changed the philosophy of the army and suspicion arose over a coup attempt by some officers. They were rounded up and sentenced to death while others managed to escape. The result was the founding of the Somali Salvation Democratic Front led by current (2008) interim President Abdullahi Yusuf Ahmed who at that time was a Colonel in the army. They were based in Ethiopia and received support from Mengistu Haile Mariam's government. It was reciprocal to Somalia's assistance to several anti-Ethiopian liberation movements such as the Eritrea People's Liberation Front, Tigre People's Liberation Front and the Western Somali Liberation Front. The WSLF became inactive after the war. Citing Compagnon, Cassanelli notes, "Organized opposition to Siad Barre's autocratic rule began in the aftermath of the abortive Ogaden campaign and continued to grow through the 1980s until virtually every region and clan had produced an anti-Barre movement."[66]

The cold war played a tangible role in extending the survival of Barre's political life. The departure of the Soviet Union and the socialist ideology had brought to an abrupt stop the flow of military aid, but the Cold War opened another door. The US, which had lost Ethiopia due to Colonel Mengistu Haile Mariam's socialist policies, needed to counter-balance the Soviet presence in the Horn and in the vicinity of the Gulf for easy surveillance of the naval movement in the area and along the Indian Ocean. The Americans were most welcome to utilize the Berbera port as a military base as long as they had the willingness to pump millions of US dollars into Barre's government coffers.

In effect, the relationship resulted in the creation of a new class of elite. Illiterates and skilled drivers in public employment were suddenly turned into prominent business elites as importers and exporters. They even benefited from (*canshuur-dhaaf*) 'duty-free' for their imports. This is the group which Compagnon describes as a "stratum of wealthy and corrupt businessmen (many of whom were penniless in the 1970s) arose from all the clans."[67] They were accorded special status because their recommendation letters to access huge and unsecured bank loans were accompanied with a letter from the higher offices indicating or rather instructing the bank "*Ka aamus*" meaning 'do not ask' the bearer to return the loan. The arrogance of this group has crossed all margins of courtesy as some of them intimidated top public functionaries and even physically assaulted diplomats, cabinet ministers as well as ordinary citizens at will (See Abdulahi A. Osman 2007 and Mohamed O. Omar 1992).

The West, particularly the US and the Arab countries, have saturated Siad Barre with funds under various categories of names, from loans to grants. Within a very short period of time, many UN agencies and international NGOs embarked on the initiation of multi-million dollar projects, some of them political with no feasibility or accountability of any nature. Bloom and Ottong agree:

"In Africa many development projects have been launched by governments who want to favor sections of society, regardless of the strict
technological or economic consideration, so there are many uneco-
nomic airlines and other prestige projects."[68]

So, for their apparent advantage, there had to be created many
prestigious projects to reward the parasitic loyals, after all, the money-
pump was running appropriately through the different pipelines, for
adequate supply. The aid funds played magnificent roles, one of them
being "Siad Barre's manipulation of clans against one another."[69] In fact
it was partly this money that played a major role in destabilizing
movements like the SSDF and lured back its officials to very good public and parastatal appointments. The teacher of the Revolution
(*Macallinka Kacaanka*) was ethnic-conscious as much as he was ethnocentric, for a study shows that by 1988 Barre's hometown Gedo had
42% households cultivating on irrigated land, while the entire Middle
Juba region had only 4% in contrast.[70]

The cause of Barre's institutionalized looting was the flow of political money from various sources without the slightest accountability
whatsoever. According to Menkhaus and Craven:

The political interests of the donors – West Germany, Kuwait,
Saudi Arabia and Abu Dhabi - were straightforward. They sought to
use generous quantities of foreign aid to wean the Somali government
away from its close ties to the Soviet Union...

Ultimately what mattered was not whether the projects were good
investments or whether they integrated local and national needs but
whether they satisfied political elite in Mogadishu whose alliance was
sought. High officials in the Somali government were quick to take
advantage.[71]

By taking advantage, the officials did not only suck dry development funds, they even went as far as using their offices and influence
(like their predecessors) to loot privately owned Bantu land in the riverine area. While discussing the phenomenon Farah et al write, "After
independence, a new class of Somali entrepreneurs began acquiring
land for irrigation, using their government connections and, if necessary, force, to claim land..."[72]

After the defeat in the Ogaden war, and with a fund flow from numerous international sources, an internal war was waged on Bantu land in the Shabelle and Juba riverine areas. The colonial land laws enacted for the deliberate purpose of expropriating Jareer land, and upheld in the post-independence civilian administrations, were reinforced by Siad Barre's Land Reform Act of 1975 which re-emphasized the ownership of all land by his government, so that he could allocate his clients enough plots right on the bank of the rivers while the owners would work on it as hired squatters. According to Barre and his entire Jileec government, this was the "justice and equality" which the "Blessed Revolution" was born to achieve for its people, specifically the Jileec.

Through these laws, a scenario was created where land alienation projects were implemented under the donor funded national projects, and all to the dismay of the indigenous Jareer land owners. Scholarly studies have revealed the coercion, oppression, persecution and fraudulent formulas employed in the acquisition of the Bantu land. In fact, Barre's men and sections of the pseudo-nobility got engaged in land grabbing competition. And whoever among them that talked of "acquiring" an agricultural land was praised as *"dirac dirac-dhalay"*, which translated means: "brave son of a brave man", a term usually reserved for a notorious looter and a fugitive camel rustler.

In order to stifle and contain the Bantu into a permanent economic vulnerability, Barre established the Agricultural Development Corporation which, controversial to development, had an institutional mandate to purchase all cereal produce at its own fixed rates and sell back to the same producers at inflated prices, because competition was undermined by the existence of the ADC. As Ahmed Q. Ali (2004:166) highlights, "Farmers were ordered to sell all their harvest to the [ADC] agency. The new price was fixed arbitrarily by the agency...Farmers were re-buying their products with tax added" (Emphasis added). Luling reports, "The prices of the ADC were impossibly low, hence farmers to raise money began to switch from grain to other uncontrolled crops."[73] She also notes, "One ex-Italian plantation was owned by the Prime Minister (Jileec outcast), another by the Minister of Foreign Affairs, another by the President's daughter. Two very large ones belonged to Kuwaiti Arabs."[74]

One has to note here that land means to the agriculturalist what livestock means to the pastoralist. But the Somali regimes have not made introduction and enactment of laws classifying livestock as state property, like they made to dispossess the Bantu of their land. Yet when droughts and famine hit some parts of the pastoral regions, the pastoralists and their camels were airlifted in a national rescue campaign and relocated/implanted in the riverine land. It was the collaboration between these pastoral aliens and their kinship in high government positions close to state project funds that encouraged the influence on farm raiding, causing the intensification of expropriation. Sedentary cultivators were shrunk to squatters without legal rights to their ancestral land, by means of forgery and fraudulent title deeds acquired by the well-connected total men of the day.

"No equality for the 'Adoon'"

A community which has been denied its rights for centuries and exposed only to suppression and deliberate under-development cannot suddenly rise up and race against another that enjoyed unlimited opportunities for sacrosanctness throughout the centuries, when the former was undergoing all kinds of stigmatization and the historical hardships of time. The Jareer, like other oppressed peoples elsewhere, were tolerating sequenced systems of oppression of varied degrees and of multi-ethnic/multi-racial domination. In his essay about black oppression in America, Aldon Morris imparts, "Basic to all such systems is a ruling hegemonic consciousness and the denial to the oppressed of important rights and privileges routinely enjoyed by the dominant group."[75] The same was taking place in Somalia; not against racial contrast of white against black, but black against black!

The Jareer/Bantu in Somalia has not known an easy life like his counterpart Somali Jileec 'brother'. Whether free-born/autochthonous, or whether manumitted or fugitive ex-slave, the Bantu/Jareer were all lumped as slaves and suppressed at the bottom line of the social strata. They have been denied economic advancement, political participation as well as social equality in the academics. In the burden of these societal mischiefs, it couldn't be simple for this community to register and legalize the ownership of their land, although they had not had ownership - or expropriation-related phenomena prior to the Italian colonial occupation and the subsequent neocolonialist civil regimes of post-independence preceding the dictatorial rule of Mohamed Siad Barre.

Under Italian and Somali rules, the Bantu person was situated in a situation much contrastable to Derrick Bell's[76] postulation of American

177

society, that it would be highly unlikely for a white court to exercise any kind of justice unless it suited white interest. This could accurately be said of the Jareer situation, only that in the Somali instance, the Jileec pastoral Somalis take the place of the 'white-court'. Seeking remedial recourse from the law could often worsen the matter. It has been evidenced severally that expropriation victims who sought redress frequently ended up in jail. (See the survey chapters on Jareer abuse in this volume.)

While still within the context of this discussion, I contend against reports of scholars and others who seem to purport Barre's 'equality and justice' policy. Many have the misconception that Barre had introduced policies, laws and acts to uplift the status of the Jareer.[77] Obviously, this is not just a misconception but also a miscalculated ideological error against Barre, notorious for his disgust of the community just like his predecessors. A clarification of this, despite the ample evidence in this and other chapters, must be made for more comprehensive understanding.

First of all, there was no Jareer who ever occupied a ministerial position or any other top administrative office in any government [in] Somalia, from the corrupt neocolonialist civil regimes to Barre the dictator. So that circle was a restricted area the Jareer Bantu was not allowed to approach; it was again an all-Jileec affair.

Second, there was no single Jareer citizen in the Supreme Revolutionary Council but, to everybody's knowledge there was Tumal/Midgan – Madhiban representation in the SRC and in a manifold of other capacities in Barre's administration and before him. The Tumal, Madhibaan, Midgaan, Yaxar are outcasts I discussed earlier in Chapter One. In spite of the ranks of friendship, Samatar, the top outcast official in the SRC, was suffering from that social inferiority – if not him, members of his community certainly were. For Barre to acquire Samatar's and other outcast officials' loyalty, he had to lift up their inferior social status so that their peers and juniors would accept the delegation of duties and top-down instructions as given by the outcast superiors.

Third, the Jareer, for all known social purposes, are despised, oppressed, taunted, and derogated as inferior, but are not the outcast accused of feeding on decayed animal meat or contracting unpropitious marriage with undesirable women from low women (whatever these mean to anyone!). They are, in the social stratification hierarchy, at a low level of the strata but not as outcasts. Therefore, in a sense, equality would 'uplift' the outcasts into the social strata of whichever level, where the Jareer had already been situated – albeit the low level. At this stage, we see a vertical status mobility of the outcasts (Jileec group) but not a reciprocal accommodation for the Jareer up the other rungs of the ladder near where the 'noble' claiming Jileec people were situated.

Fourth, due to the kind of bias in equality and mobility, a Jareer *'Laashin'* poet commented as to evaporate the misconception of a status lift for the Jareer and enlightens:

"Jilac ii Jareer Jimeeye, Janaraal Jaalle Siyaad"
Jugaa ku Jirtee, ma Jiro Janaraal Jareer eh.[78]

Translation:
Comrade General Siad's (misinterpreted) equality of the Jareer and the Jileec Lacks even the vaguest sincerity, as there exists not a Jareer General.

I think the verse and the above elaboration about Siad Barre's equality rhetoric should be sufficient argument disproving the existence of any equality, in any sense, of Jareer and Jileec, except in the Qu'ranic sense which is hardly in practice in Somalia. The rush for Bantu land and the unabated looting scheme should further provide substantial evidence of declining equality as powerful outcasts were among the expropriators, raiders and acquirers of Bantu land. One good example of Barre's philosophy of equality for the Bantu is exposed here: A Jareer Colonel was proposed for promotion on merit after a long period of service in that rank. A general (deceased during the Somali National Reconciliation Conference) close to Siad Barre went with him to the Presidency with delight and explained to the President in detail of the achievement of the Jareer Colonel in his military career, reminding the president that they had previously talked about the issue and relevant papers prepared to the effect.

The late General concluded with a request to the President to promote the colonel to the rank of General as Siad Barre frowned at the embarrassing silence, because the request and the briefing took place in the presence of the Jareer Colonel. It was clear to the Jareer Colonel that although the General had discussed the issue with the president, he had not explained to him that the concerned officer was of ethnic Bantu origin. Like someone from a long slumber, but with a cunning smile, the President retorted, "Please, advise me to do for the officer whatever else on earth, but don't advise me to decorate him with the rank of general."

Traditions of this nature are also related about Samatar opposing similar promotions recommended for long serving Jareer officers. Therefore, the purpose of equality was to serve those who would sit at the same table with Barre and other high ranking officials of his pastoral group, all within the same cohort of Jileec composition, but not the Jareer or 'Adoon' who are kept at bay and away from the decision-making circles.

In urban areas, the Jareer were subject to discrimination and exploitation. They provide the largest number of technicians, as a result of early grandfathers' migration from the villages in avoidance of conscription and forced labor by the Italian colonists. More often than not, auto-mechanics who maintained cars were imprisoned because they asked for their money days after failure of payment. Masons and building contractors who accomplished their duties were upon completion warned not to risk "rotting"[79] in prison for persistently asking for the balance of their payment. It was clear that Barre's people were "balancing" the burden on the Jareer, whether rural or urban, wherever they might have been in the country.

At the height of frustration and injustice, a group of Jareer people organized themselves and, with assistance and recommendation from insiders, secured an appointment and met Siad Barre one evening in 1985. When he listened to their complaints, together with a few of his aides, he said he knew everything and promised that he would address the problems. Before their departure, he asked whether the Jareer would send fifty cadets to the military academy, but one old man replied, "Jaalle Siad, the learned (Jareer) who have been in the army for about 20 years are not going above the ranks of Major and Colonel, what can you do for them?" The President had no answer, but another appointment would be set on his personal invitation for about six elders from the community. It was held after about eight months but did not bear any fruits.

The suffering escalated. More farms were looted as more donor funds came into the country. Those who were close to '*Maandeeq*' would milk it more often than the others. It was 'every man for himself' in the "Land Rush in Somali…"[80] as "Somalis of certain clans with the support of the state could confiscate land without any due process."[81] The Italian colonists, the post-independence neo-colonialist civilian regimes and the dictatorial rule of Siad Barre, all operated from the ideology of oppressing and distancing the autochthonous Jareer community from the corridors of power in a plot to nullify their aspirations for economic advancement and submerge their ethnic identity. But what followed was worse.

The civil war: doom of Darood dynasty or hollowness of Hawiye hegemony?

Supplement to ethnic-based internal rivalries within the army, the aftermath of the Ogaden war saw the first organized local movement against Siad Barre. The Somali Salvation Democratic Front (SSDF), who belonged to the Majerteen sub-clan of the Darood clan, diverted a colossal quantity of weaponry for use by their movement. Under the leadership of current interim President Abdullahi Yusuf and his kinship, the SSDF was based in Ethiopia and waged its attacks, alongside regular Ethiopian forces, from Ethiopian territory, and captured several Somali towns bordering that country. The hundreds of millions of cold war dollars, later played a great role in seducing and re-attracting the Majerteen on board, some of whom were considered to occupy economically "fertile" (*jaga qoyan*) positions with lots of money to manage, unaccountably. In time, they acquired the legitimacy to join in the looting of public funds and private land grabbing, abandoning their earlier motives that had put them against the lowly educated dictator.

In the north, the Isaq formed their clan movement, the Somali National Movement (SNM), in preparation for secession. In 1988, the SNM waged several attacks on army positions. It experienced a bloody war and large casualties in a civilian massacre. Barre utilized the full force of the army, including aerial bombardment in the most inhuman nature. The agony from that wound and others endured over the decades would later make part of the justification for Isaq desertion from the Somali Republic and their withdrawal from the 1960 unity.

The northern regions were no longer a part of the Republic but were treated as the 'enemy zone'. The military action and the southerners' new discourse of *"xabbadi-keento"* (immigrants brought by the bullet), to their northern brothers and sisters were messages for consideration but the best message was tailored in the Isaqs' response to the southerners as *"xabbadi-sugto"* (those waiting for the bullets). The Isaq were right, although their sociolinguistic discourse might have missed the analysis of a majority of the southerners.

When in the final hours of 1990 the war began in the capital, the Isaqs' prediction was turning imminently into reality. Several clan elders approached Barre to save the 'country' from turmoil but the dictator stood by his word that only by the barrel of the gun he would step down, since that was the formula by which he came and not by election or elders' negotiation. Stubborn and fierce urban militia composed of poorly organized youngsters consisting of *ciyaal-koolo* glue-snuffers, *ciyaal-derbi* street boys and *caseeye* or *baalishle* shoe-shine boys, initially engaged Barre's soldiers for the first few days of the war. It was a cat and mouse sort of street fighting, which quickly signaled the lack of conviction in the President's men. Within three days or so, bodies of Barre's soldiers of the pseudo-nobility were strewn in almost all the main streets of the capital. The regular militia came, reinforced their urban counterparts and finally extruded the vicious dictator from the presidency. He later holed up himself in Garbaharrey, his self-made home village.

The war picture depicted the Hawiye clan against the Darood clan of Siad Barre. It seemed that without Barre in Villa Somalia, the presidential palace, it marked not only the end of the dictator's era, but looked to many like the demise of the last Darood dynasty of almost a quarter of a century. Several attempts by the ousted self-ennobled Darood to retake the capital failed, and Barre took a short sojourn as asylum seeker in Kenya before he was given sanctuary in Nigeria, where he later died with all the disgrace of pastoral dictatorship. It was disgrace in many aspects; that he even sought protection in Jareer lands (Kenya and Nigeria) where his 'nobility' as *Nasab* 'Pure noble' was devalued by his status as asylum seeker under "Adoon" rules away from the land of the 'nobles'.

Although the Hawiye fought and toppled Barre with disgrace, intra-clan feuds, jealousy and lust for power undermined their effort and political ideology, if at all they had any. The song of war calling for the amalgamation of the Hawiye nation to ethnic-cleanse the Darood once and for all, was now futile. The Darood were gone, but the Hawiye proved to be political non-starters of the highest degree, though they could amend the ripped state had they engaged some of the best learned brains they have in the Diaspora. Intra-Hawiye wars proved more detrimental to peace. The lyrics of a clan war song, '*Maanta maanta, maanta Hawiye israacye maanta*' improvised from a national song (*Maanta, maanta, manta, madaxeen banaane manta*) which translated means, 'today we are at liberty' from colonial rule, was implausible. The Hawiye became the first-hand witnesses of their own political and ideological vanity. While the so-called politicians were failing to coop-erate into a consensus, the militia resorted to a massive looting and raping spree in each area they captured from Barre and from each other. Because members of the Hawiye were armed and so 'respected' each other, the unarmed minorities and the oppressed were every mili-tia's easy target.

In the urban areas, the Jareer were forced out of their houses so as to accommodate members of the armed militia. The Reer Xamar and Reer Barawaa communities also suffered drastically under the armed militia. In the riverine zone, mature crops were burnt; grains stored under the ground (*bakaar*) were opened and looted. The militia forced the Jareer villagers out of their houses, gang-raped the women, killed the men and practically "inherited" the farms. Situations were wit-nessed where armed militia announced that a bullet was more costly than the life of the Jareer.[82] On many occasions the Jareer were forced to work without pay on their own farms at gunpoint, while the produce was taken by the Hawiye militiamen. Describing the mayhem in po-etry, a Jareer 'Laashin' said:

> *Basal ii Baraajis Bur-soorne ma haasto*
> *Beerteeya Bexeeysaan baahi oola jiifti.*[83]

Translation:
> I have neither vegetables nor a meager lump of '*soor*' the staple maize-meal
> And I stretch out in hunger while abundant grains grow on my farm.

The only recourse and consolation was sought from God, the Al-mighty, as the tribulations magnified and the armed bandits metamor-phosed the productive villages into slave quarters and death camps. Ahmed's words explain the situation when he imagines, "The villain is more powerful than the victim who must search far afield for mecha-nisms to redress the injustice. The helpless victim, more often than not, resorts to a curse by presenting his/her case to God."[84] In her communication to God, a Jareer poetess produced this verse:

Cariiri adduun ii Ciilaan ku Jiraa
Casiis-Alla-weenaan Ciidankeey ka yeeli [85]

Translation:
> I am submerged in the resentment and oppressiveness of the world I made
> Almighty God my army.

The militia blocked the passage of relief food to the suffering Jareer and Reewing/Digil-Mirifle in the inter-river locations. Even the Jareer urbanites were discriminated against in the feeding camps. Charles Geshekter remarks:

Somali nomads were notoriously prejudicial against these dark skinned people against whom they hurled racial slurs. In 1992, a nurse with the Save the Children Fund was shocked to hear Somalis admit they would "rather see our children starve than feed alongside these smelly Bantu."[86]

While this purports to portray the paradigmatic behavior of "homogeneous" and Islamic society supposed to cater for the needy and the weaker, it seems more indignant when in reality those seeking better treatment in the feeding centers are the cause of all the devastation, since they have been ruling from the time of the so-called civilian regimes to the civil anarchy. They were now discriminating against people whom they had been persecuting over the years after their sheer arrogance and unwise nomadic thinking destined them to be fed by the international community alongside their age-old victims.

When Ramjee Singh tells us that, "Gandhi saw God in the starving millions of India,"[87] unfortunately Muslim Somalis could not respect their faith and see God in the millions of the Jareer suffering under their harsh oppression as these oppressors are accused of:

Soowjaa kufsateen Siifna waa dhacdeen
"Salaama – caleykum" mi'iigu Sireeysid. [88]

Translation:
> You ravished our women and subsequently looted our fertile farmland
> We shall no longer be deceived by your Islamic imitativeness.

The arrival of the so-called UN Peacekeepers under the logo of UNOSOM was supposed to change the status quo, but their damage to the Jareer community was in many aspects even more enormous and painful. As I.M. Lewis wrote, "UN Officials have had to recruit the gunmen as 'guards' in effect, paying protection money to save food for the hungry."[89] But it is in fact this money that contributed to the expansionism of the militia who used the UN dollars to frustrate the lives of the unarmed Bantu people in the urban as well as in the rural areas.

Menkhaus and Prendergast studied the situation, before revealing the social effects the UNOSOM operation took on the riverine communities and the benefit it rendered to the armed clans:

The faction leaders, ...especially Aideed...greatly benefited from rents, security contracts, employment, currency transactions and a variety of other fringe benefits courtesy of the UNOSOM cash cow. One Somali elder remarked, "UNOSOM came to save us from the warlords, and ended up aligning with them.[90]

The Jareer population experienced the bitter side of Somali annihilation, psychologically and materially. They were caught in between a looming disaster and crossfire of which they were neither causal nor participants. Estimating the effects according to the perception of their assessment, Menkhaus and Prendergast report, "Perhaps a third to a half of the Bantu population has disappeared from the Juba Valley; they either died or remain in displacement."[91]

Although Kenneth Menkhaus had written about a Gosha history of prosperity in their pre-colonial years of self-autonomy as young polities under their own visionary rulers like Mzee Nasib Bundo, his later contrast was disheartening:

"One hundred years ago, the ex-slave communities along the Juba river, despite rudimentary technology and chronic harassment from surrounding pastoralists, produced regular yields of surplus grain which they sold to trading posts of the Sultanate of Zanzibar".[92]

Later, the scholar had to write:

"Ironically, although the imposition of centralized state authority has been responsible for many of the Gosha's crises, the disintegration of the contemporary Somali state has proven even more ruinous to the riverine community.[93]

185

After the degree of aggression escalated, those with no means had to remain behind and provide the workforce, testing their psychological and physical endurance. They had no choice but to accept the unacceptable inhumanity. What might be of a great psychological concern is the nature of aggression, something to which the Bantu/Jareer are not accustomed. Whenever the militia thugs suffer a certain defeat, or undergo difficulty from a stronger group or individual, the full brunt of their anger is unleashed on the innocent and unarmed Bantu people in a form of displaced aggression. It reminds one of Hilgard et al., as they define, "Sometimes the person responsible for the frustration is so powerful that an attack would be dangerous. When circumstances block direct attack on the cause of frustration, aggression may be 'displaced.' Displaced aggression is an aggressive action against an innocent person or object rather than against the actual cause of the frustration."[94] The opted solution, therefore, is victim to the situation and a combination of tools varying from apathy to obedience.

Conclusion

If Italy engineered the colonial craft in its art of expropriation, the first president dashed the aspiration of the Jareer community and dampened their cause by orchestrating the re-seizure of their land and by disregarding their rights as equal citizens. The first president was, as chairman of the SYL and Italy's choice as such, instrumental in the isolation of Jareer candidates in Bantu settled areas in a plot to distance them, so as to avert any possible motion in parliament for land repossession and reparations for atrocities committed under the colonial rule of the fascist Italian regime.

In his part, Abdirashid Ali Sharmarke strengthened and in fact expanded the rate of corruption, though he finally fell victim of its consequences. Mohamed Siad Barre and Mohamed Ali Samatar avoided going into Somali history as the first Jileec leadership who decorated generalship onto a Jareer. They effectively maintained a 'noble'-'outcast' Jileec solidarity and isolated the Jareer away from power.

The atrocities and anarchy of the civil war have intently uprooted the Jareer, with more stigmas and apparently wanton acts of massacre resulting in a massive displacement inside the country and an exodus into refugee life in neighboring countries. The international community attempted to help Somalis establish a state, but the more they tried to bridge the gap the more uncompromising the Somalis became. In the next chapter, the discussion will focus on the reconciliation conferences of Somalia, particularly the nature of the 14th Somali National Reconciliation Conference 2002-2004 held in Kenya.

Notes and references

1. Gassim, Mariam Arif., Somalia: Clan vs. Nation. Printed in UAE (2002:30).
2. Hagi Mohamed Barrow, interview in Golween, Somalia, 2003.
3. Okolany, D. H., "Ethnicity and 'Culture of Eating' in Uganda", in Ogot, B. A., (ed.), Ethnicity, Nationalism and Democracy in Africa., Maseno University College: Institute of Research and Postgraduate Studies. (1996:196).
4. Samatar, Abdi I., "Destruction of State and Society in Somalia: Beyond the Tribal Convention", The Journal of Modern African Studies, 30, 4 (1992), pp.625-641 Cambridge University Press.
5. Sabine, George S., and Thorson, Thomas L., A History of political Theory. Oxford & IBH Publishing Co. (1973:163).
6. Samatar, Abdi I., "Destruction of State and Society in Somalia" op.cit. pp.634-635.
7. UNDP – Human Development Report -- Somalia. 1998:27.
8. Pierli, F., Presbitero, U., and Muko, R., "Ethnicity and Human Development: The Missing Link", in Jong, Albert de (ed.), Ethnicity: Blessing or Curse? Pauline Publications Africa. (1999:42).
9. Lipset S. Martin, Political Man. New York: Doubleday (1960:51-54).
10. Menkhaus, Kenneth., "From Feast to Famine: Land and the State in Somalia's Lower Jubba Valley", in Besteman, Catherine., and Cassanelli Lee V., (eds.), The struggle for Land in Southern Somalia: The War Behind the War. Haan Associates, (2000:133-153).
11. Bloom and Ottong, op.cit., p.6.
12. Ibid., p.37.
13. Ahmed, Ali J., "Daybreak is Near, Won't you Become sour?" in Ahmed, Ali J., op.cit., p.151.
14. Getui, Mary N., "At Variance But In Harmony", in Jong, Albert de, (ed.), op.cit., p.13.
15. Ali, Ahmed Qassim., "Land Rush in Somalia," in Kusow, Abdi M., ed., op.cit., pp.155-176.
16. Ibdi.
17. Ibid.
18. Aziza Abdi Dhurow, a Jareer poetess of Dhajalaq Village, Afgoi District.
19. Garre Oobooy, a Jareer poet of Afgoi District.
20. Madina Mugabe, a Jareer poetess of Golween, District of Merca. Madina is

the mother of intellectuals Jamal, Kassim & Jamal Jr. Hagi Mohamed Barrow. A broad   collection of her poems exists and may be revisited elsewhere.

21. Abdullahi Hussein Buufow (alias Mashiido) of Afgoi. He was popular in Istunka.

22. Samatar, Abdi I., and Samatar Ahmed I., op.cit.

23. Held, David, Models of Democracy (2nd edition) 1966. Cambridge: Polity., cited in Anthony Giddens., Sociology. Second Indian Reprint 2002.

24. Gassim, op.cit.

25. Ibid., p.27.

26. Maryin Yusuf (alias Maryin Yaawisoow) of Dhajalaq, Afgoi District.

27. Sayid – Ali A. Eno, a Jareer scholar in comparative Islamic – Christian religions. Sayid – Ali is a cleric devoted to religious teaching and is no longer a performing poet.

28. Ismail Aliyow Baxaar. The verse was selected from a collection of poetry Baxaar had recorded in audiocassettes, mainly about the first regime.

29. Abdullahi Buurow Dhalmaasho, interview in Eldoret, Kenya, Jan. 2003.

30. Gassim, op.cit., p.42.

31. Dualeh, op.cit., pp.48-49.

32. Ibid., p.48.

33. Aw Eedeng Kheer, interview in Baidoa, 2003.

34. Garre Oobooy, recollected from Hagia Halima Essow in Atlanta, U.S.A. 2004.

35. Mohamed Osman Mahdi; a returning officer during both national elections in the 1960s.

36. Abbas Ismaan; was a vigilante at the time of the election. My interview took place at "Dagaayga" bank of the river in Afgoi. 2004.

37. Mohamud Osman Mahdi was a returning officer. He is the brother of Mohamed Osman Mahdi cited in No. 128 above. They both share the same experience.

38. Gassim, op.cit., p.42.

39. "Inter-River Economic Exploration – The Somali Republic 1961" A study conducted by the International Cooperation Administration; Washington 25, D.C., (p.ix),

40. Ibid., (p. vii)

41. Ibid., (p. xvi).

42. Osman Kamula Mofi, a former police officer in post-colonial Somalia. Mofi's statement about the visits of the top Kenyan politicians from KANU and KADU parties is supported by a pamphlet titled "The Somali Republic and African Unity", Printed by East African Printers (Boyds) Ltd. Nairobi. Published on the Authority of the Government of the Somali Republic, September 1962. Kenya National Archives, Nairobi.

43. Ibid. Personal discussions on various occasions in Nairobi.

44. Ibid. Mofi's statement was a reconfirmation of Omar Abdulle's version of the political and professional antagonism against the Jareer/Bantu community in Somalia.

45. Stevie Wonder, "Black Man" a song in the double Album 'Songs In The Key of Life' 1976.

46. Mazrui, Ali A., Cultural Forces in World Politics. James Currey Ltd., Heinemann Kenya, Heinemann Portsmouth. (1990:122-123).

47. Mazrui, Alamin., Kilio Cha Haki. Longhorn Publishers. (1981:4).

48. Das and Choudhury, op.cit., pp.240-241.

49. The song was interpreting the aspirations of a large number of candidates who were targeting parliamentary seats and subsequent appointment to a cabinet portfolio. These were positions based on ethnicity and clan chauvinism.

50. Gassim, op.cit., p.62.

51. Mansur, Abdalla O., "Contrary to a Nation" in Ahmed, Ali J., ed., op.cit., p.115.

52. Hassan Mohamed (alias Hassan Maanlaawe) a family friend who was a good observer of political issues in colonial and post-colonial Somalia. He was twice incarcerated by Kacaanka for criticism and political utterances. He had an extensive knowledge of the political situation of those days.

53. Omar Abdulle, personal discussions in Nairobi, 1997.

54. Halima Hussein Hassan (alias Halima Essow) currently a resident of the U.S. She was advised by her relatives to maintain refrain from such sensitive criticisms about the Revolution.

55. Wright, Sue., Language Policy and language Planning. Palgrave – Macmillan. (2004:1)

56. Gramsci, Antonio, a selection from Cultural Writings in Forgacs and Nowell Smith (eds.), London: Lawrence and Wishart. 1985, cited in Sue Wright, op.cit., p.167.

57. Mathur, Kanwar B., Intercultural Communication: An Agenda for Developing Countries. Allied Publishers Ltd (2001:19)

58. Aitchson, Jean., Linguistics. Hodder & Stoughton (1999:108).

59. Abercrombie, David., Elements of General Phonetics. Edinburgh University Press. (1990:18-19).

60. Holmes, Janet., An Introduction to Sociolinguistics. 2nd edition. Longman; an imprint of Pearson Education Ltd. (2001:132).

61. Kusow, Abdi M., "Somalia's Silent Sufferers." In this article, Dr. Kusow elaborates on an embarrassing situation of 'communication breakdown' between a well known Somali professor (northerner) and a Reewing Maay-Maay speaker. The Professor, despite his belief of Somali 'monolinguality', had to be provided with a translator to help him understand the question posed to him by the Maay speaker in a meeting in Canada.

62. Holmes, Janet, op.cit., p.101.

63. Coupland, Nikolas., and Jaworski, Adam., Sociolinguistics: A Reader and Coursebook. Palgrave (1997:7).

64. Mahdi Mohamed Issa, personal discussions in the 1980s.

65. Lewis, I. M., "In the Land of the Living Dead", op.cit.

66. Cassanelli, Lee V., "Explaining the Somali Crisis," in Besteman and Cassanelli, eds., op.cit., p.22.

67. Compagnon, D., "Political Decay in Somalia: From Personal Rule to Warlord-ism," Refuge 12 (5): 8-13; 1992.

68. Bloom & Ottong, op.cit., p.13.

69. UNDP – Human Development Report -- Somalia (1998:28).

70. Merryman, James., "The Economy of Gedo Region and the Rise of Smallholder Irrigation," in Besteman and Cassanelli, eds., op.cit., p. 84.

71. Kenneth Menkhaus and Kathryn Craven, "Land Alienation and the Imposition of State Farms in the Lower Jubba valley," in Besteman and Cassanelli, eds., op.cit., p.162.

72. Farah, I., Hussein, A., and Lind, J., "Deegaan, Politics and War in Somalia", in Lind, J., and Sturman, K., eds., op.cit., p.335.

73. Luling, V., Somali Sultanate, op.cit. p.155.

74. Ibid., p.158.

75. Morris, Aldon., "Centuries of Black Protest: Its significance for America and the World," in Hill, H., and Jones Jr., J. E., (eds.), Race in America: The Struggle for Equality. The University of Wisconsin Press. (1993:38).

76. Bell, Derrick., "Remembrances of Racism Past: Getting Beyond the Civil Rights Decline", in Hill, H., and Jones Jr., J. op.cit., pp.73-82.

77. Luling, V., Somali Sultanate; op.cit., p.251.

78. Abdi Ali recited this verse from his father, a Jareer civil servant who did not experience promotion for about 30 years of Somali rule.

79. Abdullahi Sheikh Hassan, discussions on several occasions in Hodan, Mogadishu in the 1980s.

80. Ahmed Qassim Ali, in Kusow, ed., op.cit.

81. Ibid., p.155.

82. A Study on the Human Rights Abuse Against the Bantu. The Bantu Rehabilitation Trust (BRT) – Somalia, sponsored by ACORD. 1995.

83. Mohamed Ali Isman, currently Sultan of the Jareer in Eastern Afgoi.

84. Ahmed, Ali J., Daybreak is Near, p.135.

85. Halima Hussein Hassan (Essow), more collection from Hagia Essow will be used in other upcoming works.

86. Geshekter, Charles., "The Search for Peaceful Development in a Country of War: Global Restraint on 20th Century Somali Socio-Economic Development", in Janzen, J., ed., op.cit., p.13.

87. Ramjee Singh, "Vision of World Poverty: the Gandhian Perspective." A paper to the 14th World Conference of World Future Studies Federation, Nairobi, July 25 – 29, 1995, cited in Henry Odera Oruka, in Graness, A.,

and Kresse, K., eds., Sagacious Reasoning. East African Educational Publishers. 1999.

88. Abdullahi Abdulkadir (Aw – Jaalle), extracted from his collection of cassettes in Saudi Arabia, 2003.

89. Lewis, I.M., "The Land of the Living Dead," op.cit.

90. Kenneth Menkhaus and John Prendergast, "Political Economy of Post-Intervention Somalia", Somalia Task Force, Issue No. 3. April 1995.

91. Ibid.

92. Kenneth Menkhaus, Ph.D. Dissertation, op.cit., p.2.

93. Menkhaus, Kenneth., "From Feast to Famine," op.cit., p.151.

94. Hilgard, E. R., Atkinson, R. C., and Atkinson, Rita L., Introduction to Psychology. Sixth edition. Oxford & IBH. (1975:436).

Chapter 5

DEMOGRAPHIC FABRICATION AND ETHNIC MARGINALIZATION: LOOKING INTO THE BACKGROUND OF THE ENIGMA

"Any society that discriminates against any sector of its population is denying itself the opportunity to develop the best talents to engage in the fierce international competition that is upon us," Ramphele Mamphela.[1]

For nearly two decades now, Somalia has not had an effective central administration. Several peace conferences were held, but no tangible solution has been achieved, one which can contain the senseless war that has ravaged the poor Horn of Africa country. These peace initiatives have been truncated by factors which were not exhausted as substantive, but which stand as the realities perpetually hindering every endeavor. To develop a lasting solution in the case of Somalia's chaotic situation of a multi-faceted, multi-interest based war will possibly remain as one of the most perplexing traumas of the century. It will not keep consuming the time and thinking of the people in the Horn and in the Africa continent only, but equally the concerned world community as a whole.[2]

In dealing with this tragedy one has to identify, comprehensively, the symptoms of the problem before one can expect a considerable agreement to be achieved and fulfilled by the concerned warlords and their armed factional clan militia. I suggest this to be a possibility because, considering the approaches employed throughout the period of the conferences and the ground gained so far, the shortcomings exceed attempts to "superficially" reduce a gap which is growing in defiance.[3]

When the war broke out in Somalia initially, it had a certain image; an image which was calculated on the conscience of the masses versus the ill administration of an adamant dictator. As it gained momentum and the uprooting of the dictatorial regime became imminent, an abrupt loss of track and diversion from the original philosophy prevailed. A vision of tribalism, clanism and the opportunistic settlement of old feudal scores were deeply injected into a delicate situation that required the thinking of sane minds in their approach toward the occupation of the administrative vacuum.

193

Despite the mass confrontation to topple Barre's "*Kacaanka gaa-murey*" (matured revolution), all the active organizers and financial contributors to the war had their own hidden agenda, whether individually or collectively.[4] Suffice it to say that, most probably, all of these active human ingredients had more hidden agendas individually than they had any collectively.

At certain view the prolongation of the war, and the failure to implement the acts and articles signed in the memorandums, clearly show the contradiction between the articles signed and the hidden agendas. Despite that, every war chieftain responded by sacrificing the lives of thousands of youths from his sub-clan and clan. During this course of hatred, large amounts of money received as contributions from the rich clansmen, and from businesses and as "consultation fees"[5] from international organizations, are consumed while a lot of it is diverted to the build-up of war arsenal, mainly for the disadvantage and dehumanization of the unarmed communities.

The war in Somalia, like other wars elsewhere, has enriched a large number of people who hadn't previously thought of migrating from their areas of inhabitance in '*miyiga*', the remote rural areas. The change of living, from rural to urban, was merely facilitated by the gun and the dependence on sub-clan and clan in defending the culprit at any possible cost, morally or in terms of manpower. Practically, they've proved beyond reasonable doubt that the best way of surviving is with the gun in the hand and clansmen by the side. These factors are believed to be the 'authority' to legalize looting, robbing, raping, confiscation of property (movable and immovable), abduction, killing and other disgusting crimes that pass with impunity.[6]

Although in many parts of the world confrontations of civil war have been experienced, the mayhem in Somalia may not be contrastable. Ultimately, in the case of the Somali civil war, a lot of factors are fanning the fire as active ingredients. It is due to a multitude of factors, local and foreign, each with an interest to achieve, that the Somali peace endeavors have become more of a verbal rhetoric than a reality. For example, we have over four or five foreign players with each particular party having several hidden agendas. When, to that, you add the number of the Somali factions and individuals with comparably ulterior motives, you lose direction of where the country is heading. The material fact, though, remains that the Somali role players, whether crowned as 'heroes', 'leaders', 'great men' or by any other description, have shown themselves void of patriotism. Subsequently, that loss of patriotism has earned them a great loss of morality, distinctly represented by the simultaneous failures to implement the articles and charters laid down and agreed upon by themselves in every peace negotiation meeting.

Another aspect undermining the peace initiatives is the approach. Since the Somali warlords have shown no regard for mercy and courtesy, they shouldn't be regarded as being higher than any other participant in the conference. Their attitude denies conformity with the sound culture that regards humanity with dignity. It seems as though their average thinking hasn't been detached from the "sheer arrogance and egoism belonged to the culture of uncouth pastoral attitude".[7] In this case, modern diplomacy, intellectuality and application of sophisticated human and international relations and ideas of peace building are above the comprehension of a "wicked people who do not possess the qualitative characteristics of lordship, in any better sense of the word, except in that of warlordship."[8]

Through the tidings of history, we read about the Somali people as being a homogeneous society of the same culture, - a rich culture -, same religion and also the same language. Indeed this has proved to be an erroneous concept, which misinterpreted the realities about the heterogeneity of the Somali nation. Possibly, the organizers of the peace meetings employ their techniques and tools on the basis of that misguided concept,[9] which does not show the way to a better solution. The 'self-sameness' theory does not itself have a real cultural base of commonality to all.[10] Individuals and institutions with variety of thought tested their doctrine in the Somali peace context in versatile ways, yet no sign of peace. Billions have been spent in favor of speculations for peace but no tangible achievement has been seen to this day. Conflicting objectives and philosophies also contributed to the failure in bringing a solution leading to the establishment of a Somali state and a lasting peace![11]

The negative observation is by no means an interpretation of an inner hatred for peace in the country but the whole approach does little to win anybody's admiration.[12] During the 14th Somali National Reconciliation Conference in Kenya Mohamed Daahir Afrax, the Somali author, wrote about how certain officials of the international community were skeptical about the attitude of the Somali people as he quotes: "*Caqli ay ku heshiiyaan hadday leeyihiin horay u heshiin lahaayeen,*" meaning "Had they been bestowed with the wisdom to reconcile, they would have done so earlier than now." (My Translation)

From the outset, every initiative has targeted the building of a peace bridge across what we reiterate as being the "major clans", better termed as the armed clans. Among them, they have fought, devastated and driven every sector of the Somali civilization into the doldrums. They have killed, maimed, mutilated and dismembered each other and anyone else in the country, showing individual sub-clan strength for the accumulation of firearms, warfare and military superiority. During the course they have wiped out their clan youths, illiterate as well as intellectuals, and still seem not to have diagnosed the symptoms allowing them to have a prescriptive dose for treatment. Under the umbrella of warlords and supporters anointed with spiritual clanism, millions of USD worth of military hardware and arsenal were invested in. It brings us then to contemplate the English saying that "One man can lead the horse to the water, but twenty can't make it drink," because it exactly describes the current Somali situation since certain sectors of the society have no interest in peace. Afrax's book, launched during the early months of the 14th SNRC, discusses the subject in detail.

Still, given the phenomenon of loss of trust, more effort and guarantees for inclusion, participatory development, justice, equality and morality must be a prerequisite if the minorities, the unarmed and the ethnically oppressed communities are to be persuaded. These communities cannot put their trust in clans that have denied the existence of multiracial identities and cultures and resorted to the killing of innocent unarmed people.

Of the numerous so-called local level peace initiatives, hardly any inclusion or equal participation was considered for these communities, particularly the Jareer. This humiliating practice by the concerned parties can be deemed as eschewing this community on ethnic grounds. In a previous conference in neighboring Djibouti in early 1990s, a leader of this community, the late Mohamed Ramadan Arbo, was even denied equal presentation time as the other leaders; "it was understandable since the chair was Aden Abdulle Osman,"[13] the first president, "a character notorious for his anti-Jareer sentiments."[14]

Clanism at the heart of intellectualism

A few years later after the start of the war, a peace organization that was the dream child of some powerful international institutions willing to provide financial back-up and expertise found itself melting sooner than it could gain any momentum. The so-called ring-leaders (intellectuals), couldn't agree categorically on a few basic suggestions set by the prospective financiers as a guideline for the operation and good performance of the organization. The 'intellectuals', with all their intellect and superb academic background, could not converge into a genuine consensus over the composition of the members to the secretariat, the delegation of duties and the location of their headquarters.[15]

In reality, the financiers were initially unaware of the hidden agenda of the peace propagating 'intellectuals' whose individual concepts, principles and ideologies differed much from their illusive utterances and outer exposure. A close scrutiny by the international body, and very careful observation of the attitude of the 'intellectuals' during discussions culminated in the dissatisfaction of the prospective donors. In one of the peace workshops in a neighboring country, their conflicting motives and ideological confrontations caused a major embarrassment to the well-wishing international agencies and neutral individuals.[16] From the proceedings, the general hostility brewing in the atmosphere among the 'intellectuals' - teaming up into groups adverse to one another, and convening clandestine meetings in the odd hours of the night, discussing strategic measures to sabotage proposals moved by the rival team - sparked reflections of unreliability on the learned Somalis.[17]

After failing to hide clan sentiments, motivation and interest, the 'intellectuals' imprudently resorted to pulling in and recommending for a top post for one of their kinship, so that in the event of necessity, each of them would rely upon those from their own clan to push forward any of their proposals.[18] The Somali intellectuals have in their capacity failed to deliver. They have derailed the expectations of the masses from its course. They played a large part in the divergence between the clans by preaching a culture of war instead of encouraging an application of a culture of peace. Quite often, the Somali intellectual has banked on the frail institution belonging to the philosophy of tribalism at the cost of "disadvantaging nationalism,"[19] shrinking the prospective organization into a clan-based entity exploited by what Ahmed Qassim Ali would describe as "docile intellectuals"[20] satisfying the whims of their kinsmen.

By compromising the intellectual ethics, the clan based Somali erudite has betrayed the indispensability of the values of the society, a reason why many are not respected above the clan level. Somali intellectuality, on the basis of tribal bias, is faced in recent years with what Mohamed Eno warned against about two decades ago when he wrote, "Lose the support and dedication of the people, and you lose all possibilities for building the community and the nation."[21]

Through the ill fate of the tribal politics of war, they failed to create an honest endeavor that amalgamated the masses into a dynamic force of peace keepers. Unfortunately, they were swept up in the whirlwind and high tides of clan power brokering, unfolding a full-scale machinery of disintegration and disorientation under the influence of their intellectuality. They drew a demarcation line between the generalization and the specification of *'dadkaaga dhinac ka raac'* (flow the tide) [22] whose connotation in Barre's era was the masses in general but given the token of one's closest partrilineal kinship after the dictator's ouster. Some 'intellectuals' were quoted as saying that whatever they have learned they did so for the tribe and not for the nation.

The reiteration by some agencies to wage a culture of peace might be welcome but, does the Somali pastoral culture embrace peace?[23] If it does, why has it not employed this culture to send the peace message home?[24] The acceptance of a defeat is sometimes a gesture of courageousness and for this reason a challenge to seek change and innovation, a motivation to perform better. It is a process experienced by human nature, but one whose acceptance seems a burden to the average clan-oriented Somali society. As a whole, the former regimes, the warlords and the armed clan militia, everyone is exonerating himself or herself from the acceptance of the causal ownership of the problem; the courage to bear the responsibility and therefore to pioneer the solution. In doing so, they are scared of losing many rights since according to Allan Paton, "A person guilty of injustice has partially and temporarily forfeited his rights…"[25]

Racial supremacy and aspects of apartheid

Although South Africa has succeeded in the eradication of the

Apartheid form of administration, Somalia has embarked on creating one in a new phenomenon developed under a pastoral philosophy named the 4.5 (Four-point-Five) clan power sharing formula. The puzzle, however, lies in the avoidance of having to substantiate the basis for its introduction, rather than the goal it is to achieve. But what can be deduced from the system is that the socio-political goal of the so-called 4.5 clan power-sharing system is a clear indication of the Apartheid nature of the Somali society. It is a new device for mental oppression. Its aim is fostering in the Jareer mind the acceptance of a socially imposed inferiority in comparison with self-exaltation of the "nobility", suppressing the former into "a politically and socially limited life,"[26] as the situation was in the heyday of Apartheid in South Africa.

In this system, the Jareer are destined to survive under stiffly controlled social and economic segregation, and the chronic disabilities associated with them "from the crade to the grave."[27] Notorious experiments of this type of system are probably the testing ground for an eventual introduction of decrees and laws that will constitutionalize "...a systematic and quite definite policy of Apartheid,"[28] leading to the execution of acts such as: The Somali Bantu Inferiority Act; The Jareer Re-enslavement Law; The Bantu Education Act (like it was in South Africa); The Right to the Bantu Land Expropriation Law; the Jareer-Animal Equality Act" and many other laws that will please the supremacy status of the non-Jareer populace of Somalia.

The 4.5 system is a typical replica of the defunct South African Apartheid policy, where Black natives were not allowed election to the houses of Native Representatives of White-European origin. In essence, when one group decides the limitation of the political participation of another group, it is nothing but an effectively legitimized subjugation. It encourages segregation, which is paradigmatic of racist societies where "Onto the neck of a subject people they daily add a yoke which increases to unbearable limits the strain already caused..."[29]

The elicitation provided for this precarious plot of minority – majority clans, to the general populace, presumes a divergence related to a quantitatively numerical composition of the people differentiated. But in fact, it is not true and there is no concrete evidence to support that. It is possible then that if the Jileec had constituted a significantly larger number than the Jareer, in other words for the nation to have been provided with sufficient agricultural produce, it would have been impossible for the Jareer to have produced adequate surplus for feeding their

Jileec counterparts who are alleged to be nine times their number.

Historical findings as well as sociological theories do not support the idea of rudimentary societies of a *few* (minimized to less than 10% in Somalia!) feeding a larger number, unless the numbers of both concerned communities were almost at equilibrium, the difference being marginal if at all the feeder community is considered fewer. Oberg[30] supports this theory in his discussion regarding the ratio of pastoralists against agriculturalists in Ankole in Uganda, while Maquet[31] postulates similarly for the Hutu and Tutsi communities of Rwanda.

By this notion, ethnic qualities and physical appearance play a role in being [a] Somali. It is inadequate to be just an indigenous born and bred in the country. A Somali has therefore to possess certain physical qualities and culture unrelated to Negritude or agrarian mode of production. For one to fall in the category of Somaliness one has to be slender, not stout; has to have a pointed nose, not flat or broad one; has to have soft hair, but not hard, thick or curly; and after all one has to subscribe to the culture of nomadic pastoralism as the right properties to Somaliness.

These characteristics, which are mainly natural, have been recognized as part of the unbendable yardstick by which Somaliness is literally defined, regardless of birth, indigenity, or long sojourn in the country. The stratification, in this variety, is nurtured from the belief that a Jareer, whatever his intelligence, status or personal characteristics, cannot be treated as a Somali (See Eno & Eno 2007, 2008). Before he can assume that identity he has to transform his physical and biological composition into properties acceptable [to] the dominant Jileec Somalis. As long as these qualifying parameters are absent, then a Jareer-Bantu can not be called a Somali but a *"Habash"*, an *"Adoon"*, a *"Biddo"*, *"Beyle-Sanbuur"* and a *"Sankadhudhi"*, pejorative epithets implying Africanity or Negritude, as opposed to 'Arabness' and 'nobility'.[32]

The most deceitful element that bears colossal apartheid proportion was envisaged in the national document that sets the laws and principles of the country for its citizens, the constitution. This document, the Somali constitution, granted more citizenship rights and opportunities to a Somali born and bred in neighboring Kenya, Ethiopia, and Djibouti or in any other country than an autochthonous Jareer/Bantu born and bred in Somalia. As we saw earlier, Mariam Arif Gassim and Omar Eno have both consented to the easy access of this category of "Somalis" to top government positions, owing to the codification of the constitution which is fundamentally based on "pro-Somali", "anti-Jareer" objectives and interpretations. More importantly, former Somali Ambassador Hussein Dualeh provides concise but quite conscious evidence on that as he admits: "I had to give Somali passports to these young Somali Kenyans..."[33]

At all events, Eno's and Gassim's testimonials aside, the history of the participation in the post-independence Somali cabinets and top administrative ranks portray clear evidence; Jileec communities of all the distinguished ethnic backgrounds, with the exception of the Jareer/Bantu, have assumed these responsibilities. The outcast groups, though considered outside the social strata, had very powerful representation and at times enjoyed a status second to the most incumbent position (Eno & Eno, forthcoming). Therefore, the ironic statement in Jacques Maquet's general theory that, "people born in different castes [*in here Jareer and Jileec*] are unequal in inborn endowment, physical as well as psychological and have consequently fundamentally different rights,"[34] also accurately matches the Somali situation. (Clarification in parentheses mine)

For whatever reasons, Italy did a duplication of what Britain had done in South Africa, by distancing power at independence from the oppressed autochthonous people and into the hands of the oppressors. But while Britain in 1910 had not given a written constitution to South Africa for reasons apparent, Somalia at minimum had in 1960 a constitution whose content was engrained with the principle Somali ideology of Jareer and Jileec as people in the same nation but ethnically separate and socially unequal.

For all practical purposes, the Somali-Italian policy of post-independence "democracy" functioned on two effectively compounding factors: (1) Italy's fear of a Jareer retaliation over Italian colonial atrocities upon acquisition of independence, and (2) The Somalis' socio-psychological belief of being above black Africans (psychological food for Somali self-ennoblement). The interplay, among others, of interests between these two factors (Italian and Somali) has created a wider social gap in independent Somalia. The idea was built firmly on a legitimation of Jareer/Bantu "African" inferiority at the advantage of Jileec/Somali "Arab" superiority.[35] As a consequence; it laid the foundation for a political circle impermeable for the Jareer. The policy was aimed at fostering the multiplication of antagonism and the grouping up of all the Jareer into a nation of slaves as a mechanism for the deprivation of their equal status to the Jileec.

The necessary scapegoat fabricated for such social stratification had to be adjusted on ethnic grounds, where Somalis predominantly downgrade Africanism or Negritude in favor of Arabism and lighter pigmentation, one whose tutelage displays the Jareer as a people who "know nothing and ...have nothing of value."[36] We are faced here with a situation which Allan Paton, commenting on the European conquest in Africa, describes thus: "even those who had no gifts of invention whatsoever, came to consider themselves the superiors of all other people."[37] While not undermining or degrading any human race whosoever, one wonders if the average Somali would think of his ethnic or racial superiority as being above the African, against historically recorded truths denouncing even the often purported white genius or racial supremacy. An example clarifies the situation as Cicero writes to Atticus in the First Century B.C.:

Do not obtain your slaves from Britain because they are so stupid and so utterly incapable of being taught that they are not fit to form a part of the household of Athens.[38]

And Said of Toledo writes in the Eleventh Century:

Races north of Pyreness are of cold temperatures and never reach maturity; they are of great stature and of a white color. But they lack all sharpness of wit and penetration of intellect.[39]

But Max Muller contrastively indignifies racial supremacy:

"I have declared again and again, that when I say Aryas (Aryans) I mean neither blood nor bones nor hair nor skull; I mean simply those who spoke an Aryan language. When I speak of them I commit myself to no anatomical characteristics. To me an ethnologist who speaks of Aryan race, Aryan blood, Aryan eyes and hair, is as great a sinner as a linguist who speaks of dolichocephalic [narrow-headed] dictionary or a brachycephalic [broad-headed] grammar."[40]

Of the three main human racial ramifications, namely: leucodermi (white-skinned), xanthodermi (yellow-skinned) and melanodermi (black-skinned) which practically correlate with Caucasoid (white), Mongoloid (yellow) and Negroid (black), the last fits the group under discussion, but may not satiate the Somali nomad who is of a black Negroid by pigmentation and of African origin but in a long crave for identity transformation, probably ignorant of the fact that "The range in each group is very large and some groups of whites are darker than some Negroes."[41]

The myth of Somali majority clans: baseless pastoral fabrication

Race is a contentious subject which varies in its interpretation; but the controversy grows even deeper in the Somali situation. Considering the apartheid 4.5 clan segregation system, we are faced with the question of whether the Somalis base the superiority or supremacy in account of physiological, biological, psychological, historical or theological factors.

The argument extends beyond the appearance and physical features as seen externally. These simply represent biological substances. These variables are acquired through inheritance, and therefore one has no control over the determination of those properties. Nor do I make assessments based on how someone looks. I am thinking in terms of achievement, civilization, discoveries and inventions, a contribution to humanity attributed as the end product of Somali intelligence so as to validate superiority related to world class intelligence, a contribution to humanity, and not by strata one gave to himself out of formless illusion. But as long as we keep trading [only] with unproven genealogical myths, the ethnic hygiene of nomadic nobility is yet to prove excellence above self-made beliefs.

Observing the lack of any appreciable contribution to the achievement of mankind, Somali pastoral nobility may generously share Ruth Benedict's emphasis that "While certain groups of a given race forge ahead...other groups of the same race may remain primitive nomadic herdsmen."[42] With no tangible share in world achievement or any other praiseworthy mark in the historical dictionary of human society, Somali nobility fits into Bendict's latter group.

A large number of Somalis and believers of Somalia as an egalitarian pastoral democracy may not agree with my contentious coining of Apartheid to Somali social life, a theme that leads us to defining the term "Apartheid" as was put by the natives of where it originated. In Moses Mabhida's definition, among others:

> The word means segregation, discrimination and so-called separate
> development... The idea of segregation is based on a fallacious theory

derived from Calvinistic religion, which is very widespread among the Boer population, who do so far as to claim, on the basis of quotation from the Bible, that the black man was created to be the slave of the white man.[43]

Several other sources also suggest the term as meaning segregation, keeping races apart, and as a kind of institutionalized social separation and discrimination between groups within a society thus one group denying the other the opportunities to political decision-making, academic advancement, economic development as well as social mobility. However, an examination of the above definition presents a very rich degree of similitude between the system of segregation and discrimination against the masses of Bantu/Jareer ethnic community in Somalia and those in Apartheid South Africa. The most vivid significance of the similarities rests in (a) The belief in inequality between the different races of Jareer and Jileec, hence Negroid and Non-Negroid; (b) That both dominant groups (South African whites and Somali nomads) also base their subjugation and Apartheid philosophy on theological grounds, comparatively Christianity in the South African situation, and of course Islam in the case of Somalia.[44] Whatever the sphere and magnitude, the common denominator for both situations rests in the exploitation of a self-dignified group against the autochthonous population.

Recent historical fact demonstrates, however, that whereas after national and international condemnations of Apartheid (Somalia being among the anti-Apartheid forces) South Africa has realized the eventual hand-over of rule to the natives, Somalia has in retrogressive contrast shamefully and callously moved onto a legitimating process by the adoption of a 4.5 (four – point – five) clan stratification and clan supremacization scheme, abominable evils of ethnic/racial oppression and discrimination that are now history in South Africa. The objective of the system is instrumental to the experimentation process through which an ultimately legal Apartheid policy might be formulated and implemented in the Somali peninsula.

To better understand it, the mechanism is framed in the context of an erroneous but general myth of clan division in which all the people are categorically put into significant and insignificant tribal groups at first. The so-called Somaloid groups (Cushites turned Arabs), the significant tribes, are said to contain 4 'major' clans constituting the separate entities of Hawiye, Darod, Dir and Isaq, excluding the occupational outcast groups discussed in the opening chapter of this study. Hypothetically, this major-minor clan myth is based not on a demographically proven fact but on a myth imagined and executed by a lustful Jileec subgroup of the Somali society.

Perceptually, the socially legalized notion of "major and minor" clans has no basis on a scientifically conducted population study carried out on per head clan demography, but rather a nomadic layman's wishful process of imagination. This is true because to this date, no single clan or sub-clan has even a rough statistical estimate of the demographic constitution of its membership. No postcolonial census has been implemented in Somalia to establish 'per head' constituents of a tribe or clan so that we could justify "majority" and "minority" tribes in respect of their numbers.

Myths, concoctions, crave and cowardice

For the purpose of this brief discussion, I consider demography not necessarily in the aspect of an abstract spatial distribution per se, as it may frustrate the objective due to heavy and unproportional migration that became a cause of demographic disequilibria in the days after independence. We may require considering the academics' perspectives that approach the topic as follows:

1. Peter R. Coxi: "...the study of statistical methods of human population involving primarily the measurement of the size, growth and diminution of the numbers of the people, the proportions of living being born or dying within the same region and the related functions of fertility, mortality and marriage."[45]

2. H. Stenford: "...the vital statistics of human population (especially birth, death and migration)..."[46]

3. W.G. Barkley: "The numerical portrayal of human population..."[47]

Our variable object of focus here is the statistical distribution of each sub-clan and clan within the Republic of Somalia as determined deductively from the outcome of a head-count of its composite membership. With regard to this issue, the "majority" and "minority" clan concept cannot apparently harmonize itself with objective statistical reality. Illustrative evidence (possibly an existing one of a rare kind) can be traced to colonial documents and as referred by academicians. Insofar as we know, the Somali census conducted in 1986 by the military government did not regard clan affiliation, owing to the regime's denouncement and subsequent eradication ("burial") of tribalism. The British anthropologist most celebrated as an "authority" on Somalia, Ioan M. Lewis, visited the subject of tribal statistics descriptively in quantitative terms, referring to relevant studies carried out by the colonial administrations in the respective Somali territories of those days.

For the purpose of illustration, one must refer to the 5 separate territories according to I. M. Lewis:[48]

No.	Territories	Total Somali Population
1	French Somaliland (1948)	25,000
2	British Somaliland (1950)	640,000
3	Harar Territories (1938)	350,000
4	Somalia (1939)	1,436,706
5	Northern Frontier Province of Kenya (1948)	2,519,206

The most crucial revelation in Lewis' work, however, is carried in what he gives as: "the latest estimate for Somalia ...2,258,084."

The British scholar has referred two distinctive figures for Somalia, (presumably Italian Somaliland); the former figure as "1,436,706" and the latter which he calls "the latest estimate" as "2,258,084". Why are the two sums hugely disproportional? What is Lewis' justification? The scholar illustrates the response (in a footnote!): "This estimate, made for the British Military Administration (from Italian sources?), appears to include the Negroid groups although they are [not] explicitly mentioned, for the Italian estimate for 1952, which [does] gives a total "autochthonous" population of 1,275,584." For the confirmation of his source, Lewis gives (Rapport du gouvernement Italien a l'Assemblee Generale des Nations Unites sur l'Administration de Tutelle de la Somalie, 1952, p.269.)

Though these figures look good enough to disprove the Somali myth of 4 major clans, when the Negroid Jareer/Bantu autochthons constituted a "population of 1,275,584" out of a total southern Somali population of "2,258,084", a difference of the two figures leaves us with an autochthonous Negroid majority of 293,084 heads more than the Jileec total in the south, at that time. Even with these figures, there can

be no certainty that the Italians have submitted the results before doc-
toring them drastically to reduce further the number of the Negroid,[49]
considering their mutual relationship with the Somalis, particularly the
Somali Youth League (SYL) party. I am of the opinion that, after the
necessary tampering, the Italians could not decrease the number of the
Negroid autochthons further than 1,275,584 in spite of its lead of almost
300,000 people more than the southern Somaloid groups put together.

In a videotaped workshop for Somali intellectuals in Mogadishu,
(a copy of which is in my library) one of the participants namely Eng.
Abdilaziz Siidow, mentions how the results of a census by a French
institution was shelved by the nomadic leaders in Barre's military regime after astonishing results displayed the Lower Shabelle Region
alone leading all the regions of the north combined together. Barre's
military junta suffered a slap in the face because the majority of the
Lower Shabelle residents constitute the "autochthonous" Negroid
population, residues of the pre-Cushitic Sabaki/Bantu-speaking tribes
who migrated from Shungwaya to the Tana and coastal areas in present day Kenya.

It is remarkable mentioning that the Jareer people are not unconscious of their numerical enormity but had no means to reveal that.
The main reasons were obviously political and academic marginalization, among others; a political voice would have set an approach in the
decision-making ranks for the publication of the true tribal statistics,
while the academic area would provide opportunity for research and
further reading to unearth the long entombed truth. It is not, at this
end, out of mere fantasy or unknowledgeability that the Bantu elites on
several occasions reported their number approximately at 40% (count-
of-the-thumb too, we may say) of the average population of Somalia.[50]
Just to supplement to the Bantu claim, I quote Professor Abdi Ismail
Samatar[51] saying, "When a proper census is conducted, believe me, the
.5 (point five) community will be 1.5." I may note here, too, that the
distinguished Somali scholar was a strong voice advocating against
inequality and injustice, the phenomena that marred the proceedings of
the 14th Somali National Reconciliation Conference in Kenya.

Though there is often an inclination to rely on the documented
word as more accountable, we can draw from the Bantu elders' statement that, "between 30 and 40% of the population in Somalia are
Bantu" while not entirely overlooking their cautious manner as they
admit that "no reliable statistics exist."[52] Considering the aforemen-

tioned statistical documents and other oral and audiovisual material, I politely disagree with Perouse de Montclose in the distribution of unsubstantiated descriptive data without referencing. A report cites de Montclose as this:

> "According to Perouse de Montclose, the Bantus of southern Somalia represent a minority whose marginality is more easily seen. They represent less than 2% of the inhabitants of the country.[53]

Possibly unaware of Lewis' referred studies on the Somali tribal censuses, the Bantu elders' summative 30% - 40% stays more consistent with the available records than several scholars' and UN officials'[54] imaginative numerical marginality of the Negroid autochthons of Somalia. It is in relying on such speculative figures by incautious officials and scholars that strengthened the unfounded pastoral claims of statistical majority.

As I have indicated earlier, the classification of the vast Jareer populace into the "minority" communities stands as yet another attempt to restrengthen the legalization of their oppression as an insignificantly rightless population of a 'few' living among an extensively larger group who ascribe to a genealogically rightful people from the self-ennoblement. The plain truth invites for a more careful academic reconsideration of the subject related to Somali tribal census and comprehensive clan statistics before jumping haphazardly to the unfounded conclusion of Jareer/Bantu minority clan and Jileec/Somali majority clans. The suggestion of the Bantu as minority may occur, in my opinion, only when contrasted to a cumulative of all the Somali Jileec communities as one group, and not against a sub-clan or clan. To substantiate the argument, considering the Jareer as a minority group may be possible exclusively in the aspect of Jileec-Jareer comparison; not in one Jileec clan i.e. Isaq, Darood, Hawiye, or Digil-Mirifle as separate clan entities numerically exceeding the entirety of the Jareer population.

A situation similar to the general Jileec philosophy regarding the statistical impregnation of selected clans is clearly defined in Bloom and Ottong when they contend, "Unfortunately, some governments have deliberately double-counted some groups and left out others in order to swell unfairly particular voting groups."[55] I may draw subsequent attention to the fact that unlike other African countries, the swelling of the Somali clan/tribe figures is more multi-purpose and much deeper-rooted. Apart from voting, whose main focus lays on garnering more parliamentary entrants and representatives, here the philosophy is more dangerous in that it entails "the automatic alienation of one particular race or African ethnic group -- from their recognition as citizens with equal social rights, to the absolute denial of the existence of their identity."[56] This explains the reason why a majority of scholars have portrayed Somalia as a uniquely homogeneous nation of same Arab origin, entirely speaking one language, celebrating the same nomadic culture and a unanimous subscription to the Islamic faith.

Strata awareness at childhood

In general perception, the propagation of homogeneity, self-sameness and oneness in culture and so on and so forth cannot veil the verity that the Somali nomad is very contradictory as much as he is hypocritical, discriminative, racialist, ethnocentric as well as segregative in attitude. This negative psychosocial behavior is intrinsically hemmed in the social fabric of the Somalis and conditioned in them throughout the period of their development. As they grow, these patterns are gradually but firmly modified to characterize part of the indispensable determinants of their moral development. When it concerns the degradation and alienation of the Jareer/Bantu in particular, it is conditioned sufficiently also throughout the methods and stages of learning specified by psychologists. It thus functions as an unnegligible part of the attitude formation process.

The behavior, whether acquired as a result of classical conditioning,[57] subliminal conditioning,[58] instrumental conditioning[59] or whether by observational learning,[60] has become causal for the elements stimulating the stereotyping and social prejudice against the Jareer community. Seeing the situation from that social environment, we may believe Elizabeth Hurlock[61] who perceives that although it is not well developed, "Social discrimination appears early in childhood," particularly when studies suggest that, "Most prejudices come from imitating the attitude and behavior of parents, teachers, peers, neighbors."

The practice of social prejudice dominates the cognitive development of the child because, as Hurlock defines: "This influence is greatest during childhood and the early part of adolescence, the time of greatest psychological plasticity.[62]" At such an early age of plasticity, the Somali child is very well educated by his most immediate social environment about the 'nothingness' of the Jareer/Bantu and their place at the lowest rank of the social structure.

Such immoral and discriminative behavior appears vividly in school as the Jileec children bully, degrade and disdain their Jareer peers as aliens intruding into the social group at school because "These expectations are spelled out for all group members in form of laws, customs and rules."[63] The acquisition and maintenance of these characteristics are common during and after the period of socio-emotional development in adolescence in that the relationship with the parents, peer kinship, "contribute to an adolescent's identity development,"[64] in constructing sufficiently the negative concepts about the Jareer. It later transdevelops into the creation of an abstract ethnic image formed of "Jareer inferiority", and "Jareer subordinacy" as contrasted to "Jileec superiority" and "Jileec superordinacy", creating a concrete base for the formation of rigid ethnic stratification and the development of subversive attitudes of ethnic discrimination, ethnic-based prejudicial behaviors and indulgence in identity self-esteem.

Augmentation and escalation of segregation, alienation, degradation, persecution and marginalization have cost the Somali Bantu community massive underdevelopment interspersed in all specters of their social life. These mainly affect their social identity, political participation, economic growth, academic advancement and cultural entity, not sparing their human dignity.

My perception of identity regarding this discussion does not mean the psychological interpretations of "identity" and/or "identity confusion" per se in the concerns of one's search for and adoption of a career[65] in life and personal achievement that are usually born out of innate motivational stimulus of desire and willingness to overcome challenges. The undercurrent of the discussion relates to the ethnic group, the tribe, the clan, sub-clan and the patrilineal moiety which one is aware of by ascription, and learns from the parents' tutelage through recitation of the genealogical path of names leading to an apocryphal eponymous father, while a child is still at pre-adolescent stage. Primarily, in the Somali social life, this identity is the mother from which all other identities emanate and virtually nurtured to distribute and distinguish the variant classifications.

On the other hand, the socio-ethnic doctrine determines that in the further north and northeastern part of the country sit those at the top of the Somali ethnic groups, a social rank equivalent to that of the Brahmin of India. In the Somali myth, the Isaq and Darod consider themselves as the ordained "super-nobles" while the Hawiye and Digil-Mirifle take their places at the subsequent "lower" levels in that order but above the Reer Hamar (Banadiri) and Barawaans who rest in almost the same place, atop of the Jareer at the bottom-most.

Conclusions

One of the most enduring myths in Somalia is also related to clan size. Although no one can provide a conclusive data on the particular of a Somali clan, the Somali nomadic pastoral has made, with the help of the regimes, the whole world believe that he belongs to the largest clan group in the country. This mockery data has become a tool to stratify the communities in the country as majority and minority clans in order to accomplish hegemonic gains. In addition to that, the introduction of a new Apartheid in the name of Four-Point-Five is seen by the Bantu Jareer people and other peoples currently classified as minority as the beginning of a strategy aimed at legalizing and permanently upholding a rigid measure of social segregation that benefits the majority-claiming section of the society without showing the basis for that unfounded numerical majority, especially when it lacks the necessary census to support it. The next chapter discusses the impact of the fabricated clan sizes and the negative effects of an amorphous conference in which the Apartheid 4.5 clan power sharing system is used as a tool for gaining more parliamentary representation for certain clans and as a barrier for limiting the representation of other segregated clans.

Notes and references

1. Mapmhela, Ramphele., "Combating Racism in South Africa: Redress/Remedies," in Hamilton et al (eds.), Beyond Racism: Race and Inequality in Brazil, South Africa, and the United States. Lynne Rienner Publishers. 2001:71.
2. Eno, Omar A., "Somalia's Recovery and Reformation: Transcending the Rhetoric of Clan Politics," a paper presented at the 47th African Studies Association meeting, New Orleans, USA., November, 2004.
3. Ibid.
4. See Chapter Four of this study.
5. *"Consultation fee"* is a term used by the international agencies. It has

a hidden overtone of "bribe." It covers monies they pay to the warlords for the purchase of their safety and for warlords' approval for operation in the areas they control.

6. Eno, Mohamed A., "The 14th Somali National Reconciliation Conference," a lecture presented in a seminar at Portland State University, November 2004.

7. Eno, Mohamed A., "A Structure In Search of Function: The IGAD Product." A paper presented at the Somali Bantu Intellectuals' Forum, held at CTC, Jan. 18, 2005, Mogadishu, Somalia.

8. Eno, Mohamed A., "Clans, Warlords and Peace-building: The Somali Phenomenon," a paper presented at the Rwanda Peace-Building Workshop, 1997.

9. Ibid.

10. See Chapters Two and Three of this study.

11. Eno, Omar A. "Who will surface the hidden agenda in the Somali peace problem?" A seminar paper presented in a workshop for the Somali Bantu participants in the Somali National Reconciliation Conference in Kenya, 2003.

12. Afrax, Maxamed D., Dal Dad Waayey iyo Duni Damiir Beeshay: Soomaaliya Dib Ma u Dhalan doontaa? Daabacaadda koowaad. Printed by Maji Matamu Printers Ltd., Eldoret, Kenya. 2002, p.31.

13. Ismail Aliyow Baxaar: interview in audiocassettes recorded in Jeddah, Saudi Arabia, 2002.

14. Ibid.

15. Mohamed Abdi Bulhan (alias Buulle), in a peace workshop in Nairobi, 2003.

16. Ibid.

17. Ibid.

18. Mohamed Farah Muudeey (Booroow), participant in a Somali Peace meeting in Addis, 1996.

19. Khadija M. Harganti, a discussion in Eldoret, 2003.

20. Ali, Ahmed Qassim, "The Predicament of the Somali Studies," in Ahmed, Ali Jimale., (ed.), The Invention of Somalia, op.cit. p.78.

21. Eno, Mohamed A., "How Wide Is The gap? Heegan Newspaper, Friday, Jan, 27, 1984.

22. Translation of Ahmed Qassim Ali, as above No, 20.

23. Aheda Mkomwa, discussion with Somali Bantu women in Kakuma Refugee Camp. 2004.

24. Ibid.

25. Paton, Allan., "The Christian Approach to Racial Problems in the Modern World." A Christian Action Pamphlet, (second edition). 1959:7.

26. Christian Action pamphlet, "The Dispossessed: the human tragedy of Apartheid". Published by the Christian Action. p.8. Kenya National Achieves.
27. Ibid., p.11.
28. Ibid., p.8.
29. Ibid., p.10.
30 Oberg, K. "The Kingdom of Ankole in Uganda," in Fortes, M., and Evans Pritchard., eds., African Political System. London: Oxford University Press. 1940.
31. Maquet, Jacques J., "Inequality In Rwanda," in Berghe, Pierre L. van den, ed., Race and Ethnicity in Africa. East African Publishing House, 1975: 79-89.
32. Eno, Omar A., "The Untold Apartheid Imposed on the Jareer/Bantu People in Somalia," in Adam, Hussein M., and Ford, Richard., eds., Mending Rips in the Sky: Options for Somali Communities in the 21st Century. Lawrenceville: Red Sea Press Inc., (1997:209-220).
33. Dualeh, op.cit., p.141.
34. Maquet, Jacques J., op.cit., p.88.
35. Extract from a videotaped seminar for Jareer/Bantu elders as mentioned in preceding chapters.
36. Besteman, Catherine., Unraveling Somalia: Race, Violence and the Legacy of Slavery. University of Pennsylvania Press. 1999:114.
37. Paton, Allan., op.cit., p.3.
38 Benedict, Ruth., Race and Racism. London: George Routledge & Sons Ltd. (1942:5).
39. Said of Toledo (a Moorish savant), quoted in Lancelot Thomas Hogben; Genetic Principles in Medicine and Social Service. London: William & Norgate, 1931, p.213) quoted in Ruth Benedict., Race and Racism.
40. Max Muller quoted in Biography of Words and the Home of Aryans. London, (1888, p. 120.)
41. Benedict, Ruth., op.cit., p.23.
42. Ibid. p.13.
43. Mabhida, Moses., For International United Action to End Apartheid – The Curse of South Africa. W.F.T.U Publications Ltd. 1962, pp.7-8.
44. See Chapter Four of this study, particularly Sheikh Hassan Barsane's statement protesting against abolition of slavery.
45. Raj, Hans., Fundamentals of Demography: Population studies with special reference to India. Surjeet Publications. (2001:11)
46. Ibid.
47. Ibid.
48. Lewis, I. M., Peoples of the Horn, op.cit., p.50 (including the footnote).
49. Hagi Mohamed Barrow, interview in Golweyn as in previous chapters.
50. Report on Minority Groups in Somalia: Joint British, Danish and Dutch

Fact-Finding Mission to Nairobi, Kenya, 17-20 September, 2000, p.30.

51. Abdi Ismail Samatar, quoted in Somali Workshop at Lenana House, Nairobi, July 10, 2003.

52. Report on Minority Groups in Somalia as in No. 51 above.

53. Ibid.

54. Ibid.

55. Bloom and Ottong, op.cit., p.76.

56. Enow, Marian A., "Alienation and Marginalization in Somali: The case of the Somali Bantu." A paper presented in a Somali Bantu Seminar in the USA, 2004.

57. Baron, Robert A., and Byrne, Donn., Social Psychology. (Tenth edition), Prentice-Hall, India. 2003:121.

58. Krosnick, J. A., Betz, A. L., Jussim, L. J., and Lynn, A. R., "Subliminal conditioning of attitudes." Personality and Social Psychology Bulletin, 18, 152-162. (1992),

59. Baron & Byrne, op. cit., p. 122.

60. Bandura, A., Self-efficacy: the exercise of control. New York: Freeman, (1997)

61. Hurlock, Elizabeth B., Child Development. Sixth edition – Tata McGraw-Hill edition. (2002:244-246.)

62. Ibid., p.229.

63. Ibid., p.387.

64. Santrock, John W., Psychology. 7th edition. McGraw-Hill (2003:153).

65. Marcia, J.E., "Ego identity development," in Anderson, J., (ed.), Handbook of Adolescent Psychology. New York: Wiley. 1980. (Also see Marcia 2001; Erik Erikson 1969).

Chapter 6

ENDORSING APARTHEID IN A NATIONAL CONFERENCE: THE 4.5 FACTOR

In Somalia's chaotic situation where armed conflict and related social disintegration have marred the realization of the basic necessities of life, it has become important to explore and discover a domain in which to restore the lost glory of the nation and the harmonious co-existence of the diverse communities. Since the collapse of the dictatorial rule of Siad Barre in 1991, the Horn of Africa nation has been held at ransom under the siege of gun-toting youths, unruly clan bigwigs and so-called clan elites with political immaturity. But in the indefinite journey towards peace and reconciliation among the vulnerable communities of the defunct state, the so-called facilitators have time and again missed the chance to implement the principle requirements of reconciliation in both contemporary as well as traditional approaches in the unfolding events through the processes.

After about 13 national peace and reconciliation initiatives proved dysfunctional, the regional member states of the Inter-Governmental Authority for Development (IGAD), and well wishers among the international community considered yet another attempt to convene a Somali conference. The objective was to bring together the various communities to overcome the curse of statelessness. The lack of a functioning central authority in the country has even tremendously affected the security situation of the neighboring countries, from the smuggling of illegal arms and narcotics,[1] and trafficking of illegal immigrants (human cargo), to the fighting in Somalia of "Proxy wars between Ethiopia and Eritrea."[2]

The prevalence of these ills and evils, compounded with disaffection with the Arte initiative of Djibouti which raised Abdikassim Salad to power, meant that Ethiopia found itself with an opportunity to stage-manage a situation many countries were reluctant to involve themselves in. It embarked on a multidimensional campaigning for the convention of the conference. Her aim was, among other things, to use all possibilities to aid herself in the maneuvering and manipulation of the proceedings in Eldoret and Mbagathi. By all means, the effort regarding the convention of the conference was seen as a commendable initiative by IGAD member states whose Council of Ministers assigned the Frontline States of Ethiopia, Djibouti and Kenya to plan and organize the conference jointly, while Kenya accepted to be the host.

The flow of the arriving contingents of delegates created the commotion and crisis that persistently haunted the receptionists and the organizers alike, especially in the provision of accommodation and catering. Barely a few days into the Conference the number of delegates sprouted up from the "official" 400 or so participants to a soaring 800, most of them equipped with official invitation letters. As one delegate remarked, "Participation has become for purchase."[3]

Within the first three days or so, it appeared that the majority of the participants in IGAD's original list had most probably been selected on terms of "who is for" and "who is against"[4] a certain frontline State. Occurrences of mysteries were discernible, one of them being how certain names were quickly plucked and others inserted into the list of participants. As it seemed, there was no proper criterion used for the selection of the delegates to the various categories for participation except the one mentioned above. An example of this nature is the civil society, which consisted of participants from diverse walks of life, from former warlords and war financiers to former ministers responsible for engulfing the country into war.

"Mafia-like gangs and syndicates"[5] were colluding to doctor vital documents supposed to be in the custody of the officials of the IGAD Technical Committee. Prominent stake-holders commenced their campaign from the outset, garnering support of one kind or another. The attitude has drawn the attention of the Chairman who announced in a full house plenary that "A lot of things are going on. Dollars have reached even my doorstep."[6] It was an open secret that collusions and business transactions were occurring in the corridors of the hotels and offices. Every financially potential warlord or prominent personality of the clan or sub-clan bought their way through to compromise the inner circles of the Conference administration, in order to implement individual interests.

Condoning the culprits

The butcherers of the masses, in the name of warlords, were welcomed in a high style with exception. They were provided with posh cars and luxurious private residences. They were not treated like the perpetrators they were in the genocide in Somalia, or same as other culprits of genocide like Charles Taylor. It seemed that the condoning of their criminality was treated as a mediating device for reconciliation. Unlike a reconciliation conference, most of the warlords were in a holiday mood relieving them of the stressful pressure they usually undergo in the country. The special treatment IGAD accorded them has increased rank for the warlords. In addition, diplomats from certain countries acted as consultants for some of the warlords, thereby laying roots for alliances for power play.

Telling the wrongdoers about their shame straight in the eyes would have helped them move a step forward towards the acceptance of responsibility for the mischiefs and massacres they had committed against the Somali society. This step would help them overcome the trauma that has led them to the commitment of those atrocities. But they were not helped to reach that important stage of self-lamentation. Instead, they were honored above all the other participants and conferred on them the status of 'leaders', although the only associable characteristics of leadership in their portfolio rests in that of killership.[7]

Disorganized conference

Uganda's president, Yoweri Museveni, once warlord himself, remarked about the conference as a "...long and torturous process..."[8] Indeed it was more torturous to certain groups than he knew, but the president did not mention that it was due to a collective foul-play by IGAD, representatives of the international community as well as members of the Somali delegates and warlords. Collectively, all the factions mentioned played a part in the undesirable circumstances leading to the prolongation of the process as an amorphous exercise. It was even more torturous to the oppressed, unarmed communities like the Jareer, the minorities and the outcasts who were denied equality in the eyes of the international community.

One of the most disgusting natures of the Conference was disorganization. Frustration and boredom grew immense due to the absence of scheduled agendas before hand. Most of the meetings were arranged in a humdrum state, either conducted prior to a short notice or, at most, communicated to the concerned delegates that night on the bulletin board in Sirikwa Hotel, which accommodated the offices of the IGAD Technical Committee and a section of the delegates. The other participants who were put up in other hotels had to be informed by a friend. Others would find out about any event after reaching Sirikwa the following morning.

In the course of the exercise, especially in the early stage, each member of the Technical Committee (TC) focused on an area of its interest:-

1) Ethiopia gathered its effort on recruiting a formidable group of clients abiding by its policy toward Somalia in order to secure a large number of votes for its preferred candidate in the event of the presidential election. Commenting on this concern, Samatar and Samatar reveal, "Ethiopia and allies continued to try to gerrymander both the composition and quantity of the delegates."[9] This was true because the initial list of the participants was drawn according to the recommendations and approval of this member of the Frontline States. Likewise, Adan Mohamed's statement reads in clear support of Samatar and Samatar as he writes, "The latest center of dispute was the claim that Djibouti and Ethiopia were unduly interfering with the talks for their specific interests."[10]

II) Kenya, being the host country and also seeing its partners' undiplomatic attitude, concentrated on entering into shady business deals with the hoteliers and transporters of the delegates. As the local media later reported, unscrupulous agreements were signed and fattened bills and invoices were concocted and paid for, eventually leading to shame and scandal prompting the donors' reaction and displeasure. It was cooled off in the diplomatic corridors and by relieving the first chairman of his duty together with a section of his team. The change ushered in the appointment of career diplomat ambassador Bethuel Kiplagat. Subsequently, the conference was conveyed from Eldoret to Mbagathi on the outskirts of Nairobi. This coincided with the completion of the Second Phase of the Conference in which selected teams comprising six committees completed their delegated tasks.

III) Djibouti, the mentor and host behind the 13th Somali National Peace Conference project behind the grooming of Abdikassim Salad to the presidency, was playing soft and shadowy diplomacy. Whispers were in the air about their wish to help reinstate Salad again for another term. But theirs was not as visible as Ethiopia's role that broke all the diplomatic lines.

Deficiencies disdained

The shifting of the conference to Mbagathi, Nairobi, envisaged a strategic move to reflect a shift in significance, following regime change in Kenya. Another viable reason was, according to the newly appointed Ambassador Kiplagat, "...to change the image of the conference and give it wider and positive media coverage."[11] True to his word, the conference was in a desperate need of a good Samaritan because the nature of events in Eldoret were deplorable, only comparable to the routine activities in the lawless Bakaraha market.[12]

On the other hand, although Kiplagat's scheme to minimize the cost of the conference and improve its image could be commendably credited to both his professionalism and good intentions, he couldn't save himself from falling into Ethiopia's trap of manipulations. In his lenient manner he once indicated, "...whatever the case, I want to keep Ethiopia on board."[13] Perhaps he was not contemplating at the time the costlier consequences of keeping Ethiopia on board.

Further worse, Ambassador Kiplagat's long career in the world of diplomacy and international relations proved blunt when he couldn't persuade or convince Ethiopia on the appointment of professional reconciliators who could apply a meaningful, ethics-based, unbiased and actual form of reconciliation. However, after the commotion and complaints became unbearable, it was no longer secret as Farida Karoney reported how, "Critics have accused the moderators in the Nairobi talks of concentrating more on power-sharing than reconciling the various factions."[14] Obviously, the agenda IGAD had put in place, particularly the intention of Ethiopia, was power-sharing. The deficiency from the lack of reconciliatory measures ripped off all institutions of the conference without sparing the well-respected Somali clergy.

The Somali clerics arrived already split into factions (or sects?) such as Babu-Sufi, Islah, Itihad, Ahlul-Sunna Wal-Jama'a and so many other names. They criticized and frequently called each other names, a behavior which doesn't augur well with either Islam or the objectives of reconciliation. Astonishingly, in the opening sessions of the meetings, especially in the plenary and civil society gatherings, the clerics were at the forefront reciting verses from the Holy Qur'an; they supplicated, and advised the delegates to maintain unity and Somaliness. But when it came to nominations to committees, they would put the Holy Book aside and settle their differences the belligerent Somali way before returning to the verses and traditions.

Extrinsic moral integrity versus intrinsic moral hypocrisy: a paradigmatic Somali social behaviour

Upon completion of the First Phase, marred by complaints, irregularities and confusion, Six Committees were formed to discuss, deliberate and report on respective areas of important national interests. Of these, Committee One, charged with the task of drafting a Provisional Charter, split into two sub-groups. The Committee, which included heavy weights in the legal profession, failed to consent on mainly three core issues: -

a)   Classification, interpretation and acquisition of citizenship;
b)   Adoption of the Federal system of governance; and
c)   Adoption of the national language.

Group A believed in:
(People, Religion and Language)
1.   The people of the Somali Republic are one and indivisible, part of the African people and the Arab nation.
2.   The law shall establish the manner of acquiring or losing citizenship. No Somali citizen or his offspring may lose his citizenship on account of acquiring citizenship of another country.
3.   Somali and Arabic shall be the official languages of the Somali Republic.[15]

(Organization of the State)
1.   "The structure of the State shall be decentralized and shall consist of:-
(a) Central authority
(b) Autonomous regional and district authorities.
(c) Authority of the independent agencies."[16]

Group B had a different opinion, presenting its ideology as follows: -

The Federal Republic

1. The Somali Federal Republic comprises of:-

    (a) A Federal Government.
    (b) State Government.
    (c) District and village governments.[17]

Article 5
The official languages of Transitional Federal Republic of Somali (sic) (Maay and Maxaatiri) Arabic and English as second languages.[18]

Article 7 – Citizenship
The following are citizens of the Somali Federal Democratic Republic:-
Any person who is a native of the Federal Democratic Republic of Somalia or any person who is born native of the Federal Republic.

> i) Any foreigner/s who was born in the Federal Republic ten years before its independence and has continuously state (sic) in Somalia.
> ii) Any foreigner who was born in Somalia after independence and one of his/her parents is a native of the Federal Republic of Somalia.
> iii) Any person who was born outside the Federal Republic whom one of his parents or grandparents are or were native of the Federal Republic.
> iv) Any person who was granted the Federal Republic citizenship in accordance with the law.
> v) No one shall qualify for the Federal Democratic republic citizenship by name, knowledge of Somali language, or short residence in the Republic.
> Citizens of the Federal Democratic Republic can have double nationality.
> vi) Any person who obtained citizenship on the conditions mentioned in paragraph 6 of this article shall lose the citizenship of the Federal Republic.
> vi) The means of acquiring and losing the federal Democratic Republic citizenship of Somalia shall be set by law.[19]

In brief analysis, Group A was in favor of the defunct theory of Greater Somalia according to which, Somalis born in the periphery of the Somali Republic i.e. in Kenya, Ethiopia and Djibouti would enjoy equal citizenship rights and status as Somalis born in the Republic. The rival Group B was in principle against this idea as those Somalis born in the neighboring countries make a constituent part of other jurisdictions, which are independent sovereign states.

The other contentious issue was the language. Group A preferred Arabic to be on equal footing and importance with Somali Maxaatiri as the official languages, an issue which does not command proper societal justification except to please the Arab League countries. Against that concept, Group B had a case to press for Maay language which is spoken as a mother tongue and lingua franca in almost all the Southern regions of the country, rather than the importation and imposition of Arabic, a language that is alien to the average Somali man or woman.

Group B, the Digil-Mirifle proponents of the Federal system of governance, had a long dream for Federalism rooted in colonial days. The political leaders of the community unequivocally expressed their sentiment to delegates from the Four Power Commission visiting Somalia for an opinion-gathering and fact-finding mission regarding the UN Trusteeship and subsequent independence. Touval visits the federalism political ideology of the Digil-Mirifle:

> "On the question of the constitutional form of the proposed union, however, the H.D.M.S. (Hizbi Democratic Mustaqal Somali) retained a distinct point of view, advocating for a federal constitution for the future Somali state. "This position was reiterated in 1958 when Jelani Sheikh bin Sheikh, at that time the party president, said in a speech to the party convention that "the party has become convinced that the only method of unifying the Somalis...is through a federal constitution which accords full regional autonomy."[20]

From another community/political leader, Touval brings to our attention:

> Sheikh Abdullah, then the party president, when asked by the Soviet member whether "he is not interested in the political activities of the country," replied: "I have only interest in the Digil Mirifle." In answer to another query, he stated: "When we asked for the trusteeship, we only meant for the country where the Digil Mirifle live, not the rest of the country. We do not mean the rest of Somalia."[21]

The controversial division of the Charter Committee into two polar sub-groups is historically laden in the pre-independence political phi-losophies of sections of the Somali society. Group A, therefore, stood for the reminiscent ideology of the SYL whose members were oppo-nents of the federal system, with a tendency for a centralized unitary system of government and a Greater Somalia ideology, which Hussein Ali Dualeh claims "died a natural death"[22] when Djibouti declined to join the Somali Republic upon attainment of independence in 1977. In any case, one year preceding independence, July 1959, then Prime Min-ister Abdullahi Issa was quoted as saying:

> In the interest of union among the Somali and in the interest of the very safeguarding of the Nation, the Government herewith declares that it does not pursue any regionalist or federalist goal, because unity alone can ensure the durable existence of a Somali national life.[23]

It was these two faculties of thought that had a hard political tussle for over 12 months, a scenario which on several intermittent occasions brought the Conference to the verge of collapse. To save the situation, an arbitration committee, various harmonization committees and a re-treat session were established as the approach towards a solution, but the contention was solid. Eventually, a harmonized Charter was agreed upon in a situation where the Digil-Mirifle won the day: a) They succeeded in the adoption of Maay-Maay as an official superordinate language parallel with its Maxaatiri counterpart, and b) Federalism was confirmed as the administrative political ideology of a Federal Somali Republic.

Notwithstanding the disputations, disparities and disinclination over the subjects mentioned above, both sub-groups of the Charter, including several of the other committees, were unequivocal about power sharing based on ethnic marginalization. They were all in sup-port of the official legalization of inequality among the different com-munities of the Somali society, particularly where the stakes related to the Negroid/Jareer. With the exception of the Committee on Economic Recovery, Institutional Building and Resource Management and the Committee on Regional and International Relations, all the other 4 Committees including the divided two sub-committees on the Charter believed in the 4.5 social inequality system and the tutelage of dishon-est members at the 13th Somali Reconciliation Conference held in Arte, Djibouti.

Ironically, the draft reports of these Committees, which were to map out guidelines for the way forward, were decoratively enriched with terms such as "justice", "equality", and "rights" not less than thirty times, without the morality to consider the controversy within their respective documents since the so-called 4.5 clan power sharing formula contrarily purported injustice, inequality and rightlessness. It becomes more deplorable particularly when some of the proponents of the discriminatory 4.5 phenomenon of Apartheid consist of respected personalities with life-long careers in the legal and jurisprudence professions, with some of them alleged to have participated in the construction of the 1960 constitution!

Dissonant to the ethics of their profession and knowledge, these committees imprudently spearheaded the culture of betrayal and violation of the human and civil rights of a section of the society. They deliberately ignored the preservation of rights and dignity of the people. Somali delegates from all walks of life, without the exclusion of high ranking officers, women, lecturers, intellectuals, religious leaders, clan elders, notables, lawyers/advocates, politicians, medical doctors, engineers and representative members of the civil society, were not only unanimously silent about this inexplicable marginalization against the Jareer/Bantu population, but indeed they all advocated for its consequent approval. Other "intellectuals" who harmonized several versions of the two disputative Charters have also celebrated the repetition, reiteration and upholding of the 4.5 clan power sharing formula ceremoniously as if it were the Holy word of God.[24] Even a section of the Somali scholars like Professor Mohamed Hagi Mukhtar glorify the 4.5 system as an "important accomplishment" in that, according to him, it is based on the "relative size, power and territorial rights" (Mukhtar 2007:123-130) of the communities separated; factors that are far from the reality as we know it, since the segregation implies a categorization of the communities as Somali and less-Somali.

Remarkably, it was only after its omission and denunciation by the first official and IGAD appointed Harmonization Committee, under the Co-Chairmanship of Professor Abdi I. Samatar of the University of Minnesota and Professor Mohamoud Jama of the University of Nairobi and their dedicated committee members, that the number 4.5 symbolically disappeared from the final draft Charter, which was indeed embedded with code and content transposed from the version of the Samatar–Jama Harmonization Committee. But literally, the system was effectively in practice as a major formula for appointments at all levels, from members of parliament to cabinet portfolios.

Despite the sound harmonization task the Samatar–Jama group did and the appreciation of members of the international committee who attended during the launch and presentation of the document, a member of the IGAD TC has pledged to disregard and obstacle the document because this committee did not contain a person of their choice. In preference, the Technical Committee member persuaded the rest to adopt a variety of lower quality versions produced through its backing and designed to depreciate and sabotage the first harmonized official Charter. The Samatar–Jama version, unlike the others, was produced through a process of unbiased, genuine, professionally and scholarly deliberated sessions in which neither the meager economy of the country nor the public aspiration was undermined. But because Ehiopia did not have an ally in the committee, it had to campaigm hard for discrediting the precious document, which it finally succeeded in total disregard of the views and good intentions of the chairman, representative members of the international committee as well as the other members of the Frontline States

The Somali delegates and the IGAD Technical Committee of the Frontline states, Kenya, Djibouti and Ethiopia, chose not to remember the evils of segregation and discrimination in South Africa and elsewhere, Somalia included, and advice against its continuance. In several sessions of the civil society meetings, IGAD TC and the so-called Leaders' Committee meetings, members of the Bantu/Jareer participants in the Conference proposed motions to strike off the 4.5 system of segregation. However, it was absolutely impossible to convince the Somali delegates about equality of the citizens in spite of its acknowledgement in the charter. In the civil society, the mention of a reverse from 4.5 displeased members from the armed clans. It would end up in a heated argument and debate and the meeting would break up.

In order to overshadow the sensitive topic of inequality and injustice, the IGAD Technical Committee in conjunction with Somali armed clans, embraced the Apartheid method of clan categorization and adopted the misleading term "all inclusive", betraying the world community. In actual fact, the lackluster named Somali National Reconciliation Conference was devoid of any equality for the Jareer community from day one. Underneath the superfluous "all inclusive" pronouncement was, in many respects, an innate ideology of segregation;

that of "inclusive but unequal." The context lodges in its underbelly a Jileec modified version of the American racial policy of "separate but equal."

The clans that share inclusivity as well as equality are those recognized as the "pure" Somalis by nomadic standards. This time, northern 'super-nobility' was disregarded and instead had to force the bitter pill down their throat. They had to accept it, especially after a show of military power had ousted them from state rule and the prestigious Villa Somalia where they manipulated over the years the milk from 'Maandeeq'.

After their military supremacy was symbolized in the removal of Dictator Siad Barre, the Hawiye achieved genealogical mobility, a status whose prerogative for decision-making previously remained within the jurisdiction of northern "nobility", which had self-stationed itself at the top. But this mobility, according to the ousters of Barre, would remain insufficient without employing an excessive push of downward mobility against the Jareer so that the status gap and rights and equality between the "very" Somali and the "less" Somali was visibly demarcated as much as it was extensively widened. The Jareer, the Reer Xamar (Banadiri) and several sub-groups of the outcast Gaboye and Baidari group were lumped together to share half of the equivalent of one Somali clan's share. Accordingly, the highest group would garner less than 0.3 of the symbolic 0.5 allocated to the totality of the artificially made "minority" groups.

The Reer Xamar (Banadiri), the occupational outcasts, the Bajuni and the Barawaans are marginal in number compared to the Jareer, according to the last colonial census. The Bantu/Jareer or "autochthonous" Negroid in the South are greater in number than the rest of the entire Southern Somali Jileec clans. Evidently, therefore, the case of squashing the numerical supremacy of the Jareer and deliberately grouping them with the numerically minority is a concept to undermine their right to equality. Whatever the fabrication, the reason is at any rate related plainly to ethnicity. Somaliness, according to genealogy, is refined and defined by the physical features of the people concerned. In this regard, the Jareer, being of distinct Negroid features and African origin, cannot be equated to the Somali,[25] the offspring of "Quraishite" Arabs, notwithstanding their African skin pigmentation and Cushitic origin of recent establishment.

In the case of the Reer Xamar (Banadiri), one may argue of statistical minority because their confederation does not constitute a large population, although one may again claim otherwise due to lack of census data to determine their exact demography. The Barawaans can be put more or less at par with the Reer Xamar, although even for them, no exact population quota is confirmed. But remarkable to this study is that both groups are in the Jileec classification of family (see chapter one), notwithstanding their dumping into the 'minority' category, an entailment referable to their being out of the parentheses of Somaliness by genealogy.

The occupational outcast groups, Tumaal, Reer Xasan, Yaxar, Madhibaan, Midgaan, Muse Dherio etc. are Somalis, or at least [were] Somali 'nobles' (nasab) before the invention of their alleged imperfections as detailed in the Chapter One above.

Maay and Maxaatiri languages: on equal footing at last

In another dynamic socio-political turn-around, the Digil-Mirifle, traditionally despised and considered below their northern Jileec brothers, have emerged achievers of tremendous victories in the social, military and political domains. They were adorned with new respect and recognition they would have never achieved earlier. They got their new social place of equality after taking up arms and liberating the Reewing land from Aideed's Habar-Gidir sub-clan of the Hawiye clan. After Aideed's humiliating defeat and other preceding triumphs over certain Darod sub-clans, the Reewing Resistance Army (RRA) and its followers became a robust group to reckon with. In Conferences convened prior to the last two or three meetings, the Digil-Mirifle confederation was not awarded the same equal participation and posts as the Dir, Hawiye and Darod.

Understandably, therefore, the Digil-Mirifle adamancy on the adoption of the Federal system and the official super-ordination of the Maay language were invigorated firstly by the military might that erected the Reewing community as equals rubbing shoulders with their Samale brethren. Only after military might and ethno political equality were realized by the community were the other social issues tabled for debate, discussion and consequent approval. It would be beyond imagination for the northerners to have lifted Maay language to official status and equal to the Maxaatiri language in any circumstance, but the Reewing community's possession of the gun negotiated a new identity for the community as a robust group to reckon with.

The charter theme drove a precarious wedge between the Maay and certain communities of Maxaa speakers, creating a dreadful stand-off and a stalemate that almost disbanded the conference. Thus, the proposal that each group works on its own draft charter has enlivened the inspiration of the multi-ethno-genetic Digil-Mirifle confederacy and the will for their political identity through the exercise of their age-old federalism ideology - a prestige in vertical identity mobility by virtue of their language of culture. Among other things, the factors lending tremendous back-up support to the Digil-Mirifle argument were:-

a) Their acquisition of militia power-base which put them militarily on par with the other armed militia, and

b) The logical dilemma of which language would qualify to a status of lingua franca – the vastly spoken local Maay language acquired as first and mother tongue by communities of native Somalis, or the alien and imported Arabic, which has to be learned as a third or foreign language?

Most of the proponents of the mythical monolinguality faculty of thought shied away from responding to this question. The Reewing have logic as a main instrument to push for their cause. Eventually, Maay had to be recognized as a national language, a prestige which was long overdue.

Somaliland shunned participation

At a glance, a disparity arises between the misleading 4-word title or theme, 'Somali National Reconciliation Conference' and the actual occurrences that prevailed in the course of the conference, especially when taken into consideration the points elaborated below:-

a)   Owing to massive foreign domination and manipulation under the umbrella of IGAD, the conference was not Somali-driven. Worse though, it was contrary to the original concept which reads in a report: "The IGAD Council of Ministers emphasized that the Somali Peace Process should be Somali-owned and Somali-driven".[26] In his words, chairman Mwangale confirmed IGAD's role by retorting, "The approach of the Frontline States is not to prescribe solutions but create a basis for dialogue,"[27] though unfortunately, it remains to everybody's knowledge that neither dialogue nor reconciliation has taken place.

In contradiction, Hussein Aideed's emotional statement on a local TV station that "The whole process is driven by circulars of instructive statements," and that the IGAD TC should remain "...as facilitators, not as managers,"[28] portrays the deception and twist administered on the initial guidelines as given by the IGAD Council of Ministers. Aideed even went further to censure the IGAD Frontline States as people who have "...neither will nor desire to continue the conference."[29]

b) A major stakeholder and part and parcel of the Union of the Republic of Somalia, the administration of the Northern brothers, Somaliland, was not officially present. Many farsighted Somali delegates and notables reiterated the necessity of Somaliland's presence at the conference. Similarly, earlier reports confirm IGAD's willingness to bring Somaliland on board, but that was later undermined. According to the initial proposal:

> "The Ministers re-affirmed a need to invite Somaliland to the conference and requested the TC makes efforts to invite Somaliland to attend the conference. They however recognized that Somaliland is not to be equated with factions and that the invitation to Somaliland be worded differently from that of other Somali parties."[30]

Sadly, sheer reluctance and hidden agenda on the part of the IGAD Frontline States have denied the Somali people the opportunity to nationalize the conference. The controversial case surrounding Somaliland's participation suggests the motive that the invitation was deliberately withheld by an IGAD member among the Technical Committee as a last resort 'lucky-card' to be used for subversive bargains in the enhancement of a particular party's future gains.

c) Because the Conference started with the factional philosophy of gaining numerical supremacy of participants, which overshadowed all other sectors of the proceedings, and consequently ended with the same, there was no mention-worthy form of reconciliation convened or achieved. Professor Abdi I. Samatar issued a clear comment on the episode in a workshop in Nairobi, affirming, "We had facilitators, not reconciliators."[31]

In the 2-year life span of the conference, neither the organizers (IGAD) nor the donors are praise-worthy for fulfilling the requirements of reconciliation necessary to put on track a society so dividedly disgruntled along tribal lines and polarized by centuries of feuding ven-

detta that funneled xenophobia reigned along with hatred and antagonism.

d) Although it was dubbed a conference, the proceedings of the
gathering left a lot to be desired. The Conference had no identification
of a workable day-to-day agenda.

e) On several occasions, the delegates were locked out of their
rooms and denied meals in their respective hotels for delay or lack of
payment.

f) The warlords severely disturbed the conference, pursuing the
settlement of conference related disagreements on wars inside the
country, thus contravening a cease-fire agreement[32] undertaken at the
early stage of the conference and signed by all the warlords and faction
leaders.

g) Apart from the Somali faction leaders, huge misunderstand-
ings among the Technical Committee have on varied occasions brought
the Conference to a complete halt. Ethiopia has technically often retreated from the conference whenever things went contrary to its de-
sires, thus causing more trauma and delay.

On the other hand, while not entirely disagreeing with Abdi
Samatar in his statement of IGAD as facilitators and not reconciliators,
my own experience and observation as an official participant in the
Conference reveal more than that. In a broad spectrum, "Facilitation is
the process of helping a group complete a task, solve a problem or
come to agreement to the mutual satisfaction of the participants."[33] Facilitation, in this paradigm, requires some tools and skills, which are
essential to equip the facilitator so that he/she is aware of the multiple
implications of the process. Secondly, considering the importance of
the conference and its input in human and material resources, and the
aspirations entwined in the intrinsic national morale, IGAD should
have foreseen as prerequisite the engagement of professional facilitators and mediators to manage and consult the proceedings of the conference for the attainment of desirable goals.

From day one, the Frontline States have compromised the traditional principles of facilitation. By this, I mean to note that IGAD's role
during the 2 - year long process of the Conference was in no way focused on the tradition of "what would serve the group best?"[34] but
rather what would best serve an individual faction subscribing to
Ethiopia's interests. As such, the true qualities for the achievement of
effective facilitation were lacking in their totality. By far, rather than as

pure facilitators, certain members of the IGAD Technical Committee and other 'friendly' countries misconceived their role and put themselves on equal rivalry with each other and again with the disputing Somali factions.

Practically, the nature of gerrymandering has made IGAD another stakeholder in the status of a faction, facilitating their own participation in multiple roles, maneuvering and manipulating the proceedings and influencing the decisions. Apparently, there exists a bulk of evidence to support that they were biased against certain factions and individual participants, while at the same time serving as consultants to the opposing rivals. Copies of complaints to the Technical Committee and press reports suggest persistent anomalies of bias and ring-leadership, supporting the reports in some of the local media.[35]

The missed points

Among other factors, core issues worthy of ample consideration have been neglected:

1) Face-to-face dialogue:-
    a) Intra-clan level,
    b) Inter-clan level, and
    c) National level.

2) Acceptance of responsibility by the warlords and all those who played a role in the flare up of the catastrophe in Somalia and the butchering of thousands of people who are unaccounted for.

3) Seeking forgiveness by the warlords in a measure to accept their responsibility for the mass murder that took place in the country.

4) Conference facilitation and mediation by Somali intellectuals from the country and Diaspora - whether through clan representation / participation or otherwise, and assisted by foreign experts.

5) Knowing the warlords' prerequisite for voluntary disarmament; the variables persistent.

6) Discussion over the hindrance of the restoration of confianza and peace building.

7) Limitation of foreign interference, manipulation and gerrymandering.

8) Minimization of the agitation towards the concept of power

sharing during the reconciliation exercise.

9) Emphasis on a time frame to implement the reconciliation process.

10) Assessment, evaluation and up-to-date reports on the development of activities in order to get an early warning and diffuse possible subversion against the process.

11) The ownership of legally binding documents by all the appointed representatives of the sub-clan/clan, rather than only by the warlords/faction-leaders the majority of whom did not practically represent the whole sub-clan or clan.

12) Equal participation for all clans/national stakeholders.

13) An appropriate holistic approach to the transformation of the culture of war into a culture of peace, with prominent roles for the unarmed, neutral communities who had not participated in the atrocities that devastated the nation.

Widening the animosity margin

As Dee Kelsey and Pam Plumb have observed, "Often we jump the gun by trying to solve a conflict before we have identified its roots."[36] The nature of the Somali conflict is complex. It is somehow shortsighted and a grave misconception as it is trying to deal with it from one angle. It shouldn't be seen just as a contemporary war instigated by the inequitable distribution of insufficient resources. We have to consider that part of the prolongation of the problem is also related to problems inherited from colonial days. Yet more of it goes deeper into age-old clan animosities and a quiet struggle for identity supremacy among the multiple clans and sub-clans.

However, Committee Six did its best to envisage what it saw as part of the problem underlying the conflict, but the IGAD Technical Committee did not pay the report much attention. The report said in a part, "The underlying sources of conflict have their origin in the pre-colonial period."[37] Once a committee report has highlighted an important source of the problem, it was IGAD's duty to focus on it and help the clans trace a solution. Instead, the concept of the war was mismanaged by 'straight-jacketing' the source of Somalia's undoing as a mere "resources and underdevelopment,"[38] as believed by even some African Presidents. The conference did not attempt to address the inter-clan and intra-clan identity conflict that was evident during the entire life of the Conference. In fact the scholarly observation that "…the superiority complex of one group over another, mainly based on cultural differences"[39] was exposed as another aspect of the root causes to the conflict but the 'facilitators' of the 14th Somali National Reconciliation Conference overlooked it. Truth exists in that part of the divided loyalties was provoked by mismanagement, greed, nepotism and ethnocentrism indulged in by those at the helm, but it lures also a synchronous combination with other segments and series of cultural predicaments, which trailed down the line of Somali pastoral history.

Looking back into the history of Somalia, one may deduce that inter-clan and intra-clan animosities and a living culture of war were the order of the day. As Douglas Collins remarks, "The Auliahan are fighting the Marehan, the Garre are fighting the Galgail, the Uadan are fighting the Geledi, the Omar Mohamud are fighting the Habr Ghidir and the Shifta are fighting for the hell of it."[40] This statement is only one out of many more written about the bellicosity of the Somali people and the depth of the roots of their antagonism against one another.

Perceptually, it was the unfolding of a series of feudal events and other monumentalized traditional animosities in a continuum that burst their banks in an abrupt explosion in search of a healing for stockpiles of psychosocial trauma. These internal wounds have been bulging into voluminous masses over the decades; and the unleashing of that wrath broke all hell loose that containing it boggles many the minds. It is in fact the failure to diagnose the remote causes from the immediate causal that swerved the precision of the focal point in the conflict.

The Somali conflictants were born into a culture of war, and more often than not, battles fought in rural areas extended to urban towns, executing vengeance on innocent citizens, for a crime committed elsewhere by an unknown kinsman. Likewise, minor personal urban grudges were shifted to remote villages "away from the law" and bloody wars flared up as a consequence. Looking at the problem only as a conflict over resources was the first mistake, while the lack of expert facilitators and reconciliators supported by expert Somalists (Somalis and foreigners) [41] was another of IGAD's deleterious and premeditated discrepancies. The attitude of one-eyedness has led to the unnecessary prolongation of the Conference and the formation of a government that would exist in structure but not in function. The legitimation of Mogadishu as the capital in the readings of the Charter[42] adopted by the Conference did not easily become plausible.

Undermining and absence of discussions to unearth the nitty-gritty of the above social dynamics envisages an acute delusion and that the crux of the matter still remains unattended to. The thesis of my argument is supported by incidents which created more havoc than could harmonize reconciliation, as new factions were formed and others married into coalitions and alliances within the process of reconciliation!

The Igad role in the emergence of pacts and new alliances during the conference

1)   The Transitional National Government (TNG) split into two groups: a faction led by then Interim President Abdikassim Salad, and its rival arm called TNG (*Asali*) original, which was headed by Abdikassim's then Prime Minister, Hassan Abshir Farah.

2)   What was once a strong alliance comprising 8 factions, well known as G8 (Group 8), suffered an abrupt political puncture, shrinking its membership to a toothless 3 – with Mohamed Kanyare and Omar Mohamed 'Finish' of the Hawiye clan and Mowlud Ma'ani of the Jareer community, bewildered as the stout foundation of their coalition was pulled off its balance.

3)   The civil society splintered into two parties spearheaded separately by Asha Hagi Elmi (Hawiye) and Shariff Salah (Digil-Mirifle).

4)   The National Salvation Council which was also an "off-spring" of the 14th SNRC in Kenya was dominated by the Hawiye, with the exception of Jama Ali Jama and Ahmed Omar Jees who both belong to sub-clans of the Darood clan family.

5)   Abdikassim's section of the TNG was also a Hawiye control-zone save one member each from Ortoble, Lelkase and Dhulbahante, all Darood sub-clans, and an insignificant number from other clans.

6)   The Jowhar administration of strong man Mohamed Dhere and the Puntland administration (faction of ex-Colonial Abdullahi Yusuf, now Interim President of the Federal Republic of Somalia) made a tactical coalition with the robust Somali Salvation and Reconciliation Council, formed after Arteh and with very strong backing from Ethiopia, to counter-balance and frustrate the Djibouti-backed Abdikassim and his dormant interim government. The 2 new comers (Jowhar administration and Puntland) stretched the SSRC coalition's subscription to a strong membership of 17 factions.

7) Out of the 25 signatories (including Abdikassim) of the National Salvation Council, 17 factions united into a separately independent coalition. Five of the remaining 8 factions chaired by Abdikassim Salad, Bihi, Muse Sudi, Osman Atto and Barre Hirale, instituted an amalgamation, with Abdikassim Salad's TNG arm standing as the power-house. The other 3 consisted of the factions left aloof after the crumbling of the G8; their leader was Mohamed Kanyare Afrah.

8) A noteworthy elaboration here is that although the National Salvation Council was composed of 25 groups or signatories, they were tolerating differences elsewhere on interest and ideological basis, because 17 of those factions were automatic subscribers to the Abyssinian philosophy and school of thought, while 8 groups were inclined to a Djiboutian school of thought, i.e. TNG thinking.

9) The Digil-Mirifle confederation of communities was also affected, although some of their prominent leaders were cautious and secretive, giving an impression of 'neutrality'. However, Sheikh Aden Madobe, Deerow and Shariff Salah were opined as having a tendency toward the Ethiopian camp. Habsade, categorized as a prominent figure in Moallim Madobe's territory, was emitting signals of affiliation with Abdikassim.

10) Ex-Colonel and RRA factional chairman Mohamed Hassan Shati-gadud had a devastating head-on collision with Ethiopia after an RRA splinter group was midwifed against him in his own area during the course of the conference. Shati-gadud blamed his former ally, Ethiopia, for masterminding the intra-RRA division, particularly at a time when he was in Kenya participating in the reconciliation conference. Later, Sheikh Aden Madobe had to be invited officially as a faction leader alongside Shati-gadud, because Ethiopia would rely on his vote for its presidential candidate. Also, he could be used to disrupt things for Shati-gadud in case of the latter's disagreement with his former sponsor.

Igad and factional relationships

1. **Daarood**
   a) Harti
      1) Dhulbahante
      2) Warsangeli

3) Marjerteen
4) Ortoble
5) Lelkase

All except few backed Ethiopian despotism in the conference.

b)   Absame - Majority of the Absame were for Ethiopia although a marginal number opposed.
c)   Marehan- Part of the Marehan showed a very loyal subscription to Ethiopia while others were hard-core opponents.

2. The marginalized / oppressed "less" Somali communities

The oppressed and marginalized groups, the "unequals" and/or the "second-class citizens", in other words, the 0.5 communities, mainly supported the Ethiopian backed "fraternity". Of the 3 Jareer-Weyne groups, approximately a 2/3 majority was for Ethiopia, "as a political tactic to (a) encounter Mowlud Ma'ani's treacheries and alliances, and (b) have a strong wall to lean on against Somali antagonism that was continuously frustrating Jareer participation."

3. Dir

About 80% of the Dir at the conference were supporters of the Ethiopia – steered policy towards Somalia.

4. The Digil-Mirifle

The Digil-Mirifle were mostly in harmony with Ethiopia. Very few of them at times strained relationship with the Frontline State. All the same, eventually they had more factional 'leaders' representing them, despite the creation [of] wider hostilities and intra-clan fighting at home in the course of the reconciliation conference.

5. The Hawiye

Most of the prominent Hawiye warlords maintained good relationship with Ethiopia although some entertained Arab policy affiliation with Egypt. Strong G8 proponent, Mohamed Kanyare Afrah of the Murusade sub-clan of the Hawiye clan was in extreme disagreement with Ethiopia, but his coalescing with Ethiopia's choice for the top seat, Abdullahi Yusuf Ahmed, in the waning days to the presidential election, opened another chapter in the study of Somali coalitions, alliances as well as inter-clan and intra-clan politics of interest.

Under this setting, Abdullahi Yusuf's election as President was not a surprise, considering the campaigning he engaged from day one of the conference. He had several advantages including a) the political back-patting and blessing he enjoyed among the IGAD Frontline States, b) his close relation with some of the Hawiye factional leaders, and c) his generosity 'open-handedness', all of which contributed to the project of his majestic ascension up the ladder where the Hawiye clan failed to protagonize in the management of milking Maandeeq (the she-camel).

Project 14

The long, tough and controversy-ridden Somali peace process culminated in the formation of a Transitional Federal Parliament, which as a consequence elected an interim president. Inauguration, oath-taking and ululation marked the outcome of the conference in spite of the inherent paradoxes. The outcome was predictable as Siad Barre's army colleague ex-Colonel Abdullahi Yusuf Ahmed was crowned as the interim president in October 2004. But a subsequent negative development was delivering an unavoidable message to the Somali people. In the sprawling Eastleigh estate in Nairobi, opposing crowds of Hawiye and Darood demonstrated in the streets in the night: One group, expectedly the Darod, welcomed the outcome while the other side, Hawiye, was obviously denouncing it. It was a near-clash as flying stone-bullets were exchanged before elders restored tranquility. It was a clear surfacing of the impasse in the underneath, which the 'Reconciliation' conference had failed to carry on aboard. My premonition related to this episode was informed by the predisposition that yet another looming bad omen would endure Somalia.

A well perceived dialectic chronicling serious criticism has opened among certain circles of the Hawiye, depreciating the result of the process as "from Darood to Darood."[43] As one of the Hawiye political backbenchers put it, "Such a result adduces the time, lives and resources devastated in the war to overthrow Barre (a Darood) as unde-serving and incommensurate with the result.[44] In the other end, the Darood expressed satisfaction and jubilation as they re-established themselves unobtrusively at a position they adore obsessively for its prestige, a seat whose occupation they have always believed to be their divine right.

The negative implications of an anticipated conference failure

There was a lot into this conference than the eye could meet. In-deed it continued on an indefinite time limit. Coupled with that was the colossal funds consumed to the tune of millions of US dollars. Therefore, the exercise was a political project of regional as well as in-ternational dimensions.

The IGAD Technical Committee of the Frontline States on the one end, and representatives of the international donors on the other, had a load on their back and a duty to implement a project whose end prod-uct was so anxiously awaited. Wreckage of the conference might have cost certain officials their jobs. Enquiries into the causes of the collapse would have revealed devastating discrepancies and the destinations of monies unaccounted for, but which monies now are covered under the shadow of this concrete indicator which is the morphological existence of a parliament, a president and of course a cabinet structure to steer the government institutions and their obligations. These remain to be no more than structures, installed for circumvention, which are now in dire perplexity of how and where to commence the required institu-tional functions a government is expected to provide.

The traumatic pressure in the forethought of the precarious conse-quences entangled in the demise of the conference, preoccupied the officials appointed for the management of this 14th Project dubbed So-mali National Reconciliation Conference. The devastating heat from the abortion of the Conference would have to a large extent jeopard-ized the credibility of the entire IGAD membership under whose aus-pices the international community committed voluntarily amounts of domestically needed resources. In a sense, therefore, the propitiation and appeasement with which the warlords and faction heads were ap-proached every time they pulled out of the conference had an underly-ing strategic connotation to pre-empt the opening of Pandora's Box.

With no tangible reconciliation eminently undertaken during the two-year span of the Conference, there is no doubt that the centuries old wounds were left rotting below the visible surface, while 'prestige' Project 14 dealt with only the dressing of the puss spread on the external. In doing so, IGAD had to create an opportunity to conclude the Project and therefore, borrowing from Ali Jimale Ahmed, "opted for the easy way out."[45]

The international community: effortless efforts

The international community commendably responded to requests to help curb the debacle the world community and the regional countries were having difficulty coping with as a result of Somalia's anarchy. They have responded with an intervention in financial sponsorship for the conference and they lived unto their word in their tolerance for the hefty amounts of funds expended.

Although this was a justified good gesture of human philanthropism, they should have also made it their concern that the exercise was carried out smoothly in accordance with the principles of facilitation, mediation and reconciliation. By doing so, the financial sponsors would have stood in a better position to conduct the monitoring of the program and its evaluation according to the successive stages and their outcome. At least they should have provided experts in the areas encompassing the process, to steer, consult and advice in the various aspects of the Conference in order to follow the fundamentals prerequisite to a successful reconciliation.

From an external evaluation, the Somali National Reconciliation Conference, alias "Project 14", consummated a game of robotics than accommodating the true ideals of purposeful politics. Technical and financial blockades have on several occasions brought the exercise almost to its knees. On several occasions, the delegates were abashed and disgraced as hoteliers flashed them out of their hotel rooms in demand of payments for earlier services provided in accommodation and meals.

Considering the magnitude of the conference, the international community should have taken the responsibility to engage expertise in terms of conference management, mediation and reconciliation methods -- in general, the engagement of Somalist scholars with profound erudition of the diversity of the Somali community of nations and their respective cultures. They should have also welcomed and appreciated the expertise of distinguished Somali scholars both from inside the country and the Diaspora so as to allow the interplay between the local and foreign expertise enrich each other to benefit the conference.

Unfortunately, this opportunity was not seized since the intellectuals were elbowed out of active participation, at times mistreated and often disgracefully humiliated,[46] owing to the heavy handedness of an IGAD TC member, namely Ethiopia. The negative attitude towards the Somali scholars' input was premeditation by the Frontline States who made it their mandate capacitating and further deepening the Somali clan hostilities. Subsequently, intellectual participation was initially limited while the importance of their presence was eventually withdrawn and ignored altogether. The principled among these scholars have pulled out from the exercise while the others had their role reduced to (kutuba-qaad) as personal secretaries to the warlords.

With the neglect of these useful factors, the good intentions of the donors have been thwarted by the monopolization and manipulation by IGAD as the stage-managers. But the donors were not unconscious of the obstructive impasse in the Conference. They have received numerous copies of complaints by the factions and individual participants informing them of the sterile path of the exercise and the emotions inherent to the intense political climate.[47] There was an inexcusable and unprecedented neglect in their part, to say the least.

There is no question that the conference has widened the multi-dimensional psychosocial trauma, which has been afflicting excruciatingly on the Somali people. The solution, in my opinion, did not lie in the formation of a state, but rather in the creation of a viable reconciliation process in which every person would overcome his or her grief. Competition for resources, identity and cultural supremacy only make way for bias, prejudice and hatred, factors through which social confianza and societal bonds cannot be attained. For Somalia, the way forward is in the restoration of the lost love, rebuilding trust in one another – regardless of one's ethnic background - and the preservation of the un-compromisable unity that was once the symbol of the country.

In the 14th Somali National Reconciliation Conference, the idea was initiated by IGAD, the conference was managed by IGAD, the 'facilitation' was made by IGAD, the Interim Somali government was molded by IGAD, yet the officials IGAD had delegated the expedition of the conference were diplomats with no possession of a reconciliation record in their portfolio. This factor is another clear representation of the conundrum that haunted the exercise. If under this reality we ask the question: Has any praiseworthy reconciliation been conducted in the 14th SNRC? The true answer is NO. Reversibly, if we may please ourselves metaphorically with an end product, we can reframe the question to suit our illusive dogma and put it this way: Was a government installed? The answer is YES. Then to the latter response we may ask: why is the government neither functioning nor seated together in one place in the capital of the country if indeed it was born out of an effective reconciliation conference and a public-driven project?

As Eno enlightens, "We have to evaluate the situation in pursuance of what the variable was before the conference, and whether the conference, as the vehicle, has achieved that. If the variable in our search prior to the conference was in the structure of an institution, one was indeed formed; but if it was laid in reconciliation and a functioning institution, veritably this is yet very far from being achieved any time in the near future."[48]

Conclusion

This chapter presented a descriptive reflection of ethnic divisions and social discrimination and marginalization. From claims of Arab origination and pre-Somali presence of autochthonous Jareer/Negroid or Bantu population in Somali in the previous chapters, the discussion has landed us into a very recent phenomenon of "4.5 clan power-sharing formula". When we scale these hypotheses against the universal belief of Somali homogeneity, monolinguality, monoculturality and monotheologicality, we may be allowed the tendency to deviate our understanding from that which was, but to give an equal observation to the other version of a more real Somalia.

This version exposes us to yet another extensive debate of: Who is a Somali and by what criteria is the paradigm of Somaliness determined? The birth of the view related to this question was partly caused by the 4.5 clan superiority-inferiority and partly by the Jareer outcry against discrimination and alienation. In order to find out the truth or otherwise about these claims, the study has considered a quantitative survey to explore in-depth the magnitude of these claims. The next segment lays its concern on the rot underneath the phenomenon of

Somaliness and the apparent ethnic marginalization hidden in the soft underbelly of "Somali homogeneity" in perspective of the autochthonous Zenj/Negroid race of Somalia.

Notes and references

1. Mohamed, Adan., "Somali Peace Talks proving futile: External interference and petty squabbles to blame for stalemate," Daily Nation. March 7, 2003.
2. Farah et al , in Lind, J., and Sturman, K., eds., op.cit., p. 327.
3. Marian Awes, a Jareer participant in the Conference whose name was later expunged mysteriously from the list after she had been officially invited.
4. Yusuf Ali (Baasaay), a participant in the first phase of the Conference, 2003.
5. Ibid.
6. Elijah Mwangale, first Chairman of the IGAD Technical Committee of the Frontline States to the Somali Reconciliation Conference. (Also see Maxamed D. Afrax's book 'Dal Dad Waayey' op.cit.,p.96.)
7. Mohamed A. Eno "The Predicament of the 14th Somali National Reconciliation Conference and the IGAD Factor," paper presented at a seminar for Somali Bantu/Jareer participants in the SNRC in Kenya, 2003.
8. Yoweri Museveni, (President of Uganda) in his speech at Moi International Sports Centre, Kasarani, during the inauguration of the interim president of the Federal Republic of Somalia, 2004.
9. Samatar, Abdi I., and Samatar, Ahmed I., "Somali Reconciliation," an Editorial Note in Ayaamaha Press on line. http/:www.ayaamaha.com(downloaded on 10.29.03)
10. Mohamed, Aden, ibid., as No. 66 above.
11. Bethuel Kiplagat, second Chairman of the IGAD Technical Committee, in a speech elaborating the new initiatives to improve the general climate of the conference, Sirikwa Hotel, Eldoret, December 2002.
12. A chaotic marketplace in Mogadishu where all kinds of businesses take place, from foodstuff to modern weapons.
13. Bethuel Kiplagat, in a discussion with the Harmonization Committee, Nairobi, 2003.
14. Farida Karoney, "Somalia hopes for peace after decades of war." (Special Report), Daily Nation, (Nairobi) Sep. 17, 2003.
15. Federalism and Provisional Charter – Committee One [Group A] (ARTICLE THREE - p.2). Nairobi, 2003.
16. Ibid. p.8.
17. Federal Transitional Charter. Article 2.(Group B)23 March, 2003. p.1.
18. Ibid., p. 2.

19. Ibid., pp.2-3.
20. Touval, op.cit., pp.96-97.
21. Ibid., p. 96.
22. Dualeh, op.cit., p.43.
23. Touval, p.97.
24. Eno, Mohamed A. "A Return of Apartheid to Africa: The Somali Case," paper presented at the Africa Peace-Building Workshop held at Sports View Hotel, 2004.
25. See Chapters One, Two and Three..
26. http/:Somali-civilsociety.org. "Somali National Reconciliation Conference."
27. Ibid.
28. Hussein M. F. Aideed, talking in a press conference televised by Citizen T.V News bulletin in Kiswahili and in English, 20th March 2004.
29. Ibid.
30. Somali Civil Society website as in No. 91 above.
31. Abdi Ismail Samatar, "The IGAD Peace Process: The Betrayal of the Somali People," a seminar paper presented in a Somali Workshop held at Lenana House, Nairobi, July 2003.
32. Article 2 of the Declaration on Cessation of Hostilities, Structures and Principles of the Somali National Reconciliation Process. (Signed by the warlords in Eldoret on 27th October, 2002.)
33. Dee Kelsey and Pam Plumb., Great Meetings! How TO FACILITATE LIKE A PRO. Hanson Park Press. Second Printing. (1999:7)
34. Ibid.
35. Daily Nation, Sep. 17, 2003.
36. Kelsey and Plumb, op.cit., p.120.
37. Report of Committee Six of the SNRC on Conflict Resolution and Reconciliation.
38. Yoweri K. Museveni – as above.
39. Jong, Albert de., Ethnicity: Blessing or Curse? op.cit., p. 13.
40. Collins, Douglas., A Tear for Somalia; op.cit., p.23.
41. Samatar and Samatar., "Somali Reconciliation", op.cit.
42. The Transitional Federal Charter of the Somali Republic. 2004.
43. Muse Mohamed Absuge, alias Jeesto, personal discussion in Nairobi, a few days after the new interim president Abdullahi Yusuf was sworn in, October 2004.
44. Ibid.
45. Ahmed, Ali Jimale, Daybreak Is Near…, op.cit., p.140.
46. Mohamed A. Eno "A Structure In Search Of Function," op.cit.
47. Ibid. (Also copies of these documents and numerous others on different subjects related to the Conference are in possession of this author.)
48. Ibid.

Chapter 7

AMID ETHNIC MARGINALIZATION AND IDENTITY CONFUSION: WHO IS A SOMALI AND WHAT DETERMINES SOMALINESS?

"Some sociologists argue that exclusion from citizenship remains a central feature of modern day racism…" [1] - Anthony Giddens.

If Joseph Arthur de Gobineau (1816 – 1882) thought of superior intelligence and morality for whites as contrasted to blacks, whom he considered as being of a low capability close to animal nature, Somaliness draws a lot from that narrative and thought. This is true because they attribute the same characteristics to Jareer-ness or Negritude, although the concept of race itself is an idea which suggests that no race is free from contact with another.

What makes the Somali situation more unbelievable is the perceptual retention of homogeneity and the unthinkable notion underlying a black race practicing racial supremacy against another. The scenario is quite unlike black-white distinction as experienced in South Africa, U.S.A. or Brazil or any other country where racial diversity is constructed on the basis of color difference. In Somalia, particularly for the incompetent 'nobles', ethnic identity is the main source from which all other streams of identities emerge. Therefore, in their belief, the maintenance of genealogy-based ethnic superiority is sacrosanct because it is the sacred pillar on which Somali 'nobility' is constructed. Once that is undermined, it means the crumbling of the foundation of pastoral pseudo-nobility.

One of the ethno-traditional philosophies embracing this paradigm is clearly manifested in the interplay between identity politics and political identity. These two can be defined as being in support of Kusow's narrative of genealogy-based and territory-based Somaliness, tools Kusow argues measure the degree of one's attachment to the place and the birth of 'pseudo-nobility'. Though Kusow approached the phenomenon in its sociological perspective describing it as "a continuous process of exclusion and inclusion," [2] the effectiveness of the impact of "a process of simultaneous exclusion and inclusion" (with all its undercurrents and crosscurrents) could again be elaborated in the perspective of political sociology where the centrality of '*Maandeeq*' was concentrated to selected socio-ethnic segments of the society.

The centrality therein, by precision, functions as the central powerhouse where identity politics determines the distribution, recognition, inclusion as well as exclusion of social identities into or out of "the social boundary of Somaliness."[3] And since it is the control zone effecting recognition and stratification of multi-ethnic identities, it is, by that virtue, the distribution point of the milk from Maandeeq, in other words, the legitimating process through which one was graduated to enable him/her to drain the national economy dry.

It is important to note that though social categorizations had their implications; one cannot overlook the fact that ethnic members representing the various sub-groups in the bracket of Somaliness have assumed top national responsibilities varying from diplomatic positions to key cabinet posts, despite Kusow's constructive narratives and regardless of their genealogical and/or geographical location of Somaliness. From Ras Aseyr to Ras Kamboni, all the communities in the country (including the outcasts, Banadiri and Barawaan) have in one regime or another or in all regimes had their members serve in a high position and in multiple capacities, except the Negroid Jareer/Bantu (See Mariam A. Gassim 2002; Eno and Eno 2008; Osman 2007). A recategorization of the ethnic composition opens wide the belief of those appointments not being without some basis of Jileec (Somali-Arab) supremacy compared to Jareer (Bantu-African/Negroid) inferiority.

The identity confusion of the Somalis in general and the Jareer frustration in particular lead one to the more confusing bifocal question: who is a Somali and by what criteria is the paradigm of Somaliness/Somalihood determined?

Abdi Kusow, the Somali erudite, debunked an oft-hidden side of Somali social reality. The multifarious characteristics of Somaliness entail the existence of conflicting kaleidoscopic identities. This blend of artificially inter-married concomitant identities of presumed Arabness, according to Abdi Kusow, observes genealogical affiliation and geographical location. But looking at both identities -- regardless of the distance one may be from the eponymous ancestor and birth place of 'nobility' and its dignified camel culture -- one still remains within "the social boundary of Somaliness"; if not genealogically, at least socially, politically, academically and economically.

For example, the Barawaans and the Banadiris may fall in the periphery of Somaliness by lineage but may celebrate social intermingling in the form of legally constituted marriages with any of the clans, be them 'more' Somali or 'less' Somali. If in all other probabilities they are disqualified genealogically, at least their 'other' identity (the non-Somali) has been accepted and allows them a social interaction as mentioned. Secondly, their lack of genealogical identity as Somalis has not denied them acceptance and participation in the important political decision-making positions and top public responsibilities, not to mention their benefit in academic advancement from state sponsored overseas scholarships.

The outcast groups though prone to discrimination and social exclusion in certain ways have not been completely outlawed from inclusion and recognition in other ways. Powerful figures of prominence like Samatar (former Vice President and Defence Minister) and former cabinet minister Salxaan are the example among many from such groups who have held incumbent positions of various capacities, while others served remarkably in the diplomatic missions. Additionally, we have the Hawiye, Digil-Mirifle and other communities whose Somaliness is considered 'contaminated' either by genealogical distance or by geographical span, but with potential recognition as shown in the manifestation of their membership as among the "major" Somali clans, whatever that may mean.

Whichever way we analyze, it may be claimed that all the above communities have a consolation of some sort within which their Somaliness is recognized, unlike the Jareer who neither held any responsible posts at any one time at the national level nor experience social harmony or acceptance in social affiliations or in any other institution to bind them to the other communities forming part of the texture of the social fabric. By their Negroid origin and African appearance, the Jareer/Bantu are unique in the social construct of Somaliness, geographically and genealogically. As we have seen from the elaboration made in some of the preceding chapters, and complementary to the relevant postulate by Kusow, Somaliness is also about the look, the physical anatomy and cultural characteristics, issues related to racial/biological and environmental phenomena.

While the Jareer protest about exclusion, marginalization and identity deformation other communities are affected by identity confusion resulting from impurity to the "process of simultaneous exclusion and inclusion." Even those clans who claim nobility by Arab forefather share a great degree of the confusion particularly now that scholars have revealed their agnatic affiliation with Cushitic groups within the Horn area. The following sets of extracts are quotations from various Somali and non-Somali scholars and intend to display the confusion in Somali identity and genealogical disarray. By far, the academics make a revelation that the territory where Somaliness and the Somali survive and where all the business of inclusion and exclusion is conducted, is not historically a Somali territory as we shall read from the following paragraphs:

(1) "The Somali race seems to be the most recently arrived of all the inhabitants of north-east Africa. Their early history is extremely obscure, and that of Somaliland before their arrival is no less so."[4]

(2) "The Asha of Somali proper...tribes are all descendants from two Arab Sheikhs in the twelfth or Thirteenth century."[5]

(3) "Although the Somalis claim they are homogeneous, the exact origin of their race remains mysterious."[6]

(4) "The proto-Reewin groups were probably the first Cushitic group to enter what is the southern part of modern-day Somalia."[7]

(5) "We can infer that Reewin...are to be regarded as the true ancestors of all the Somali-speaking groups today."[8]

(6) "All Somali claim Quraishitic descent, some through Samale, their eponymous ancestor, others independently through Isaq, Darood, Ajuran or others who were or have been reinterpreted as Arab Sheikhs."[9]

(7) "By a procedure similar to the genealogical parasitism by which they have attached themselves to Quraish, they [Somalis] now have to incorporate others into their own genealogy."[10] [Clarification in parenthesis mine]

(8) "The real origin of the Somali people, is wrapped in mystery."[11]

(9) "The dawn of the Somali race, could be placed about twelve or thirteen hundred years ago."[12]

(10) "The Somali people belong to one of five main Kin-based "clan-families," a confederation of genealogically un-related clans. There are no blood-links or other affinity between these five clans, or for that matter between the smaller clans. [13]

(11) "The commonality is the language and the religion. Each and

every Somali knows his genealogical descent until his patriarch by heart. It is called "Abtirsin." This genealogical descent shows that the five main clans, have no blood-links whatsoever.

(12) "Historians do also differ, as to when the different clans, took up their modern national name "Somali," or for that matter the meaning of the word "Somali."[14]

"This gives credence to the oft-repeated theory, the name "Somali" was an invention of the Muslim Imam of Harar, Imam Ahmed Bin Ibrahim Al-Ghazi, known to the Somali as Ahmey (sic.) "Gurey," the left-handed.[15]

"...As to why the Imam chose the name "Somali," is a mystery."[16]

(13) "The most interesting aspect about the obscurity of the Somali name, though, is its different oral interpretations."[17]

(14) "The first appearance of the name Somali in a written historical record was in the victory-claim song of Negash Yeshak (1414-1429) of Ethiopia over the neighboring Islamic Sultanate of Adal...Another document containing Somali elements is found in the Arab chronicle dealing with the Jihad wars of Ahmed Gurey. The Somali groups which are found in this chronicle are the ones that are found in today's northwest Somalia."[18]

(15) "In classical times the Somali were known as "Berbers," a designation which survives in the name of the town of Berbera. The usage runs through the writing of the Arab geographers of the Middle ages."[19]

(16) Many of the immigrant Sheikhs to whom the Somali trace descent cannot be shown to have been historical personages, but they are nonetheless type of historical figures, and while individual ancestors cannot be shown to have existed or to have left Arabia and settled in Somaliland at determined dates acceptable to the criteria of historical veracity, history shows that there has been a constant movement of this kind."[20]

(17) "The Somali people comprise a vast system of segmented groups which it is convenient to call nation, tribal-family, confederacy, sub-confederacy, and tribe.

"The Somali nation is composed of two parts, the Somali and the Sab. Strictly, the word "Somali" does not apply to the Sab, who say themselves that they are "Sab", and are so described and distinguished by the "Somali"; nor is the "Sab" group subsumed under the name "Somali" in the total genealogy of the Somali nation. The Sab stand opposed to the Somali and are grouped with them only at a higher genealogical level, when the two ancestors Sab and Somali are traced back in Arabian origins, in the total genealogy of the inhabitants of Somaliland."[21]

"At a higher level of inclusiveness, all the Somali peoples, both Somali and Sab, trace descent to the Qurayshitic lineage of the Prophet Mohammed. Somali genealogies are extrapolated to the Prophet and Founder of Islam."[22]

(18) "The story of the peopling of southern Somalia is still unclear, and a matter of controversy, which has recently taken on a political colouring."[23]

"But it was probably not until sometime in the first millennium CE that speakers of the language in its earlier forms began to occupy the region. The consensus among scholars at present is that the Somali people originated in what is now southern Ethiopia, and from there gradually occupied most of the Horn of Africa, carrying with them the Somali language (which in the process evolved into its various dialects) and displacing or mixing with and incorporating whatever peoples may have been there already."[24]

(19) "The idea of a common 'Somali' identity was clearly not current in the southern clans, except among a few learned men until about the colonial period, and the name 'Somali' was not used…"[25]

(20) Even the learned, though they agree that there is a common scheme of descent, differ as to how it works. With regard to the genealogy of the 'Samaale' clans the genealogies are reasonably consistent (though there are still disagreements, for instance as to whether the Darood are Samaale). When it comes to the 'Sab' clans, however, disagreements are numerous, and not one but several schemes of classification compete, as if the model of the 'total genealogy' turns out to be a poor fit when applied to this society.

"…However, the various genealogical schemes that have been recorded contradict one another, as though, rather than a common tradition, we have the work of different organizing minds who at various times and places tackled the problem of fitting these groups into the approved genealogical mould. No two scholars record the same arrangement. The genealogical structure of the southern Somali is like an image which from a distance appears solid, only to break up on closer view into a multitude of shifting components.[26]

(21) "According to more recent studies (Haberland 1963; H. S.

Lewis 1966; Braukamper 1980b) the Oromo cradleland has to be looked for in the southeastern highlands of Ethiopia. The Somaloid, who are linguistically related to them and who expanded into the lowlands before they did, may have originated in the same region (Fleming 1964; Schlee 1987a).[27]

(22) "But it is their Arabian ancestry which traditionally is their greatest pride. Ultimately all Somali genealogies go back to Arabian origins to the Prophet's lineage of Quraysh and those of his companions. Yet they do not think of themselves as Arabs, or except in religion, as culturally Arabian. Indeed paradoxical though it may appear, in many ways Somali despise Arabs, especially those whom they meet in Somaliland as immigrant traders and merchants. Nevertheless, it is their proud pretensions to noble Arabian origins which unite all the Somali clans and lineages into one vast genealogical system.[28]

The evidence quoted above from various academic sources does not only analytically reflect the genealogical/identity confusion haunting the Somali people but also the recentness of their arrival in the area of present-day Somalia. An alignment of a harmonious reconciliation of these crucial paradoxes is dilapidated not just by their numerousness but even by their deepening inconsistencies. Other than those, a simultaneous shift from one genealogical clan camp to the other for reasons none other than gain of interest has complicated an accurate understanding of the Somali genealogical set up. This particular culture of clan/identity transformation, mentioned earlier in this study, has become rife in the waning period of dictator Barre's regime and the subsequent era of lawlessness and anarchy. Whatever the case of the Jileec identity confusion, there exists a clamor to configure it with the possession of the land, by calling it after their eponymous ancestor, Samaale/Soomaali.

The next few paragraphs will quote a comparative literature concerning scholars' evidence about the Jareer/Bantu or Negroid autochthons and their attachment to the land as the earliest settlers before Somali or Galla or any other known groups arrived, an ancient epoch when the nomenclature Berber or Somali had not yet been invented by the Arab immigrants and/or geographers:

(1) "In the earliest times, north-east Africa was entirely occupied by the Negro race. The aboriginal population of Abyssinia was therefore Negro."[29]

(2) "Archaeological and linguistic evidence suggests that there was also a Bantu population in the nearby fertile river valleys of the Jubba and Shabelli. The Swahili culture that evolved in this coast was the result of the contact with the Bantu culture in the hinterland..." The linguistic Somalization of the Banadir coast started around the 13th century, when the first Somali-speaking nomads appeared there."[30]

(3) "...the comparatively fertile valleys of the Juba and Shibeli were already occupied by Bantu-speaking Negroid agriculturalists."[31]

(4) The predecessors of the Eyle, who in modern times are scattered bands of professional hunters, were no doubt already there."[32]

(5) The idea of an early population of, probably Bantu-speaking, farmers has recently gained acceptance among foreign scholars."[33]

(6) These communities today consist in part of original nuclei of pre-Cushitic Negroid inhabitants of Somaliland."[34]

(7) In the south, between the Shebelle and Juba rivers and to some extent north of the Shabelle, there appear to have been three movements of population. For before the incursions of the Hamitic Galla and Somali, this region was occupied by a mixed population – the Zengi of medieval Arab geographers – who seem to have comprised two distinct elements. Sedentary agricultural tribes settled in the inter-riverine area and akin to the North-Eastern Coastal Bantu formed one component. And residues of this Bantu, and Swahili-speaking population, supplemented by slaves from further south freed by the suppression of the slave trade at the end of the nineteenth century, survive today in the Shidle, Kaboole, Reer 'Iise, Makanni and Shabelle peoples, on the Shabelle River, and on the Juba River in the WaGosha and Gobweyn. To the same group belong the Elaay of Baidoa in the hinterland, and the Tunni Torre of Brava District. The other section of the pre-Hamitic population consisted of Bushmanlike hunters and gatherers, and along the rivers of fishermen, of whom contemporary representatives are the WaRibi, and WaBooni or Booni of Jubaland and southern Somalia, and the Eyle of Bur Hacaba.

"Through contact with the Galla and the absorption of the few Galla who remained behind and through the influence of the earlier Bantu communities, the Digil and Rahanwiin tribes emerged with their distinctive characteristics. From the Bantu they adopted cultivation and from the Galla temporarily copied their system of military age-grades."[35]

(8) "Some mention must be made of the Negroid populations of

Somaliland, who in many respects form an integral part of the total Somali social structure. These communities today consist in part of original nuclei of pre-Cushitic Negroid inhabitants of Somaliland (the Zengi) and in part freed slaves of varying provenance.

"Cerulli considers that the present Bantu populations of the Juba are largely a residue of the 12 tribes of the Wanyika, described in the Book of Zengi (an Arab Manuscript), which records the colonization of the African coast...

"...Both the Hawiya and Digil despise them, and there seems good reason to regard them as a pre-Cushitic aboriginal population.

"...Cerulli compares this Brava city language to the Semitic city language of Harar; its isolated occurrence demonstrates, he considers, the presence of Bantu in this region at an early date."[36]

(9) "And in all likelihood, there were along the rivers small farming settlements of a people of distinct origin from the Somali, and much more 'African' in appearance. Probably these people were originally speakers of a Bantu language."[37]

"The Jareer people have often been thought of as all simply the descendants of freed slaves. Nobles generally think so, and the European writers who first observed Somali society in the 19th and early 20th centuries refer to them in this way, as *liberti* or freedmen.[38]

(10). "I am increasingly convinced...that the current explanation which would make the indisputably Negro population of the Shiidle, Shabelle etc. groups of slaves of the Somali, set free by their masters, can definitely be dismissed. ... as far as I am concerned, there is no doubt the original nucleus of the Shidle, Shabelle etc. populations was left behind by the Bantu, when they retreated from the region of Webi Shabelle."[39]

(11) "There is another tradition, however, Faay Muudey Shoongo, whose family belongs to the Jareer of East Afgoye, told me that 'our ancestors were born here; they did not come here.'"[40]

(12) "Ancient Arabian findings found in Brava demonstrate early presence of Zengi/Bantu people called Wanyika who were scattered in the Juba River area. They owned cattle, goats and chickens and produced agricultural products such as maize and banana. Among their main towns was called Shungwaya. The Wanyika community which the Arabian findings reveal lived very long centuries ago in the inter-riverine area of Juba and Shabelle whose running waters facilitated for them their engagement in farming."[41]

(13) "The second group of Bantu/Jareer people in Somalia are linked and believed to be the remnants of the Mijikenda people who migrated to the Tana River in modern Kenya...These Jareer people reside mainly along the banks of the Shabelle River in southern Somalia...[42]

"Aside from those groups who migrated to the Tana River (in present Kenya), there were those who remained behind, and continue to live in their present locations in southern Somalia..."[43]

(14) "We may reckon those [Bantu/Jareer] tribes in all probability represent remnants of a pre-Somali population...."[44]

(15) "Before the Somali penetrated the area in the sixteenth and seventeenth centuries, a population of Bantu-speaking cultivators inhabited the river lands...

Distinctly Negroid in physical type, whereas the Nobles have the "Hamitic" features typical of the Somali in general, these people are probably in part the descendants of the original farming population of the area, the Bantu-speaking "Zanj" of the Arab chronicles."[45]

The extracts of the above scholarly works provide a brief demonstration revealing the nub of the truth about Jareer predominance and therefore ownership of the territory now known as Somalia, in an ancient period prior to the arrival of even the Galla who had preceded the Somalis in the area. The two sets of extrapolations have been compared in order to accommodate the view of the agrarian cultivator who has been outside the social construct of Somaliness, a genealogical reality that bears fruits in many ways.

My view regarding the above furnished exrtrapolation has no intention of making a claim for genealogical absorption of the Jareer/Bantu into Somaliness, an identity already struggling with enough burden of its own. Nor does this view entertain a desire to claim the bridging of the geographical distance to the birthplace of Somaliness, criteria and categories which certain Somalis seem to use as the yardstick for measuring the degree of Somaliness or 'purity' accorded to specific clusters of the society. The rationale of the subject, to a broader hypothesis, invites a different perspective from which to view the matter.

We have already seen, based on the evidence in the previous chapters, the inadequacy for a Jareer to be born or to have been born in Somalia to qualify for Somaliness without bearing the necessary supporting properties, either physiologically, biologically or   genealogically, geographically (the latter two as hypothesized by Kusow) or a combination of any of them and even all of them. Given this state of affairs, and out of the perplexity of identity confusion, two provocative hypotheses emerge; hypotheses that do not disagree with the existence of the two proximity measurement tools for Somaliness highlighted by Kusow as (a) "Genealogical" proximity to the founding fathers of Somaliness, to two or more immigrant Arab Sheikhs, and (b) "Geographical" proximity to the location where the Arab Sheikhs were causal or rather independent variables to the birth of Somaliness in distinct areas in the north.

These hypotheses propose the possible use of other Somaliness assessment tools, which have validity in their own nature without infringement to Kusow's formula; just like the hypothesis of Jareer and Jileec. I present the first one as the "proximity of physiological properties to Somaliness" and the second as "Proximity of historical precedence of human habitation in the territory."

The two sets of illustrations above were referred as a guiding framework for the underpinning validity of the construction of the last two hypotheses. For example: numerous Jareer/Negroid people have been assimilated and subsumed into the genealogies of certain Somali tribes, and so transferred the count of their patriarchal lineage to that of their assimilators, but yet find themselves outside the system. In this chronicle, the Jareer is already there, accepted for attachment into the lineage ascending its trace to the ancestor, but the property exposed in his/her physiology hinders actual penetration into the social texture, even after overcoming the genealogy barrier. The broad nose (*sanka buuran*), the hard/thick hair (*timaha adag; timaha jareerka*) and the muscular African/Negroid features (*jir-dhismeedka murqo-murqaha*) indicate other criteria used to measure acceptability as a "Somali", for the Jareer/Bantu stock in this case.

The second premise is an alternative that persisted in practice in the days preceding the dominance in the land by the Somaloid stock.[46] It recognizes the right of ownership to the earliest settlers, the Negroid/Jareer or autochthons who were the earliest occupants as supported by academic works, a few of which were established above.[47] Therefore despite the frail name "Somali" in its symbolic nature of today, Puntland/Bantuland or Biladul-Bantu is for the Jareer/Bantu aborigines as far as precedence and earlier settlement is concerned.

Since Somaliness as a name or origin had not taken root as a result of the Somalis themselves but by the making of Arabs – Sheikh Isaq; Ismail Jabarti, Ahmed Al-Ghazi (Gurey) etc. or by other foreigners - and since culturally they are made up of compositions of distinct tribal groups of nations as we see them today,[48] the genealogical solidness or solidarity in homogeneity has fallen apart. But what constitutes Somaliness and who is really a Somali? When, where and how does Somaliness function? Why is the motivational thrust lenient towards the clan institution but comparatively insufficient or void towards Somaliness and the Somali nation? What do these nations of clans share in common and what factors stimulate that commonality?

First of all, one has to realize that, as an identity, Somaliness is an emblematic metaphor designed out of the image of a nomad's dream; one who was not satisfied with who he was and what he was. It is an abstract image providing refuge for people who are not happy with who they are and what they are, but who from the cradle to the grave, are in search of a better identity than who they are and what they are. A Somali, according to nomadic social psychology, is driven not by loyalty to a nation (Somali nation), and at times not even by the often-worshipped lineage or patrilineal kinship, but primarily by his own intuitive self-interest and egoism as and when it serves him. Neither is he limited by human/cultural values, nor does he observe self-dignity. The personal drive and self-esteem of the Somali pastoral character are those typical of a nation-less, cultureless mercenary. Instances of this have been widely seen during the period of anarchy following Barre's ouster.

As has become knowledge, a Somali and his Somali nation are easily separable, but a Somali and his tribal nation remain inseparable. According to pastoral thinking, the thesis is simple to explain: Somalia as a nation may not undertake for an individual citizen certain morally binding things which the clan may embark on implementing for the sake of an individual member of the kinship. For instance, Somalia would not allow itself to have suffered the magnitude of devastation befallen on it by its "Somali" citizens unless those involved were not genuine members of the citizenry and loyal to Somalia.

Contrastively but also constructively, the very annihilators of Somalia could not inflict (as far as history is concerned) similar destruction on the territories of their respective tribal nations, but instead they defended their abodes of tribal territories against outsiders from other tribes or sub-tribes. Thus the Somali sentiment for the two nations, the remote and the immediate – the Somali nation and the tribal nation respectively - are staked in two divergent horizons. Hence the immediate nation, which is the clan and its abode, is of more value to the Somali than the remote nation that pulls together a mixture of tribes, distant tribes which other wise have the potential to unite on short notice at the call for common defense against a presumed common enemy.

These nations of clan families and even sub-clan institutions are separate and diverse sub-group entities. Although Dualeh (see Chapter 1) suggests the Somali commonality in the spheres of language and religion, my contention envisages a reality about Somali multilingualism (*Maay, Maxaatiri, Af-Jiido, Af-Garre* etc) as all spoken by Somalis but yet not intelligible with one another. Concerning faith, the majority of the Somali people are Muslims (more so metaphorically than practically) but that should not negate the factual existence of Somali Christians, despite the insignificance of their number. Therefore inside the presupposed external commonalities are in fact expansive breeding grounds for true divergences and diversities that puzzle the outsiders, academics and non-academics. But the average Somali, the pastoral democrat, would prefer it to be left untouched, lest the internal rot pollutes the external environment unknown to it.

The other thesis I promulgate, within the context of commonality, focuses on the separation between:

a) Commonality shared as a result of common cultural values, common historical tidings, common identity, common national spirit as well as other common factors mitigating positive social/human behavior, and,

b) An alliance, an amalgamation constituting layers of pastoral scums in a pseudo-unity, when the doctrine is hinged on the causing of death to human lives and destruction of property for the sake of individual or tribal greed. This amalgamation or temporary fluid solidarity often promoted in the wake of a threat from an enemy or in an unprecedented attack against an "assumed" enemy, doesn't appeal to the good blueprint of a global commonality shared by all Somalis. Instead, notwithstanding the generalized name/identity 'Somali', such barbaric acts should be seen and taken as matters particularly limited to the cultural representatives of the concerned culprits and not as a general attitude that all Somalis share. In brief, it is an alliance of unison based on mean rapacity for spoils that more often than not drives the 'Somali people', 'Somali nation' to war and justifies, temporarily , a reason for the resurrection of "Somaliness" which in all other circumstances is "laid to rest"[49] in the living Somali nomad who self-aggrandizes himself as 'noble'.

According to the agrarian Jareer/Bantu social thought:
Maal ninkiisaa ka naxaayo,
Mood ninkiisaa Maro saarto.

Translation:
Wealth is well protected by its owner, and
A deceased is best covered by a kin.

This verse or saying, prefigures the unfolding view in the next few sentences as it subsequently entices one to draw a line between categories of Somalinesss and Somalis, much unlike the nomad's version. Somalis of different cultural beliefs are always lumped together as an unwholesome group despite the wholesome culture of the other group and their sacrifice for the well-being of the country. Whenever a culturally contaminated individual commits a barbaric act, he contaminates the dignity of nations of tribes with whom he shares the remote nation 'Somalia' but not his immediate tribal nation which is responsible for arming him.

Throughout the rough periods of social evolution in Somalia, the Bantu/Jareer people have been at the forefront from nation building to the struggle for independence. Because they make the highest number of technicians, their contribution to the various sectors and sub-sectors of development and in nation building has been unmatchable, though unappreciated by the nomadic culture. Their role toward boosting the economy, especially in the sector of agricultural production has been remarkable. Unfortunately, these were mistranslated to inferiority, a status adjusted as *modus operandi* to execute the lowest menial duties.

Although the Bantu human resource has been the key to the little change the country was undergoing in development, they were the subject of oppression and social injustice and discrimination. Yet they had to develop the courage for perseverance due to their attachment to the land, a property that later became up for grabs, through expropriation and looting, rather than developing.

Whatever the interpretation, the Jareer have refrained from participating in the primitive acts of demolition and dilapidation in the country, whether in the process of misappropriation of public funds or in the process of civil war. In a way, this was not because of anything else but the philosophy that "These people have come, so they will go; but the land is ours and it will forever stay with us." This touching statement is not from the thought of an educated person, but a young Jareer/Bantu man in his late teens at the time. He was pushing a wheelbarrow for a living at the height of the civil anarchy in December 1991, as he concluded: "We are the ones who built this country before, and we shall build it again once they are gone; our hand knows how to do it."

This is where I draw the line of Somaliness, between the one who built the country and yet stays firm, dedicated and determined to build it again, regardless of the hardships of abuse, degradation, underdevelopment, discrimination, and other social evils; and the one who kept bombarding it relentlessly for over a decade and a half, one who seeks superiority, pride and self-aggrandizement by destroying lives and properties alike, and then finally migrating to anywhere where he can join the dole queue.

The mythical genealogy, geography and physiology aside, it is the aboriginal owner of the land, the autochthonous Bantu/Negroid that has always worked in this country with all his dedication and unreserved effort. It is him/her that resisted all burdens and tolerated hardship in the course of nation building, and yet possesses the vigor, high morale and spirit to re-build it. This intrinsic feeling of citizenship, and genuine native sentiment, is the kind of intuitively driven motivation a true citizen can pledge his/her allegiance towards his/her nation, but not in sharing a merely symbolic nomenclature whose origins are mysterious and is used 'effectively' and collectively only when the scheme is to cause harm to others, internally and externally.

According to the Jareer/Bantu girl, whether we call her Adoon, Xabash, San-buur, Sankadhudhi, Biddo, Beyle-san-buur, Ooji, Dhal-Goleed, Mashuunguli, Boong, Meddo or any other degrading epithet, Somaliness is not embraced in foolish pride "*Laankruusar gado, soo bari galleey*"[50] [Buy a Land Cruiser, but wander and beg for maize.] According to her, the nexus between the citizen and his/her nation is not manifested in the looting of the public coffers; not in "killings, politically-motivated rape of women and the robbery of state treasury,"[51]; not in organizing unruly clan militia to gang-rape innocent virgins as witnessed in Hodan District in Mogadishu;[52] not at all in the wanton killing and dehumanization of the elderly, the unarmed and the vulnerable such as women and children.

In the view of the Jareer girl, civil morality is not represented in the heart and mind of one who expresses satisfaction in creating and living in perpetual anarchy, but in one whose sweat mingles with the irrigation water as it trickles from his face and hands in the course of digging his/her farm, generally tolerating and facing gallantly the hardship in nation building. It is through the preservation of decent attachment to the country and the citizenship that the spirit for national love and nation building are portrayed, not in the cowardly association with the gun, a fact contrary to the principles of development.

A mind associated to a hand carrying a gun will not have its thinking beyond the easy use of that gun, hence a dual deprivation to development: (1) Because it has to carry the gun, it can not afford the delivery of other tasks, and (2) Because it is carrying the gun for use, it has to fulfill the "duty" of killing which is the reason behind carrying it, and in this course, kill one who was building or would build the nation.

Ever since the wake of independence, the Jareer community has complained about exclusion, inequality and social injustice, oppressions whose roots could be traced back to the pre-colonial era. However, after independence, the recognition of the existence of these oppressions and the possibility to bring them into the limelight beyond the national boundaries was curtailed in the thick clouds of an unholy doctrine of Somali homogeneity that misled many scholars and the world at large.

As we have seen throughout this study, the Somali nation constitutes nations of disintegrated communal clans or entities of diverse origins, some with undisputed ancestry whilst others had the exact origin of their race described as remaining mysterious. Concurrently, ethnic groups among these nations have had their identities deliberately misplaced by adjoining them to one of Somaliness, which in turn heeds a mythical belief of being a branch from an Arabian root. In any case, what is more undisputable lies in the distinction between Jareer and Jileec, the characteristic paradigm of classifiction assuming Negritude/Africanness and non-Negritude/Arabness respectively.

This characteristic identification has become a rigid basis for the creation of an eponym-ased genealogical stratification ofsuperior/noble clans (Somali-Arabs) and an inferior/ignoble race (Negroid-Africans).

As a consequence of that, coupled with colonial interference and support, the Jareer of Negroid African/Bantu origin have been denigrated as a subject people unworthy of any attributable social esteem and achievement – a community destined for exploitation and subjugation and therefore created for benefiting the superior Jileec race of the 'nobles' who perceive the Jareer as their god-given servants!

In the outside world, without the exception of even distinguished scholars, Somalia had an erroneous image of a nation of one homogeneous race. For that matter, it was unthinkable that racial discrimination, ethnic marginalization and acts of apartheid could prevail among such a unique people from the same forefather. It was under the pretext of this misbelief that other factors about Somalia were deliberately either overlooked or discouraged. It is however worthwhile mentioning that a number of Somalist scholars who conducted field research in the country, particularly in the inter-riverine zone, have noted an early recognition of the reality about the pervading social distinction of what was otherwise promoted by I. M. Lewis as a homogeneous egalitarian society of a pastoral democracy.

The works of Catherine Besteman, Kenneth Menkhaus, Virginia Luling, Omar Eno and Lee Cassanelli, to mention a few, are the most remarkable in recent times, although these could only be conducted by foreigners and/or published outside Somalia during the military regime of late dictator Siad Barre, except Eno's works which approached the issue from a different socio-historical perspective after the collapse of the military rule. At any rate, it was during the civil war that the majority of the international community became aware of the massive apartheid maneuvers that shaped the Somali social system.

Prevalent among those who raised the alarm about the existence of race-related discrimination were international relief workers operating in the country. In addition to this were advocacy initiatives to end the rebirth of slavery in the banana plantations in Lower Shabelle region in mid 1990's, heavily mounted by the Jareer/Bantu elite in the Diaspora, the local media (Ali Muse Abdi and Mohamed Shiil being the journalists in the forefront) and SAMO (Somali African Muki Organization), the political organ of the Jareer, have reshaped the universal view about Somali homogeneity and cultural pastoralism as the revelation of the truth was no longer preventable.

Later, an academic overturn from homogeneity was justified and a proven heterogeneity emerged. Under this circumstance, the Jareer exploited the opportunity not only in contributing to the prevalence of ethnic diversity but the persistence of ethnic marginalization and social exclusion similar in form to Apartheid as practiced in South Africa.

The disclosure pertaining to the unexpected factor of Somali heterogeneity was further aggravated by the more devastating revelations concerning the practice of elements of apartheid in Somalia. These two factors have attracted a myriad of criticism and denial from the Somali proponents of the self-same school of thought on the one hand and the foreigners of similar belief about Somalia on the other. When the contention over the episode increased, the non-governmental organization, Bantu Rehabilitation Trust (BRT) undertook a survey on the human rights abuse against the Somali Bantu.

Conclusion

The phenomenon underlying the multifacial characteristics entangled with Somaliness is complex as are the qualifications allowing one into Somaliness and the variety of measures of disqualification preventing certain groups from 'trespassing' into the social "purity" of Somaliness. But as we have seen, the Jareer concept of citizenship teaches an affectional attachment to the country, the land, the territory. It informs the interactive owner-territory relationship that distinguishes the builder and feeder of the nation from the killer and destroyer of the nation; one who has always been the eater of nationhood and violator of sovereignty.

The unequalness of Somalis to Somaliness and the oppression and social discrimination lurked under the fabricated mass of homogeneity, have become causal to focus part of this study to quantitative evaluation of the reasons and nature of discrimination prevailing in the country. The next chapters will provide the findings and results of a survey data collected to analyze aspects related to the episode of marginalization as presented by the victims.

NOTES AND REFERENCES

1. Giddens, Anthony., Sociology. 4th edition. op.cit., p. 253.
2. Kusow, Abdi M., "Contested Narratives and the Crisis of the Nation State" in Kusow, Abdi M., (ed.), op.cit., pp.1-13.
3. Ibid.

4. A Handbook of Abyssinia, op.cit., p.145.
5. Ibid.
6. Mukhtar, "Islam in Somalia" op.cit.,p.19.
7. Kusow, "The Somali Origin: Myth or Reality" op.cit., p. 93.
8. Ibid., p.95.
9. Schlee., op.cit., p.225.
10. Ibid., p.226.
11. Dualeh, op.cit., p.9.
12. Ibid.
13. Ibid., p.10.
14. Ibid.
15. Ibid.
16. Ibid.
17. Kusow, "The Somali Origin" in Ahmed, A. J. (ed.), op.cit., p.85.
18. Ibid., p.82 (see also Guidi I., "Le canzione ge'ez-amarina in onore di Re Abissino." RAL 5: 1889, hymn 2.)
19. Lewis, Peoples of the Horn, p.13.
20. Ibid., p.14.
21. Ibid., pp. 14-15.
22. Ibid., p.17
23. Luling, Somali Sultanate, p.15.
24. Ibid., pp. 15-16.
25. Ibid., p.85.
26. Ibid., p.84.
27. Schlee, op.cit., pp.81-82.
28. I. M. Lewis., A Pastoral Democracy, op.cit., p.11.
29. A Handbook of Abyssinia, p.104.
30. Kassim, Mohamed M., "Aspects of the Banadir Cultural History" in Ahmed, Ali J., ed., op.cit., p.30
31. Hallett, Robin., Africa to 1875., op.cit., p.105.
32. Luling. A Somali Sultanate, op.cit., p.16.
33. Ibid., p.116.
34. Lewis, I. M., Peoples of the Horn of Africa, op.cit., p.41.
35. Lewis, I. M., A Pastoral Democracy. op.cit. pp 22 & 25.
36. Lewis, Peoples of the Horn, op.cit. pp.41-43.
37. Luling, V., Somali Sultanate, op.cit.,p.16.
38. Ibid. p.115.
39. Cerulli, E., Somalia: Scritti vari editi ed inediti. Volume 2, Roma: Istituto Poligrafico dello Stato. (1959: 116-7).
40. Luling, Somali Sultanate, p.116.
41. Salim, Hamid Al-Sayid., Al-Sumaal – Qadiiman wa Hadiithan. Vol. I. Mogadishu, 1965:296. (Translation mine).
42. Eno, Omar A., "Landless landlords" op.cit., pp.137-38.

43. Ibid., p.138.
44. Bulletin of the International Committee of Urgent Anthropological and Ethnical Research., pp. 28-29. No.3, 1960., assisted by UNESCO.
45. Luling, V., "Colonial and Postcolonial Influences on a South Somali Community" op.cit.
46. Notes from a video-taped workshop for Somali Bantu elders in Mogadishu, Somalia, 2003.
47. See also chapter Three of this study.
48. Mansur, Abdalla O., "The Nature of the Somali Clan System," in Ahmed, A. J., (ed.), op.cit.
49. Osman Abdi Osman (alias Oska), personal discussion in Atlanta, USA, Nov. 2004.
50. Title of a radical song by Saada Ali, criticizing Siad Barre's government in late 1980s before the break out of the civil war, when the competition for looting the public treasury was at its peak.
51. Ahmed, Ali J., Daybreak Is Near; op.cit. p.133.
52. This event took place in 1991 in Hodan, Mogadishu, after a Somali employer misplaced her gold necklace. She suspected that her Bantu/Jareer house-girl had stolen it. After the poor girl pleaded her innocence the employer called her relatives in the militia and handed the girl over to them "as a revenge for my necklace." After a few hours the poor under-age girl was seen crying and screaming of pain with blood trailing down her legs as she walked back to her house. The chain was found while the girl was still undergoing her ordeal. By the time the employer's message reached the militia, the poor girl had already lost her virginity in the gang-raping spree of the militia. This author and the residents in the area between *Baar Raaxo* and *Suuqa Siigaale* of Hodan District know this ugly episode and others, which cannot be recounted here.

Chapter 8

8.1. RACIAL DISCRIMINATION IN THE UNDERBELLY OF RACIAL HOMOGENIZATION: UNEARTHING THE UNTOLD APARTHEID

"O mankind! We created you from a single (pair) of a male and a female, and made you into nations and tribes, that ye may know each other (not that ye may despise each other). Verily the most honored of you in the sight of Allah is (he who is) the most righteous of you..."[1]

Race is a biological concept, which classifies people by inherited characteristics such as color of hair and skin, physique, etc. This would have no particular importance if people were content to be physically different but socially equal.[2] – Margaret Peil and Olatunji Oyeneye

The survey was conducted in the Diaspora as well as in 9 regions in the country where the Jareer/Bantu are the dominant settlers. About 200 questionnaires were sent to be filled in each of the nine regions. The Diaspora here consists of the Somali Bantu in Kenya, Tanzania, Saudi Arabia, Italy, Canada and the U.S.A. In the East Africa region, Tanzania and Kenya, the questionnaires were personally administered, while the mailing system was used for countries outside the region. The targeted samples in the Diaspora consisted of 400 interviewees; 300 from within the East Africa region and 100 in Arabia, North America and Italy. Although it was possible to mail more questionnaires to anywhere in the region, this investigator was not in possession of the addresses of all the Diaspora Bantu.

The rate of return was high due to several factors, from common ethnic interest and loyalty to training of female and male data collectors familiar with the social culture and sociolinguistics of the subjects. The total number of questionnaires distributed was 2,200 with 2,116 returned, a little higher than 96%, whereas 84 questionnaires, approximately 4% were unaccounted for. From the Somali Bantu Diaspora in East Africa, the rate of return was 93% compared to 76% of their counterparts elsewhere in Europe, Arabia and North America. Within the country, the average returned questionnaires was 1,759, not capturing

41 questionnaires of the 1,800 target cases. By all means, an almost 98% return rate for the group makes the findings more stable and reliable.

8.2. Apartheid and abuse of Bantu/Jareer rights: Survey findings and results (with illustrations in tables and charts)

8.2.1 Personal Data

A sample population of 2116 responded to various questions. They consisted of male and female members of the Bantu ethnic community (Tab. 1 & Fig. 1). The average age for men was slightly over 48 years while that of their female counterparts stood at a little above 40 years. Men made up 62% compared to 38% for female. Of the total population, 24% of men were single and 38% married men. A further observation of the female respondents reveals that, of the total population, 11% single and 27% married while the entire female subjects were numerically equivalent to the married men at 38%.

Table 1
Bantu population analysis studied in Somalia and diaspora

BANTU POPULATION ANALYSIS STUDIED IN SOMALIA AND DIASPORA					
CATEGORY	NO	PERCENTAGE			
No. of Female	804	38%			
No. of Male	1312	62%			
Male Single	508	24%			
Male Married	804	38%			
Single Female	233	11%			
Married Female	571	27%			
Mean age for Male		48.6 Yrs			
Mean age for Female		40.3 Yrs			

Figure 1

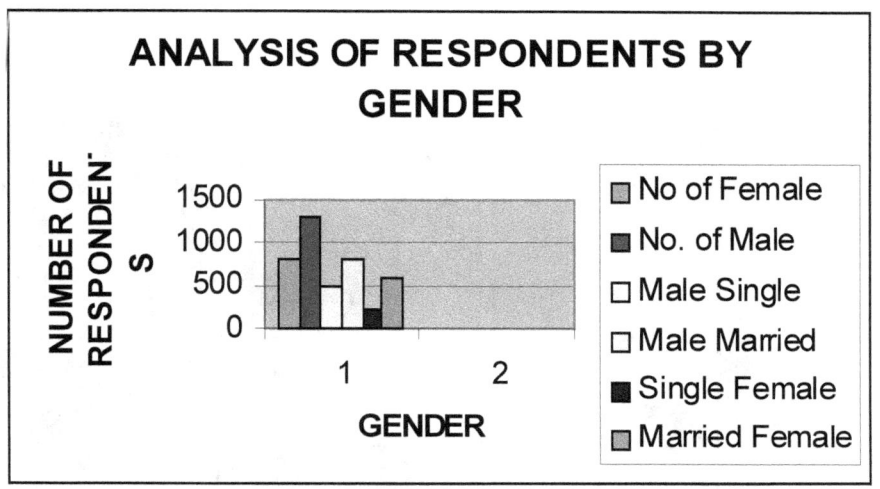

8.2.2. Analysis by level of education

Approximately 87% of the Bantu respondents (Tab. 2 & Fig. 2) had not undergone formal education while the majority among the literate, about 9%, had not studied beyond elementary school or 4th grade. About 2% had an opportunity to join intermediate level 5th – 8th grade, though later less than 2% reached secondary school. An insignificant number, much less than 1% of the Bantu interviewees have had an opportunity for higher education at tertiary level.

Table 2

Level	Male	Female	Total	Percentage	
Uneducated	1156	692	1848	87.333%	
Elementary	104	81	185	8.743%	
Intermediate	25	19	44	2.08%	
Secondary	20	9	29	1.371%	
Tertiary	7	3	10	0.473	*
TOTAL	1312	804	2116	100%	

- Very insignificant

Figure 2

ANALYSIS OF RESPONDENTS BY LEVEL OF EDUCATION

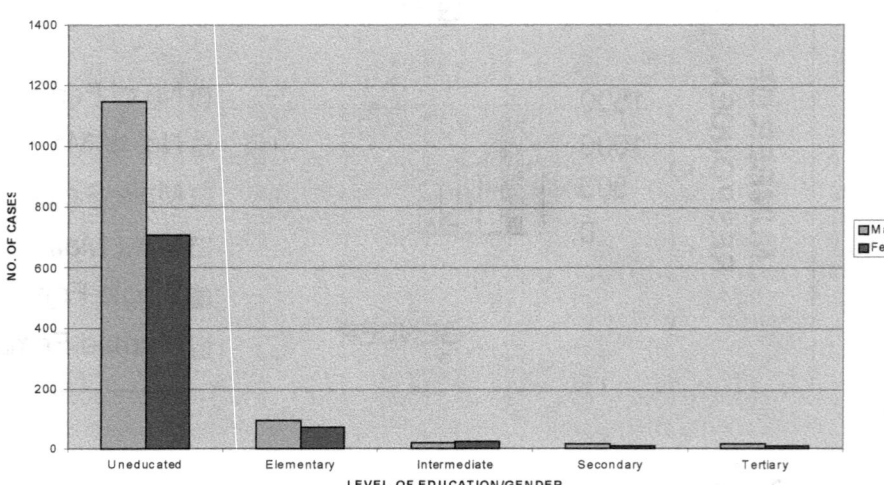

8.2.3. Nature of abuse

Within the concerns of the variable concentrating on the nature of abuse experienced, over 99% have complained of suffering from *inequality/injustice* (Tab. 3 & Fig. 3) under their ruling Jileec/Somali counterparts. *Persecution* was undergone by 89% of the cases analyzed while the variable regarding '*denial of education*' registered with 98% of the population, showing a convincing agreement with the Education Analysis enumerated in (8.2.2) above.

Denial of Job Opportunity was suffered by 99%, the perceivable implication being due to the lack of education as well as job placement. Over 98% of the Bantu interviewees who had worked in the country reveal denial *of promotion as a difficulty. Denial of business opportunity* was experienced by 98% of the sample studied.

An insignificant portion of the population (less than 1%) was analyzed for '*Jail without trial*' *while* **Social degradation** stands at a response of 98% abuse rate.

Table 3

Nature of abuse of Jareer/Bantu community

Nature of abuse	Cases	Percentage
Persecution	1883	89%
Denial of Job Opportunity	2095	99%
Denial of Promotion	2084	98.50%
Denial of Education Opportunity	2074	98%
Denial of Business Opportunity	2023	95.60%
Inequality/Injustice	2108	99.60%
Jail without trial	21	0.01%
Social Degradation	2074	98%
Rape	21	1%
Physical Abuse/Torture	607	59%
Confiscation of property	1716	81.10%

The victims of rape make up 1% of the entire subjects studied but a further analysis of the females (the specific target) raises the figure higher to approximately 3%.

About 81% of the interviewees, or 1716 cases, have had some form of their *property y confiscated*, irrespective of any particular period, while 59% expressed to have undergone *physical /moral* **torture**.

Figure 3

ABUSE

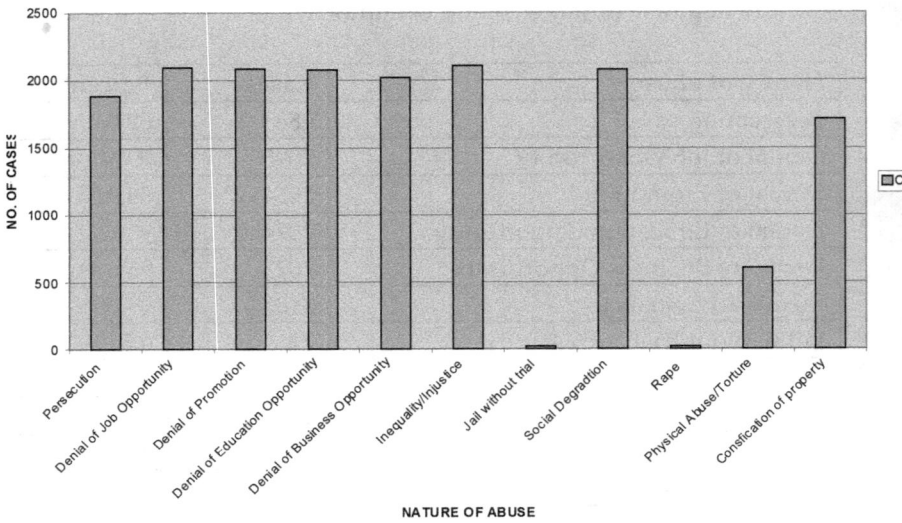

NATURE OF ABUSE

8.2.4. Reasons for abuse

In view of the question investigating the reason for their abuse, 1967 cases (Tab. 4 & Fig. 4) confirmed it was due to their *ethnic diversity and background*, 58 replied as to both *political and ethnic* implications and 91 cases had it only as a *political opinion*. As percentages of the total population, the first figure corresponds to 93%, the next 3% and the last as 4%.

Table 4

Reasons of abuse/Violation	Cases	Percentage
Political Opinion	91	4
Racial/Ethnic Reasons	1967	93
Both	58	3
Other Reasons	-	-
TOTAL	**2116**	**100**

Figure 4

ABUSE

REASONS OF ABUSE

8.2.5 The worst era of abuse

Six percent of the entire sample group and 100% of those who were in their teens or twenties during the colonial period claimed to have experienced colonial atrocities and violation of their human rights. This means that out of 129 interviewees in this category, only one respondent had not experienced any colonial violation of his/her rights, while 128 responded positively to have suffered colonial abuse, as displayed in Table 5 and Fig. 5.

The period 1960 to 1967, under the presidency of Aden Abdulle Osman, is equivalent in the score of abuse to the era of his successor, Abdirashid Ali Sharma'arke, 1967 - 1969. These two eras of post-colonial civilian administrations have each scored an abuse rate of 68% against the Bantu/Jareer population under study.

The leadership of Siad Barre recorded nearly 89% and, as such, the highest cases of Jareer rights abuse in any given Somali state, compared to his two predecessors of the civilian regimes, 1960 to 1969. However, a further analysis in terms of age group reveals that over 90% of the subjects in Barre's era have suffered an abuse of some kind. Bantu rights violation hit record peak in the period of civil anarchy from 1991 to the 2005. About 98% of the overall respondents are unanimous about their ill fate in this period with the infliction of atrocities of all sorts.

Table 5

Era	Year	Cases	Percentage
Italian Colonial Era	1950-1960	128	6.04%
Aden Abdulle Osman	1960-1967	1439	68%
Abdirashid Ali Sharma'ke	1967-1969	1439	68%
Mohamed Siyad Barre	1969-1990	1667	88.80%
Civil War/Anarchy	1990 to date	2074	98%

Figure 5

ERA OF ABUSE

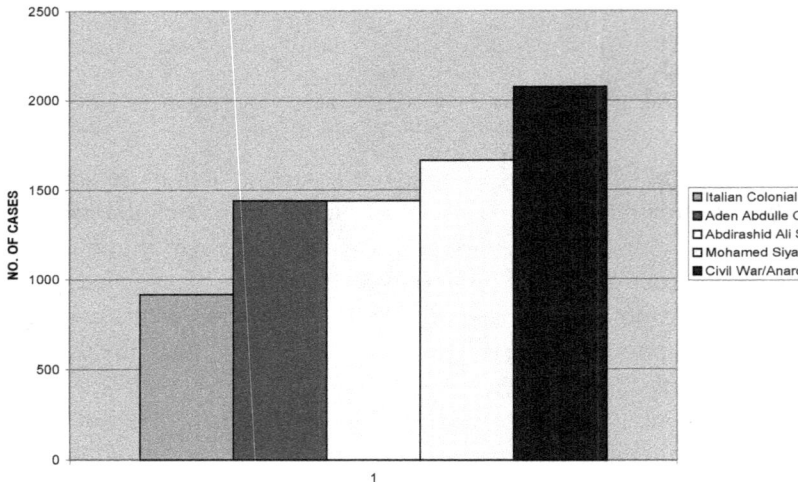

YEARS OF ABUSE

8.2.6. Solution for abuse/violation

(A) Reaction to abuse/violation

About 1,662 cases or 79% of the overall respondents (Tab. 6 & Fig. 6) stated *obedience/perseverance* as a self-developed mechanism to neutralize the abuse they were subjected to; to live with it and be conditioned in compliance. Twenty-one percent have sought *relocation* elsewhere away from where they had suffered the abuses.

Table 6

REACTION		
Reaction to Abuse	Count	Percentage
Obedience/Perseverance	1662	79
Relocation	454	21
TOTAL	**2116**	**100**

Figure 6

REACTION TO ABUSE

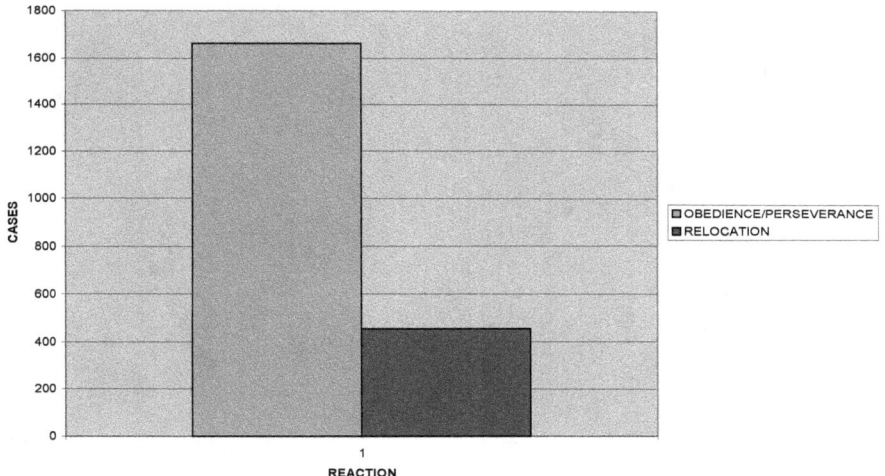

(B) Remedy to abuse/violation

Ninety-six percent of the victims, 2,038 cases (Tab. 7 & Fig. 7) did not dare try to seek remedy compared to 4% or 78 respondents who sought some kind of legal intervention to heal their grievance. Despite the attempt, however, a zero representation reported to have achieved any legal redress. Subsequently, 99% admit the abuses are still continuing compared to one percent who said it has been discontinued.

Table 7

ACTION	REMEDY				
	YES	PER.	NO	PER.	TOTAL
Seeking remedy	78	4%	2038	96%	2116
Provision of remedy	-	0%	78	100%	78
Discontinuation of abuse	25	1%	2091	99%	2116

Figure 7

REMEDIAL ACTION

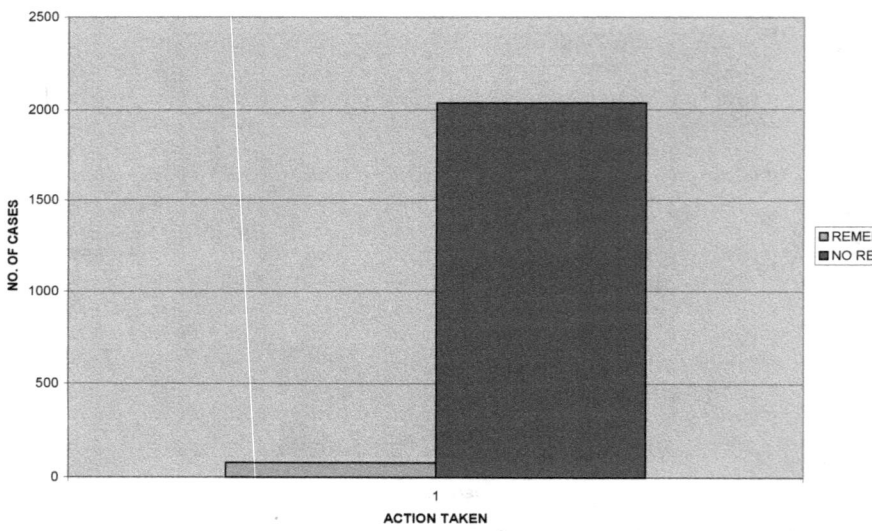

ACTION TAKEN

Notes and references

1. The Holy Qur'an, (Sura Al-Hujurat 49:13), English translation of the meanings and commentary. Revised and edited by The Presidency of Islamic Researches, IFTA, Call and Guidance.
2. Peil, Margaret, and Oyeneye, Olatunji., Consensus, Conflict and Change: A Sociological Introduction to African Societies. East African Educational Publishers. (1998:83)

274

Chapter 9

ELABORATING THE ACTS OF MARGINALIZATION

1. Analysis

The result shows a general overview of the Somali Bantu/Jareer sample group. The composition of the respondents represents interviewees from all walks of life and selected randomly. It shows the number of respondents who replied and the related gender representation, ensuring that single as well as married male and female Bantu/Jareer were represented in the study.

The chart and table on education analysis estimate the meager opportunity of academic acquisition for the average Jareer male and female. According to the statistics, this has been an area of neglect by all the authorities in the country, colonial, civilian as well as the dictatorial military regime. The findings support the desire of the Jareer people to seek academic advancement, however, they could not continue for reasons related to various other elements of oppression indicated in the study.

With statistical figures as high as revealed in this section, the Bantu/Jareer people undergo intolerable abuses and rights violation of multiple characteristics. The variables investigated and results encourage us to consider the existence of Apartheid, call it racial or ethnic. The revelations assume the prevalence of this phenomenon in "orientally homogenized" Somalia. The versatile natures of abuse and violation also reveal the magnitude of the inherent human suffering this community lives under.

Whatever the propagation of the oriental/colonial scholars, be it Somali homogeneity or pastoral totality, the oppressed voices of the Bantu/Zenj Jareer autochthons have sent their messages as an overwhelming majority declare they are abused, violated, segregated and dehumanized because of their ethnic background, which is racially and biologically distinct from that of the pastoral Somali.

The factor under observation in this sub-section leaves us with an inferential probability that the seven years of Osman's rule had an abuse rate equal to the two years of Sharma'arke. The deduction by far presumes a possibility for a much higher rate of abuse had the second president continued to lead the country a corresponding period to Osman's era. Sharma'arke, like his predecessor, was notorious for alienating the Jareer. He denied them to represent their constituencies on SYL ticket. The Negroid Jareer population of Somalia say they have undergone violation of their rights and human dignity across all the eras in the context of the survey, from colonial period to the current anarchy.

The higher rate of Bantu rights abuse in Barre's rule of 21 years compared to a total of nine years shared between the first and second presidents as seven years and two years respectively, might have been influenced by the ethnocentric dictator's longer period in power. None has a record of observing their well being and significance of their social role as feeders and builders of the nation. The highest rate, in the sense of frequency, of the human rights violation of the Jareer, according to the analysis described, have reached record peak after the ouster of Barre and in the current *civil anarchy*.

Owing to the enormity of the oppression and the multiplicity of its characteristics and sources, state and social, the Jareer had to condition themselves to obedience and submission. Theirs was, as they utterly disclosed, a vulnerability which attracted inexplicable types of aggression, misplaced or otherwise (in psychological context). Seeking remedy and redress to the violations has created more traumatic distress as it led to more oppression. Relocation is a remedy somehow interpretable to displacement within the country and refuge elsewhere in the neighboring countries and/or across the continents. One suggestion for discontinuation of the violation, as responded by a section of the respondents, could be they have either fled the country or relocated/displaced to another area.

2. Discussion

As the findings of the study reveal, **education** has been a crucially scarce commodity for the Jareer people, encouraged by a continuum of multiple negative factors. Some of these factors include: (a) Lack of educational establishments in areas heavily inhabited by the Bantu/Jareer. (b) The few agricultural towns, where elementary schools were established, did not have intermediate level institutions, so it was an economic constraint for an undeveloped, rudimentarily equipped traditional farmer to afford upkeep to educate a child in the capital or in any other urban centre. (c) It is not harmonious for the urban dwellers from this community to study in Jileec-dominated schools owing to stereotyping, bullying, harassment and beating by gangs of their Jileec/Somali peers. (d) Stereotypes, names and epithets by some class teachers damaged the motivation and self-esteem of the Jareer pupils and therefore a reason for an early dropout from school. (e) Lack of teacher's motivational remarks for the Jareer/Bantu pupils' outstanding performance. (f) Reference of negative examples and attributes to the Bantu/Jareer culture and community by schoolteachers. (g) Teachers' unfairness to the Jareer students in assessments, marking and grading of exam papers, and (h) Teachers' harsh, unequal punishment and embarrassment of students from the Jareer community: -

Case No. 9.2.1

Abukar Ali Abanur was a very bright Jareer pupil in our 2nd grade in Hodan Boys School. After very good performance in the first term, Abanur has become a subject of punishment both by the teacher and students on daily basis. Our teacher really used to punish the boy, harsher than any other pupil in the class. At times, he was penalized for other boys' misdeeds. During the third term, the boy did not return; instead, his father saw it safer for the young Abanur to be apprentice in an auto-mechanic workshop.

As seen here, apart from the dreadful economic straits, the environment of the school society was emotionally demotivating, hostile and psychologically traumatizing to the Jareer child for whom the quality of his ethnic properties became a reason for his denigration and alienation from the academic arena at an early age. One such evidence is here: -

Case No. 9.2.2

An Italian teacher one day called for his Jareer student's parent. When the two met, the teacher advised, "Try to transfer your son to another school. In this school, he will not move to the upper grade no matter what." The student's father was perturbed as he was told, on confidential note, "The Somali teachers are hard on him without any valid reason. We can't help the situation but we have to be honest with you. The boy is brilliant and active but that is his disadvantage. I am sorry!

Consequently, these negative trends have contaminated and tremendously frustrated the domains of the elements stimulating the Jareer desire for education. The effects of prejudice from the environment of the school institution tallied apparently against the Jareer learner's emotions, which again caused scars of psychological wounds by diminishing the potential of his/her intellectual ambition and academic performance in general. The results of Jareer/Bantu alienation in the school environment do not provide a clean bill of health to the education authorities and society in general, as academic evidence has shown the difficulties the community has been experiencing in the education sector to date. In Somalia, academic participation is seen as a sacrosanct privilege reserved for the non-Jareer who quite often felt disturbed by outstanding Jareer performance:

Case No. 9.2.3

When school headmaster Abdalla Ali Murshid announced the highest scorer in the centralized leaving exam of Casa Popolare Elementary School was "Mohamed Abdulkadir Eno" (this author), a parent from the north could not take it. As I was passing near him to the podium to shake hands with the headmaster, I heard my left-handed northerner classmate's father saying "Ma kan adoonka ah baa caruurteena ka badiyey?" translated which means "How is it possible that this slave one has outscored our children?" When I reported the incident at home, my parents counseled and encouraged me, a long story beyond this study, but one that has inspired me all the way to this academic stage.

Looking into **Denial of job opportunity** and/or **promotion** in the civil service, it is not at all uncommon for a Jareer with qualification either to wander unemployed or be displaced in an institution and post irrelevant to his academic or skills background. The Jareer constitute the governments' popular preference for transfer in remote areas and positions shunned by the 'noble' pastoral officers in the civil or public service. The fact that none from this community had ever held ministerial portfolio, high diplomatic office or any other top administrative posts in the parastatal institutions as General Manager, Director General, or even a General in the army, reveals self-axiomatically the socio-ethnic place of the Jareer. This is another factor that may be linked to the possibilities that the few who were employed in insignificant of-fices and posts were not worth the while for promotion to a level or an opportunity commensurate only to the prestige of a Jileec/Somali 'no-ble'.

The interpretation of **business** in this study is in its wider scope, contrary to 'business' in the narrow sense of limiting it only to an ex-change of items or products. The adjunct aim behind the Jareer denial for education is obviously treated as a prerequisite for denial of busi-ness in the sense that an opportunity for potential performance, an academic expertise in a certain discipline, could make a difference for a Jareer. From the other aspect, mass confiscation of privately owned Bantu agricultural land from colonial time to date, also features in the denial of business as the right of one's occupation to work on his farm and sustain his family was violated. Another interpretation could yet be related to the deliberate lack of development policy for the small-scale subsistence farmer, a move that would create prosperity and pos-sible business interaction and advancement for the Jareer agricultural-ists. The responses seem high for the variable, considering the Bantu/Jareer community's cultural domain in agriculture, but denial remains a paramount obstacle to Jareer achievement. Certain presiden-tial decrees and state laws and acts were not "meant" for the benefit of the Jareer/Bantu:

Case No. 9.2.4

Siad Barre's military regime declared importation of agricultural equipment "duty-free", but when a Jareer imported a tractor, model "SAME Centauro 45", it took over six months to clear it from the port. The reason: "Duty-free was not meant for people like you", the "you" referring to Bantu/Jareer.

Denial of business opportunity is related also to various villages inhabited by the community that were disenfranchised through the private allocation and diversion of the 'communal main canals' (Keli-Gumeed) that irrigate their farms. Forced conscription of the youth, the backbone of the human resource of the nucleus family, into the army, constitutes another major deprivation affecting the family pro-duction business and productivity and hence denying them an oppor-tunity to conduct their business potential un-interfered:

Case No. 9.2.5

Mohamed Abdi Roble, alias Maadeey Barakaale, and his younger brother Ali, were very talented auto-mechanics in Mogadishu. As a result, their workshop attracted a large number of patrons. A Jileec workshop owner in the neighborhood was not pleased with their competition. The two brothers were severally but alternatively locked up, day in day out, for reasons beyond their understanding, until one day when they saw their arresting officer repairing his car in their neighbor's garage. This time the officer was brief but clear, "You and your brother will either come and work in this workshop, or move your garage elsewhere." Maadeey and Ali reported the matter to their area police station. After a few days, they were traced to their residence, put under custody in their area police station before they were handed over to the higher-ranking police officer against whom they sought redress. When they were released after about 2 weeks, the two Jareer brothers closed their business down and traveled to Saudi Arabia where they are currently residents.

The Somali authority's ill treatment to Jareer education is manifested in this demoralizing incident:

Case No. 9.2.6

A young Jareer man got scholarship to study abroad. Upon reaching Mogadishu International Airport for departure, his passport and ticket were retained at the Immigration counter and he was sent back "upon instructions from the higher authority, which you will be told in your office tomorrow." The following day, he was told, "The arrangement was made due to 'name mix-up', but in fact the scholarship was not for you." In a week's time, he was transferred to a remote pastoral area as assistant veterinary technician although he had graduated as a draughtsman from the Polytechnic. After failing to adjust to his new job for about two months, he came back to Mogadishu and became self-employed.

Imprisonment without trial in a court of law was not punitive measures for an ordinary citizen tolerating (as the Jareer did) and abiding by the dictatorial nature of the Somali Revolutionary Socialist Party. A possible reason in the nature of this kind of punishment is in its exclusiveness for political dissidents and others categorized as reactionary (*dib-u-socod*) with an undertone of anti-revolutionary (*Kacaan-diid*) sentiments. The Jareer community, as far as the social politics and political sociology of Somalia is concerned, are situated well beyond the hem of associating, approaching or indulging in activities facilitating competition for political and/or economic power. The low rate of the score in this factor seems to have been interpreted in political significance, which does not of course overrule the fact that many of the community members have experienced this particular version of oppression and injustice, especially the few that had done some of the other non-political social issues that had an overburdening effect on their lives, such as seeking legal action against expropriators.

Alternatively, certain arrests had no mentionable reasons to justify as preferring a crime against the arrested; this personal experience is one of many such unsubstantiated arrests:

Case No. 9.2.7

A Jareer youth was supposed to travel to Dar es Salaam on Somali Airlines, which suspended the route after issuing him with the ticket. They advised him to re-route to Seychelles and from there to take Air Tanzania up to Dar es Salaam, which they made the reservation accordingly. After boarding the aircraft, two policemen entered the plane hastily and ordered the young man to disembark. He thought he hadn't identified his luggage or something. They escorted him out of the terminal and into the office of the commanding officer at the Airport Police Station, a Police Captain named Mohamed Hassan. He interrogated the boy about the trip to Seychelles where, according to the captain, only "white tourists go." The Jareer youth explained the circumstances leading to the rerouting to Mahe, Seychelles, and also to enquire and confirm the same from his carrier. The Captain was not convinced as he kept telling the young Jareer man, "you, being a 'simple' Jareer, what are you going to do in Seychelles, a place for rich white tourists?" He ordered one of his junior officers by the name 'Musse' to arrest the Bantu boy. After he stayed in custody for two days, a friend, Abuu Makhafaay, a goldsmith, contacted his friend, Col. Ali "Apollo", then a prominent Judge in the Military Court. When Captain Mohamed Hassan failed to prefer any crime against the young man, as requested by "Apollo", the Jareer prisoner was summoned in the Captain's office. Upon releasing him, the Captain insulted the youth in anger for freeing him; indecent words that are unprintable here!

Cases are uncountable where Bantu/Jareer technicians executed tasks and contracts before ending up in cells upon claiming their wages and payment after completion of the task. Others were **sentenced** in Kangaroo courts convened by a District Commissioner or Chairman of the District Security Officer or Party Bureau Chairman and his hand-picked committee who had no legal jurisdiction whatsoever to officiate, judge or sentence, all in absolute violation of the law of the land. Neither had these officials undergone professional training in law to enable them officiate in legal matters, nor were the accused allowed to appoint and be represented by a lawyer. Everyone in the public offices exercised their authority negatively against the Bantu–Jareer, as per their pleasure.

To put it more explicitly, the diversity of African origin has become sufficient reason for the Negroid autochthons to suffer discrimination, prejudice, stereotype, segregation, epithets and marginalization, all culminating in their stratification as second-class citizens, with half or less the right of the pastoral Jileec citizen in a recent social stratification phenomenon called '4.5 clan power-sharing system.'. The existence of ethnic-based degradation and discrimination provides yet again a reason to believe the existence of fission of multi-ethnic heterogeneity much at variance with the artificially midwifed homogeneity that nurtures pastoral Jileec self-ennoblement. Social degradation, in essence, as well as in effect, functions as a paradigmatic reality in the lifeblood of Somali social vein, exclusively more active in the Jareer/Negroid-inferior and Jileec/Somali-superior customary law of social stratification. Central to degradation are a divergence of factors, but core among them is the ethnic distinctiveness of the Bantu/Jareer, according to the findings of the survey and as evidenced in the dialogue between the two neighbors (Case No. 9.2.8.) below, a clear presentation of the Somali social psychology towards the social place of the Jareer:

Case No. 9.2.8

Two Jareer brothers were heading to school smartly dressed in their school uniform, when a neighbor, Asha Hajin, approached their mother to remind her: "Why do you waste so much time educating children who will never take up a public office." This neighbor's overtone was a reflection of the stigma with Jareer-ness and the low social status it carries in everyday Somali social life. The Jareer mother replied wisely, "Once they are educated, they will not need a post in public office; they may as well be self-employed."

In another extremely unbelievable incident, as envisaged in the next case, we see how the Jileec-ness factor played an effective role against Jareer-ness and an innocent man made casualty of gross injustice:

Case No. 9.2.9

One day, around 3 o'clock in the afternoon, a crowd was after a thief who had snatched a gold chain from a teen-age girl. A Jareer boy was fast and caught the thief. When the case came up in court, the crime was turned over to the Bantu/Jareer witness who had caught the thief. The neighbors of the Jareer victim of justice later discovered that the police officer preparing the case and the girl, who was the complainant, happened to agree to incriminate the innocent Jareer witness rather than having the Jileec thief behind bars. They sentenced the Jareer young man to serve an illegal sentence. The witness-turned-criminal spent four months in prison. Upon completion of his illegal jail term, he had to leave the country in disgust of the injustice he had encountered.

Case No. 9.2.10.

Yusuf Haji Ibrahim (alias Prof. Yusuf) was a talented Jareer teacher in a high school in Mogadishu. He failed one of his students who wasn't doing well in his subject. On his way home one day, he was waylaid by a gang from the kinship of Yusuf's student. The Jareer teacher was interrogated, degraded and maliciously abused in the presence of a crowd of his students before the gang of five men physically battered him. He puked blood and became unconscious before the men drove away in their Toyota Land Cruiser with the student. He was hospitalized for about three months. Upon his return to work the student's parents insisted that Yusuf be transferred to another school because his presence in the school would demean the pride of their nobility. He was transferred to teach in an elementary school although he was a graduate of the College of Education with qualification to teach in secondary school.

Appropriation and **confiscation** of Bantu property, movable and immovable, has been a daily dilemma. However, there is little disagreement about expropriation and confiscation of Bantu/Jareer property across the extension of colonial era through the current civil anarchy. In one such state-sponsored violation, **Hussein Kulmiye Afrah**, then Minister for Internal Affairs, and founding member of the Supreme Revolutionary Council (Golaha Sare ee Kacanka), was sent in 1971 to speak to complainants in the Lower Shabelle Region who were protesting against losing their land to the government's agricultural Crash Programmed Scheme. After listening to the unending complaints of the Bantu/Jareer farmers, he had to tell the thousands of villagers unsympathetically, that even the Italians had expropriated their (villagers') land with neither consent nor compensation, therefore they had no right whatsoever to oppose state policy or to protest against it.

Case No. 9.2.11

A new expropriator of a mango plantation (a top official) came to the wholesale market in Afgoie and said to a Jareer broker, "I have mango plantation; how much is a mango?" The Jareer broker asked in a friendly remark with a smile of irony, "If you don't know the price of mangoes, how could it be that you own mango plantation." The stranger left and returned after about 30 minutes or so with a few police officers. The Jareer broker was jailed on 'Emergency', without trial, for "bad conduct" toward a high official of the government.

The Italian colonial regime was the mother that first invented the sequestration of Bantu agricultural land when it designed a blueprint to boom the metropolis economy via the exploitation of appropriated Jareer land worked by forced Jareer human resource. Subsequently, the civilian regimes of independent Somalia borrowed a leaf from their colonial masters as members of parliament, cabinet ministers, the incumbent in the top seat and others in their respective administrative posts waged a huge campaign to seize land directly or by means of dubious and undercover transactions. Some of these alleged transactions involved colonial concessionaires as a clever mechanism to claim legal acquisition and right to ownership of land properties formerly looted or appropriated from the original proprietors. This is to reveal that certain prominent personalities claim to have acquired their agricultural farmland from former Italian concessionaires while they were very well aware of the circumstances under which the colonial settlers had acquired the Bantu land.

Ironically, these dignitaries have "purchased" the plantations [in] Somalia from the colonial land-looters and land-grabbers instead of condemning colonial atrocities including slavery and expropriation. It becomes more shocking when after sovereignty those in the top leadership claim the acquisition of such properties from the colonialists despite the fact that they (colonialists) had expropriated from the Jareer citizens, thus arising a reason to doubt the moral integrity and degree of statesmanship and loyalty of the leadership of the first civilian regime. In more explicit terms, the Jareer poets' verses bear more significance in delivering the strong message of doubt over the Italy-SYL relationship on the one hand, and the acts of neocolonialism that became the order of state administration in newly independent Somalia.

During Barre's military regime, the expropriation of Bantuland, particularly in the riverine areas of Shabelle and Jubba, has become an easy target legitimized through state acts, laws and by-laws for state as well as individual plunder and fraud empowered either by ethnic attachment to the ruling clan or by personal authority of a top official in an administrative position, or connection with one. Confiscation of Bantu property, including buildings and even household properties, has amazingly become one of the easiest acquirable materials of value from 1991 in the wake of the civil anarchy.

Very many respondents show to have suffered physical and/or moral abuse, most of them probably during the period from 1991. Physical and moral abuse, although persistent in all other administrations, be them colonial, civilian or military, crossed the limit in the recent past in the unruly chaos and crisis led by the warlords and their armed ethnic/clan militia. One example on each could be drawn from: (a) Physical torture while working wagelessly as slaves on banana plantations in Lower Shabelle, and (b) Moral torture by witnessing the gang-raping of women relatives by the armed militia who first hold the Jareer male under gun-point; those who couldn't stand the immorality or reacted to it were summarily executed.

The indication in the statistics invites us to believe that out of 804 female samples, about 21 have apparently suffered as victims of rape, and that most of these cases were respondents from Lower Shabelle, Lower and Middle Jubba as well as the Refugee Camps in Kenya. The question concerning rape may not have presented all the truth. Although women interviewers were active in establishing rapport, it is not culturally easy for a female Jareer to narrate her ordeal about rape. Accordingly, there is likelihood that many rape victims shied away from sharing their abuse due to cultural reservations or avoidance of related psycho-traumatic emotions as almost all these rape victims do not access any trauma counseling to heal their wound.

Case No. 9.2.12

In the turbulent days of the civil war somewhere in Lower Jubba Region, a lady from one of the armed clans that occupied the area talked about how she admires the voice of the Imam (leader) of the mosque in the area as he calls for the prayers, and how she dreamed about him one night. The armed youth couldn't take the idea of their female dreaming of a Jareer, despite his piety, and summoned the clergyman to substantiate why the lady had dreamed about him. The man had no answer as he knew nothing about what was going on. The armed youth kept repeating: How can our female dream about you? But the Bantu man had no answer to give about someone else's dream. The armed gang then shot him several times and tied his mutilated body onto a tree for the whole day before his relatives were allowed to bury him late in the evening with a penalty to pay for the 11 bullets that were used to kill the cleric.

Remarks

This chapter and the preceding one have constructively but also empirically disagreed with the idea of Somali homogeneity and the other self-sameness universally misleading about the heterogeneity and multi-ethnicity of the communities in this Horn of Africa peninsula. Within the strict confines of this study, and as proven from the perspective of quantitative findings, ethnic marginalization in the form of Apartheid is highly prevalent in Somalia as instituted against the sections of the distinctly Negroid/Jareer community, affecting all aspects of their social life, politically, academically as well as economically.

Conclusion

Within its limits, this study has attempted to distinguish between the Jareer and Jileec peoples of Somalia, as well as the distinct Jareer groups, touching on the controversies surrounding Somali genealogy and homogeneity. The alleged 'oneness' of the Somali people, as often narrated in the history of their origin, language and culture, is nothing more than a social myth. It is typical of other world myths which are enduring and fast disseminated, and in time become a solid component of the social belief. Therefore, without proven relationship to Arab ancestry, and with emerging realities of multiple cultures and languages, the self-sameness hypothesis is weaker than earlier scholars have argued.

However, what is not yet clearly known is the reason behind the adoption of this 'oneness'. Partly it could be due to Somali predilection to associate with the emerging power and civilization of Islam and its root from Arabia that influenced the early Somalis to adopt genealogical Arabness. In the mind of the Somali nomad of that time, Arabness was superior compared to the African identity in his neighborhood. According to his thinking at that day, a closer consanguinity relationship with Mohamed, the Prophet of Islam, would give him a reason for support from Muslim rulers so he could attack and hold conquest over the Christian and pagan rulers in the vicinity. Traditional myth aside, the idea of an entire community 'recreating' themselves from a couple of visitors, without significant proof to strengthen that claim, stays hypothetically implausible. Therefore I argue that the raison d'être of Somali pastoral's self-attachment to Arabness was to secure his long-sought after noble identity 'above' Africanity. By this, he concocted a biological reason for denigrating those who identify with Africanity.

If we consider Somaliness according to territorial citizenship, scholars are unequivocal about the recentness of Somali appearance in the Horn. Even before the appearance of the Somali people, the Cushitic groups who came to this part of the Horn of Africa found that the Bantu people had already been dominant in the area. These were Galla who forced the Bantu to migrate into Tana and coastal towns in modern Kenya. There is likelihood, according to distinguished scholars, that the residues of those early Bantu aborigines are the present day inhabitants of the inter-river areas, the stock popularly referred to as Jareer, Bantu, Zenj, Negroid, and epithets like Habash, Adoon, San-

buur, Sankadhudhi etc. The traditions, oral literature, archival documents as well as linguistic evidence, as elaborated in this study, are in
support of the thesis disagreeing   with the oriental/colonial scholars'
homogeneity narrative that lumps all the distinct identities into a symbolic one-Somali people and culture.

Yet, a sociological approach to the Somali clan system and its functions extensively highlight the complexity of the evolving phenomenon
of Somaliness and the variety of criteria for qualification to that identity. Without undermining the existing postulates measuring Somaliness, the Jareer perspective of Somaliness lends credence to antece-
dence in the inhabitance of the territory by the Negroid/Zenj, despite
the accident of the mysterious nomenclature "Somali/Somalia" and its
fast gain in popularity.

As discussed in one of the chapters, the Jareer/Bantu concept of
Somaliness is beyond the easy fabrication and falsification of identities,
simultaneously constructing and deconstructing kinship at one's liberty, ultimately becoming cause for destructiveness. The Jareer thought
of identity or Somaliness is shaped around dignified constructiveness
in nation-building, pacifism, human respect and moral values. These
variant qualities of the Jareer and Jileec depict the different characteristics of the social cultures as well as social psychologies of the Somali
society; more specifically the divide between belligerent pastoral destructiveness compared to pacifist agrarian constructiveness.

The prevailing suggestion is that perhaps the idea of a self-same
Somalia has in part pleased the post-colonial political dominance of
pastoralists over the agrarian population. In time, it has become a basis
for the divide between a socio-economically disadvantaged Jareer at
the bottom rung and a more advantaged Jileec in the Somali social
strata. Political and economic disadvantages on the one hand, and social degradation and exploitation on the other, have to a greater degree
contributed to the constraints hindering the Jareer community from
advancement in all areas of social development.

Ethnic stratification, social prejudice and social exclusion have consequently culminated in the establishment and constitutionalization of
a rigid system of Apartheid in the name of "4.5 clan power sharing
formula". Without elaborating any viable reason for its adoption, the
"4.5 formula" has become the Somali people's only exception and
meaningful method for explicitly determining the class, status and social destiny of the Bantu–Jareer community as "officially" lower in

rights and citizenship than their pastoral Jileec counterparts. The system, though, contradicts with the harmony and social integration expected from a society widely celebrated for its 'homogeneity'. Conversely, it has become an effective vehicle for accelerating ethnic polarization and marginalization.

Concerning their social status and causes of their degradation, the Bantu–Jareer have expressed the existence of oppression in spite of the self-sameness supposed to be the pastorals' socio-psychological food for domination. With that note, I intend to declare the existence of a wide heterogeneity in which the ethnic-Bantu population undergoes a constitutionally orchestrated social exclusion. Exerted between two evils of a kind, colonial exploitation and Somali domination of a similar end but of distinct natures and magnitude, the Bantu/Jareer community endures a myriad of societal damages in the forms of oppression, persecution, discrimination and other inhumane atrocities of Apartheid nature.

For the enhancement of this alienation strategy, it was deemed crucial, among other things, to engage a state policy based on political structures without Jareer representation. The policy was again supplemented by state neglect towards the development of agriculture, an area that would achieve potential economic advancement for the community. It was this devastating political strategy that has inflicted the Jareer community a drastic limitation in the development of their potential in the economic domain and more destructively also in the academic realm.

Under the growing overlap of this socio-ethnic paradox, one needs to prove Somali homogeneity and monoculturality by first disproving the ethnic diversity of the Bantu Jareer people from that of the Somali Jileec, physically, culturally and genealogically. Consequently, if "Somaliness" amounts to the automatic portrayal of identity for a clique with certain physical, cultural and genealogical properties specific to them, it becomes inevitable to invent a "Somaliness" that addresses and accommodates the other communities in the country who are characterized by identities distinct from those qualified with Somaliness in its current description as determined and distributed by the dominant nomadic units north of the capital.

Looking at Somalia from the true perspectives of its social realities is a subject rather complex and versatile in nature. Mine is possibly a tip of the iceberg in disentombing all that nomadic Somalia has entombed about the different Somali identities living in the country. The situation is rather aggravated by the myths and fabrications world renowned scholars have recorded about the country, mainly relying on and re-producing nomadic thoughts and traditions. The great desire to correct past historical anomalies, and the need to preserve the existing realities are adequate reasons for extensive research on the communities in this country. Adamancy to stick to the current historical mendacity will not only narrow the scope of knowledge retrievable on Somalia but may in time cause genocide to the entire cultures and civilizations of the non-nomadic communities in the country.

Appendix 1: Summary of cases answered in every region and in the diaspora

No.	REGION	CASES ANSWERED
1	Lower Jbba	196
2	Bay	197
3	Gedo	196
4	Middle Shabelle	194
5	Hiran	195
6	Bakool	194
7	Banadir	198
8	Middle Jubba	194
9	Lower Shabelle	195
10	Diaspora	357
	Total	**2116**

Appendix 2: Areas where interview was conducted

1	Lower Jubba	Kismayo
		Jamame
2	Hiran	Belet-weyne
3	Lower Shabelle	Afgoi
		Marka
		Shalambod
		Golween

4	Bay	Baidoa
		Bur-Hakaba
5	Middle Shabelle	Balcad
		Jowhar
		Mahadaay
6	Middle Jubba	Jilib
		Dujuma
		B/Karim
7	Banaadi/Mogadishu	Waaberi
		Wadajir
		Hawl-Wadaag
8	GEDO	Luuq
		Baardheere
9	Bakool	Xudur
		Tayegloow
10	Diaspora	U.S.A.
		Canad
		Italy
		Saudi Aabia
		Kenya
		Tanzania
		Tanzania

DISTRIBUTION BY AREA OF ORIGIN

No.	Towns	Number of **Cases**
1	Afgoi	26
2	Aw-Gooye	8
3	Buulo-Gaduud	13
4	Buur-Hakaba	48
5	Baladul-Kariim	20
6	Belet Weyne	39

7	Baarow Weyne	16
8	Baasaay	22
9	Baidoa	45
10	Balcad	23
11	Baraawa	6
12	Bariire	2
13	Barsane	6
14	Bu'aalle	14
15	Buulo Burte	13
16	Buur-Heybe	25
17	Buulo	11
18	Cumar Beere	6
19	Dujuuma	41
20.	Buulo Mareer	27
20	Diinsoor	9
21	Fagan	24
22	Gaafaay	21
23	Gaduudeey	14
24	Garsaale	16
25	Goobween	26
26	Hargeesa	21
27	Jalalaqsi	10
28	Jamaame	40
29	Jambaluul	12
30	Janaale	21
31	Jilib	91
32	Jowhar	82
33	Kalaanga	37

34	Kamsuuma	45
35	Kamtirey	47
36	Kawasan	53
37	Kismaayo	153
38	Kobon	24
39	Kudha	81
40	Kulmis	21
41	Luuq	8
42	Maandheere	22
43	Mafula	20
44	Maagle	3
45	Mahadaay	34
46	Makalaangoow	29
47	Marka	32
48	Mareerey (Middle Jubba)	88
49	Mareereey	17
50	Mashaqa	29
51	Migwa	25
52	Miyooni	37
53	Moofi	30
55	Mugaambo	57
56	Qallaafo	22
57	Qoryooleey	25
58	Raqayle (Middle Shabelle)	17
59	Saakooki	28
60	Saakow	23
61	Sabaato	36
62	Sablaale	26

63	Sanguuni	19
64	Shalambod	15
65	Sabatuuni	19
66	Wanla Ween (Daafeet)	23
67	Waajid	19
68	Xawaadleey	16
69	Xudur	15
70	Yoontooy	36
71	Jilib-Marka	11
72	Maagaay	13
73.	Tayeegloow	8
74.	Waaberi	17
75.	Wadajir	25
76.	Hawl-Wadaag	13
	TOTAL	**2116**

Bibliography

Abercrombie, David. *Elements of General Phonetics*. Edinburgh University Press. (1990).

Afrax, Maxamed D., <u>Dal Dad Waayey iyo Duni Damiir Beeshay: Soomaaliya Dib Ma u Dhalan doontaa?</u> Daabacaadda koowaad. Printed by Maji Matamu Printers Ltd., Eldoret, Kenya. (2002).

Ahmed, Ali Jimale., "<u>Day Break Is Near, Won't You Become Sour?</u>" in Ahmed, Ali J., (ed.), <u>The Invention of Somalia</u>. Red Sea Press Inc. (1995).

_____ *Daybreak is Near...: Literature, Clans and the Nation-State in Somalia.* Red Sea Press. (1996).

Ahmed, Christine C., "Finely Etched Chattel: The Invention of a Somali Woman", in Ahmed, Ali Jimale, (ed.), *The Invention of Somalia*. Red Sea Press. (1995)

Aidarus, Sharif Aidarus Ibn Shariff Ali, *Bughyat al-Amal – fi-Tarikh– As Sumal*. Mogadishu, Stamperia A.F.I.F. (1955).

Aitchson, Jean., *Linguistics*, Hodder & Stoughton (1999).

Ali, Ahmed Qassim, "The Predicament of the Somali Studies," in Ahmed, Ali Jimale., (ed.), *The Invention of Somalia*. Red Sea Press (1995).

_____ "Land Rush in Somalia," in Kusow, Abdi M., (ed.), *Putting the Cart Before the Horse*. Red Sea Press. (2004)

Al-Idrisi, Abi – Abdalla Muhammad., *Kitab Nuzhat al-Mushtaq fi-ikhtiraq al-Afaq*. MS Pococke 375, Arch. OC 2, Bodlein, Oxford.

Allport, G., *The Nature of Prejudice*. Reading, MA: Addison – Wesley (1954).

Ali, Mohamed Nuuh., <u>'Somali History: Linguistic Approaches to the Past,'</u> in Kusow, Abdi M., (ed.), *Putting the Cart Before the Horse*. Red Sea Press (2004).

Allen, James de Vere, "Shungwaya, The Mijikenda, And The Traditions." International Journal of African Historical Studies; vol. 16(3) (1983) pp. 455-85.

Bandura, A., *Self-efficacy: the exercise of control*. New York: Freeman, (1997).

Baron, Robert A., and Byrne, Donn., *Social Psychology*. Tenth edition. Prentice-Hall, India.(2003).

Barr, A. S., Robert, A. Davis and Palmer O. Johnson. *Educational Research and Appraisal*. Chicago: J.B. Lippincott Co. (1953).

Bell, Derrick., "Remembrances of Racism Past: Getting Beyond the

Civil Rights Decline", in Hill, H., and Jones Jr., J. (eds.), *Race in America: The Struggle for Equality*. The University of Wisconsin Press. (1993).

Benedict, Ruth. *Race and Racism*, London: George Routledge & Sons Ltd (1942).

Best, John W., *Research in Education*. New Delhi: Prentice-Hall of India Pvt. Ltd. (1977).

Best, John W., and Kahn, James V. *Research in Education*, Seventh edition. Prentice Hall of India – Private Limited. New Delhi. (2004).

Besteman, Catherine L., *Unraveling Somalia: Race, Violence and the Legacy of Slavery*. University of Pennsylvania Press (1999).

_____ "Land Tenure, Social Power and the Legacy of Slavery in Southern Somalia", Ph.D. Dissertation, The University of Arizona. (1991).

_____ "The Invention of Gosha: Slavery, Colonialism and Stigma in Somali History," in Ahmed, Ali J., (ed.), *The Invention of Somalia*. The Red Sea Press Inc. (1995)

Bricchetti, Robecchi., *Dal Benadir, Lettere illustrate alla societa Antischiavista d'Italia*. Milano (1904).

British Naval Staff *A Handbook of Abyssinia*, vol.1, Intelligence Division. (1917).

Burton, R., *First Footsteps in East Africa*. London (1894).

Cassanelli, Lee V., "A Historian's View of the Prospects for Somali Reconstruction", in Janzen, Jorg., (ed.), *What are Somalia's Development Perspective?*, Berlin: Das Arabische Buch (2000).

_____ "Explaining the Somali Crisis" in Besteman C. L., and Cassanelli, L.V., (eds.), *The struggle for Land in Southern Somalia: the War Behind the War*. Haan Associates (2000).

_____ *The Shaping of Somali Society*. Philadelphia: University of Pennsylvania Press. (1982)

Champion, A.M. "The Agiryama of Kenya," Royal Anthropological Institute Occasional Paper No. 5 London, (1967).

Cerulli, E., Il Libro degli Zenji," in *Somalia, Scritti Vari Editi ed Inediti* (3 vols. Rome, 1957 – 1964).

_____ *Somalia, Scritti editi ed inediti*, vol.III Roma: Istituto Poligrafico dello Stato (1964)

_____ *Somalia: Scritti vari editi ed inediti*. Volume 2, Roma: Istituto Poligrafico dello Stato. (1959).

_____ *Somalia: Scritti vari editi ed inediti*. Vols. I, II, III. Roma (1957).

Chhabra, S.S., *Fundamentals of Demography* Surjeet Publications (2001).

Chiesi, Gustavo, and Travelli, Ernesto., *Le Questioni del Benadir*. Milano: Bellini. (1904).

Chittick, H. Neville., "The Book of the Zenj and the Mijikenda". International Journal of African Historical Studies IX, 1 (1976).

_____ "An Archaeological Reconnaissance of the Southern Somali Coast," Azania, IV (1969).

Christopher, William. "Extract from a Journal by Lt. William Christopher," (commanding the H.C. Brig. Of War Tigris on the East Coast of Africa). May 8th (1843). Journal of the Royal Geographical Society (1844).

Collins, Douglas., *A Tear for Somalia*. Jarrolds Publishers London Ltd.(1960)

Compagnon, D., "Political Decay in Somalia: From Personal Rule to Warlordism," Refuge 12 (5): (1992).

Coupland, Nikolas and Jaworski, Adam., *Sociolinguistics: A Reader and Coursebook*. Palgrave (1997).

Das, Hari Hara and Choudhury, B.C., *Introduction to Political Sociology*. Vikas Publishing House PVT Ltd. Second Reprint (2002).

Declich, Francesca, "Fostering Ethnic Reinvention: Gender Impact of Forced Migration on Bantu Somali Refugees in Kenya. Cahiers d'Etudes Africaines, 157, XL-1, (2000)

De Vecchi di Val Cismon., *Orizzonti d'impero: Cinque anni in Somalia*. Milan: Mondadori. (1935)

Doke, C.M., - "The Earliest Records of Bantu" reprinted from Bantu Studies – vol. XII, No. 2; June (1938)

Drake-Brockman, R. E., *British Somaliland*. London: Hurst & Blacket Ltd. (1912)

Drew, J. C., *Introduction to Designing and Conducting Research*. Second edition. The C.V. Mosby Company, Toronto, (1980).

Dualeh, Hussein Ali., *Search for a New Somali Identity*. Printed in the Republic of Kenya. (2002)

Duyvendak, J.J., 'China's Discovery of Africa'. London School of Oriental and African Studies. Occasional Paper (1949)

Ehret, Christopher., "Cushitic Prehistory" in Bendar, Lionel (ed.) *The Non-Semitic Languages of Ethiopia*. Ann Arbor: The University of Michigan (1976)

Eno, Mohamed A. "Understanding Somalia Through the Prism of Bantu Jareer Literature" in Ali J. Ahmed and Taddesse Adera (Eds.) *The*

Road Less Traveled: Reflections on the Literatures of the Horn of Africa. Trenton NJ: The Red Sea Press. (2008)

_____ "Inclusive but unequal: The Enigma of the 14th SNRC and the 4.5 (Four-point-Five) Factor" in Abdulahi A. Osman and Issaka K, Souare (Eds.*) Somalia at the Crossroads: Challenges and Perspectives on Reconstituting a Failed State.* Adonis and Abbey Publishers Ltd. (2007)

Eno, Omar A., "Somalia's Recovery and Reformation: Transcending the Rhetoric of Clan Politics" in Abdulahi A. Osman and Issaka K, Souare (Eds.) *Somalia at the Crossroads: Challenges and Perspectives on Reconstituting a Failed State.* Adonis and Abbey Publishers Ltd. (2007)

_____ "The Abolition of Slavery and the Aftermath Stigma: the case of the Bantu/Jareer People on the Benadir Coast of Southern Somalia," in Gwyn Campbell (Ed), *Abolition and Its Aftermath in Indian Ocean Africa and Asia.* Routledge, London and New York. (2005)

_____ 'Sifting Through a Sieve: Solutions for Somalia', in Janzen, Jorg (ed.), *What Are Somalia's Development Perspectives?* Proceedings of the 6th Somali Studies International Association (SSIA) Congress. Berlin, Dec. 1996. Das Arabische Buch – Berlin (2000)

_____ "The Untold Apartheid Imposed on the Jareer/Bantu People in Somalia," in Adam, Hussein M., and Ford, Richard., (eds.) *Mending Rips in the Sky: Options for Somali Communities in the 21st Century.* Lawrenceville: Red Sea Press Inc. (1997)

Eno, Omar A. and Eno, Mohamed A. "The Making of a Modern Diaspora: The Resettlement Process of the Somali Bantu Refugees in the United States" in Toyin Falola and Niyi Afolabi (Eds.) *African Minorities in the New World.* Routledge, Taylor and Francis Group (2008)

_____ and Eno, Mohamed A. "The Journey Back to the Ancestral Homeland: The Return of the Somali Bantu (Wazigwa) to Modern Tanzania" in Abdi M. Kusow and Stephanie R. Bjork (Eds.) *From Mogadishu to Dixon: The Somali Diaspora in a Global Context.* Trenton NJ: The Red Sea Press, Inc. (2007)

Eriksen, Thomas H., 'Ethnic identity, national identity and intergroup conflict: The significance of personal experience' in Ashmore, Jussim and Wilder (eds.), *Social Identity, Inter-Group Conflict, and Conflict Reduction.* Oxford University Press (2001)

Farah, I., Hussein, A., and Lind, J., "Deegaan, Politics and War in Somalia", in Lind, J., and Sturman, K., (eds.*), Scarcity and Surfeit: The Ecology of Africa's Conflict.* Institute for Security Studies (2002)

Farah, Nuruddin. *A Naked Needle,* London: Heinman (1976)

Fleming, H.C., "Baiso and Rendille: Somali outliers," Rassegna di studi Etiopici, XXC (1964).

Gassim, Mariam Arif. Somalia: Clan vs. Nation. Printed in U.A.E. (2002)

Geshekter, Charles. "The Search for Peaceful Development in a Country of War: Global Restraint on 20th Century Somali Socio-Economic Development," in Janzen, J., (ed.) *What are Somalia's Development Perspectives?* Berlin: Das Arabische Buch (2000)

Getui, Mary N., "At Variance but in Harmony" in Jong, Albert de, (ed.), *Ethnicity: Blessing or Curse?* Paulines Publications Africa. (1999)

Good, Carter V., Barr, A.S., and Scates, Douglas E., *Methodology of Educational Research.* New York: Appleton – Century Crofts Inc. (1941)

Goode, William J., and Hatt, Paul K., *Methods In Social Research.* New York: McGraw-Hill Book Company. (1952)

Grottanelli, V.L. *A Lost African Metropoli,* Afrikanistische Studien Berlin, (1955)

Gupta, Dipankar., *Interrogating Caste: Understanding Hierarchy and Difference in Indian Society.* Penguine Books, New Delhi. (2000)

Guillain, Captain C., *Documents sur L'histoire, le geographie et la commerce de L'afrique orientale,* 3 vols., Paris: Arthur Bertrand, (1856)

Hallett, Robin., *Africa Since 1875.* Surjeet Publications. Second Indian Reprint. (1999)

Hatch, E. and Farhady, H., *Research Design and Statistics for Applied Linguistics* (1982)

Helander, Bernhard., 'The Hubeer in the Land of Plenty: Land, labor and vulnerability among a Southern Somali clan'; in Besteman, Catherine and Cassanelli, Lee V. (eds.), *The Struggle for Land in Southern Somalia: The War Behind the War.* Haan Associates – London (2000)

Hersi, Ali Abdirahman., "The Arab Factor in Somali History: The Origins and the Development of Arab Enterprise and Cultural Influences in the Somali Peninsula." Ph.D. Dissertation. University of California, Los Angeles. (1977)

Hess, Robert L. *Italian Colonialism in Somalia.* The University of Chicago Press, (1966)

Hewston, M. and Giles, H. 'Social Groups and Social Stereotypes', in Coupland, Nikolas., and Jaworski, Adam (eds.), *Sociolinguistics: A Reader and Coursebook. Palgrave.* (1997)

Hilgard, E. R., Atkinson, R. C., and Atkinson, Rita L., *Introduction to Psychology.* Sixth edition. Oxford & IBH. (1975).

Holmes, Janet. *An Introduction to Sociolinguistics*, 2nd edition. Longman; an imprint of Pearson Education Ltd. (2001)

Hourani, G. *Arab Seafaring in the Indian Ocean in Ancient and Medieval Times*. Princeton (1951)

Huntingford, G. W. *The Galla of Ethiopia: The Kingdoms of Kaffa and Janjero*, Ethnographic survey of Africa, North-Eastern Africa, Part 2. London: International African Institute (1955)

_____ "The Peopling of the Interior of East Africa by its Modern Inhabitants", in R. Oliver and G. Mathew (eds.), History of East Africa, Oxford: Oxford University Press (1963)

Hurlock, Elizabeth B. *Child Development*. Sixth edition – Tata McGraw-Hill edition. (2002)

Ibn-Battuta, Abu Abdalla Mohamed, *Rihlat ibn Batuta (Travels of ibn Battuta)*, edited by Abd al-Hadi al-Tazi, (1997)

Ibn A-Sibahi, - *"Awdah al-Masalik ila Ma'rifat 'l-Buldan Wal-Mamalik,"* MS. Pococke 302, Bodelein, Oxford.

Jardine, Douglas. *The Mad Mullah of Somaliland*. London: Herbert Jenkins (1923)

Johnston, C. *Travels in Southern Abyssinia*. London: J. Madden & Co., (1844)

Kassim, Mohamed M., 'Aspects of the Banadir Cultural History', in Ahmed, Ali J.,(ed.), The Invention of Somalia. Red Sea Press. (1995)

Kayongo - Male, D., and Onyango, P., *The Sociology of the African Family*. Longman, Third Impression. (1991)

Kelsey, Dee and Pam Plumb., *Great Meetings! How TO FACILITATE LIKE A PRO*. Hanson Park Press. Second Printing. (1999)

Koul, Lokesh., *Methodology of Educational Research*. Third edition. Vikas Publishing House Pvt. Ltd. Fifth Reprint (2004)

Krapf, J. L. *Travels, Researches and Missionary Labors During Eighteen Years Residence in East Africa.* London: Trubner (1860)

Krosnick, J. A., Betz, A. L., Jussim, L. J., and Lynn, A. R., "Subliminal conditioning of attitudes." Personality and Social Psychology Bulletin, 18, 152-162. (1992)

Kusow, Abdi M., 'Contested Narratives and the Crisis of the Nation - State in Somalia: A Prolegomenon', in Kusow, Abdi M., (ed.), *Putting the Cart Before the Horse: Contested Nationalism and the Crisis of the Nation-State in Somali.* Red Sea Press (2004)

_____ 'The Somali Origin: Myth or Reality' in Ahmed, Ali J., (ed.), *The Invention of Somalia*. Red Sea Press. (1995)

_____ "Somalia's Silent Sufferers" Africa News Service (Durham), January 3, 1993. (Posted to the web January 8, 2001). www.allafrica.com.

Lewis, I. M., *Saints and Somalis: Popular Islam in a Clan-based Society*. London. Haan Associates (1998)

_____ *A Modern History of Somaliland: From Nation to State*. New York: Fredrick Praeger – Publisher (1965)

_____ "Historical Aspect of Genealogies in Northern Somali Social Structure." Journal of African History, III, (1962)

_____ A Pastoral Democracy: A study of pastoralism and politics among the Northern Somali of the Horn of Africa. African Publishing Company, New York. 2nd edition. (1982), (First Published in 1961.)

_____ *Peoples of the Horn of Africa: Somali, Afar, Saho*. London: International

African Institute (1955)

Lewis, H.S. "The Origin of the Galla and Somali," Journal of African History, VII, I (1966)

Lipset, S. Martin, *Political Man*. New York: Doubleday (1960)

Low, D. "The Northern Interior 1840-84" in R. Oliver and G. Mathew (Eds), *History of East Africa Vol. I*. Oxford University Press. (1963) 321

Luling, Virginia., "Colonial and Postcolonial Influences on a South Somali Community": *Journal of African History*, Vol. 8, No. I Spring, (1976)

_____ Somali Sultanate: The Geledi City-State over 150 years. HAAN Associates (2002)

Mabhida, Moses., *For International United Action to End Apartheid – The Curse of South Africa* W.F.T.U Publications Ltd. (1962)

Mahadallah, Hassan., "Pithless Nationalism: The Somali Case", in Kusow, Abdi M., ed., *Putting The Cart Before The Horse*. Red Sea Press. (2004)

Maloba, Wunyabari., "Nationalism and Decolonization, 1947 – 1963" in Ochieng', W. R., (ed.) *A Modern history of Kenya 1895-1980*. Evans Brothers Ltd. (1989)

Mansur, Abdalla O. "Aspects of the Somali Tribal Systems" in Adam, Hussein M., and Ford, Richard., (eds.), *Mending Rips in the Sky: Options for Somali Communities in the 21st Century*. Lawrenceville: Red Sea Press Inc. (1997)

_____ "Contrary to a Nation: The Cancer of the Somali State", in Ahmed, Ali J., ed. *The Invention of Somalia*. Red Sea Press (1995)

_____ 'The Nature of the Somali Clan System', in Ahmed, Ali Jimale (ed.), *The Invention of Somalia*. Red Sea Press (1995)

Maphela, Ramphele. "Combating Racism in South Africa: Redress/Remedies," in Hamilton et al (eds.), *Beyond Racism: Race and Inequality in Brazil, South Africa, and the United States*. Lynne Rienner Publishers. (2001)

Maquet, Jacques J., "Inequality In Rwanda," in Berghe, Pierre L. van den, (ed.), *Race and*
Ethnicity in Africa. East African Publishing House (1975)

Marcia, J.E. "Ego identity development," in Anderson, J., (ed.), *Handbook of Adolescent Psychology*. New York: Wiley. (1980)

Mathur, Kanwar B., *Intercultural Communication: An Agenda for Developing Countries*. Allied Publishers Ltd (2001)

Maxamed, Cabdi M. (Goobe) and Cumar, Cabdullaahi Cusman (Shakespeare), *Cilmiga Bulshada 6*. Printed in Kenya. UNESCO (2004). (After a lot of criticism, this title was removed from schools for review)

Mazrui, Ali A., *Cultural Forces in World Politics*. James Currey Ltd., Heinemann Kenya, Heinemann Portsmouth. (1990)

Mazrui, Alamin. *Kilio Cha Haki*. Longhorn Publishers (1981)

Menkhaus, Kenneth., "From Feast to Famine: Land and the State in Somalia's Lower Jubba Valley", in Besteman, Catherine and Cassanelli Lee V., (eds.), *The struggle for Land in Southern Somalia: The War Behind the War*. Haan Associates, (2000)

_____ "Rural Transformation and the Roots of Underdevelopment in Somalia's Lower Jubba Valley", PhD. Dissertation., University of South Carolina (1989)

Menkhaus, Kenneth and Craven, Kathryn, "Land Alienation and the Imposition of State Farms in the Lower Jubba valley," in Besteman C., and Cassanelli L. V., (eds.) *The Struggle for Land in Southern Somalia: The War Behind the War*. Haan Associates (2000)

_____ and Prendergast, J., "*Political Economy of Post-Intervention Somalia*", Somalia Task Force, Issue No. 3. April (1995)

Merlen, R.H.A. Article in the newspaper East Africa & Rhodesia Jan. 13, 1949. Kenya National Archives, Nairobi. (1949)

Merryman, James., "The Economy of Gedo Region and the Rise of Smallholder Irrigation," in Besteman and Cassanelli, (eds.), *The Struggle for Land in Southern Somalia: The War Behind the War*. Haan Associates (2000)

Mohamed, Aden. "Somali Peace talks providing futile: External Interference and Petty Squabbles to Blame for Stalemate, Daily nation, March 7, (2003)

Morgenthau, Hans J., *Politics Among Nations: The Struggle For Power and Peace*. Sixth edition. Kalyan Publishers (2001)

Morris, Aldon., "Centuries of Black Protest: Its significance for America and the World," in Hill, H., and Jones Jr., J. E., (eds.), *Race in America: The Struggle for Equality*. The University of Wisconsin Press (1993)

Morton, R.F., "The Myth of Shungwaya Origins of the Mijikenda: A Problem of Late Nineteenth Century Kenya Coastal History" , *The International Journal of African Historical Studies* 5 (1972)

Muhammad, Ali S. "The Origin of the Ishaq People", *Somaliland Journal*, Hargeisa, (1954)

Mukherji, Partha Nath (ed.) Methodology in Social Research. Sage Publications, New Delhi (2002)

Mukhtar, Mohamed H., 'Islam in Somali History: Facts and Fiction', in Ahmed, Ali Jimale (ed.), *The Invention of Somalia*. Red Sea Press (1995)

_____ "Somali Reconciliation Conferences: The Unbeaten Track, in Abdulahi A. Osman and Issaka K. Souare (eds), *Somalia at the Crossroads: Challenges and Perspectives on Reconstituting a Failed State*, Adonis and Abbey Publishers Ltd. (2007)

Murdock, George P. *Africa: Its people and their culture history*. New York: McGraw Hill, (1959)

Narula, S. 'Caste Discrimination.' http://www.india-seminar.com/2001/508. (2001)

Nurse, Derek. "Shungwaya and the Bantu of Somalia: Some Linguistic Evidence, in Hussein M. Adams and Charles L. Geshekter, (eds.), *Proceedings of the First International Congress on Somali Studies*, 1980 Chico CA: Scholars Press. Pp. 54-61. (1980)

Oberg, K. "The Kingdom of Ankole in Uganda," in Fortes, M., and Evans Pritchard., (eds.), *African Political System*. London: Oxford University Press (1940)

Ochieng, William R. 'The Mau Mau, the petit bourgeoisie and decolonization in Kenya', unpublished paper, Kenyatta University, (1984)

O'Connor, James., "The Meaning of Economic Imperialism," in Rhodes, R.I., (ed.), *Imperialism and Underdevelopment*. New York: Monthly Review. (1970a)

Odetola, Olatunde T., and Ademola, Ade., *Sociology: An Introduction of African Text*. Macmillan. (1985)

Okolany, D. H., "Ethnicity and 'Culture of Eating' in Uganda", in

Ogot, B. A., (ed.), *Ethnicity, Nationalism and Democracy in Africa.*, Maseno University College: Institute of Research and Postgraduate Studies. (1996)

Omar, Mohamed O. *The Road to Zero.* Haan (1992)

Palmer, Norman D., and Perkins, Howard C., *International Relations.* Third revised edition; A.I.T.B.S. Publishers and Distributors, (2002)

Pankhurst, Sylvia E. *Ex-Italian Somaliland.* London (1951)

Paton, Allan. *"The Christian Approach to Racial Problems in the Modern World."* A Christian Action Pamphlet, (second edition).(1959)

P'Bitek, Okot. *Artist the Ruler: Essays on Art, Culture and Values.* East African Educational Publishers. Reprint (1994)

Peil, Margaret, and Oyeneye, Olatunji. *Consensus, Conflict and Change: A Sociological Introduction to African Societies.* East African Educational Publishers (1998)

Montclose, Marc – Antoine Perouse de, " Minorities and discrimination, Exodus and reconstruction of identities: The case of Somali refugees in Mombasa." The French Scientific Research Institute for Development through Cooperation. (1997) www.ceped.ined.fr/cepedweb

Pierli, F., Presbitero, U., and Muko, R., "Ethnicity and Human Development: The Missing Link," in Jong, Albert de (ed.), *Ethnicity: Blessing or Curse?* Pauline Publications Africa. (1999)

Raj, Hans., *Fundamentals of* Demography: Population studies with special reference to India. Surjeet Publications. (2001)

Revoil, Georges., *La Vallee Du Darror,* Paris: Challamel Aine, Libraire - Editeur, (1882)

Rodney, Walter. *How Europe Underdeveloped Africa*, East African Publishers (2001)

Ronnell, Rodd., *British Military Administration of Occupied Territories in Africa.* Londra. (1948)

Sabine, George S., and Thorson, Thomas L. *A History of political Theory*, Oxford & IBH Publishing Co. (1973)

Salim, Hamid Al-Sayid. *Al-Sumaal – Qadiiman WA Hadiithan* Vol. I. Mogadishu, (1965)

Samad, Asha S. 'Brief Review of the Somali Caste Groups' – Statement to the Committee on the Elimination of Racial Discrimination, The International Dalit Solidarity Network. (2002). http;//uk.geocoties.com/internationaldalitssolidarity/cerd/Somalia2002.html.

Samatar, Abdi I., "Destruction of State and Society in Somalia: Beyond the Tribal Convention", The Journal of Modern African Studies, Cambridge University Press (1992)

_____ *The State and Rural Transformation in Northern Somalia 1884 - 1986.* Madison: University of Wisconsin Press. (1989)

Samatar, Abdi I. "The IGAD Peace Process: The Betrayal of the Somali People," Seminar lecture given in a Somali Workshop, Lenana House, Nairobi, July (2003)

Samatar, Abdi I., and Samatar, Ahmed I., "The Material Roots of the Suspended African State: Arguments from Somalia." The Journal of Modern African Studies, 25, 4(1987)

Samatar, Abdi I., and Samatar, Ahmed I., "Somali Reconciliation," An Editorial Note in Ayaamaha Press on line. http/:www.ayaamaha.com(downloaded on 10.29.03)

Santrock, John W., Psychology. 7th edition. McGraw-Hill (2003)

Schlee, Gunther. *Identities on the Move: Clanship and Pastoralism in Northern Kenya.* Gideon S. Were Press, (1994)

Singh, Ramjee "Vision of World Poverty: the Gandhian Perspective." A paper to the 14th World Conference of World Future Studies Federation, Nairobi, July 25 – 29, (1995)

Somali-civilsociety.org. "Somali National Reconciliation Conference." http/:somali-civilsociety.org.

Somali National Reconciliation Conference: "Article 2 of the Declaration on Cessation of Hostilities, Structures and Principles of the Somali National Reconciliation Process." Eldoret (2002)

Somali National Reconciliation Conference, "The Transitional Federal Charter of the Somali Republic." Nairobi (2004)

Sorokin, Pitirim. *Contemporary Sociological Theories.* Kalyani Publishers; Reprint (2000)

Sorrentino, Giorgio. *Ricordi del Benadir.* Naples: Trani – (1912)

Spear, Thomas T. "The Kaya Complex – A History of the Mijikenda Peoples of the Kenya Coast to 1900, Kenya Literature Bureau, Nairobi (1978)

_____ "Traditional Myths and Linguistic Analysis – Singwaya Revisited" La Trobe University. (1977)

Sutton, J. E. G., "Early Trade in East Africa"; Historical Association of Tanzania. East African Publishing House. (1973)

The East African Standard, "Support for Kenya Somali Claim for Asiatic Status," 18th August, (1930). (KNA)

The Holy Qur'an: (*Sura Al-Qasas 28:18-29*) English translation of the meanings and commentary. Revised & Edited by the Presidency of Islamic Researches, IFTA, Call and Guidance. King Fahd Complex for the Printing of the Holy Qur-an.

The Holy Qur'an, (Sura Al-Hujurat 49:13), English translation of the meanings and commentary. Revised and edited by The Presidency of Islamic Researches, IFTA, Call and Guidance.

Tidy, Michael, and Leeming, Donald *A History of Africa 1840 - 1914.* Volume Two. Arnold Publishers. (2001)

Touval, Saadia., *Somali Nationalism: International Politics and the Drive for Unity in the Horn of Africa.* Harvard University Press, Cambridge, Massachusetts (1963)

Turton, E.R. "Bantu, Galla and Somali Migrations in the Horn of Africa – A Reassessment of the Juba/Tana area." *Journal of African History* 16,4 (1975)

UNDP – Human Development Report -- Somalia (1998)

UNDP – Human Development Report -- Somalia (2001)

Wa Thiong'o, Ngugi. *Decolonizing the Mind.* East African Educational Publishers (1996)

Wright, Sue. *Language Policy and language Planning.* Palgrave - Macmillan. (2004)

Archival materials, journals and newspapers

A communication letter from the District Commissioner's Office, Wajir, Northern Province, 19th April, 1948. (Kenya National Archives – Nairobi)

A communication letter from the District Commissioner's Office, Kismayu, , signed by the Assistant to the Provincial Commissioner. (Kenya National Archives - Nairobi). December 2nd, 1916

ASMAI – Archivio Storico del Ministero degli Affari Esteri, (Roma, Italia) (1905)

ASMAI, pos. 59/1, f.5. Yusuf Ali's declaration in Alula, April 7, (1889)

ASMAI, pos. 75/1, f.3. Incoronato report No. 90, Zanzibar, Dec. (1893)

ASMAI, pos. 75/6, f.56, Onorato Di Monale report, Feb. (1903)

ASMAI, pos. 59/1, f.8. Launay (Berlin) communication to Crispi, in March (1889)

ASMAI, position 55/1, f.4, Filonardi report, (Zanzibar October (1886)

Filonardi communication from Zanzibar to Crispi, the Italian Prime Minister. 'Libro Verde', doc. 2, p.27. (1888)

ASMAI, pos. 75/1, f.3, Filonardi Report No. 171. Provisional Ordinance for the government and Administration of Territory Under the Protection of Italy. ; Sep. 16, (1894)

A study by The International Cooperation Administration., "Inter-River Economic Exploration," The Somali Republic; Washington 25, D.C., (1961)

Bulletin of the International Committee of Urgent Anthropological and Ethnical Research. pp. 28-29. No.3. assisted by UNESCO. (1960)

Christian Action pamphlet, "The Dispossessed: The Human Tragedy of Apartheid." Published by the Christian Action. (Kenya National Archives, undated).

Citizen T.V News Bulletin in Kiswahili and in English, 20th March (2004)

Cottoni communication to Brin, July 1892, Zanzibar. ASMAI, pos. 55/5, f. 37 (1892)

Hertslet, E. The Map of Africa by Treaty (Third Edition) London, His Majesty's Stationery Office, (1890)

Hertslet, E., The Map of Africa by Treaty, III, 948, 1091 – 93; London Post, November 21, (1889).

Filonardi-Rosasco Report 'Libro Verde', doc. 29, annex II, p.69 (1891)

Mackinon's communication to Crispi, ASMAI, pos. 55/1, f. 8. August, London (1888)

Republic of Somalia. The Somali Republic and African Unity. Printed by East African Printers (Boyds) Ltd. Nairobi (1962)

Stevie Wonder, "Black Man" a song in the double Album 'Songs In The Key of Life.' (1976)

Treaty of Protection 'Libro Verde', doc. 11, annex 1, p.40. (1889)

Papers, Reports and Studies

Ali Jimale Ahmed, "Off the Beaten Sterile Trail," A paper presented at the 47th African Studies Association, New Orleans, U.S.A. November (2004)

Bantu Rehabilitation Trust (BRT) – Somalia "A Study on the Human Rights Abuse Against the Bantu", sponsored by ACORD-Somalia. (1995).

Commander Sorrentino, Report of Commander Sorrentino , Zanzibar, January 22, 1892.

Committee One, [Group A] "Federalism and Provisional Charter (ARTICLE THREE)." Nairobi: Somali National Reconciliation Conference (2003).

Committee One [Group B] "Federal Transitional Charter (ARTICLE 2)" Nairobi: 14th Somali National Reconciliation Conference (2003)

Committee Six Report of Committee Six on Conflict Resolution and Reconciliation. Nairobi, 14th SNRC (2003).

Joint British, Danish and Dutch Fact-Finding Mission to Nairobi, Kenya Report on Minority Groups in Somalia: , 17-20 September, (2000)

Mohamed A. Eno "A Structure In Search of Function: The IGAD Product." A paper presented at the Somali Bantu Intellectuals' Meeting (2005)

Eno, Mohamed A. "A Return of Apartheid to Africa: The Somali Case," A paper presented at the Africa Peace-Building Workshop , Nairobi, (2004a)

_____ "The 14th Somali National Reconciliation Conference," A lecture presented in a seminar at Portland State University (2004b)

_____ "The Predicament of the 14th Somali National Reconciliation Conference and the IGAD Factor," A paper presented in a seminar for Somali Bantu/Jareer participants in the SNRC in Kenya, (2003)

_____ "An Approach to the Nature of the Somali Conflict," a paper presented to the Workshop on Conflict-Resolution for the Great Lakes Region, Nairobi (2002)

_____ "Clans, Warlords and Peace-building: The Somali Phenomenon," A paper presented at the Rwanda Peace-Building Workshop (1997)

_____ " Warar Qubane ah ; Waxa isku soo dubarriday Eno," Wargeyska Runta Bogga 4aad. 5th – 20th Juun, Cadadka 11aad. (1996)

_____ "Jawaab", Wargeyska Runta – 16-30 Maajo, (1996)

_____ "All Roads Led to Istunka (A Grand Mock-Fight at Afgoi)" in Heegan Newspaper. (1986)

_____ 'The Istunka Festival – A traditional Mock-fight at Afgoie. Heegan Newspaper. (1984)

_____ "How Wide Is The gap?" Heegan Newspaper, Mogadishu: Friday, Jan 27, (1984)

_____ "Historical Background of 'Istunka': A Mock-Fight at Afgoi", Heegan Newspaper, Mogadishu (1980)

Eno, Omar A., ' "Gosha/Heer-Goleet" (people of the forest): Runaway slaves in the Juba valley of Southern Somalia.' A paper presented at the International Conference on Slavery, Unfree Labor and Revolt in Asia and Indian Ocean Region. University of Avignon (2001)

_____ "The Reasons Behind the Somali Tragedy and the Vulnerable Minority Groups, Particularly the Bantu/Jareer." A paper presented at the African Studies Association in Orlando, Florida, USA. (1995)

_____ "Who will surface the hidden agenda in the Somali peace problem?" A seminar paper presented in a workshop for the Somali Bantu participants at the Somali National Reconciliation Conference in Kenya, (2003)

Enow, Marian A., "Alienation and Marginalization in Somali: The Case of the Somali Bantu." A paper presented in a Minority Rights Seminar in the USA (2004)

Grottanelli, Vinigi., "I Bantu del Giuba nelle tradizioni dei Wazegua." Geografia Helvetica, VIII, 3, (1953).

Guadagno, Marco., Xeerka Beeraha/Diritto Fondierio Somalo. (1981)

Gupta, Dipankar., 'Caste, race, politics'. http://www.india-seminar.com/2001/508.

Hazard, Domitille, "Mohamed Kadir: N'oubliez pas moon people," Faim Development Magazine; No. 126, November (1996)

Kimaryo, Jacob L., "East African Coastal Historical Towns: Asiatic or African? January 13-15, 2000, University of Goteborg, Goteborg, Sweden. A paper presented to the Conference: U-landsforskning (2000).

Karoney, Farida, "Somalia hopes for peace after decades of war." Daily Nation, (Special Report), Sep. 17, 2003.

Lewis, I. M., "The Land of the Living Dead". Sunday Times, August (1992)

Oral Interviewees & Traditionists

Abbas Ismaan Sadiiq
Abdi Ali
Abdullahi Abdulkadir (Aw Jaalle)
Abdullahi Buurow Dhalmaasho,
Abdullahi Hussein Buufow (alias Mashiido)
Abdullahi Sheikh Hassan
Abdullahi Soomoow (Ul-Qalin)
Abukar Abdullahi Mungai
Abukar Ali Abanur
Aheda Mkomwa
Aziza Abdi Dhurow
Bukow Ahmed
Diinle Aliyow
Edeng Kheer
Garre Oobooy
Hadija Msharemo Mwali
Hagi Adam Kheerow
Hagi Hassan Mohamoud (Adimow)
Hagi Mohamed Abdi Roble (alias Maadeey Barakaale)
Hagi Mohamed Barrow
Hagia Halima Hussein Hassan (alias Halima Essow)
Hassan Faqay
Hassan Mohamed (alias Hassan Maanlaawe)
Ismail Aliyow Baxaar
Juma Bakari
Juma Chivalo
Khadija M. Harganti
Madina Mugabe
Mahdi Mohamed Issa
Mahmadey Ismaan
Marian Awes
Marian Yusuf Ali (alias Maryin Yaawisoow)
Mberwa Muya Mberwa
Mohamed Abdi Bulhan (alias Buulle)
Mohamed Ali Isman (Weershe)
Mohamed Farah Muudeey (Booroow)

Mohamed Hamisi
Mohamed Hussein Hassan (Jawaani)
Mohamed Osman Mahdi
Mohamed Ramadaan Arbo
Mohamoud Osman Mahdi
Muridi Mahi Mumin
Muya Mkomo
Omar Abdulle (ex-Col.)
Omar Muya Mberwa
Osman Kamula Mofi
Sa'di Mumin Hassan
Sakaawa Abu (alias Abti)
Sayid–Ali Abdulkadir Eno
Shariff Abdinassir Elmi Shariff Mohamed (alias Quleel)
Shariff Hussein Shariff Mohamed
Shariff Osman Shariff Samad Shariff Ali
(See Mukhtar 2007:123-130).
Shiikhe Ismaan Sadiiq
Yusuf Ali (Baasaay)
Yusuf Ali (Yaawisoow)

A

Abai River, 30
Abu, Sakawa, 54, 55, 61, 63, 109, 176, 302, 314
Abyssinia, 16, 30, 31, 52, 58, 59, 60, 109, 121, 132, 252, 264, 298, 302
Adoon, 65, 80, 88, 90, 100, 116, 178, 181, 184, 201, 260, 289
Afgoie, 34, 35, 36, 41, 61, 78, 81, 82, 83, 88, 93, 103, 109, 119, 146, 285, 311
Agaumeder, 30, 31
Agricultural Development Corporation, 170, 177
Amarani, 52, 94, 108
anti-Jareer by policy, 155
Arab Sheikhs, 16, 249, 256
Arabia, 9, 18, 20, 21, 23, 27, 28, 30, 38, 39, 51, 52, 102, 147, 148, 149, 154, 176, 192, 213, 250, 266, 267, 281, 288
Arabized Somali nomads, 87
Arabo-Persian immigrants, 37
Asia, 19, 37, 104, 139, 300, 311
Awiya, 30, 31

B

Baidoa, 109, 189, 253, 292, 293
Baiso, 21, 28, 60, 301
Banaadiri, 15, 55, 56
Banadir, 55, 62, 87, 107, 253, 264, 291, 302
Baraawans, 53
Barawaans, 15, 51, 52, 53, 55, 56, 58, 212, 228, 248
Barawanese citizenship, 53
Barre, Siad, 11, 12, 53, 76, 120, 121, 122, 127, 129, 157, 160, 164, 166, 167, 168, 169, 172, 173, 174, 175, 176, 177, 179, 180, 181, 182, 183, 184, 188, 195, 199, 208, 216, 227, 236, 239, 252, 257, 262, 265, 272, 273, 277, 280, 286
Barsane, 115, 116, 117, 215, 293
Berlin Conference of 1884 - 1885, 105
Bimaal, 108, 113, 114, 115

Boong, 90, 260
Boran, 21, 28, 33, 34
Britain, ii, 105, 106, 107, 108, 111, 136, 142, 202, 203
British Naval Army, 95

C

Cecchi, Antonio, 106, 109, 110
Chimbalazi, 52
Chivalo, Mzee Juma, 95, 104, 313
Christian culture, 31
Cushitic neighbors, 34

D

Daarood, 11, 84, 237
Dalits of India, 46
Dar-es-Salaam, 95, 104
Dhabarweyne, 55
Dhoobooy, 115, 119, 120
Dhulbahante, 84, 236, 237
Diaspora Bantu, 92, 266
Digil, 16, 23, 26, 29, 34, 40, 55, 59, 84, 87, 88, 132, 143, 151, 168, 185, 210, 212, 223, 224, 228, 229, 236, 238, 248, 253, 254
Digil-Mirifle, 23, 26, 29, 34, 55, 59, 84, 87, 88, 132, 143, 151, 168, 185, 210, 212, 223, 224, 228, 229, 236, 238, 248
Djibouti, 39, 107, 197, 202, 217, 219, 220, 223, 224, 225, 226, 236
Donbira, 16, 18, 21
Duruma, 67

E

Egypt, 34, 37, 106, 238
Eritrea People's Liberation Front, 175
Ethiopia, 22, 28, 29, 33, 35, 39, 40, 51, 57, 60, 107, 121, 132, 133, 173, 174, 175, 182, 202, 216, 217, 219, 220, 223, 226, 231, 232, 236, 237, 238, 241, 250, 251, 252, 300, 302

F

France, 105, 106, 107

G

Gaboye community, 48
Galla, 21, 22, 28, 60, 69, 76, 78, 85, 86, 91, 101, 103, 110, 132, 252, 253, 255, 289, 302, 303, 308
Garbaharrey, 183
Germany, 105, 106, 110, 176
Gosha people, 18, 94, 95, 96, 97, 100, 104
Greater Somalia, 136, 142, 144, 173, 223, 224
Gupta, Dipanka, 46, 47, 48, 62, 301, 311

H

Hashemite, 23, 50, 51
Hawiya, 31, 40, 254
Hersi, Ali Abdirahman, 19, 20, 24, 30, 34, 38, 58, 59, 60, 61, 75, 76, 77, 102, 301
Horn of Africa, i, iii, 9, 30, 51, 56, 58, 59, 60, 62, 101, 102, 103, 194, 216, 251, 264, 287, 289, 300, 303, 308

I

ideology of Arabness, 30, 38
IGAD Council of Ministers, 230
Imperial British East Africa Company, 107
Inter-Governmental Authority for Development, 12, 216
Iskaashato, 11, 55

J

Jareer of Gosha, 98
Jileec, 10, 12, 15, 25, 26, 27, 40, 49, 53, 58, 78, 79, 80, 84, 85, 86, 87, 88, 89, 90, 92, 93, 100, 116, 119, 124, 134, 135, 138, 141, 142, 151, 154, 158, 161, 165, 168, 169, 177, 178, 179, 180, 181, 188, 201, 202, 203, 205, 206, 208, 209, 210, 211, 227, 228, 247, 252, 256, 261, 262, 269, 278, 280, 281, 283, 284, 288, 289, 290
Jimale, Sheeikh Ali, 10, 16, 22, 25,

58, 59, 60, 103, 120, 127, 147, 148, 149, 150, 214, 240, 245, 297, 304, 305, 310
Juba valley, 74, 93, 95, 97, 99, 104, 108, 154, 311
Jubba, 34, 65, 66, 81, 90, 92, 132, 145, 188, 191, 253, 286, 287, 292, 295, 304

K

Kenya, 12, 22, 33, 39, 51, 52, 53, 56, 58, 59, 60, 63, 67, 69, 83, 89, 101, 102, 103, 105, 107, 133, 142, 146, 148, 149, 183, 188, 189, 190, 196, 202, 207, 208, 209, 213, 214, 215, 217, 219, 220, 223, 226, 236, 237, 244, 255, 266, 287, 289, 293, 297, 298, 299, 303, 304, 305, 306, 307, 308, 309, 310, 311
Kismayo, 106, 107, 108, 292
Kiswahili, 56, 72, 94, 244, 309
Kusow, Abdi, 10, 24, 25, 28, 59, 60, 62, 67, 89, 101, 103, 105, 146, 148, 189, 191, 192, 246, 247, 248, 256, 264, 297, 300, 303

L

Laas Caanood, 11
Lower Juba, 26
Luling, Virginia, 10, 17, 36, 37, 42, 61, 78, 82, 92, 93, 102, 103, 177, 191, 262, 264, 265, 303

M

Maay language, 26, 29, 33, 41, 82, 223, 229
Mad Mullah, 114, 122, 123, 146, 147, 302
Madhibaan, 15, 44, 179, 228
Majerteen sub-clan, 182
Makalango, 98
Manyasa, 93
Marshall Plan, 134
Meddo, 260
Mengistu Haile Mariam, 175
Middle Juba region, 176
Middle Shabelle, 26, 103, 291, 292,

295

Mijikenda, 67, 68, 71, 73, 74, 89, 90, 100, 101, 255, 297, 299, 305, 308

Mkomo, Mzee, 94, 104, 314

Mogadishu, 12, 37, 38, 55, 56, 61, 63, 65, 68, 70, 72, 73, 77, 95, 100, 102, 103, 106, 107, 109, 110, 114, 115, 117, 119, 120, 121, 125, 127, 128, 143, 147, 148, 153, 154, 163, 165, 169, 176, 191, 208, 213, 235, 244, 261, 265, 281, 284, 292, 297, 300, 307, 311

Moorshe, 55

N

Nassib Bundo, 96, 97, 98

National Assembly, 160, 168

Negritude, 201, 203, 246, 261

Negroid Jareer people, 55

Negroid-Africans, 262

Non-Bantu, 15, 40

Non-Negroid, 15, 205

Nurse, Derek, 66, 67, 70, 71, 101, 305

O

Ogaadeen, 84

Ogaden, 96, 97, 98, 99, 100, 107, 123, 174, 175, 177, 182

Oromo, 21, 28, 33, 34, 35, 61, 252

Osman, Aden Abddulle, 10, 51, 76, 110, 121, 126, 127, 137, 150, 151, 153, 155, 156, 157, 158, 159, 160, 162, 163, 164, 165, 167, 175, 189, 190, 197, 236, 247, 265, 272, 273, 276, 277, 300, 305, 314

Osu of Nigeria, 46

P

pastoral democracy, 44, 139, 157, 204, 262

Persia, 52

Pokomo, 67, 71, 73, 89, 90

Portugal, 105

Q

Qur'anic right, 85

Qureishite, 16, 19, 31, 43, 50, 57

R

Rahanweyn, 88

Reer Banu-Hashem, 18

Reer Hamar, 56, 94, 108, 212

Reer Xamar, 15, 52, 56, 58, 184, 227, 228

Reewing, 16, 26, 29, 30, 50, 57, 58, 74, 84, 88, 89, 90, 91, 125, 148, 168, 185, 191, 228, 229

Revoil, Georges, 20, 59, 306

Rodney, Walter, 94, 104, 306

S

San-buur, 260, 289

Sankadhudhi, 90, 201, 260, 289

Save the Children Fund, 185

Segeju, 67

Seychelles, 282

Shabelle, 26, 40, 55, 60, 65, 66, 77, 78, 81, 89, 90, 104, 108, 117, 124, 137, 154, 163, 177, 208, 253, 254, 255, 262, 285, 286, 287, 292

Shariffoow, 36, 82

Shungwaya, 56, 67, 68, 69, 72, 74, 75, 78, 100, 101, 102, 103, 208, 254, 297, 305

Somali African Muki Organization, 262

Somali Bantu, 9, 25, 65, 66, 68, 69, 74, 77, 78, 93, 100, 102, 105, 200, 211, 213, 214, 215, 244, 263, 265, 266, 276, 300, 310, 311

Somali culture, 9, 31, 77

Somali National Reconciliation Conference, 12, 180, 188, 196, 209, 213, 227, 230, 234, 240, 241, 242, 244, 307, 310, 311

Somali outcasts, 46

Somali Salvation Democratic Front, 175, 182

Soomaali khaldaan, 42

South Africa, 200, 202, 205, 213, 215, 226, 246, 263, 303, 304

Southern Somalia, 60, 69, 104, 107, 133, 188, 298, 300, 301, 304, 305, 311

T

Tanzania., 53, 56, 101, 104, 308
Taylor, Charles, 42, 218, 300
the Bajuuni, 52, 67
Tigre People's Liberation Front, 175
to Quraishite Arabs, 10
Toyota Land Cruiser, 284
Tuni, 88

U

UNESCO, 101, 121, 265, 304, 309
United Somali Congress, 11
UNOSOM, 186
USA, 62, 134, 147, 213, 215, 265, 311

W

Wa-Gosha, 18, 95, 97, 105, 132
Wanakoocha, 95
Western Somali Liberation Front, 174, 175

X

Xabash, 260

Z

Zanzibar, 56, 106, 107, 108, 110, 145, 146, 187, 309, 310
Zaramo, 93
Zenj, 55, 56, 68, 69, 74, 75, 76, 86, 102, 243, 276, 289, 299

www.ingramcontent.com/pod-product-compliance
Lightning Source LLC
Chambersburg PA
CBHW070559270326
41926CB00013B/2363